*International African Seminars*
*New Series, No. 4*

# HOUSING AFRICA'S URBAN POOR

# INTERNATIONAL AFRICAN SEMINARS

*New series*

# HOUSING AFRICA'S URBAN POOR

EDITED BY
**Philip Amis** and **Peter Lloyd**

Manchester University Press
Manchester and New York
*for the*
INTERNATIONAL AFRICAN INSTITUTE

Distributed exclusively in the USA and Canada by St. Martin's Press

Copyright © International African Institute 1990

*Published by* Manchester University Press
Oxford Road, Manchester M13 9PL, UK
*and* Room 400, 175 Fifth Avenue,
New York, NY 10010, USA

*Distributed exclusively in the USA and Canada*
*by* St. Martin's Press, Inc.,
175 Fifth Avenue, New York, NY 10010, USA

*British Library cataloguing in publication data*
Housing Africa's urban poor.—(International African
  seminars: New series; no. 4).
  1. Africa. Urban regions. Housing
  I. Amis, Philip   II. Lloyd, P. C. (Peter Cutt), *1927–*
  III. International African Institute   IV. Series
  363.5'096

*Library of Congress cataloging in publication data*
Housing Africa's urban poor / edited by Philip Amis and Peter Lloyd.
    p.   cm. – (International African seminars; new ser., no. 4)
    ISBN 0–7190–3020–X
    1. Urban poor – Housing – Africa.   2. Urban poor – Housing –
Government policy – Africa.   I. Amis, Philip, 1956–   . II. Lloyd,
Peter Cutt. III. International African Institute. IV. Series.
HD7287.96.A4H67   1989
363.5'8'096–dc20            89–12657

ISBN 0–7190–3020–X *hardback*

Photoset in Linotron Plantin
by Northern Phototypesetting Co, Bolton

Printed in Great Britain
by Biddles Ltd., Guildford and King's Lynn

# CONTENTS

# FIGURES AND TABLES

## FIGURES

## TABLES

# CONTRIBUTORS

*Tade Akin Aina* studied sociology at the University of Lagos, the London School of Economics, and the University of Sussex. He is currently a Senior Lecturer at the University of Lagos and has been a member of the University of Lagos Human Settlements Study Group – a multidisciplinary research team on human settlements – since 1980.

*Philip Amis* was until recently a Lecturer in the Development and Project Planning Centre of the University of Bradford. He is now a Lecturer in the Development Administration Group, School of Public Policy at the University of Birmingham.

*Seth Opuni Asiama* lectures in Land Economy at the University of Science and Technology in Kumasi, Ghana. He was awarded a PhD at the University of Birmingham for his work on land reform in Ghana. His research interests include the social and economic implications of housing in Third World countries, and he has written many articles in scholarly journals.

*John Campbell* conducted fieldwork on urban development and politics in southern Ghana for his doctoral thesis at Sussex University. Between 1981 and 1985 he was a Lecturer in Sociology at the University of Dar es Salaam, Tanzania; and later Visiting Research Fellow at the University of Sussex. His interests range from urban politics to urban planning and housing policy.

*Michel Coquery* is Professor at the French Institute of Town Planning, University of Paris VIII. He has worked extensively on urban planning and development in West and Central Africa for the past two decades.

*Michael Edwards* was educated at the Universities of Oxford and London, where he was awarded a PhD for his work on renting in Colombia. In 1982 he joined VSO as a Development Officer, moving in 1984 to become Oxfam's Representative for Zambia and Malawi, based in Lusaka. He is currently spending a year at the Guruder Peeth ashram in Ganeshpuri, India, where he works as a volunteer on village development programmes. He maintains a continuing interest in renting and rental housing.

*Galila El Kadi* has been carrying out research for ORSTOM since 1984. At present she is seconded to Cairo to the Institute of Urban and Regional Planning where she undertakes teaching and research work. Author of a thesis on spontaneous urbanisation in Cairo, she has been involved in several working groups on the subject of land and real estate and has written numerous articles on the subject in Egypt. She has just completed research into 'The city of the dead in Cairo', which for some years has been a reception centre for the urban poor in Cairo. Since 1986 she has been carrying out research with IURP on medium-sized towns in Egypt and their role in national and regional planning.

*Philippe Haeringer* is Director of Research at the French Institute of Scientific Research for Development in Cooperation (ORSTOM), France. He has carried out research in Central and East Africa and his present work is in Egypt. He was instrumental in instituting analyses of urban politics in Black Africa and in devising an 'anthropology of town life'. He was co-leader of the CNRS/ORSTOM group 'Towns and townspeople of the Third World'.

*Diana Lee-Smith* is an architect from the UK who has lived and worked in Kenya since 1975, mainly on low-income housing planning, policy and evaluation. She is a founder member of Mazingira Institute, Nairobi, a non-profit research institute, and of Settlements Information Network Africa, of which she is the Editor. She has worked as a consultant for the United Nations, the World Bank, USAID, IDRC and the Kenyan government. She has held academic appointments at five universities, in Kenya, the USA and Canada, and worked as an architect in three European countries.

*Peter Lloyd* is Professor of Social Anthropology at the University of Sussex. He has published widely on West Africa and Latin America and is the author of *Slums of Hope?* (1979) and *The 'Young Towns' of Lima* (1981).

*Theophilus O. Okoye* is Reader in Geography at the University of Nigeria, Nsukka. His main research interest is in urban geography and regional planning. He has carried out studies of medium-sized cities in Eastern Nigeria and their role in regional development. His publications include *The City in Southeastern Nigeria*.

*Thomas Pennant* was a Lecturer in Sociology at the University of Malawi from 1977 to 1983. From 1983 to 1985 he was a Visiting Research Fellow in the Urban and Regional Studies Unit of the University of Kent at Canterbury, and now teaches Economics at a school in London.

*Frej Stambouli* is Professor of Sociology at the University of Tunis. His research and publications focus on urbanisation and social movements in North Africa. He is currently engaged, with an international research team, in a comparative study of social movements in Africa, Asia and

Latin America.

*Richard E. Stren* is a Professor of Political Science at the University of Toronto, where he holds a cross-appointment at the Institute for Environmental Studies. From 1984 to 1987, Professor Stren co-ordinated a comparative research project, involving seven African research teams, entitled 'African Urban Management', with support from the IDRC. His major recent publications include *African Cities in Crisis* (edited, with Rodney White) (Boulder, Colorado, 1988) and (with Clare Letemendia) *Coping with Rapid Urban Growth in Africa* (Montreal: McGill University, 1986).

*Paul Teedon* is a Lecturer in Geography at Wolverhampton Polytechnic, and is at present completing PhD work on low-cost housing provision in Harare, Zimbabwe.

*Unni Wikan* is Professor of Social Anthropology at the University of Oslo. She has carried out fieldwork in Egypt, Oman, Papua New Guinea and Bali. Her publications include *Life Among the Poor in Cairo; Behind the Veil in Arabia – Women in Oman; Tomorrow, God Willing,* and *Managing the Heart to Brighten Face and Mind: culture and experience among the Balinese.*

*Saad Yahya* is Associate Professor of Land Economics in the Department of Land Development, University of Nairobi, where he has also served as head of the department, and Dean of the Faculty of Architecture, Design and Development. His main area of interest is urban land policy.

# FOREWORD

The successful appearance of this book might be deemed a monument to persistence. The idea of organising an International African Seminar on the important – and timely – topic of housing the African poor first arose in April 1983 in discussions with Professor Peter Lloyd, who kindly agreed to assume academic responsibility for the project. We decided that the best way to proceed productively was to begin with a preliminary survey of the existing literature. We were fortunate to find in Philip Amis a suitably qualified young specialist to carry this out, and managed to secure the requisite financial support for this survey from the ESRC, to whom we record our gratitude.

Following Philip Amis's report in 1984, and based on the key issues arising from it, the IAI proceeded to seek funds for a seminar and, possibly, a linked research project. The search proved particularly protracted. We could not locate a source of support for the research project, and thus concentrated on securing funds for the seminar which we had initially hoped to hold in Cairo. Eventually we secured a very welcome promise of support from the International Development Research Center, Canada, by which time it had become clear that we could not hold the meeting in Cairo, and the location was accordingly changed to Mogadishu, with enthusiastic support from the Somali authorities. By this time, the Swedish Agency for Research in Developing Countries (SAREC), which had generously supported the Institute's 1983 seminar in Botswana on Traditional Medicine, again came to our aid as co-sponsor.

The seminar was due to be held in Mogadishu in November 1986. Ten days before the seminar was to take place, when all the travel arrangements for the participants had been completed, with air tickets dispatched, and when one seminar participant had already left North Africa en route to Somalia, the Somali authorities informed us that they could not receive us on the agreed date. In these circumstances, and with the understanding co-operation of our sponsors, the seminar location was switched to the London School of Economics. As can be imagined, this caused severe logistical problems, but with the co-operation of my colleagues at the

London School of Economics and the good offices of the Pro-Director, Professor Robert Pinker, we were able to welcome all but one of the invited participants here in London on the appointed day. In addition to its Secretary, Jackie Hunt, and the then Research Officer, Robert Dodd, the Institute owes a very substantial debt to Peter Lloyd and Philip Amis for taking this unanticipated complication in their stride and for making the seminar a particularly successful meeting where we advantageously enjoyed the participation of a number of UK-based Third World housing specialists who joined us at short notice. (In particular John Turner and Sally Burrows, who gave short presentations, and Caroline Moser, Antony O'Connor, David Satterthwaite and Anne Varley, who acted as discussants.) As with our other seminars, we relied on participants to provide such translation as proved necessary, and I wish to record our debt here particularly to Professor Richard Stren from Canada whose bilingual talents proved invaluable.

The substantive contents of this volume speak eloquently for themselves and are well served by Philip Amis's excellent introduction. I wish finally, therefore, simply to thank him and Peter Lloyd on behalf of the Institute for creating and sustaining this seminar and bringing it to the fruitful conclusion of the present volume.

I. M. Lewis                                    September 1988
Honorary Director
International African Institute

# Introduction    Philip Amis

# KEY THEMES IN CONTEMPORARY AFRICAN URBANISATION

The aim of this introduction lies in the title; namely to highlight the key themes in contemporary African urbanisation. This will hopefully provide the context for the chapters that follow on housing in urban Africa.

The first section will give an overview of African political economy. The next two sections will focus more directly on issues of urbanisation and housing. The final section will preview the articles in the collection and try to provide a synthesis of the overall arguments contained in the volume.

## AFRICA, 1960–85: POLITICAL AND ECONOMIC TRENDS

The road from decolonisation has not been an easy one. The optimism of the 1960s associated with decolonisation and rapid economic growth has been dissipated. Between 1965 and 1973 the average annual growth rate for low and middle-income sub-Saharan African states was 3·7 and 8·5 per cent respectively. In the later period 1973–84 the average annual growth rates declined to 2 and 1·6 per cent respectively (World Bank, 1986: 180–1). The five nations of North Africa, with the exception of Egypt (3·8 and 8·5 per cent), show a similar trend. This decline is partly a function of recession in the global economy, but also has important internal dimensions (Berg, 1981).

While the overall economic growth rate has declined since the mid-1970s, the downward trend in agriculture and food production has been much more alarming. At a standardised base of 100 in 1969–71 the average index of food production per capita for Africa (not including South Africa) in 1982 was only eighty-seven (Commins et al., 1986: 22).

These figures clearly indicate the major problem for Africa: the failure since 1960 to increase agricultural productivity. This is in sharp contrast to the experience of Asia and Latin America. When considering the prospects for long-term economic growth, the importance of this and the low level of technology employed in African agriculture cannot be underestimated.

Commentators from across the entire political spectrum emphasise the importance of agricultural development in the process of capitalist and socialist economic development (Moore, 1967; Hyden, 1980; Berg, 1981). The causes of this failure are numerous and structural. They include, among others, unfavourable international trade terms, foreign exchange shortages, the rise in the price of petroleum products, low farm prices, overvalued exchange rates, inefficient parastatal organisations and a misplaced industrialisation policy (Lofchie, 1986: 6–11).

Nevertheless, whatever the reasons, both external and internal, the prospects of African development, which seemed promising in the immediate post-independence era, have been shattered. The state of Africa is the worst facing humanity; in the World Bank 1987 low-income category (< $400 per capita GNP), fully twenty-three out of the thirty-seven states are African. The average life expectancy at birth in these countries in 1984 was forty-eight years. Indeed the average figure for Africa as a whole (population weighted) was fifty-one years. In only seven countries (which represents 23 per cent of the continent's population) was the figure greater than fifty-five years. These figures compare unfavourably with other low-income nations, notably China and India, whose life expectancy is sixty-nine years and fifty-six years respectively. Indeed, such south–south comparisons in agricultural production and economic growth reveal the paucity of African development. A small anecdote will suffice; in 1960 Ghana's per capita income was higher than South Korea's. In 1985 the latter's per capita income was six times the former. Between 1960 and 1985 the spectre of famine shifted from India to Africa; in 1960 Africa was in food surplus while India was under an ever-present threat of famine, but now the situation is reversed. This is tragedy enough, leaving aside the potentially long-term irreversible ecological damage which may now be occurring in some regions of Africa.

Many readers may find that this apocalyptic version of Africa fits unhappily with a growing literature documenting the establishment of capitalist relations in Africa (Iliffe, 1983; Sender and Smith, 1986). There appears to be indeed a profound paradox; at the moment Africa's economy is breaking down; suddenly there is debate over the potential for capitalist development. These two interpretations may not be inconsistent, dealing as they do with different areas of social reality. Nevertheless it is also likely that there is a deeper connection which unfortunately still remains to be specified. At its crudest it is not clear whether Africa needs 'more' or 'less' capitalism. However we must be careful in such discussions not to assume a uniform monolithic form capitalism should take; each situation must be locally specified.

While Africa has been in the vanguard of the present economic crisis it is not alone. The international agencies' shifts in approach since the 1950s neatly encapsulate the changes in attitudes. The discourse of the mid-1960s was 'modernisation' and 'take-off'; the emphasis was large-scale urban industrial projects; in essence the Marshall Plan which rebuilt war-destroyed Western Europe could build Africa. (Indeed it actually was to involve the same agencies.) This was reinforced by the political enthusiasm of decolonisation, and, for example, in the West, the optimism of the Kennedy administration in the United States. The faith that science and technocrats could forge a new world had never been higher.

Critics in the late 1960s in the developing world began to criticise this view, in particular the failure of 'trickle-down' to occur. By the early 1970s the emphasis was more on modest, intermediate technology, and on the integration or encouragement of the 'informal sector' and, under McNamara, an attempt to focus directly on the alleviation of poverty (Sandbrook, 1982). This basic-needs strategy was partly political in terms of redistribution, but also economically pragmatic; attempts to improve overall welfare would encourage economic development and growth. Increased welfare and economic growth were seen as complementary rather than mutually exclusive. A cynical interpretation of basic needs would be that it represents an implicit acceptance of the failure of development and the possibility of sustained social transformation in the Third World. In this interpretation basic needs is a minimalist response to alleviate poverty while long-term development is postponed. Nevertheless it is from this era that the World Bank's urban shelter programme evolved.

The change of political attitudes in the West, with the electoral victories of Thatcher and Reagan, the ascendancy of monetarism together with the 1980s economic recession and subsequent debt crisis, has dramatically shifted the emphasis again. The international agencies, in particular the World Bank (IBRD), have increasingly abandoned their traditional project focus; instead they have moved closer to the International Monetary Fund (IMF) with their joint Structural Adjustment Programmes (SAPs) which are aimed at policy reform in return for balance of payments support.

The content of IMF austerity packages is well known; they include, among other things, a devaluation of the currency, a reduction in the role of the state and parastatals, a reduction in subsidies and import controls and an increase in agricultural prices. These adjustment programmes have generated considerable debate and hostile comment from some academics (see the July 1986 issue of *Development and Change*, Vol. 17, No. 3). Indeed in some circles the IMF has become a fifth horseman of the apocalypse. This is not the place to continue this debate; however, there are some themes which are relevant. Firstly, the present approach is the most pessimistic in development thinking since the Second World War. The emphasis is not developmentalist as such but is merely an attempt to balance the books in order to prevent default.

The second theme, which may even be more contentious, is that it represents a significant increase in the West's (or developed world's) attempt to control African states. The idea of 'conditionality' is to pressurise governments to accept loans in return for certain policy reforms – which in many cases are opposed by host nations. The process has no democratic underpinning at all. It is worth mentioning and is particularly relevant to the urban sphere that such 'leverage' may achieve reforms which humanitarians would applaud; namely the prevention of demolition of unauthorised housing. Two of the chapters in this collection (Stren and Campbell) are partly concerned with the relationship between international agencies and national governments.

The result of these trends, combined with the effects of the recession reducing Africa's room for manoeuvre, is likely to have increased the West's control in Africa. Indeed we might postulate that the developed world now has more control in Africa than at any time since the decolonisation process started.

The negative impact of the 1980s recession, and by implication that of Structural Adjustment Policies, is beginning to emerge. Infant mortality rates (IMRs), after declining systematically for four decades, are beginning to falter and in some cases increase (Cornia *et al.*, 1987). Within Africa the rate has increased in nine out of thirty-six countries between 1980 and 1985. It is significant to note that these are aggregate figures which may hide a substantial deterioration for certain groups. Secondly, this worsening situation is not exclusively limited to states experiencing civil disorder. Thus while the situation worsened in Ethiopia, Uganda and Mozambique it also worsened in Kenya, Tanzania, Somalia, Mali, Morocco and Zimbabwe. The international agencies are very slowly beginning to address themselves to the distributional impact of such adjustment policies.

While the basic facts of Africa's economic (and specifically agrarian) crisis are well known, there are other important economic changes which have occurred since the 1960s which have received almost no attention[1] (Sandbrook, 1982: Weeks, 1986). The changing nature of the urban–rural relationship has passed almost unnoticed. In a nutshell, much academic policy thinking is based upon the historical experience of the 1960s; namely the existence of a relatively privileged urban sector with a large urban–rural differential. Economic processes have by the 1980s made such a view untenable and misleading.

The 1960s model, which itself was a legacy from the colonial system, contained a high wage and privileged urban sector (the labour aristocracy thesis) and a large urban–rural divide which stimulated migration (the Todaro model), juxtaposed with an undifferentiated peasantry. In this model the 'urban' has been seen as exploiting and growing at the expense of the rural (Lipton, 1977). The problem is diagnosed as urban bias. The urban poor, squatters and the informal sector are left to languish between the two sectors.

In the 1960s this model did, to an extent, accurately reflect reality. In particular the colonial legacy of labour stabilisation, the creation of a moderate middle class and the subsequent replacement of expatriate personnel. The provision of subsidised public-sector housing was a key element in this general strategy. However, independent African states were increasingly subject to internal pressures which undermined these policies. Firstly by the late 1960s – with a general abandonment of colonial restrictions in labour movement – African cities began to experience 'open unemployment'. Indeed it was partly in response to these conditions that Keith Hart was to discover the 'informal sector' in the back streets of Accra (Hart, 1973). The famous ILO mission to Kenya which popularised the term was in fact a response to the Kenyan government's request for a mission to solve their 'unemployment problem' (ILO, 1972). The general result was pressure towards the creation of urban employment and political pressures towards egalitarianism, which was associated with much populist rhetoric. The result was to change the late colonial policy. The emphasis shifted from labour stabilisation to employment creation. As an example, in 1972 the Kenyan government delinked the minimum wage from calculations about subsistence requirements. This was one cause of some important trends in the African labour market which were discernible by the 1980s. John Weeks, in a seminal but as yet unpublished paper for the ILO, has documented these trends for all the nations of sub-Saharan Africa (Weeks, 1986).[1]

The first trend which he identifies is a real decline in urban wages since the early 1970s. In many cases income levels have halved in real terms. The second and related trend is a general decline in urban employment security and benefits – in our context the increasing decline of employer housing is significant. The next trend, which has not been widely understood, is that the urban–rural income differential has sharply *reduced* and in some nations – Tanzania, Uganda and Ghana – has actually been reversed. Another relevant trend is the increasing blurring of the distinction (in income or wage terms) between the formal and informal sectors. This was implicit in the policy suggestions of the early 1970s but seems to have come about without any conscious state action (ILO, 1972). Wikan's paper on Cairo provides an extreme example of such blurring; she documents 'informal' sector construction workers earning substantially more than formal white-collar workers.

The result of these trends, combined with the increasing economic differentiation of rural areas, is that overall inequality in *both* the urban and rural sectors has increased. This is consistent with the view that as capitalism continues to penetrate and develop African political economies are being structured around capital and labour. This is more important than previous distinctions such as traditional/modern, rural/urban and informal/ formal sectors. The 1960s rural–urban model, despite its continuing influence on policy-makers, is in fact no longer tenable. It is a contention of this introduction that the importance of these shifts for African political economy have not yet been understood or explored. This move away from the 1960s model is one of the most important themes in contemporary African urbanisation. Indeed it is tempting to suggest that the large urban– rural divide in Africa in the 1960s was a historical anomaly associated with rapid economic growth, decolonisation and the political need to create a middle class. The changes that have subsequently occurred could be inter- preted in terms of adjusting to a more balanced development process.

Two points are worth emphasising; firstly, in the present global recession the African urban poor are an increasingly vulnerable group. This is exac- erbated since IMF policies in terms of limiting subsidies, increasing food prices and restricting wage levels are disproportionately borne by the urban poor. The comfortable assumption that they are politically able to protect themselves is not borne out by their decline in urban incomes since the mid-1970s. The general argument, crudely put, is that the urban elite, through their ownership of assets and/or political connections, can cushion themselves from the impact of the economic downturn. Meanwhile those in the rural areas may survive through a strategy of reverting to subsistence.[2] Indeed within this formulation in East Africa the extent and irreversibility of proletarianisation is crucial in explaining the vulnerability of the urban poor (Amis, 1986). It is the room for manoeuvre the urban poor have which may structure their political responses. Such survival strategies may include among others moonlighting, obtaining resources from rural areas, urban farming and moving household members between urban and rural homes. Wikan's paper on Cairo shows how women continue working after marriage for economic reasons although this is seen as being culturally unacceptable.

The second important point to make is that despite this reduction in the urban–rural differential its impact on migration is as yet unclear. Indeed the nature of the present recession may accelerate urbanisation in some cases but may limit it in others. In monitoring these developments the lack of reliable data and censuses is significant. This problem tends to accentuate itself at the end of decades as many nations tend to have censuses at the beginning of decades. Thus while speculative and anecdotal, there do seem to be indications, at least within East Africa, that urbanisation has slowed significantly. Secondly, within the urban system secondary cities may well be growing faster than capital cities (Hardoy and Satterthwaite, 1986).

Africa's agrarian crisis, the shift in rural–urban balance and the increas- ing economic vulnerability of the urban population are clearly important politically. In recent times political demonstrations and food riots have occurred in the following capital cities: Cairo, Tunis, Monrovia, Lusaka, Khartoum and Nairobi (Lofchie, 1986: 5). The problems of urban food are directly linked to changes in governments in Liberia and Sudan but also lie to a large extent beyond Tanzania's protracted negotiations with the IMF (Nyerere, 1986). The incidence of food shortages together with an increasingly vulnerable urban population is indeed a potent mix. A recent collection also associated with the International African Institute has been associated *precisely* with the problem of *Feeding African Cities* (Guyer, 1987). It is hoped that this volume will provide a complementary study.

The problem of urban food is made increasingly acute as the ability of countries to finance food imports declines. In 1974 sub-Saharan Africa imported 3·9 million metric tons of cereals; by 1985 this figure had risen to 10·2 million tonnes (World Bank, 1987: 212–13). This latter figure has been estimated to be approximately the total grain requirement of Africa's urban population (Lofchie, 1986: 3). In the same period food aid has increased from 0·9 million tonnes in 1974 to 4·8 million in 1985. The debt problem of Africa has also considerably worsened. In 1974 the low-income nations of sub-Saharan Africa faced an annual cost of debt repayment of under $500 million; in 1984 the figure was $1·4 billion and is still rising. Likewise the average debt service ratio increased from 7 to 30 per cent (Lofchie, 1986: 6). Furthermore the harsh reality is that while locally these figures are crippling, in international terms (excluding Nigeria and Egypt) these debts are insignificant. As such African states have a very limited bargaining power with the IMF and the global financial community.

This overall economic situation clearly lies behind many of Africa's political problems; instability, corruption and repression. However, there is also an independent political strand in the present economic crisis. It is argued that post-colonial African society faces a legitimacy crisis, the solution of which often depends upon some form of 'personal rule'. This personal rule is sustained by a combination of clientelism (economic rewards for supports) and coercion (for opponents). The result is authoritarian and personalised states whose very operation, unless closely controlled, is likely to be counter-productive to economic development (Sandbrook, 1986). Within the African context it is unfortunately not difficult to identify such states dominated by some form of personal rule.

This destructive process has increasingly entrenched itself but has also been considerably accelerated by economic decline – itself an outcome of the process. The main premise behind this original argument is a familiar one; namely that African states, with few exceptions being colonial creations, are not national states; rather they are predominantly multi-ethnic or polyethnic. The greater the length of time since decolonisation the more the anti-colonial nationalist coalition has been weakened. Secondly, the peasantry is relatively unintegrated into a capitalist economy. The question then is, in the absence of either a convincing 'nationalist' or 'capitalist' appeal, how is legitimacy achieved and the state held together (Sandbrook, 1986: 321)? In this situation authoritarian 'personal rule' has increasingly taken over where legitimacy has been gained by clientelism and coercion. With few exceptions this has resulted in arbitrary decisions by the bureaucracy to the detriment of long-term planning. The administration is unable to function in a rational fashion. The state, as has also been argued for India, is unable to isolate itself from specific political requests and promote a coherent development strategy (Bardham, 1984). The result is to undermine the state's operations and economic development. When resources are scarce, since legitimacy rests on economic patronage, even this form of legitimacy is undermined. The result is even more fierce competition to consolidate or take over political control.

While many may disagree with the precise specification or causes of it there can be little doubt that Africa faces a political crisis that depends upon but also fuels its economic crisis. The political crisis ultimately concerns the ability of the state to function and administer. The pressures are from many sources: financial, external (IMF and international agencies), opposition elements (ethnic, military or civilian), generational (young post-colonial) and the dispossessed (urban and rural). Economic developments since the mid-1970s in almost all cases will have increased these pressures.

The most striking result of Africa's twin crises, agricultural production and political instability, is the enormous increase in refugees.[3] Table 1 gives UNHCR estimates for selected African countries.

Table 1
Refugees in selected African nations, 1985 (000s)

| | |
|---|---|
| Algeria | 167 |
| Angola | 91 |
| Burundi | 268 |
| Ethiopia | 86 |
| Somalia | 700 |
| Sudan | 1,164 |
| Zaire | 283 |
| Zambia | 104 |
| Zimbabwe | 63 |
| Other African countries | 160 |

*Source:* Office of the UN High Commission for Refugees (UNHCR).

In certain situations these refugee populations are significant in terms of the local population. In Somalia the ratio of refugees to local population is 1 in 7, in Burundi 1 in 15 and in Sudan 1 in 18.

It is worth mentioning that for refugees in conditions of famine the decision to move, which often involves moving towards urban centres, is rational. On the Great Bengal Famine in India in 1943 Sen notes, 'there is little doubt that a destitute who had found his way into Calcutta had a much better chance of survival than anywhere else in Bengal' (Sen, 1981: 57). The reasons are often located in the political importance of urban areas, or put another way, the state's greater difficulty in ignoring the problem.

The refugee is, in many respects, the extreme case of the migrant. The processes are similar; namely the rational response to a declining situation being to move to increase economic opportunities. The refugee movements across Africa in certain circumstances are creating a form of proto-urbanisation. The refugee camp and the shanty town have much in common. It is to the wider processes of urbanisation that we now turn.

## URBANISATION: APPROACHES AND RESPONSES

In this section we shall begin by examining the process of urbanisation in Africa. We shall then give a brief overview of academic approaches to the subject. This will be followed by a discussion of the relationship between urbanisation and urban problems. In the last section we shall examine the changing nature of the African state's response to migration. The changing responses to urbanisation since the 1960s are important in understanding the changing nature of housing provision.

Africa is the least urbanised yet most rapidly urbanising region of the world. Table 2 gives the data for selected African nations.

In 1960 there were 7 cities in Africa with over 500,000 inhabitants. In sub-Saharan Africa there were only two – Kinshasa and Lagos. Twenty years later there were fourteen such cities in sub-Saharan Africa and a further nine in North Africa; thus twenty-three cities in Africa by 1980 had populations in excess of 500,000 (World Bank, 1987: 266–7). The UN estimates are staggering; with the possible exception of North Africa growth rates are expected to remain at 5 per cent per annum. Thus in 2000 – less than twelve years away – there will be eighty-nine cities in Africa in excess of 500,000 inhabitants and fifty-four cities with over a million (Blitzer et al., 1980). The estimates for individual cities are also startling. By the year 2000, Cairo's population is expected to reach 13·2 million, Lagos 8·3 million, Kinshasa 8 million and Jos 7·7 million, while Dar es Salaam, Nairobi, Khartoum, and Addis Ababa will all be over 4 million. Overall it is estimated that the percentage of those living in urban areas in Africa will increase from 29·7 to 39 per cent by the year 2000 (Bruntland, 1987: 237).

When faced with such figures there are two responses. Firstly, disbelief in such predictions, and secondly, alarm at what they mean for the future of African cities. Population projections are notoriously unreliable; Hardoy and Satterthwaite have questioned such projections, noting that they are

Table 2
Urbanisation data for selected African states (population >5 million)

| | As % of total population | | Average annual growth rate | |
|---|---|---|---|---|
| | 1965 | 1985 | 1965–80 | 1980–85 |
| Ethiopia | 8 | 15 | 6·6 | 3·7 |
| Burkina Faso | 6 | 8 | 3·4 | 5·3 |
| Mali | 13 | 20 | 4·9 | 4·5 |
| Mozambique | 5 | 19 | 11·8 | 5·3 |
| Malawi | 5 | — | 7·8 | — |
| Zaire | 19 | 39 | 7·2 | 8·4 |
| Niger | 7 | 15 | 6·9 | 7·0 |
| Angola | 13 | 25 | 6·4 | 5·8 |
| Rwanda | 3 | 5 | 6·3 | 6·7 |
| Somalia | 20 | 34 | 6·1 | 5·4 |
| Kenya | 9 | 20 | 9·0 | 6·3 |
| Tanzania | 6 | 14 | 8·7 | 8·3 |
| Sudan | 13 | 21 | 5·1 | 4·8 |
| Guinea | 12 | 22 | 6·6 | 4·3 |
| Senegal | 27 | 36 | 4·1 | 4·0 |
| Ghana | 26 | 32 | 3·4 | 3·9 |
| Zambia | 24 | 48 | 7·1 | 5·5 |
| Chad | 9 | 27 | 9·2 | 3·7 |
| Uganda | 6 | 7 | 4·1 | 3·0 |
| Mauritania | 7 | 31 | 12·4 | 3·4 |
| Morocco | 32 | 44 | 4·2 | 4·2 |
| Egypt, Arab Rep. | 41 | 46 | 2·9 | 3·4 |
| Côte d'Ivoire | 23 | 45 | 8·7 | 6·9 |
| Zimbabwe | 14 | 27 | 7·5 | 5·0 |
| Nigeria | 15 | 30 | 4·8 | 5·2 |
| Cameroon | 16 | 42 | 8·1 | 7·0 |
| Botswana | 4 | 20 | 15·4 | 4·5 |
| Tunisia | 40 | 56 | 4·2 | 3·7 |
| Algeria | 38 | 43 | 3·8 | 3·7 |
| Sub-Saharan Africa (w) | 13 | 25 | 6·2 | 5·7 |
| Developing economies (w) | 24 | 31 | 3·9 | 3·8 |
| Low-income economies (w) | 17 | 22 | 3·6 | 4·0 |
| Middle-income economies (w) | 37 | 48 | 4·4 | 3·5 |

Note: (w) = weighted.
Source: World Bank, 1987: 266–7.

composed of simple extrapolation based upon an assumption of uniform linear economic transformation (i.e. that the underdeveloped world will repeat the experience of the developed world). This latter view has been widely discredited; nevertheless these projections are effectively made independently from processes of economic change (Hardoy and Satterthwaite,

1986). Given the present economic recession and the previous discussion there do seem to be very clear reasons why we might expect the rate of urbanisation in Africa to decline. To suggest otherwise is to implicitly admit that urbanisation is totally unrelated to economic change. Again we can note the tendency, in the absence of contemporary data and censuses, to be dominated by the experience of earlier periods (i.e. the 1960s and 1970s). In what follows we shall give an overview of academic approaches and responses to African urbanisation; as we would expect this partly mirrors the changing empirical reality.

At the outset an apology is appropriate; this review is almost exclusively concerned with the Anglophonic literature. The lack of interaction between the Anglophonic and Francophone literatures is both deplorable and remarkable. At the risk of excessive simplification, Anglophonic African urban studies have tended to be individualistic and empirical, being dominated by anthropology as a discipline (Mercier, 1973). The problems of adaptation to urban life and the urban–rural divide have been dominant themes. Meanwhile the Francophone literature has in general been more theoretical, focusing on structural characteristics of processes within urban areas.

In the 1950s and early 1960s the issue was the migrants' adjustment to urban life. The focus was upon tribal associations, traditional society and rural–urban links. The approach is almost explicit in Mayer's classic study *Townsmen or Tribesmen* (1961). As the urbanisation (and decolonisation) process continues the literature becomes influenced by two forces: firstly the growing emergence of an African urban working class, and secondly a growing radical tradition or political economy approach to African studies. The latter was strongly influenced by the 'dependencia' school of Latin America (Frank, 1969).

Within the African context the focus was on the making of an African working class, and its political and economic significance to the overall political economy (Sandbrook and Cohen, 1975). We would also situate studies of the informal sector within this overall approach. The focus shifts from the cultural aspects of urbanism towards the investigation of the process of proletarianisation. There is much implicitly in common here, although the links are never made, with Castells's devastating critique of Western urban sociology (Castells, 1976). African urban studies, like urban studies and development studies in general, takes on a more explicitly Marxist tone. Indeed within Latin America urbanism and African historiography there is discussion of a 'new paradigm' or a 'new wave' (Gilbert *et al.*, 1982; Crush and Rogerson, 1983).

The aspects of such a new approach are an emphasis on class formation, the state and capitalism which seems to have much in common with contemporary Francophone approaches. The latter, however, seem to have a greater interest in processes of urban real estate, space and residential differentiation (Mercier, 1973).

At the risk of excessive elaboration, we may detect another shift in African urban studies in the 1980s.[4] In part this is a reflection of wider general trends. In the last decade, there has been a sustained critique of underdevelopment theory by Marxists. This has been on two fronts; firstly that underdevelopment theory has underestimated the 'progressive potential' of capitalism and secondly that it has been weakly grounded in historical research (Warren, 1980). The result has been research with an increasing attention to specific historical detail, but retaining and located within an overall political economy framework. Gavin Kitching's work on *Class and Economic Change in Kenya* (1980) is perhaps the classic of this genre. This seems to be a clear move forward from attempts at wide theoretical generalisation. As a consequence, in a period of economic recession the focus in the urban sector has often been on strategies of survival (Murray, 1981).

It is perhaps appropriate to end this rapid overview of contemporary African urban studies by noting that the changes in trends and approaches we have outlined are by no means universal. Indeed, unfortunately, intellectual inertia often seems greater than change. In what follows we shall examine the relationship between urbanisation and urban problems. This is important as this relationship is often misunderstood; the result is to partly obscure the dynamics of urban society and our understanding of the creation of urban problems.

It is common in discussions about African urban areas to start with the rate of urbanisation. The image, whether intended or not, is that of hordes of migrants descending upon urban areas, which are almost immediately diagnosed as having a 'problem' in absorbing this influx. In this interpretation the migrants are flooding both the urban housing and labour markets. At the very least these new immigrants will put a strain on existing resources. Within Africa this is the prevailing political response and ideology. A related and more sophisticated ideology has grown up which perceives urban areas as exploiting the rural areas and considers that this process has hindered development (ILO, 1972; Lipton, 1977).

While the majority of this work accepts that these statements are only valid in specific historical circumstances, the confusion has arisen because these observations have tended to be seen as universal statements. This is reinforced by the seemingly self-evident truth that migration does exacerbate urban problems. It is thus a very short step to assume that there is a causal and necessary connection between increased migration and urban problems. As we shall see, the apparent simplicity of this common observation hides considerable complexity. Indeed it is pertinent to note that in certain situations rural–rural migration exceeds rural–urban migration, but with a seeming absence of this relationship. This is clearly a function of the visibility of urban problems (Hill, 1986: 123).

The relationship between migration and urban problems presupposes a static model, limited information and an aggregated model of society. We shall now consider these three assumptions in turn.

The most simple and compelling version is that rural–urban migration creates, through an increase in numbers, excess demand for urban services. The strength of this argument and its weakness are immediately apparent. To deny the logic of this position is to deny any legitimacy to market forces. However, this 'excess demand' interpretation is by definition the mirror image of an 'insufficient supply' interpretation. It is a contention of this introduction that it is misleading to disaggregate these explanations. Thus the assumption becomes qualified that the relationship between migration and urban problems holds in a situation where the supply of urban services remains untouched, declines, does not increase, or does not increase fast enough; or, to anticipate, does not increase fast enough for a specific group. To accept this is to undermine the simplicity we started with.

The confusion has arisen because in most empirical cases studied the provision of legal or formal sector urban services did not increase as quickly as the increase in overall demand. However, little attempt was made to evaluate the contribution of unauthorised provision of services. In the model they were simply ignored, particularly in a qualitative sense. The well-documented rapid physical growth of unauthorised settlements within African urban areas should make us suspicious about the case concerning the lack of provision of low-income housing and urban services. It is not clear that the housing problem, with this physical growth, is simply either that of 'excess demand' or 'insufficient supply'. It firmly suggests that the problem may be in the eye of the beholder.

A related assumption of the conventional view of migration exacerbating problems is that of limited information. Thus the would-be migrant, like the refugee, is thought to be unaware of the prevailing urban conditions. In the terms we have used the 'excess demand' information does not seem to be transmitted into the rural areas. The implicit assumption seems to be that, 'if they knew' they would not come. This idea is flawed: there is a substantial flow of information between the urban and rural spheres (Koenigsberger, 1976). The administrators' position is ambivalent: 'poor information' explains the migrants' mistaken idea to move. At the same time improvements in urban housing and services are to be limited since they are thought to increase migration which will undermine any improvement. The news that the streets are not paved with gold does not get through (poor information) but any news of modest improvement gets through (good information). Good news travels; poor does not.

This is contradictory. The exchange of information between town and country within Africa is excellent (Parkin, 1976). To the individuals concerned migration is perceived correctly and is a personal gain (ILO, 1972). Presumably urban services are part of an individual's evaluation. This brings us to the final assumption behind the conventional view; an unaggregated society. To tackle this issue we shall consider what constitutes a problem, and secondly the advantages and disadvantages of the migration process for different economic groups.

The African urban administration may see uncontrolled chaotic urban growth. This seems to be the official view; it is interesting to consider the elements of this interpretation. At the simplest there is the planner's professional dislike of uncontrolled and unplanned growth. For the state administrator this may represent a problem in that it implies a high level of illegality. Aesthetic considerations are relevant in the definitions of a problem partly on their own account, but mainly in terms of international tourism and image. This problem is exacerbated in many African cities by their pretensions to be 'international' centres. The frequent tidy-up campaigns in African cities that are associated with international conferences and the like are ample evidence of the importance of such considerations.

The more sophisticated interpretation sees the problem in terms of public health. At a humanitarian level, this is a problem in its own right. However, the official view will also contain the element that public health problems are infectious and cannot be contained, and as such the existence of such a problem is a threat to all individuals, including the administration. Finally the administration may perceive the problem in terms of political dissent and potential conflict, especially when faced with food problems. However, while such migration may increase the chances of dissent, it may also increase the potential for patronage.

The individual may experience problems predominantly associated with gaining access to housing and the quality of the housing. It is important to point out that the problem as perceived from the individual (migrant) level is by no means congruent with the official definition of a problem. Hence we are in agreement with Portes that

Internal migration and urban growth are intrinsically neither good nor bad. Such assessments depend upon the specific social context and, in particular, on the point of view one adopts with respect to the different classes and institutional actors. A case can be made that, in the short run at least, the present trends of rural–urban migration and urban concentration are functional for a wide assortment of groups. (Portes, 1985: 110)

He then proceeds to list the advantages; firstly for the individual migrant in terms of economic opportunities; for private firms by increasing the urban market, increased labour supply (downward pressure on wages) and indirectly reducing labour costs – by limiting the reproduction of labour power. Rural landowning interests benefit from the presence of a safety value by reducing land pressure and peasant mobilisation. The urban administration and politicians benefit by an increasing urban population amenable to patronage, especially in terms of land allocation and recognition and mobilisation. Within Africa we might also add the escape from rural destitution. Furthermore, urban incomes and resources earned are often reinvested in rural areas (Portes, 1985: 110; Collier and Lal, 1986). However, in the long run the negative aspects are associated with the 'quality of life for the mass of the urban population' (Portes, 1985: 110). It is these issues which we are concerned with in the final section.

While Portes does not see a necessary connection between migration and unregulated settlements, he does see a relationship between immigrants and the forcing up of rent levels (p. 111). Secondly, the price of legal housing is moving out of reach of the majority. In this situation, 'illegal occupation of land and the spontaneous self-construction by the poor emerge as the only viable alternative' (p. 112). Thus he correctly notes, 'the emergence of squatter settlements is not the consequence of so-called excess numbers, but of a given wage structure' (p. 112).

This emphasis on the wage structure and the importance of patronage is consistent with our earlier discussion of the changing nature of the urban–rural relations within Africa. Thus when considering the process of African urbanisation it is important to realise that there is no *necessary* connection between rural–urban migration and urban or housing problems. In a recent paper using an entitlement approach I have attempted to show this for the Nairobi housing market (Amis, 1987). Secondly, it is important to understand the factors that do affect the housing market. It is in this context that we should consider urban poverty, the commercialisation of unauthorised housing, the informal building industry and the urban land market.

In this section we shall examine different African states' responses to urbanisation. We shall build up two ideal types of such responses; namely a repressive and a *laissez-faire* model. This will make it easier to analyse the changes in political responses to unauthorised settlements that have occurred. The state's response to urbanisation is a key determinant of the availability of different housing forms.

The repressive model is characterised by the following features that tend to be mutually reinforcing. Firstly and most importantly, there is an attempt to control or prevent rural–urban migration; secondly, access to urban land by market mechanisms by the urban poor is limited (i.e. there is an extremely unequal urban land distribution) and thirdly, there is a generally well-developed legal system and a well-enforced system of property ownership. In such a situation the urban poor are forced to occupy land illegally, i.e. they are obliged to squat – usually in direct confrontation with the state.

The *laissez-faire* model is characterised by two main features: the lack of any state attempt to control rural–urban migration, and a generally less-developed legal system – often there is a confused system of property ownership or at least a poorly established notion of private property. In this model the distribution of urban land is generally characterised by greater equality. The urban poor can either purchase land, or if they occupy land 'illegally' their dwellings are not likely to be demolished – since in this case, unlike the repressive model, the state has no strong legal and property system to defend. In this situation of sanctioned non-commercial occupation or access to land via the market it is likely that small-scale rental sector will develop, since there is security for capital investment. However, it is unlikely to be particularly profitable as it is relatively easy for others to have access to urban land, thus making this sector relatively extensive.

At the risk of oversimplification we can define the applicability of these two models as follows. Within Africa, we may characterise the settler states as repressive in their responses to urbanisation while the non-settler states adopted a *laissez-faire* policy.

It is interesting to note that there is a similar kind of distinction in the French literature. Thus Adrien-Rongier (1981) in his study of Bangui shows that urbanisation is spontaneous and that despite its illegality the state is not acting against such housing. It is interesting to note that the notion of illegality is only meaningful if the state is prepared to enforce its laws. Clearly there are elements of our *laissez-faire* model in this. However, he is also keen to emphasise that this is different from the situation in Abidjan and Dakar that Vernière conceptualises, like our repressive model, along the following lines: 'un espace conflictuel entre deux forces antagonistes, un spontanéisme populaire et la volonté étatique' (Adrien-Rongier, 1981: 94). Peil, in her comparative analysis of African squatter settlements, comes to a similar conclusion. Her central question is – why are there not any squatters in West Africa? She offers three reasons: the land tenure patterns; official tolerance of sub-standard housing; and migrants' attitudes to permanence. In essence this is our *laissez-faire* model. 'Squatting results from lack of alternatives, and . . . the choices open to the West African usually make squatting unnecessary' (Peil, 1976: 155).

In general in 1960 our two ideal-type models seem appropriate representations of the urban housing situation in Africa. However, by the 1980s the situation had changed. The key point was that the sheer scale of demographic increase in urban areas was making the repressive response to urbanisation untenable.

In this section we have examined the process of urbanisation and the responses to it both administratively and academically. In the next section we shall examine the implications of these changes for the housing market.

# AFRICAN URBAN HOUSING:
## COMMERCIALISATION AND CHANGE

In this section we shall explore the changing nature of African urban housing. We shall first consider the processes that are changing the nature of unauthorised and low-income housing. We shall focus on the commercialisation of unauthorised housing although the processes are similar in the traditional or project housing areas. This gives a general introduction and overview of the processes outlined in the case studies contained in this collection.

The conventional view of squatting in Third World cities involves the illegal occupation of land and self-construction of shelter. The settlements so formed are often seen as being politically autonomous, under a permanent threat of demolition and outside the legal system. Characteristically, the urban poor were building their own shelter with anything they could lay their hands on, on land they did not own. This was partly occurring as private capital did not find such a sector attractive for investment (Roberts, 1978: 147–8). The insecurity associated with possible demolition discouraged investment. As we shall see, once security was established and financial returns available, capital was attracted to this sector, regardless of the legal position. It is this process that has transformed African and Third World low-income urban housing.

At this stage it is useful to disentangle the two aspects generally characterising squatting, namely illegal occupation and self-construction. It is important to understand that there is no necessary connection between these two aspects. Unfortunately these two aspects have become confused; thus the illegal occupation of land and unauthorised structures have often wrongly been used to infer self-construction of housing. There are many cases where squatting does not involve both aspects. The process of self-construction applies when the provision or production of shelter and its consumption are contained within the same household unit. In this case the illegal occupation of land allows for the provision of shelter without monetary exchange. The crucial point is that the self-construction aspect of squatting can only exist in the absence of capital, since the involvement of capital will result in the establishment of commercial relations. Furthermore the general tendency of capital to penetrate and integrate new sectors and markets into a capitalist and commercial economy has been well documented.

The key point about illegality as an aspect of squatting is that it generally discouraged capital investment in this sector. It is security for capital investment that matters rather than illegality *per se*. It is the relationship between security (of which legality represents one form) and expected rates of return which influence whether capital will penetrate this sector. Indeed it is this relationship that determines whether capital will become involved in other housing areas; notably the traditional and project sectors. It is the factors that determine security and expected rates of return that ultimately are at the heart of the housing issue. It is here that we should locate the importance of the urban land market, the informal building industry, popular participation and the legal system.

Before continuing it is relevant to elaborate upon what determines security and expected rates of return for capital investment. These factors ultimately determine the commercialisation process. There are four developments that seem to have influenced security, which in one case means the *de facto* acceptance of unauthorised settlements; in other cases security may be sanctioned by the legal system.

The first and most clearly associated with this discussion has been the emergence since the 1960s of a pro-squatter literature. This was stimulated by the work of John Turner in Peru; the thrust of this new orthodoxy was that squatters solved their own housing needs themselves (Turner, 1976). Hence what was previously defined as the 'problem' might be more accurately described as part of the 'solution'. In general this literature was a plea against inhuman demolitions. These ideas were reinforced by a general shift in the 1970s in development thinking towards encouraging the informal sector, small-scale production and meeting basic needs.

The second realisation was that the process of rural–urban migration was inevitable. The rationale behind demolition was partly a belief, especially in Africa, in the 'temporary' nature of migration. Increasingly it became obvious, whatever policy was pursued, that urban growth would continue unabated. In the end there was little option but to accept unauthorised settlement (Wegelin, 1983). It was on this open door that the humanitarian lobby was pushing.

These two trends became institutionalised after 1972 when the World Bank (IBRD) became involved in urban shelter projects. This involved attempts to harness the self-evident ability of squatters to house themselves; the projects took the institutional form of squatter upgrading and site and service schemes (Skinner and Rodell, 1983.) The World Bank was also to exert pressure, usually in the form of conditionality on loan agreements, to Third World urban administrations to accept and stabilise unauthorised areas. Hence in the mid-1970s the most marginalised of the urban population was to suddenly discover that the World Bank had become its patron. This process of leverage in changing urban policy was particularly clear in Kenya and the Côte d'Ivoire.

The final development is related to the last; namely what explains the World Bank's involvement in supporting unauthorised development. The idealist view is that academic pressure with humanitarian motives combined with McNamara ideology accounts for this policy shift. This is not entirely convincing. Similarly, a crude materialist interpretation in terms of reducing wages by reducing housing costs (the reproduction of labour power) is unsatisfactory. Firstly this logic has always existed and does not explain the timing of a specific historical intervention. It also fails to explain a policy pursued and promoted in a wide variety of economic conditions (from Mexico and Brazil to Senegal and Kenya). It seems therefore that the underlying logic behind an acceptance policy must be sought at the political level. In essence the importance of political stability within the urban areas of the Third World seems important. In this context the acceptance of unauthorised settlements is a relatively painless, and potentially profitable, way to appease the urban poor in the Third World. The increasing mobility and ability of international capital to change locations at short notice are likely to make these political considerations more rather than less important. Indeed we might postulate that these changes are not unrelated to developments associated with the new international division of labour.

These, then, at the macro level, are the trends which are moving Third World administrations towards a more *laissez-faire* acceptance policy towards unauthorised settlements. Hence, whatever the precise legal position, the security for capital investments is likely to be increasing. However we must also consider the expected rates of return in this sector in order to examine the likelihood of capital investment. These rates are not easily assessed but are clearly important in attracting capital investment.

The first and most obvious point is that it is the expected rates of return in this sector in relation to alternative sources of investment that matter. These will clearly reflect the prevailing economic conditions within a specific country. However the evidence for land speculation is sufficiently widespread to suggest, in general, that housing and land are seen as attractive outlets for investment. This may reflect perceived security as much as expected rates of return. In general it seems fair to suggest that in stagnant economies and/or in periods of economic recession land and housing are likely to be seen as secure and/or lucrative outlets for investment. This is clearly the case in contemporary Africa.

The level of competition within the housing sector is also important in determining expected rates of return. Access to land and in particular the extent of monopoly in this access seem to be the most important in determining competition, i.e. the availability of alternative forms of shelter. Recent research confirms that the main determinant of shelter is the availability of urban land development, however determined. The more land that is available, the lower the returns, which implies less attraction for capital investment. (The relatively under-developed urban land market of the 1960s.) The emergence of monopoly tends to create land scarcity: higher returns with considerable attraction for capital (Angel *et al.*, 1983: 22).

Within each historical and national context it is these variables that
influence the security and rates of return for capital investment that
determine the commercialisation of low-income housing.

It is a central tenet of this seminar that the commercialisation or commodification of low-income housing is the dominant process throughout African cities. In this we are in agreement with the suggestion that contemporary processes in capitalist peripheral states are breaking down informal
housing mechanisms (Ward, 1982b: 92). There is a burgeoning literature
on similar processes in Latin America from a group at University College
London (see the work of Edwards, 1982; Gilbert *et al.*, 1982; Ward,
1982a&b); likewise the processes are well covered for Asia (Angel *et al.*,
1983). The aim of this collection is to provide an outlet for and a synthesis of
studies of similar phenomena within the African context.

## THE STRUCTURE OF THE COLLECTION:
## TOWARDS A SYNTHESIS

This volume is divided into three broad main sections. The first section
continues the themes of this introduction by examining the changing
approaches to urban housing in Africa. The second part contains the
detailed empirical case studies of individual African urban housing
markets. The third part concerns urban shelter projects and possible policy
options. Finally, Peter Lloyd provides an epilogue to the discussion.

The first two chapters (Stren and Coquery) are reports from the inside of
two major urban research projects of the 1980s. As such they provide
excellent introductions to the changing field of urban research in Africa.
Stren at the University of Toronto reports on a large Africa-wide IDRC-
funded project entitled 'African Urban Management'. In his chapter he
chronologically identifies the changing nature of the urban housing problem. Thus we travel from the conventional state housing of the 1950s and
1960s through the phase of aided self-help in the 1970s to the final, contemporary phase in the 1980s which he identifies in terms of a growing concern
with management and infrastructure. The first two phases are accepted
wisdom; namely the shift from conventional subsidised state housing
towards aided self-help. Stren's research, however, highlights a crucial
weakness in the latter policy; despite the rhetoric, recent research shows
that site and service projects require large public subsidies and have a
tendency to go to affluent groups. This was precisely the criticism of
conventional state housing policies, to which aided self-help was the
solution.

The third phase implies a retreat from new investment in housing. Thus
with the growing economic downturn of the 1980s – from which the urban

sector has suffered disproportionately – the emphasis moves to simply maintaining the existing urban infrastructure. In many African cities there is evidence of a serious decline in basic urban infrastructure (water, roads and transport). In acute recessions such large-scale investments are likely to be shelved and services cut. Hence the delivery or non-delivery of basic urban services is now of major concern.

Two comments on this analysis may be pertinent; firstly, the finance to provide urban services is often a function of local government. Hence the issue of urban service delivery is related to concerns about central–local government relations. In many countries local administration is starved of funds and autonomy lest it becomes a potential source of political opposition. This process is particularly clear in the case of Kenyan local government. The second point is that local government services, which often include water, education and health, are often relevant in terms of social indicators like the infant mortality rate. The recent decline in such indicators may partly reflect a decline in government expenditure, perhaps at the local level. The final point is that 'austerity packages' associated with structural adjustment (or recession) are likely to exacerbate central–local relations in Africa.

Michel Coquery reports from a large French research effort on African and Third world urbanisation, between 1981 and 1985, mainly based at ORSTOM and CNRS in Paris. All the French contributors in this volume were involved in this project. In his chapter he documents the changing philosophy of this research initiative by the class of 1968 stimulated (and funded) by the Mitterand electoral victory in France in 1980. The original technocratic emphasis on building materials was abandoned in favour of a detailed analysis of the process of building production. Here suddenly the problem became defined as one of concepts and discourse. Studies focusing on the language of development policies have become an important growth area in development studies recently (Clay and Schaffer, 1984). The use of labelling to reinforce overall structures of inequality has been demonstrated for low-income housing in Bogotá (Glaser, 1985).

Implicit in Coquery's chapter is the idea that the terms used to address the housing process in which the urban poor are engaged in are inadequate, in particular the confusion between the legal status and method of production. It became necessary to disaggregate 'auto-construction' into true self-help or production for others as an investment. In English the emphasis on 'self-help' has, until recently, trapped and constrained research. In a nutshell the processes of housing commodification were not visible in the dominant Turneresque discourse, partly reinforced by a World Bank ideological commitment to such terms: self-help was the dominant term, to which everything else was apparently an aberration. The author remembers being informed by a Bank consultant that 'the purest form of self-help was sub-contraction'! Nevertheless the material changes in housing were such that the Turner discourse could not hold. The new terms are partly a response to new conditions. However the concepts themselves were important; researchers liberated from 'self-help' or 'consolidators' were finding tenants, landlords and commercial relations everywhere. The French work has been synthesised and published in Alain Durand-Lasserve's book *L'Exclusion des Pauvres dans les Villes du Tiers-Monde* (1986). The title clearly suggests the new agenda.

Coquery finishes by examining the specific case of Lomé in Togo. He demonstrates the emergence of rental housing for the poor. He concludes by asking the question: is the emergence of renting a response to the economic crisis or does it represent a new structural change in urban development? The implications of other research tend towards the latter position.

The second section examines the changing nature of housing markets across Africa. The first two chapters (3 and 4) are concerned with Nigeria. Okoye's paper traces the historical evolution of Nigeria's housing policy. He documents the state's intention to intervene directly, on a large scale, in house construction in the 1975–80 period. However by 1980 only approximately 20 per cent of the planned units had been built. The policy was continued into the 1980s with the formulation in 1981 of a national housing policy, and Okoye concludes that direct construction has met with limited success while site and services schemes are seen as a policy solution. It is interesting to compare this policy with similar large-scale schemes in the Côte d'Ivoire (see Stren's chapter). The latter was the most ambitious in Africa and has in the end been abandoned, clearly illustrating the inability of the public sector to provide sufficient units.

Meanwhile, at a more local level, Tade Aina's paper shows the development of commercialised rental housing in a settlement in Lagos – Olaleye-Iponri. He identifies an extremely complex tenure relationship involving layers of sub-letting with leases of different lengths. He distinguishes the 'petty–landlord' (small and resident) from the 'enterpreneur–landlord' (large and absentee) and discusses the variation in landlord–tenant relations. He ends by calling for policies to restrict the large-scale landlords while encouraging the small.

This disaggregation of the actors in the urban development process is an important theme in the next chapter. El Kadi shows how in Cairo agricultural land on the periphery is being developed as 'informal plots' for urban (housing) use. This, however, encourages processes of speculation which result in mechanisms of exclusion for the poor.

The analysis identifies different agents in the process of 'lotissement' (subdivision and putting land on the market); at the bottom are poor/agricultural peasants selling small (i.e. less than 1 feddan (0·42 ha.)) agricultural plots for development while retaining a piece for personal use (or renting). The next tier are the 'professional' (or private?) developers buying and developing larger sites rapidly for resale. This is an extremely lucrative business with profits of around 200 per cent and a somewhat fly-by-night character. Finally at the top are 'les sociétés de lotissement' which are relatively large financial institutions involved in many different sectors, and in one case operating in many Egyptian cities. However the legal position of such operations is extremely ambiguous. El Kadi's study firstly shows that to understand the commercialisation of land and housing we must consider the different actors involved (and their class interests) and secondly identifies the processes by which semi-legal urban development can be institutionalised.

The next chapter tells a somewhat different story from the central tenements of Cairo. Unni Wikan, from her detailed anthropological work, is able with longitudinal data to examine the changing housing strategies among the Cairo poor between 1950 and 1985. In particular she documents housing strategies in a situation of excessive overcrowding, rent control and limited 'new' opportunities. These strategies involve the payment of key money, attempts to accumulate a housing deposit by both husband and wife saving and the 'forced' living together of relatives. The subordination of cultural norms – e.g. that married women should not work – to economic necessity is very apparent. Finally as a result of the longitudinal nature of the study (fieldwork over seventeen years) she is able to trace the trajectories of different groups. The middle-class families who invest in education and formal jobs are somewhat unsuccessful, while the manual families, who are often involved in the building industry, invest in property which becomes a vehicle for upward mobility. Wikan's paper reminds us that to understand housing markets longitudinal anthropological data is essential. We are thus able to understand the importance of the household, age cycles and culture in housing strategies. In this context overcrowding is almost a hidden variable in research on housing studies. It is an important household response to falling incomes which is often overlooked. Thus it is not mentioned as a household response to declining incomes in a recent review on the subject (Cornia et al, 1987). The studies in this volume provide very tentative evidence that overcrowding is on the increase in African cities.

The relationship between the overcrowded *medina*, common in North Africa, and informal plot allocation and land invasion on the city edges is again illustrated in the next chapter. Stambouli's study of Tunis shows how large-scale 'informal' development is occurring at the extremity of the urban area (14 km from the centre); furthermore this development is functional both in an economic and political sense. At the economic level it provides land and housing for development which the state is unable to deliver. Politically these developments allow ample opportunity for political patronage by party officials. Indeed the political health of the Tunisian state can almost be interpreted from the extent of invasion *vis-à-vis* informal sale by officials. The relationship, however defined, between administrative structures and commercial urban development (land or housing) is an important issue in new approaches to urban development. Assumptions of administrative involvement rather than the autonomy of communities are the starting points.

This involvement is apparent in residential land markets in urban Kenya. Yahya gives a general overview of the methods by which land is obtained by individuals in Africa (and especially Kenya). In particular he highlights the increasing shortages of public land for urban development. The recent World Bank experience with urban shelter projects in Kenya is relevant; rather than attempting to acquire land for development (private or from the declining stocks of public land) the emphasis has shifted to making agreements with existing landowners on which private rental housing is developed. We can see in this elements of an official attempt to control existing semi-legal forms of urban development.

This theme is taken up explicitly in Diana Lee-Smith's Chapter 9, which directly compares the internal organisation of an unauthorised settlement, Korogocho, and a site and service scheme, Dandora, in Nairobi. Both settlements are dominated by commercial rental units with well-defined landlord and tenant groups, and the property in both settlements represents a lucrative investment. The most interesting observation concerns the allocation process in the two systems. The 'informal' allocation in the unauthorised settlement is *more* arbitrary and inequitable than the more formal system. This example is a welcome corrective to simple assumptions that 'traditional' systems are necessarily equitable and that the process of commercialisation implies a competitive market (freedom of entry). In this context the distributional aspect of the commercialisation process is a key research issue.

While the Nairobi experience is one of a highly profitable and inequitable development of unauthorised rental housing (Amis, 1984), this is not always the case as the chapter on Lilongwe, the new capital of Malawi illustrates. Malawi, while relatively unurbanised, has had an almost conti-nuous emphasis for the last three decades on a site and service approach. This has taken the institutional form of THAs (Traditional Housing Areas) in Lilongwe. These areas have historically been associated with small-scale landlordism; tobacco farming was a much more lucrative output to large capital. The development of THAs in Lilongwe until the mid-1970s appears to have been a model of 'appropriate' and 'affordable' urban development. However various pressures, mainly associated with presi-dential prestige, have led to a process of upgrading in specific THAs in Lilongwe (Area 47). In these areas the building standards have *increased*;

the result has been to give an impetus to commercialisation. Plots were increasingly being purchased rather than allocated, tenancy became institutionalised and overcrowding increased. The result has transformed Malawi's virtuous case into something approximating a vicious circle more like Nairobi.

It is clear from the case studies that disaggregating the actors and institutions involved in these new housing markets is a central concern. It would seem that attempts to specify the logic of these processes, whether in terms of the 'articulation' of petty commodity production, or the development of the building process, is a more profitable area for theoretical discussion than to endlessly rehearse the merits or applicability of self-help housing (Nientied and van der Linden, 1985; Burgess, 1985; Gilbert and van der Linden, 1987; Burgess, 1987). The thrust of these volumes is that the latter is becoming historically irrelevant.

Nevertheless in discussing the distributional aspects of this 'new' housing we must be careful not to fall into a comfortable 'populist' position that large landlords are wicked and that small landlords are benevolent. While this may be the case, it can not be assumed, as work in Nairobi suggests (Amis, 1983). Poor landlords often have less finance for investment and are totally dependent on tenants' rent, and as such they were often as hard or harder than affluent landlords. Ideas about solidarity among the poor may be comfortable to appease the conscience of the well-off but are often untrue. Indeed the housing markets discussed here could be opening up a schism in the African working class.

The third section explicitly considers issues of housing policy and urban shelter projects. The latter are associated with the World Bank's involvement in urban shelter since 1972. There is already a growing literature explicitly or implicitly evaluating this intervention (Ward, 1982a; Skinner and Rodell, 1983; Payne, 1984). The chapters that follow cover similar ground but are more concerned with the ongoing impact of market mechanisms and what to do about them in such projects, than with 'self-help' as a policy.

The chapter by Campbell is mainly concerned with World Bank projects in Tanzania. These projects do not fulfil their objectives of providing affordable low-income housing; instead they have ended up housing a middle-income group. This point has been acknowledged elsewhere in the volume (Stren), and what is particularly interesting is the institutional impact of this urban project. Thus at one level it has become 'a white elephant' and a drain on financial resources while on the other it has increased bureaucracy and institutional confusion. The overall result has been to reduce the local authorities' ability to 'manage' Dar es Salaam.

The negative impact of project agencies on institutional development has been noted elsewhere. Indeed this problem was explicitly acknowledged in the third urban project in Kenya. This destructive impact of projects on institutions is precisely the reverse of the World Bank's 'Trojan horse' strategy to urban projects. In this interpretation the main aim of urban shelter projects has been as a vehicle through which to achieve urban policy reform which would allow the private sector, helped by appropriate by-laws, to deliver cheap, affordable and legal housing (Bunkerley, 1982). Whether the market is capable of providing this must remain at least a moot point.

In this context, and Tanzania in the later 1970s is an appropriate example, it is relevant to note that these urban poverty and shelter projects were started precisely at the moment when urban incomes began to fall and the global recession started to bite. This does not imply that a basic needs philosophy was mistaken but does suggest some possible reasons for the apparent failure to achieve stated objectives.

The chapter by Teedon on low-income housing in Harare in Zimbabwe directly addresses this issue. The perennial problem with urban projects is as follows: low-income allottee unable to repay (cost–recovery problem), sell-out (or buy-in), resulting in the project *de facto* becoming middle-income, usually involving landlordism. The precise legal situation varies but to any urban planner this is a familiar scenario. The solutions suggested and tried all involve attempts to restrict sale. Harare was no exception to this; it is the contradictions in this policy which Teedon exposes. Attempts to restrict allottees' right to sale undermines investment in housing involvements; thus they cannot work. Nobody improves (or invests in) their house without an assurance that they can recoup the capital gain. The implication is that successful tenure reform is more than freedom from demolition; it requires ownership, which includes the right to sale. Teedon's important contribution is to expose this contradiction. The policy implication is that not only is it *de facto* impossible to restrict market forces, but it is also counter-productive to attempts by low-income groups to improve their housing. At least at this level participation and market forces are complementary.

Asiama considers the problem of access to urban land for housing. This access is considered essential to strategies for housing (Angel *et al.*, 1983; Crooke, 1983). The chapter considers the options but, not surprisingly, is unable to suggest ways ahead. The breakdown of traditional tenure appears to be a truism. Asiama's paper is useful reading to correct against simple solutions. Thus even radical legislation like India's Urban Land (ceiling and regulation) Act 1976, ensuring the poor access to urban land, has, through a lack of political will, had almost no impact (Roy, 1983).

It is tempting to suggest that the urban land market in African cities is approaching an 'urban nexus' which can only be solved by state intervention (Scott, 1980). Elsewhere Lojkine has shown the contradiction between the operation of the urban land market and the development of industrial capitalism. In the end, to create a rational solution, the state must intervene (Lojkine, 1976). The city needs workers but the land market expels them. The solution to this problem, given the general poverty, the urban land market and legal systems is perhaps the major challenge facing African urban administrations. The key to the problem of affordability lies here. Whether the political will is yet available must remain debatable.

The final two chapters are attempts at synthesis. Edwards's chapter bravely asks two central questions: what causes renting? and what should we do about it? His discussion draws upon his own work in Latin America (Edwards, 1982). The answers, as we might expect, are not definitive. The incidence of renting is considered in terms of migration, household incomes and housing costs and government policy. These are then examined both in space (Africa v. Latin America) and time. He confirms that the development of small-scale landlordism is the contemporary dominant theme. He then considers the policy options which are all ultimately designed to increase 'choice'; cost-recovery, rent control and strengthening of the tenants' bargaining position. There are contradictions in all these suggestions, but the welfare of the low-income tenant is now clearly on the agenda. This in many instances involves active participation. The idea of popular participation has been influential in housing circles. Despite its much stated importance the record of active participation in project implementation is limited (Skinner and Rodell, 1983). In part this clearly reflects the inherent contradiction in many urban projects between local popular democratic participation and large-scale bureaucratic organisations like the World Bank (Seymour, 1975). However within the African context the potential for participation is also restricted, as many states identify any form of participation with political dissent (Sandbrook, 1982). Finally we should also be aware that community development can often in fact amount to a subtle form of state control (Gilbert and Ward, 1983).

It is worth noting that in most of the above instances participation has primarily been centred around owners rather than tenants. Participation with tenants, as Edwards notes, has only just begun.

The question to be asked, if we are concerned with poverty and basic needs, is whether housing interventions are appropriate at all. The difficulty Edwards has in identifying policy suggestions may reflect the difficulty in finding solutions to the 'housing problem' from within the housing market itself (Marris, 1979). This does not simply mean that nothing is possible until capitalism is overthrown; rather that to improve the welfare of the urban poor attention and investment in other areas may be more appropriate. Thus, as an example, if poor health and sanitation are the main problems of such settlements perhaps education and primary health care might be a more effective strategy.

In the final chapter Phillipe Haeringer, from his twenty-five year experience, in particular with the Côte d'Ivoire, wonders aloud about what can be done. After considering the experiences of Brazzaville, Douala, Abidjan and San Pedro (the latter was an Ivorian growth centre), he suggests partly as a result of the recession that a creative combination of technocracy and tradition has been successful in the Côte d'Ivoire. He concludes by suggesting that the future of African urbanisation will be dependent upon states' responsiveness to their peoples. We can only reply that we hope this is the case.

## NOTES

1  The Weeks paper on which much of this argument is based is in fact unpublished. I apologise for using such an obscure source, but feel its importance justifies this. Many of the arguments Weeks develops are implicit in Sandbrook's more available source.

2  This strategy assumes that such areas are not yet so desperate as to make this impossible. Clearly it implies a minimum of access to land, the absence of famine and the absence of unfavourable ecological conditions.

3  'Refugee' is an international political category. It involves the crossing of international borders. 'Internal refugees' have similar characteristics, hence this data considerably underestimates the extent of the problem. Conservative estimates put internal refugees at 1–2 million (Overseas Development Institute Briefing Paper No. 5, 1983).

4  I am indebted to J. S. Eades for this observation on African urban studies in the 1980s.

## REFERENCES

Adrien-Rongier, M. F. 1981. 'Les Kodro de Bangui: un espace urbain "oublié" ', *Cahiers d'Etudes Africaines*, 21, pp. 1–3.
Amis, P. 1983. 'A Shanty Town of Tenants: the Commercialisation of Unauthorised Housing in Nairobi 1960–1980'. Unpublished PhD thesis, University of Kent.
—— 1984. 'Squatters or tenants: the commercialization of unauthorised housing in Nairobi', *World Development*, 12 (1), pp. 87–96.
—— 1986. 'Urban proletarianization and poverty in East Africa: survival strategies and the I.M.F.'. Paper presented at African Studies Association Conference, Canterbury, Kent.
—— 1987. 'Migration, urban poverty and the housing market: the Nairobi case', in J. Eades (ed.), *Migrants, Workers and the Social Order*. London: Tavistock.
Angel, A., Archer, R., Tanphiphat, D. and Wegelin, E. (eds.) 1983. *Land for Housing the People*. Singapore: Select.
Bardham, P. 1984. *The Political Economy of Development in India*. Oxford: Blackwell.
Berg, E. (ed.) 1981. *Accelerated Development in Sub-Saharan Africa*. Washington DC: World Bank.
Blitzer, S., Hardoy, J. and Satterthwaithe, D. 1980. *Aid for Human Settlements in*

*Africa: the role of multilateral agencies up to 1979*. African Environmental Occasional Paper No. 60.

Bruntland, G. 1987. *Our Common Future: world commission on environment and development*. Oxford: University Press.

Bunkerley, H. 1982. *Public lecture* at Development Planning Unit (DPU), London.

Burgess, R. 1985. 'The limits of state self-help housing programmes', *Development and Change*, 16 (2), pp. 271–312.

—— 1987. 'A lot of noise and no nuts: a reply to Alan Gilbert and Jan van der Linden', *Development and Change*, 18 (1), pp. 137–46.

Castells, M. 1976. 'Is there an urban sociology?', in C. Pickvance (ed.), *Urban Sociology: critical essays*. London: Tavistock.

Clay, E. J. and Schaffer, B. B. (eds.) 1984. *Room for Manoeuvre: an exploration of public policy in agriculture and rural development*. London: Heinemann.

Collier, P. and Lal, D. 1986. *Labour and Poverty in Kenya 1900–1980*. Oxford: Clarendon Press.

Commins, J., Lofchie, M. and Payne, R. (eds.) 1986. *Africa's Agrarian Crisis*. Boulder: Rienner.

Cornia, G. 1987. 'Adjustment at the household level: potentials and limitations of survival strategies', in G. Cornia *et al.*, *Adjustment with a Human Face*, pp. 90–104. Oxford: Clarendon Press.

Cornia, G., Jolly, R. and Steward, F. (eds.) 1987. *Adjustment with a Human Face*. Oxford: Clarendon Press.

Crooke, P. 1983. 'Popular housing supports and the urban housing market' in R. J. Skinner and M. J. Rodell (eds.), *People, Poverty and Shelter*, pp. 173–91. London: Methuen.

Crush, J. and Rogerson, C. 1983. 'New wave African historiography and African historical geography', *Progress in Human Geography*, 7 (2), pp. 203–31.

Durand-Lasserve, A. 1986. *L'Exclusion des Pauvres dans Les Villes du Tiers-Monde*. Paris: L'Harmattan.

Edwards, M. 1982. 'Cities of tenants: renting among the urban poor in Latin America', in A. Gilbert *et al.*, (eds.) *Urbanization in Contemporary Latin America*, pp. 129–58. Chichester: John Wiley.

Frank. A. G. 1969. *Capitalism and Underdevelopment in Latin America*. London: Monthly Review Press.

Gilbert, A. (ed. with Hardoy, G. and Ramirez, K.) 1982. *Urbanization in Contemporary Latin America*. Chichester: John Wiley.

Gilbert, A. and van der Linden, J. 1987. 'The limits of a Marxist theoretical framework for explaining state self-help housing', *Development and Change*, 18 (1), pp. 129–36.

Gilbert, A. and Ward, P. 1983. 'Community action by the poor: democratic involvement, community self-help or a means of social control?' *World Development*, 12 (8), pp. 769–82.

Glaser, M. 1985. 'The use of labelling in urban low income housing in the Third World: case-study of Bogotá, Colombia', *Development and Change*, 16 (3), pp. 409–28.

Guyer, J. (ed.) 1987. *Feeding African Cities*. Manchester: University Press for the International African Institute.

Hardoy, J. E. and Satterthwaite, D. 1986. 'Urban change in the Third World. Are recent trends a useful pointer to the urban future?', *Habitat International*, 10 (3), pp. 33–52.

Hart, K. 1973. 'Informal income opportunities and urban employment in Ghana',

*Journal of Modern African Studies*, 11, pp. 61–89.

Hill, P. 1986. *Development Economics on Trial*. Cambridge: University Press.

Hyden, G. 1980. *Beyond Ujamaa in Tanzania: underdevelopment and an uncaptured peasantry*. London: Heinemann.

Iliffe, J. 1983. *The Emergence of African Capitalism*. London: Macmillan.

International Labour Organisation (ILO). 1972. *Employment, Incomes and Equity: a strategy for increasing productive employment in Kenya*. Geneva: ILO.

Kitching, G. 1980. *Class and Economic Change in Kenya: the making of an African petite bourgeoisie 1905–1970*. New Haven: Yale University Press.

Koenigsberger, O. 1976. 'The absorption of newcomers in the cities of the Third World', *Overseas Development Review*, 1, pp. 57–79.

Lipton, M. 1977. *Why Poor People Stay Poor: a study of urban bias in world development*. London: Temple Smith.

Lofchie, M. 1986. 'Africa's agrarian crisis: an overview', in J. Commins *et al*. (eds.), *Africa's Agrarian Crisis*, pp. 3–18. Boulder: Rienner.

Lojkine, J. 1976. 'Contribution to a Marxist theory of capitalist urbanization', in C. Pickvance (ed.), *Urban Sociology: critical essays*, pp. 119–46. London: Tavistock.

Marris, P. 1979. 'The meaning of slums and patterns of change', *International Journal of Urban and Regional Research*, 3 (3), pp. 419–41.

Mayer, P. 1961. *Townsmen or Tribesmen?* Cape Town: Oxford University Press.

Mercier, P. 1973. 'Quelques remarques sur le développement des études urbaines', *Cahiers d'Etudes Africaines*, 51.

Moore, B. 1967. *The Social Origins of Dictatorship and Democracy*. Harmondsworth: Penguin.

Murray, C. 1981. *Families Divided: the impact of migrant labour in Lesotho*. Cambridge: University Press.

Nientied, P. and van der Linden, J. 1985. 'Approaches to low-income housing in the Third World: some comments', *International Journal of Urban and Regional Research*, 9, pp. 311–29.

Nyerere, J. 1986. 'An address', *Development and Change*, 17 (3), pp. 387–97.

ODI. 1983. Briefing Paper No. 5. London.

Parkin, D. 1976. *Town and Country in Central and Eastern Africa*. Oxford: University Press for the International African Institute.

Payne, G. F. (ed.) 1984. *Low-income Housing in the Developing World: the role of site and services and settlement upgrading*. Chichester: John Wiley.

Peil, M. 1976. 'African squatter settlements: a comparative study, *Urban Studies*, 13, pp. 155–66.

Portes, A. 1985. 'Urbanization, migration and models of development in Latin America', in J. Walton (ed.), *Capital and Labour in the Urbanized World*, pp. 109–25. London: Sage.

Roberts, B. R. 1978. *Cities of Peasants*. London: Edward Arnold.

Roy, D. 1983. 'The supply of land for the slums of Calcutta', in A. Angel *et al*. (eds.), *Land for Housing the Poor*, pp. 319–32. Singapore: Select.

Sandbrook, R. 1982. *The Politics of Basic Needs*. London: Heinemann.

—— 1986. 'The state and economic stagnation in tropical Africa', *World Development*, 14(3), pp. 319–32.

Sandbrook, R. and Cohen, R. (eds.) 1975. *The Development of an African Working Class*. London: Longman.

Scott, A. J. 1980. *The Urban Land Nexus and the State*. London: Pion.

Sen, A. 1981. *Poverty and Famines: an essay on entitlement and deprivation*. Oxford:

Clarendon Press.

Sender, J. and Smith, S. 1986. *The Development of Capitalism in Africa*. London: Methuen.

Seymour. T. 1975. 'Squatter settlements and class relations in Zambia', *Review of African Political Economy*, 3, pp. 71–7.

Skinner, R. J. and Rodell, M. J. (eds.) 1983. *People, Poverty and Shelter: problems of self-help housing in the Third World*. London: Methuen.

Turner, J. 1976. *Housing by People*. London: Marion Boyars.

Ward, P. (ed.) 1982a. *Self-help Housing: a critique*. London: Mansell.

—— 1982b. 'Informal housing: conventional wisdoms reappraised', *Built Environment*, 8 (2), pp. 85–94.

Warren, B. 1980. *Imperialism: pioneer of capitalism*. London: Verso.

Weeks, J. 1986. 'Vulnerable segments of the labour market: urban areas of the African region'. Paper for the ILO, mimeo.

Wegelin, E. 1983. 'From building to enabling housing strategies in Asia: institutional problems', in R. J. Skinner and M. J. Rodell (eds.), *People, Poverty and Shelter: problems of self-help housing in the Third World*, pp. 106–24. London: Methuen.

World Bank. 1986. World Development Report. Oxford: University Press.

—— 1987. World Development Report'. Oxford: University Press.

## RESUME

Cette introduction apporte une vue générale des thèmes clés de l'urbanisation africaine contemporaine. Elle comprend tout d'abord une vue générale des principales tendances politiques et économiques; en particulier l'évolution des approches, de l'industrialisation, des besoins fondamentaux à l'adaptation structurelle. Les problèmes politiques particuliers sont également évoqués. La seconde partie examine le changement des réponses gouvernementales apportées au problème de l'urbanisation; en particulier, l'impuissance à contrôler la migration suivie de l'adoption d'une approche de laisser-faire. La supposition selon laquelle les problèmes urbains sont nés de la croissance du taux des migrations est remise en question. La section suivante explore les facteurs mis en jeu dans le procédé de commercialisation du logement pour la population à faibles revenus (à la fois légaux et illégaux). Il en a résulté qu'en 1980 le logement de la population urbaine pauvre en Afrique ressort des mécanismes du marché. La dernière section comprend une synthèse et un aperçu général des articles composant le volume illustrant les procédés de commercialisation et de changement au sein du marché immobilier.

# PART I
# CHANGING APPROACHES TO
# URBAN HOUSING IN AFRICA

# 1    Richard E. Stren

## URBAN HOUSING IN AFRICA: THE CHANGING ROLE OF GOVERNMENT POLICY

I intend in this chapter broadly to outline the 'housing question' in African cities since the period immediately preceding independence, and to relate this question to government policy responses across the continent. I shall argue that by the late 1980s, our understanding of the role of housing in the development process has undergone some major changes. These changes are related both to more modest expectations of the role of the state in the provision of housing in Africa, and to the elaboration of commercial networks in African cities which have been increasingly responsible for the supply of urban services to the poor.

To understand the context within which urban housing is presently situated in Africa, it is necessary first to sketch the history of housing as government policy across the continent. This history can conveniently be divided into three phases. The first of these may be called the *state housing* phase. This phase lasted from the 1950s (or just before independence) in most countries, to the late 1960s and early 1970s. During this phase, the focus of government policy was the construction of public housing estates, tight central planning controls and large-scale urban master plans. This gave way – in many, if not all countries – to the *aided self-help* phase, during which planning standards began to be relaxed and state aid was extended to (in principle) low-income groups to build and improve their own houses. This second phase overlapped with the first, lasting from the early 1970s through the early 1980s. The present phase, which began in the late 1970s when the consequences of the African economic downturn began to manifest themselves in the cities, may be called the *management and infrastructure* phase. During this phase, governments have become increasingly concerned about efficient local management and effective controls over decentralised initiatives, while they struggle to deploy resources to maintain a deteriorating infrastructural base. Although many countries have now entered the third phase, they have not necessarily totally discarded either the symptoms of, or the policy approaches characteristic of the other phases. In the remainder of the chapter, I shall explore the dynamics of each of these phases, concentrating on the interaction between the changing manifestations of the 'low-income housing problem' and the government policy response.

## PHASE ONE: STATE HOUSING

The post-war years in Africa were, in relative terms, a period of rapid social change. From stagnation during the inter-war years, and heavy administrative controls on rural–urban movement during the Second World War, the towns began to grow much more rapidly. Georges Balandier, the author of one of the earliest classics on African cities, begins his exposition with a lengthy treatment of the 'rural exodus' in Congo–Brazzaville, and the problems posed by the 'brutal growth' of urban centres (Balandier, 1985: 15–45). From a population of about 4,000 Africans on the eve of the First World War, Brazzaville had grown to a population of between 80,000 and 100,000 by 1950. Elsewhere, the capital cities of other colonies were expanding at an equally rapid pace. Although there were substantial non-African populations in most major colonial cities, the great majority, the fastest growing part of the urban population, was of African origin. As Jean Dresch put it, the African city was 'created by the whites, but inhabited by blacks' (quoted in Balandier, 1985: 15).

This enormous population growth in post-war African cities was accompanied by a more dynamic economy throughout Africa, and by legislative instruments in Great Britain (the Colonial Development and Welfare Act of 1940) and France (FIDES, or the Fund for Economic and Social Development, established in 1946) which supported economic planning, and the construction of significant infrastructural works. Such a major effort implied higher productivity of African workers. Productivity of African workers, in turn, was seen to depend on a certain level of urban welfare measures, not the least of which was the provision of adequate family housing. Indeed, large-scale projects to construct urban housing estates were a key element in the effort to create a stable African urban middle class – a particularly attractive administrative objective during the fifties all over Africa, but especially in Kenya.

Two of the hallmarks of the colonial approach to African urban housing in the fifties were the redevelopment of decaying 'core' areas combined with the removal of 'slums' or squatter areas, and the construction of large rental (sometimes tenant-purchase) public housing estates. Once the dust had settled after independence in the early sixties, these policies were pursued with even more vigour than before. In a classic Nigerian study, Peter Marris studied a large 'slum clearance' scheme covering seventy acres in central Lagos. Marris stresses the visible achievement of 'modernity' as a public goal. 'The overriding aim', he writes, 'was to rebuild the most conspicuous neighbourhood of Lagos to the standard Nigerians had set themselves, as a matter of pride, and a symbol of the progress they were determined to achieve' (Marris, 1961: 119). Most of the people who were forced to leave the redeveloped area on Lagos Island did not, for various reasons, settle in the mainland flats that had been built especially for them.

In Kenya, many of the same factors were at work. Thus the colonial Central Housing Board (originally established during the early 1950s) was transformed into a National Housing Corporation (NHC) in 1967, and given power directly to undertake housing projects throughout the country. The NHC was expected to be a more vigorous actor in the housing field than the old Board, which needed 'to have a new image in playing a role which is in keeping with the spirit of the new, independent Kenya' (quoted in Stren, 1984: 235). By the early 1970s, the NHC was building an average of about 2,000 public housing units per year, most of them in the capital city. To the south, Tanzania also established a National Housing Corporation in 1962, for essentially the same reasons. While the Kenyan housing agency operated through a tendering procedure with private sector contractors, the Tanzanian NHC hired a large staff and built directly. But over the five-year period of Tanzania's first national plan, which ran until 1969, fully 70 per cent of the 5,705 low-cost houses built by the Tanzanian NHC were replacement units, built on the site of former 'slum' dwellings that had been eradicated in downtown Dar es Salaam. Although the Kenyan NHC managed to maintain a relatively high level of production of conventional housing units throughout the 1970s (from a low of 317 in 1976 to a high of 4,085 in 1979), the Tanzanian NHC was wound down by the government. Mismanagement and corruption, an inability to keep costs down, and unavailability of low-interest funding from the Treasury were cited as the reasons for this low level of performance. From 1975 to 1980, the corporation averaged less than 100 units per year (Stren, 1984: 248). While both Kenya and Tanzania began seriously to experiment with other modalities of public support for housing, the public housing corporation was the main instrument of policy until the mid-1970s in both countries.

Across the continent, large public housing projects, accompanied by systematic eradication of 'urban blight' and the maintenance of high standards of physical development, characterised both Senegal and Côte d'Ivoire. In Senegal, SICAP (Société Immobilière du Cap-Vert) was formed as early as 1949, as a mainly public company to develop lodging in the capital. Ten years later, a fully public corporation, OHLM (Office des Habitations à Loyer Modéré) was formed for lower-cost housing. Both corporations depended largely on state subsidies, the funds for OHLM coming notably from a 2 per cent tax on the salaries of permanent workers. By 1968, the two agencies had produced close to 12,000 housing units, almost all of them in Dakar. Of this total, SICAP in the period 1951–68 produced 7,441 units in seventeen different projects in the capital city (Sommer, 1972: 65). Although the production of SICAP and OHLM declined in the 1970s, the Senegalese state carried out a major campaign to eradicate central-city '*bidonvilles*' from 1972 through 1976. Over the whole period from 1951 to 1976, more than 90,000 people were displaced through eradication measures (White, 1985: 512). And in 1976 and 1977 the state pressed further, systematically and forcefully ejecting urban marginals, or 'human encumberments' as they were called in official documents, from the downtown areas (Collignon, 1984).

The approach of the Ivorian government, while initially slower to gain momentum, and bereft of the same animus toward urban marginals as in Senegal (perhaps because the expanding Abidjan economy offered more formal opportunities to absorb such people), followed a similar trajectory. From 1955 to 1970, the state stayed in the background in the promotion of housing (Haeringer, 1985). Urban policy during this early period was characterised by Philippe Haeringer as a 'double or nothing' policy (Haeringer, 1969). Pursuing this imagery, Michael Cohen writes:

Insisting on rapid, modern urban development, Ivorian public authorities have established objectives which do not include the majority of urban population. High quality housing, building standards, capital-intensive infrastructure, incentives for growth-producing industries rather than employment-generating enterprises, and spatial planning all reflect official intentions to develop urban areas according to ultramodern standards. This policy ignores the majority of the population, providing few services which urban residents can afford or simply not providing services at all. Housing policies force people to reside in *bidonvilles* in unsanitary, crowded, and expensive conditions. Rather than improve these *quartiers populaires*, the government allocates resources to the residential neighbourhoods inhabited by the ruling class. (Cohen, 1974: 33–4)

Just after the late 1960s when Cohen carried out his research, the Ivorian state made some major efforts to catch up with the housing deficit in Abidjan. Haeringer calls the decade from 1970 to 1980 the period of 'the great leap forward'. During this period the state made a significant commitment to build 'social housing' and to equip large tracts of peripheral urban land with high quality infrastructure (Haeringer, 1985). In a massive construction orgy, unparalleled in black Africa, SICOGI (Société Ivoirienne de Construction et de Gestion Immobilière, formed out of two existing parastatals in 1965), which had built only 1,858 units in Abidjan before 1970, produced 21,897 'low-cost' units in the next decade. At this pace, it was only slightly ahead of SOGEFIHA (Société de Gestion Financière de l'Habitat, created in 1963) which built 17,912 'low-cost' units during the same period (Djamat–Dubois, N'Guessan et N'Guessan, 1983). Meanwhile SETU (La Société d'Equipement du Terrain Urbain, established at the end of 1971), by September 1979, had prepared 1,779 ha. of land in Abidjan, of which the company itself estimated 444 were for 'low-cost housing' and accommodated as many as 350,000 persons (Equipements et Transports, 1980: 227). In proportion to the population of the country, but excluding the enormous amount of private housing constructed on plots prepared by SETU, the Ivorian housing parastatals produced over four times as much housing as did the NHC in Kenya – one of the leading housing agencies in Anglophone Africa.

By the late 1970s in Côte d'Ivoire, but much earlier in most other countries, this direct, statist approach to urban housing had run its course. While it has not totally disappeared as an active option, it has been down-graded in importance and obliged to coexist with other policy approaches. Perhaps the major reason for this shift in emphasis is the enormous expense of financing and constructing fully equipped housing units, particularly at a time of economic stagnation and even recession in most African countries. A related reason involves equity. Although billed in most cases as 'low-cost' units, state-built housing has inevitably involved a high level of public subsidies to ensure that the monthly (rental or mortgage) payments fall within the range that 'low-income' families can in principle afford. In the process, and given the enormous pressure on urban housing outside the state sector, this has produced a distorted situation in which enormous benefits accrue to individuals who are able to obtain these housing units. As a result, the wealthy and the well-connected have benefited dispropor-tionately from state-built housing, in comparison with the urban poor and lower middle-income groups. While this 'bias' in public housing pro-grammes (Temple and Temple, 1980) mirrors similar biases in other sec-tors, it is particularly hard to defend in countries where the rural poor constitute the overwhelming majority of the population. In the event, an alternative approach, to which we now turn our attention, has developed in an attempt more effectively to respond to this question.

## PHASE TWO: AIDED SELF-HELP

For Africa, the origins of the aided self-help approach to urban housing lay in two apparently unrelated phenomena. The first was the massive growth of spontaneous housing. While controls over the use of residential land in African cities were relatively tight during the colonial period, the immediate post-independence period saw the inability of the formal planning system to provide adequate infrastructure and services for large numbers of rural to urban migrants. Thus by 1967 it was estimated that 36 per cent of Dar es Salaam's population lived in 'uncontrolled settlements'; during the same year, the equivalent figure for Lusaka was 27 per cent. Two years later,

Dakar had an estimated 30 per cent of its population in such settlements
(World Bank, 1972: 82). These figures, while they varied considerably
between countries, tended to rise over time. Thus Dar es Salaam had 44 per
cent of its population living in 'squatter' areas in 1972, constituting an
average compound yearly increase from 1969 through 1972 of 24 per cent
(Stren, 1975: 60–2). By 1979, the estimate of the Master Plan was as high as
60 per cent (Marshall Macklin Monaghan, 1979: 26). And Nairobi, whose
population in 'uncontrolled and illegal housing' stood at approximately 33
per cent in 1971 (Etherton, 1971: 4) had an estimated 38 per cent of its
population in such housing by the end of the decade. The growth of
spontaneous housing all over urban Africa was a reflection of a much more
general phenomenon: the 'informal sector'. The growth of this sector (on
which there is a substantial academic literature) has vitiated the effectiveness of formal planning controls and absorbed urban migrants who cannot
effectively support the cost of residential structures produced according to
conventional building standards.

The second wellspring of pressure for aided self-help came from the
international lending community, and in particular the World Bank. Given
the rising figures for 'spontaneous settlements' in cities all over the Third
World, in the face of tight planning controls, regular demolitions, and
high-cost construction programmes, the World Bank argued for a new
approach to urban development which incorporated various forms of aided
self-help (World Bank, 1972). The two 'packages' which received the most
support were sites and services schemes, and upgrading schemes.
Essentially, the first provided low-income beneficiaries with serviced plots
and help to build (or have built) their own houses; the second approach
helped house-owners in existing squatter areas obtain tenure to their land,
and to improve their dwellings. Similar approaches were followed by
USAID and by the British ODA. Over the period 1972 to 1981, the World
Bank lent some $187·5 million for shelter projects in East and West Africa
(Cohen, 1983: 15). While the Bank has been gradually shifting from sites
and services toward upgrading in its shelter projects, its overall approach of
planning for the needs of lower-income groups has had a strong influence on
the urban policies of many recipient countries. In Africa, the major
countries to have developed sites and services projects under Bank auspices
were Senegal (which obtained its major loan in 1972) and Kenya (obtaining
its loan in 1975). Tanzania's 1975 loan went toward a mix of sites and
services and upgrading, while Zambia's loan in the same year concentrated
on upgrading. In 1977, Côte d'Ivoire received the largest African urban
project loan – $44 million for a large upgrading scheme in Abidjan. Most of
the loan agreements attached to these projects have obliged the recipient
countries to carry out some reforms or to improve the administration of
their urban policies, which gives the Bank some leverage, but the evidence

on compliance in the implementation of these conditions is mixed.

Until the 1980s, there was insufficient evidence to make an adequate evaluation of the aided self-help approach to African urban housing. But starting with a classic article by Lisa Peattie which challenged the logic of sites and services as an aggregate benefit to the urban poor (Peattie, 1982), articles, books and theses began to appear, dealing with many aspects of these projects. The first major sites and services project supported by the Bank was the Cambérène project in Dakar, the agreement for which was signed in 1972. In a scheme originally designed to provide serviced plots for 14,000 low-income Senegalese families, by 1984 only 3,600 of the Dakar plots were actually occupied, while another 3,000 were under construction. Of the houses built, less than 20 per cent conformed to the original norms set for the original low-income 'target population'; the rest surpassed these norms (White, 1985: 505). Rodney White's fascinating analysis of how this happened stresses, on the one hand, the inability of the Bank to respond to the changing requirements of the Senegalese state as Senegal's economy faltered during the 1970s; and on the other hand, Senegal's determination to end the impasse, by allocating plots to upper-income groups who would be able more rapidly to build than the original target population. White concludes that the changing economic circumstances of the 1970s brought latent policy contradictions to the surface, contradictions that ironically revealed that the Bank was more committed, though less able, to help the urban poor than was the Senegalese government. In a different formulation of a similar argument, Annik Osmont suggests that the technocratic means used by the Bank to secure the position of the urban poor in Senegal were, in the final analysis, subversive of the institutional effectiveness of the Senegalese state. Insistence on technocracy as a condition for receiving necessary aid, no matter how laudable the goals, weakened the ability of local institutions to deal with their own urban problems according to their own best political judgement (Osmont, 1985).

Osmont's argument that the urban policies of both the Bank and African governments must be seen in a wider economic and political context is echoed by Mohamed Halfani, in a lengthy study of the Bank site and service scheme in Dar es Salaam. Basing his baseline data on project files, Halfani shows the discrepancy between project goals (as embodied in the signed agreement in 1974) and project outcomes (as they were measured in 1982). Significantly, while the project considerably exceeded its targets in terms of the number of squatter houses serviced in the upgrading portion of the operation, the number of serviced sites was only 80 per cent of the original target, and by 1982 (well after the anticipated completion of the project) only 39 per cent of the plots had completed houses on them (Halfani, 1986: 94-6). At this rate of completion, 'the annual production of shelter units from the project (470 houses) has surpassed the production levels of the ill-fated slum clearance programme of the National Housing Corporation during the 1960s by only 70 houses' (Halfani, 1986: 99). Halfani explains the factors behind the deflection of project objectives as part of a larger system from which the sites and services project could not be insulated. This approach (which is similar to the approach taken by other academic writers) contrasts sharply with studies carried out by the World Bank itself. In these studies, urban projects are seen as having (largely beneficial) impacts on the city in question, or even on the national economy, but project limitations are almost always explained by technical factors rather than by the political economy of the national society (Keare and Parris, 1982; Bamberger, Sanyal and Valverde, 1982). Nevertheless, the severe resource constraints faced by most African countries just as these large urban projects were being implemented must be a major area of explanation for their shortcomings (Stren, 1982).


## PHASE THREE: MANAGEMENT AND INFRASTRUCTURE

By the early 1980s, ten years after the first major sites and services project got under way in Senegal, the aided self-help approach was in trouble. As for the schemes' stated objectives of providing housing for low-income groups at a cost they could readily afford, critics charged that the actual beneficiaries of sites and services schemes were often the higher-income people which the schemes had been explicitly designed to avoid. The evidence further suggested that repayment for land and services was low (Kulaba, 1985: 91; Bamberger, Sanyal and Valverde, 1982: 139–46), and that the very success of the schemes led to higher values for land, higher rents, and the marginalisation of poor tenants from the redeveloped areas (Mitullah, 1985).

A second problem was a high level of state subsidies in these schemes. Typically, the subsidy support took the form of free administrative services (as in the management of the complex procedures in sites and services schemes), free or less than market-priced land, or low interest rates on loans for building materials. Stephen Mayo and David Gross estimate that subsidies built into the sites and services projects in Côte d'Ivoire, Senegal and Tanzania amounted to 68, 55, and 67 per cent respectively of the cost of the resources used (Mayo and Gross, 1985: 63). Subsidies were a serious problem because they prevented the replicability of schemes (since the projects could not pay for themselves), and since they reduced considerably the scope of government activity during the period from the late seventies onwards when state revenues were seriously shrinking.

But the third reason for the shift away from a concentration on aided self-help had to do with levels and quality of urban infrastructure. Roads, water and other services were either not built on time, or were not well maintained once they were installed. Thus Halfani notes the poor condition of infrastructure in the Dar es Salaam sites and services project:

Roads in the project area had huge gullies and potholes. This made driving (or walking) along these roads very hazardous, especially in the absence of simple traffic signs, sidewalks, and street lighting. Similarly, the open drainage system, which was often clogged, created a fertile breeding ground for malaria-spreading mosquitoes and contributed to general environmental pollution. This unhealthy condition prevails essentially because there is no budget allocation for maintenance and repair of the infrastructure in project sites. (Halfani, 1986: 98)

By the late 1970s and early 1980s, many African countries were having severe problems maintaining an even minimally acceptable level of urban services and infrastructure. The situation was particularly serious in most of the Anglophone countries, where hard currency for the purchase of equipment and spare parts was in short supply. Nairobi's problems with public refuse collection are a good example. In 1985, the national news magazine, the *Weekly Review*, featured a large cover photograph of a pile of uncollected rubbish, entitling the lead article 'City in a Mess' – a satirical comment on Nairobi's official slogan, 'City in the Sun'. As the magazine described the situation:

It has always been proudly referred to as the Green City in the Sun. But today, Nairobi presents a picture of a city rotting from the inside. Over the past 18 months, the main city news in the local press has been about mounting piles of stinking refuse, dry water taps, gaping pot-holes and unlit streets.
Nairobi residents have watched helplessly their once beautiful city turn into one stinking mess. In the less fashionable but heavily populated areas such as Mathare, Kibera and Kangemi, the refuse piles mount for months before the Nairobi City Commission makes feeble attempts at clearing the mess. In Eastlands, it often takes weeks. At Soko Mjinga in Kariobangi, a refuse heap a whole quarter of an acre or more in size continued to spread between houses before it was finally arrested. Even the more fashionable residential estates have not been spared. In Buru Buru, Kilimani, Plainsview and Golden Gate estates, housewives dumped domestic refuse in unattended public lots as they waited for the city trucks to empty dustbins that filled weeks ago. City health inspectors turned a blind eye. (*Weekly Review*, 25 January, 1985: 3)

Journalistic hyperbole aside, Nairobi did indeed have a serious problem with refuse collection. While the population of the city was increasing at an estimated annual rate of at least 6 per cent, the amount of refuse collected fell from a high of 202,229 tonnes in 1977, to 159,974 tonnes in 1983 – a decline of 21 per cent over six years (Nairobi City Commission, 1983). Thus over the late seventies and early 1980s, the Council was collecting, on average, almost 10 per cent less refuse per capita every year. The most important reason for this situation, according to officials operating within the system, was the deterioration of equipment. The city council's finances were deteriorating, and there was a corresponding shortage of foreign exchange available in the country. Spare parts for the city's vehicles could not easily be obtained, and new imported vehicles were much too expensive. The deterioration of the cleansing vehicles reinforced a bias in the collection system whereby central parts of Nairobi were visited on a regular basis, while more distant parts of the city (where most of the low-income population is located) were served whenever there was 'slack' in the system. One of these poorly-served areas was the first phase of the World Bank-financed Dandora Sites and Services Scheme.

Public transport is another service area which has been under severe pressure during the 1970s and 1980s. As African cities expand – mostly horizontally – the distances which ordinary workers must travel to work expand geometrically. Dar es Salaam is a good example of this trend, having grown in land area very extensively in recent years. In 1974, the national parastatal company, UDA, was created, for public transport within Dar es Salaam. But before long, UDA's fleet strength and thus its overall performance began to deteriorate. While it was able to carry 137 million passengers in 1983, this was achieved in the face of frequent breakdowns and constant overloading. From a fleet size of 374 buses of which an average of 257 were serviceable every day in 1975, UDA's fleet size fell in 1984 to 205, of which an average of only 131 were operational. The shortfall is reflected in the fact that, during the 6 a.m. to 9 a.m. peak period, 22 per cent of all waiting passengers on Dar es Salaam routes are left behind because of overcrowding on the buses (Kulaba, 1986: 49). For 1984, a consultant study estimated that UDA would need 305 serviceable buses to meet the demand; given the serviceability ratio of 70 per cent, this would mean a total fleet of 436 buses (Tanzania, 1984: 46). Given UDA's poor record in obtaining foreign exchange from the government (from 1975 through 1983 it obtained only 35·33 per cent of what it asked for), and the serious problems of potholes in Dar es Salaam's very extensive road system, the prospects were not good for an improvement in either the capacity or the running efficiency of the publicly-owned transport service.

One response to the shortfall in public transport facilities has been to permit the private sector to take up some of the slack. For many years, private-sector public transport was anathema to the socialist beliefs of Tanzania's ruling elite. For a brief period from 1972 to 1974, *sumni-sumni* vehicles were allowed to operate in order to supplement public services. The *sumni-sumni* were so named because they charged a flat fare of =50 (called a *sumni*) per trip. However they were mainly old micro-buses and minibuses in poor condition, and were driven rapidly and dangerously. They were officially banned in 1975. While various kinds of 'pirate' operators took up some of the slack, it was not until 1983 that the government permitted private enterprise again in Dar es Salaam. On 1 April, private

vehicles were permitted to operate in compliance with certain regulations –
which included an acceptable standard of mechanical fitness for the vehicle,
and a licence to operate on stipulated routes. By 1985, 300 of these large
minibuses had been registered. These vehicles were called *dala dala* after
their 5T Shs flat fare (a large silver coin called a *dala* in Swahili). The *dala
dalas* were generally smaller than the UDA buses, and operated on a smaller
number of intra-city routes. They were faster, but more expensive for
passengers (in 1985 UDA charged a flat adult fare of 3T Shs for normal
routes and 4T Shs for express routes) (Banyikwa, 1985). They rapidly took
over a substantial share of the market. While the overall level of service has
improved in Dar es Salaam with the regularisation of *dala dalas*, transport
costs are heavy for ordinary workers. Assuming a worker earned the legal
monthly minimum wage of 810T Shs in 1985, and worked a normal six-day
week (including Saturday mornings), he would have to pay a minimum of
300T Shs, or 37 per cent of his gross wage, just for public transport.
Workers who lived on the outskirts of the city and needed to take more than
one bus, or workers who took *dala dalas*, paid proportionately more. While
the trend in other large African cities is for the public bus service to be
supplemented by private operators (who often charge more and provide
more rapid, though more dangerous service) (Kapila, Manundu and
Lamba, 1982; Godard, 1985), both the expense and the reliability of mass
transport is a severe problem for low-income workers, who tend to live at a
considerable distance from major commercial and industrial areas.

A third area of concern is water. Potable water is an irregular commodity
in most Nigerian cities. In a comprehensive household survey of Makurdi
and Idah (in Benue State, with populations respectively of 144,000 and
47,200) in 1982, residents identified the poor water supply as their single
most serious neighbourhood problem. At the time of the survey (which
covered 1,525 households in both towns), only 49·8 per cent of Makurdi
residents and 30·4 per cent of Idah residents had access to piped water in
their own houses or compounds (Stren, 1985). Another more elaborate
survey of the distribution of piped water and the perceptions of water users
was carried out by the Nigerian Institute of Social and Economic Research
(NISER) in 1985. Based on a stratified random sample of 1,986 households
in Ibadan, Enugu and Kaduna, the NISER researchers found that on the
average close to one-third of those interviewed had no pipe-borne water
connections to their homes. And of those households which *did* have water
connections, 27 per cent of the Ibadan households, 40 per cent of the Enugu
households and 39 per cent of the Kaduna households reported having only
a single tap on their premises. Most of those with water connections
reported various degrees of interruption in their water supply; and 34 per
cent of the Ibadan households, 27 per cent of the Kaduna households, and
26 per cent of the Enugu households reported that their pipes were always

dry (Onibokun, 1986: 135). In the Nigerian study, there was a rough correlation between the regularity of water supply, on the one hand, and the socio-economic status of the surveyed areas. This correlation was strengthened by the likelihood of wealthier households to be able to purchase water from commercial water-sellers, and to be able to store large quantities of water in covered cisterns within their compounds.

All over urban Africa piped water is generally not available in many newly-developed, and in almost all 'spontaneous housing' areas. In such circumstances, residents of these areas – among the poorest in the city – are obliged to purchase water from water-sellers. In Dar es Salaam in the early 1970s, public standpipes were installed in 'squatter' areas, where water was available free of charge. But because of the distance people would have to walk to obtain water at the few water points, most people needed to purchase water regularly from water-sellers. I calculated that the cost in 'squatter' areas of purchasing water in this manner was ten times higher (for equivalent quantities) than in areas where piped connections had been installed for individual houses (Stren, 1975: 49). An account of the water problems of Nouakchott and Rosso in Mauritania notes that more than 65 per cent of the inhabitants have no direct access to water. Under these circumstances, the commercialisation of the water trade has resulted in extremely high prices for the very poorest:

In the shanty towns, the Government is supposed to distribute water by lorry on a regular basis. Often, however, the rounds are cancelled because the lorries are needed for emergency deliveries in the bush. In recently parcelled areas, taps are few and far between; only one in a self-help built area of Njourbel in Rosso, and that serves part of the 6,000 inhabitants in addition to the 11,500 people living in Satara [a shanty-town which sprung up in 1968]. The latter have access to no other water point, except one tap in the city and a few wells, whose waters are polluted and in any case dry up during the dry season.

A highly adapted, door-to-door trade in water has developed spontaneously since 1978. The water is contained in one or two drums transported by donkey or horse and cart. Since it is controlled neither by the Government nor by the unorganized inhabitants, this intermediate trade in water has led to highly profitable speculation. Thus, in Nouakchott, the price of a 10-litre bucket sells at 3 ouguiyas and a 30-litre jerrycan at 15 ouguiyas, whereas a household in the well-established urban area connected to the mains pays 15 UM per $m^3$ (Nouakchott price), i.e. thirty times cheaper than do people living in the 5th arrondissement.

The situation is even worse during the dry season in Rosso, which depends for its water on a reservoir filled once a year during the rainy season. The first water cart made its appearance there in 1979. The owner sold his water in the Satara shanty town at 1UM per litre, or one hundred times dearer than the price paid by people connected to the SONELEC system. (Theunynck and Dia, 1980: 224)

The difficulties in both the supply and maintenance of urban infrastructure in Africa have been compounded all over the continent with the economic downturn of the late 1970s and early 1980s. Not only have these difficulties pressed down on the 'quality of life' of African urban residents who already have reasonable housing, but they have proven an even more severe burden for urban newcomers who must often find (or construct) housing on the urban periphery where there is no infrastructure and there are no public services. In an interesting study based on work on Lima, but supplemented with research in Nairobi, Lusaka and three other non-African cities, Paul Strassman shows that the rate of housing construction in low-income areas varies directly with the speed at which basic infrastructure (especially water) is installed (Strassman, 1984). This underlines the more general argument of Johannes Linn that 'the extension of public services', by which he refers to water supply, energy, waste disposal, drainage and road circulation, 'is the most effective policy instrument for expanding the supply of urban housing, dampening land price increases, and stimulating private investment in shelter' (Linn, 1983: 183). Linn also argues that public provision of housing is one of the least efficient and least equitable means of solving the housing problems of Third World cities.

If large-scale sites and services and even upgrading projects are deficient in various important ways, and if the supply and adequate maintenance of urban infrastructure is crucially important to both the supply of new housing and the equitable enjoyment of housing facilities by urban Africans, the question turns on the organisation and delivery of services and infrastructure. In Khartoum, there is (in comparison with the situation in most sub-Saharan cities) a strong tradition of self-help in the provision of such local projects as primary schools, health centres, water reticulation networks and even roads. Such self-help activities are particularly strong in the more than ninety spontaneous housing areas scattered around the periphery of the city. While the reasons for this self-reliant behaviour may be attributed to a combination of administrative prerequisites (each area is incorporated actively into one of Khartoum's 367 local neighbourhood councils), cultural homogeneity (communities in each area tend to have common rural areas of origin) and economic necessity (the city government can offer little if the communities do not organise on their own), these poor villages are remarkably clean and well planned (El Sammani et al: 1986). The Sudanese experience, borne out of severe economic and environmental scarcity, parallels the 'popular approach' to shelter provision advocated by Jorge Hardoy and David Satterthwaite (1986: 282–4).

This 'popular approach' stresses government support for the building of necessary infrastructure, supported by decentralised planning. In the 1980s, there has been renewed interest in decentralisation in Africa, and in the proper 'management' of urban services at the local level. These questions come together in a concern with how best to structure institutions of local government in major African cities. All across the continent, whatever the colonial heritage, there is recognition that large cities must be better governed if services are to be more accessible, and if urban residents are to be more productive.

Urban government reforms have taken different turns, a result both of colonial influences and of the particular political experience of different countries. In both Côte d'Ivoire and Senegal, decades of centralisation of urban government are being followed, during the 1980s, with cautious decentralisation of functions to the local level, and a gradual democratisation of urban decision-making. Starting in 1978, a new law in Côte d'Ivoire decreed ten communes within the greater Abidjan area with local jurisdiction, and a supra-municipal body called 'the City of Abidjan'. Following the elections of 1980, there has been a gradual development of municipal competence in Côte d'Ivoire, with the elaboration of technical services within the municipal bodies, and of various executive agencies around the mayor and his administrative counterparts (Attahi, 1987). In Senegal, municipal reform began with Law No. 83–48 of 18 February 1983, which dealt with the administrative reorganisation of the Cap-Vert region. Following the dispositions of this law, Dakar was divided into three new communes, corresponding to the districts of Dakar, Pikine, and Rufisque-Bargny. Each of these urban areas is run by a mayor and elected councillors; and over all three districts is the Urban Community of Dakar, at the head of which is a 'super mayor', elected from among the three district mayors. While the urban governments of both Abidjan and Dakar are still officially 'under the close supervision' of the Ministries of Finance and of the Interior, notable efforts have been made in both countries to improve the revenue base and technical competence of the local bodies. Even in Zaire, some limited efforts have been made in the direction of loosening central government control over local government in Kinshasa.

Across the continent, both Kenya and Tanzania are moving to stabilise the delivery of urban services through some local government reorganisation. Kenya, with a relatively long tradition of urban local government, began to experience some serious problems in the late 1970s and early 1980s. A symptom of these problems was the central government's decision to close the elected Nairobi City Council in March 1983, and to replace it with an appointed Commission. When he suspended the Nairobi City Council, the Kenya Minister for Local Government mentioned 'gross mismanagement of council funds and poor services to the residents' as justification (11 March, *Weekly Review*, 1983: 4). But three years later, when the government extended the City Commission's term for another two years, the financial situation was still unstable and '[t]he problem of water shortages and uncollected garbage . . . continued unabated' (21 March, *Weekly Review*, 1986: 6). In spite of these problems in the capital (exacerbated perhaps by the central government's political difficulties with the Nairobi City Council) the Kenya government has suggested in an important policy paper that even rural development requires more investment in, and more efficient management of, urban infrastructure. 'To fulfil their role effectively in supporting regional economic growth', the government has argued in a sessional paper, 'cities and towns will have to be properly administered and competently managed, and must have adequate resources to operate and maintain public services efficiently' (Kenya, 1986: 48). Nowhere in the lengthy document is either public housing or aided self-help housing actively promoted.

The Tanzanian government has also been concerned about the question of inadequate urban infrastructure. Like Kenya, it is paying considerably less attention to housing strategies as such, and more attention to strategies for the improvement of local government and the management of urban services and infrastructure. Since the 1972–78 'decentralisation' period, when urban services deteriorated dramatically, the government has been moving towards a reinstatement of the old 'local government' system, whereby local councils have some financial autonomy from the centre, and are able to operate at least a limited range of services. But the new system began to come under severe strain in 1987, when the central government seriously reduced its grants to local authorities. Meagre resources at the local level, financial mismanagement, and a weak local government audit system all contribute to the inability of local urban councils effectively to manage their services, even though the role of local government is now accepted by both the public and the central government (Kulaba, 1986). For both housing and other urban services, Tanzania's challenge is the more efficient control and allocation of the limited resources that have been made available to local authorities.

## CONCLUSIONS

The role of housing in national development policy in Africa has undergone three main phases, from an emphasis on state-built public housing, through an aided self-help phase, to the present phase, during which the concern has shifted to the proper 'management' of services and infrastructure. Accordingly, the policy focus has moved from housing itself to the provision of services related to housing; public-sector agencies have withdrawn even further from the direct provision of accommodation.

If this is the trend, what are some of its implications? One implication is that there may be more equity in the distribution of urban capital investment. State-sponsored housing schemes (whether they are public housing estates or sites and services) are notoriously prone to 'leakage' – whereby the rich and powerful are able to take control of resources originally meant for the poor and the weak. A shift from the provision of divisible public goods (such as housing) to the provision of indivisible public goods (such as infrastructure) should (if it continues) remove at least one major source of inequity in African cities.

A second implication is that the conciliar structures of local government at the local level may be strengthened. With growing recognition in Africa that urban services must be both paid for and administered at the local level, what used to be called 'institutional development' may at last occur in large city governments. While the strength of local political institutions in Africa will for some time, be constrained by central government weakness and insecurity, a greater role for local governments in the large cities may very well imply more effective influence by the 'popular sector' for improved services and infrastructure in peripheral areas. If the pressure exerted by this sector can be ignored by central governments, it cannot so easily be avoided at the local level, where low-income residents are an overwhelming majority of the urban population.

A third implication, however, is more worrisome since it pushes in the opposite direction. Central governments are increasingly concerned with developing the institutional capacity to provide and to maintain an adequate infrastructural base. But they are also warming to the idea that private enterprise rather than local councils or parastatals might be the appropriate agency for many types of service. This represents a movement from 'areal' and 'functional' decentralisation (which might benefit the urban poor) to outright privatisation (which might not). Since the late 1960s, the marginalisation of the urban poor has meant large-scale commercialisation of land and housing markets in Africa. In this chapter, we have seen how the balance is tipping toward the private sector in the provision of mass transport. In addition, private contractors have been operating in the refuse removal business in West Africa, and in the water-supply business all across the continent. While a lot more research needs to be done on the trade-off between efficiency and equity in the provision of different kinds of services, there is a real danger that the commercialisation and market pricing of services may seriously disadvantage the urban poor. Just as, in an earlier period, market forces penetrated all sectors of the housing market, the same process threatens to overtake the supply and provision of urban services. If the weakness of African state structures which this process reflects makes it inevitable, the future shape and texture of African cities will be very different from the colonially-inspired present.

# NOTE

The arguments contained in this chapter, and some of the data cited in it, are a product of a close and fruitful relationship over almost three years with a number of colleagues – both in Toronto and Africa – who have been working with me on an IDRC project entitled 'African Urban Management'. I would like to thank Rodney White and our associates in Zaire, Senegal, Nigeria, Côte d'Ivoire, Sudan, Kenya and Tanzania, as well as the IDRC, the Social Sciences and Humanities Research Council and Project Ecoville, for their intellectual and financial support, respectively. They are not responsible, however, for the opinions expressed in this chapter.

## REFERENCES

Attahi, K. 1987. *Une évaluation de la réforme de la gestion urbaine en Côte d'Ivoire*. Abidjan: Centre de Recherches Architecturales et Urbaines, Université d'Abidjan.

Balandier, G. 1985. *Sociologie des Brazzavilles noires*. Seconde édition augmentée, Paris: Presses de la Fondation Nationale des Sciences Politiques.

Bamberger, M., Sanyal, B. and Valverde, N. 1982. *Evaluation of Sites and Services Projects: the experience from Lusaka, Zambia*. World Bank Staff Working Paper No. 548, Washington DC.

Banyikwa, W. 1985. 'Urban passenger transport services in Dar es Salaam'. Paper prepared for Nairobi Workshop on Management of Urban Services in Africa, Department of Geography, University of Dar es Salaam, 9–10 July.

Cohen, M. A. 1974. *Urban Policy and Political Conflict in Africa: a study of the Ivory Coast*. Chicago: University Press.

—— 1983. *Learning by Doing: World Bank lending for urban development, 1972–82*. Washington DC: World Bank.

Collignon, R. 1984. 'La lutte des pouvoirs publics contre les "encombrements humains" à Dakar', *Revue Canadienne des Etudes Africaines*, 18 (3), pp. 573–82.

Djamat-Dubois, M. N'Guessan, K. et N-Guessan, K. 1983. *Les logements économiques à Abidjan: une politique d'habitat du grand nombre en Côte d'Ivoire*. Abidjan: Centre de Recherches Architecturales et Urbaines, Université d'Abidjan.

El Sammani, M. O., Abu Sin, M. E., Talha, M., El Hassan, B. M. and Haywood, I. 1986. *Management Problems of Greater Khartoum*. Khartoum: Institute of Environmental Studies, University of Khartoum.

*Equipements et Transports*. 1980. 'Bilan et perspectives'. Abidjan.

Etherton, D. 1971. *Mathare Valley: a case-study of uncontrolled settlement in Nairobi*. Nairobi: Housing Research and Development Unit, University of Nairobi.

Godard, X. 1985. 'Quel modèle des transports collectifs pour les villes africaines?', *Politique Africaine*, 17 (mars), pp. 41–57.

Haeringer, P. 1969. 'Quitte ou double: les chances de l'agglomération abidjanaise'. Abidjan: ORSTOM.

—— 1985. 'Vingt-cinq ans de politique urbaine à Abidjan, ou la tentation de l'urbanisme intégral', *Politique Africaine*, 17 (mars), pp. 20–40.

Halfani, M. S. 1986. 'Urban Management and the Implementation of an Externally Financed Project, in Dar es Salaam'. Unpublished PhD dissertation, University of Toronto.

Hardoy, J. E. and Satterthwaite, D. 1986. 'Shelter, infrastructure and services in Third World cities', *Habitat International*, 10 (3), pp. 245–84.

Kapila, S., Manundu, M. and Lamba, D. 1982. *The Matatu Mode of Public Transport in Metropolitan Nairobi*. Nairobi: Mazingira Institute.

Keare, D. H. and Parris, S. 1982. *Evaluation of Shelter Programs for the Urban Poor: principal findings*. World Bank Staff Working Paper No. 547, Washington DC.

Kulaba, S. M. 1985. *Urban Growth and the Management of Urban Reform in Tanzania: second report*. Dar es Salaam: Centre for Housing Studies, Ardhi Institute.

—— 1986. *Urban Growth and the Management of Urban Reform, Finance, Services and Housing in Tanzania: revised final summary report*. Dar es Salaam: Centre for Housing Studies, Ardhi Institute.

Linn, J. F. 1983. *Cities in the Developing World: policies for their equitable and efficient growth*. New York: Oxford University Press for the World Bank.

Marris, P. 1961. *Family and Social Change in an African City: a study of rehousing in Lagos*. London: Routledge & Kegan Paul.

Marshall Macklin Monaghan Ltd. 1979. *Dar es Salaam Master Plan: technical supplements 1, 2, 3 & 4*. Toronto and Dar es Salaam.

Mayo, S. K. with Gross, D. J. 1985. 'Sites and services – and subsidies: the economics of low-cost housing in developing countries'. Working Paper B.13, Toronto: Development Studies Programme, University of Toronto.

Mitullah, W. V. 1985. 'A World Bank housing upgrading project in a Kenyan town: winners and losers'. Unpublished paper presented at the joint meeting of CALACS and CAAS, Montreal.

Nairobi City Commission. 1983. 'Introduction to cleansing services in Nairobi'. Unpublished paper. Nairobi: Public Health Department.

Onibokun, A. 1986. *Urban Growth and Urban Management in Nigeria with Particular Reference to Public Utilities and Infrastructure: final report*. Ibadan: Nigerian Institute of Social and Economic Research.

Osmont, 1985. 'La Banque Mondiale et les politiques urbaines nationales', *Politique Africaine*, 17 (mars), pp. 58–73.

Peattie, L. R. 1982. 'Some second thoughts on sites-and-services', *Habitat International*, 6 (1–2), pp. 131–9.

Republic of Kenya. 1986. *Sessional Paper No. 1 of 1986 on Economic Management for Renewed Growth*. Nairobi: Government Printer.

Sommer, J. W. 1972. 'Illicit shops in an African suburb: SICAP, Dakar, Senegal', *African Urban Notes*, 7 (1), pp. 62–72.

Strassman, P. 1984. 'The timing of urban infrastructure and housing improvements by owner occupants', *World Development*, 12 (7), pp. 743–53.

Stren, R. E. 1975. *Urban Inequality and Housing Policy in Tanzania: the problem of squatting*. Berkeley: Institute of International Studies, University of California.

—— 1982. 'Underdevelopment, urban squatting and the state bureaucracy: a case study of Tanzania', *Canadian Journal of African Studies*, 16 (1), pp. 67–91.

—— 1984. 'Urban policy', in J. D. Barkan (ed.), *Politics and Public Policy in Kenya and Tanzania*, pp. 233–64. Revised edition, New York: Praeger.

—— 1985. *Two Nigerian Towns in the Eighties: a socio-economic survey of Idah and Makurdi, Benue State*. Project Ecoville Working Paper No. 21, University of Toronto.

Tanzania, United Republic of. 1984. 'The rationalisation of urban passenger transport in Dar es Salaam'. Unpublished report, Dar es Salaam: Ministry of Communications and Transport.

Temple, F. and Temple, N. 1980. 'The politics of public housing in Nairobi', in Grindle, M. S. (ed.), *Politics and Policy Implementation in the Third World*, pp. 224–49. Princeton: University Press.

Theunynck, S. and Dia, M. 1980. 'The young (and the less young) in infra-urban

areas in Mauritania', *Environment in Africa*, 4 (2–4), pp. 205–33.
*Weekly Review* (Nairobi) 11 March 1983; 25 January 1985; 21 March 1986.
White, R. R. 1985. 'The impact of policy conflict on the implementation of a government-assisted housing project in Senegal', *Canadian Journal of African Studies*, 19 (3), pp. 505–28.
World Bank. 1972. *Urbanization: sector working paper*. Washington DC: World Bank.

# RESUME

L'historique du problème du logement en Afrique, et la réaction des gouvernements africains à cet égard, peuvent être divisés en trois phases. La première, ou phase de 'logements de l'état' va des années 50 au début des années 70. Pendant cette phase, la politique du gouvernement s'est concentrée sur la construction de complexes de logements publics, les contrôles étroits d'un urbanisme intégral, le redéveloppement de quartiers de bidonvilles, et les schémas directeurs urbains sur une grande échelle. Cette phase a cedé le pas à la phase de 'l'autonomie aidée', renforcée par les interventions des grandes agences d'aide internationale. Durant cette phase, les normes ont commencé à se détendre et l'aide gouvernementale était, en principe, accordée aux groupes à faibles revenus pour leur permettre de construire et d'améliorer leurs propres maisons. Mais, des subventions inattendues, l'incapacité d'atteindre efficacement la 'population cible', et les difficultés d'application ont eu pour résultat un changement dans cette approche. Pour corriger certains de ces problèmes d'application, les politiques urbaines se sont concentrées de plus en plus sur les questions adjacentes de gestion des collectivités locales et d'infrastructure. Cette troisième phase, que l'on peut appeler la phase de 'gestion/infrastructure', est largement documentée dans ce chapitre, avec des données comparatives dans le domaine du ramassage des déchets, du transport public, et de l'alimentation en eau. Les cas cités montrent le lien entre les problèmes de la détérioration des services dans les villes africaines et les problèmes jumeaux de l'insuffisance des ressources et de la faiblesse des institutions. Les réactions aux problèmes d'infrastructure sont en partie de laisser le secteur privé offrir certains des services; et en partie d'essayer de raffermir les institutions locales pour coordonner et mieux gérer les ressources disponibles.

# AUTOPROMOTION DE L'HABITAT ET MODES DE PRODUCTION DU CADRE BATI: L'APPORT DE RECHERCHES RECENTES EN AFRIQUE NOIRE FRANCOPHONE

La question du logement des populations urbaines pauvres, dans le contexte de pays où les modalités et les effets de l'explosion démographique ont mis un certain temps à être correctement perçus, a suscité une abondante littérature, à défaut de réponses concrètes appropriées. Il s'agit moins d'en faire ici la recension critique (on se reportera aux communications de P. Amis et de R. Stren) que de situer l'apport de quelques recherches récentes sur les processus de production de l'habitat et sur l'économie de la construction dans plusieurs pays d'Afrique noire francophone.

## L'HABITAT DES POPULATIONS URBAINES PAUVRES: UN HERITAGE CONCEPTUEL ET TERMINOLOGIQUE CONTROVERSE

L'espoir, ou l'illusion, persista jusqu'au début des années 70 qu'on maîtriserait à terme la demande du 'plus grand nombre' par des politiques dites de logement social, le plus souvent décalquées, dans leurs formes et leurs procédures, de modèles européens (financement public, offices para-étatiques de promotion et de gestion de logements économiques locatifs octroyés clés en main). Dans ce contexte, où l'offre de logements ainsi conçue ne pouvait répondre qu'à une fraction limitée d'une demande sans cesse accrue, l'habitat des plus pauvres, souvent désigné sous le terme générique de 'bidonvilles', fut longtemps considéré de façon péjorative, quand il n'était pas simplement ignoré (des autorités, des documents cartographiques . . .). Dans la relative euphorie 'développementaliste' des années 60, ces zones d'habitat précaire, irrégulier, illégal, anarchique et, pour tout dire, selon un terme qui fit fortune, 'spontané', furent mises au compte d'une marginalité appréhendée, voire théorisée, comme un effet provisoire ou transitoire de la croissance, appelée à terme à se résorber, sinon à disparaître. Une majorité d'experts occidentaux et la plupart des responsables politiques africains, après les indépendances, semblaient d'accord sur cette vision des choses: il fallait supprimer cette 'lèpre' des villes du Tiers-Monde.

Assez précocement pourtant, des chercheurs et quelques praticiens s'étaient attachés à décrypter les facteurs, les formes et l'impact de ces processus d'urbanisation dits spontanés (Dresch, 1950; Gutkind, 1960; Durand, 1963; Haeringer, 1969; Lacoste, 1970; CEGET/CNRS, 1972; Vernière, 1973). Ces auteurs, parmi d'autres, contribuèrent à forger de nouveaux concepts (habitat sous-intégré), de nouveaux outils d'investigation et surtout de nouvelles perspectives dans l'appréhension globale et la compréhension des phénomènes d'urbanisation en Afrique.

Mais il fallut, pendant une bonne douzaine d'années, la pugnacité d'un John Turner et de quelques autres experts et chercheurs qui, à partir de leur expérience en Amérique latine, multiplièrent les études de terrain, pour convaincre les organisations internationales, les gouvernements et les autorités locales que les zones d'habitat précaire, non réglementé, n'étaient pas a priori des repaires de délinquants, de paysans sans travail et sans ressources, d'opposants potentiels, même si l'on pouvait y déceler des formes évidentes de la pauvreté. De là à reconnaître l'aptitude d'une masse accrue de citadins, en l'absence d'autres choix, à prendre en mains la question de leur logement, il y avait encore plus qu'un pas à franchir. Changer de regard et de politique, institutionnaliser la dynamique de ces filières populaires de production du logement, n'était-ce pas prendre des risques, affaiblir les pouvoirs d'Etats encore jeunes, renoncer à une modernité – au reste mal comprise – dont les villes, et notamment les capitales, devaient être porteuses, susciter de nouvelles demandes sociales, de nouvelles contradictions d'intérêt, au détriment des positions acquises par les classes dirigeantes?

Du moins le tournant fut-il pris. Y avait-il au reste une alternative face à la crise économique montante et à l'endettement accru des pays du Tiers-Monde? La Conférence HABITAT (Vancouver, 1976) attesta du changement des esprits: mais reconnaître le droit à l'autogestion du processus de production du logement est une chose, en assurer les garanties et les conditions concrètes de mise en oeuvre, par des politiques appropriées, en est une autre. Les freins et les dérives n'ont pas manqué; maints projets de la Banque Mondiale ont révélé les difficultés pour atteindre ce qu'il est convenu d'appeler la 'population cible', celle des pauvres . . . et néanmoins solvables (Pasteur, 1979; Bryant 1980; UNCHS, 1981; Gilbert et Gugler, 1982; Payne, 1984; McAuslan, 1985).

Malgré leurs fortes relations réciproques, il n'y a pas coincidence stricte entre autoconstruction et pauvreté. Entre autres auteurs de langue anglaise (Morrison et Gutkind, 1982; Ward, 1982; Richards et Thomson, 1984), c'est le mérite de R. Stren (1975, 1978) et de R. Sandbrook (1982) d'avoir remis les pendules à l'heure sur cette question fondamentale de la pauvreté urbaine en Afrique. Le débat s'est largement développé au début des années 1980. De fortes divergences sur les implications des notions d'autonomie et d'autogestion, appliquées à l'habitat, invitaient alors à un opportun réexamen des stratégies du capitalisme international et des classes dirigeantes en Afrique et donc à une réflexion de nature politique sur l'Etat, encore que le transfert à l'Afrique de concepts et de termes élaborés dans le contexte des pays d'Amérique latine ne soit pas sans poser quelques problèmes (Turner, 1969, 1982, 1986; Burgess, 1978, 1982).

A cet égard – et au moins jusqu'à cette année (Stren, 1986) – on peut relever, ou déplorer, la faible perméabilité réciproque des littératures anglaise et française (rareté des traductions? caractère suffisamment constitué et conséquent de la recherche au sein de chaque aire culturelle et linguistique?). Toujours est-il que les chercheurs francophones, sans avoir à renvoyer Turner et Burgess dos-à-dos, ont de leur côté sérieusement approfondi leurs investigations depuis quelques années.

## LE RENOUVELLEMENT DES PROBLEMATIQUES ET DES METHODES DE LA RECHERCHE URBAINE DANS LES ANNEES 80

Comblant ce qui pouvait apparaître comme un retard, les chercheurs de langue française ont contribué à éclairer de façon significative les comportements et les stratégies concrètes des acteurs urbains en Afrique. Leurs travaux, qu'ils concernent les formes et les modalités de la croissance urbaine (Haeringer, 1972, 1973, 1985; CEGET/CNRS, 1972; de Maximy, 1984; Pain, 1985), le secteur informel (Hugon, 1980, 1982), les pratiques sociales liées à l'habitat (Osmont, 1981, 1984, 1985; CEA, 1981; Le Bris *et al.*, 1984, les enjeux fonciers et les formes de promotion foncière et immobilière (Tribillon, 1984; Durand-Lasserve et Tribillon, 1983, 1986), la gestion urbaine (Durand-Lasserve et Tribillon, 1985), pour ne citer que quelques exemples, sont presque tous le fruit d'équipes et de réseaux.

Prenant leurs distances aussi bien vis-à-vis d'approches macroéconomiques par trop théorisantes que de démarches strictement monographiques et monodisciplinaires isolées, ces recherches, souvent lancées à la fin des années 1970, ont permis un nouveau regard sur la question urbaine et sur les politiques de l'habitat en Afrique. Qu'elles aient pu se développer et se structurer, notamment au sein de l'ORSTOM (Office de la Recherche Scientifique et Technique Outre-Mer), du CNRS (Centre National de la Recherche Scientifique) et de plusieurs universités grâce aux incitations

d'un 'Programme Mobilisateur' du Ministère français de la Recherche de
1981 à 1985, c'est évident et ce fut positif.

Les questions soulevées, souvent en liaison avec des praticiens et des
techniciens, remirent en cause quelques certitudes passées sur la vertu des
plans d'urbanisme, si souvent dessinés a priori au nom de rationalités
extérieures et si peu attentifs aux acteurs concrets en charge de la gestion du
quotidien et du futur proche des villes. Disons aussi que la crise économique mondiale a tempéré les enthousiasmes (et les budgets) et conduit a
plus de lucidité et de modestie dans la formulation de recommandations,
sinon de remèdes possibles (Coquery, 1983; Venard, 1986).

Significative aussi se révèle l'évolution des préoccupations de ceux
qui, dans la mouvance du Ministère français de l'Urbanisme et du Logement, pensèrent que des transferts de technologie et la mise au point de
technologies appropriées, appliquées à la production à bas coût du
cadre bâti, permettraient de mieux faire face à l'augmentation drastique
de la demande de logement. On vit ainsi un organisme comme REXCOOP
(Recherche et Expérimentation en Coopération), initialement attaché à
la recherche sur les matériaux et les procédés de construction, infléchir
judicieusement ses appels d'offre, à partir de 1982, vers la reconnaissance
des structures socio-économiques et des potentialités des milieux d'accueil, sans laquelle la mise en oeuvre de ces expérimentations techniques
risquait de rester sans suite. L'attention se porta ainsi sur des thèmes tels
que les chaînes de production et les modes d'appropriation de l'habitat,
l'industrie des matériaux, l'économie de la construction, les services
urbains, les investissements publics urbains. Plusieurs dizaines de rapports
et quelques colloques sur ces questions ont singulièrement enrichi la
connaissance des structures et des pratiques, balisant de façon plus réaliste
la voie des recommandations, sinon celle des décisions.

## L'APPORT DES RECHERCHES RECENTES SUR
## L'AUTOPRODUCTION DE L'HABITAT EN AFRIQUE:
## UNE CLARIFICATION DES TERMES ET DES CONCEPTS

C'est dans ce contexte, à défaut de pouvoir ici les évoquer toutes, qu'il
convient de signaler l'apport majeur de l'une de ces études, consacrée à
l'histoire comparée de chantiers d'habitation autoproduits à Douala et à
Kinshasa (ADRET, *Construire la ville africaine*, 1984).

Le mérite de P. Canel, P. Delis et C. Girard est d'avoir enfin clarifié,
dans le vocabulaire français, la question fort ambigüe de l'autoconstruction, et d'avoir suggéré une approche pertinente du secteur dit informel de
la production de l'habitat. En retenant une démarche d'enquête apparemment simple et limitée (analyse dans la durée d'une trentaine de chantiers

de construction dans divers quartiers irréguliers), les auteurs démontrent l'inexistence d'un modèle selon lequel l'immigrant s'improviserait constructeur de son habitat. Le chef de ménage fait en réalité appel à une main d'oeuvre qualifiée, dont les critères d'appréciation reposent notamment sur l'expérience acquise par le tâcheron (ou l'équipe de tâcherons spécialisés) dans les entreprises du secteur moderne. L'étude montre aussi que la phase transitoire d'intégration à la ville, de durée variable, n'excède généralement pas six ans, au terme de laquelle l'habitat en dur de type urbain a remplacé la baraque initiale et traduit le souci de préserver l'acquis foncier (Douala).

En remplaçant le terme d'autoconstruction par celui d'autopromotion du logement, les auteurs de l'étude caractérisent non seulement la réalité d'un processus où maîtrise d'ouvrage et maîtrise d'oeuvre sont distinctes mais aussi la diversité possible des stratégies des maîtres d'ouvrage ou promoteurs. Dans les quartiers périurbains, une majorité de chefs de ménage ont fait construire pour se loger eux-mêmes; mais plus on se rapproche des quartiers sous-intégrés du centre, plus on rencontre de constructeurs dont les opérations ont d'autres buts que le logement de leur famille; habitat locatif, usage commercial, petites activités productives.

L'une des préoccupations majeures des constructeurs maîtres d'ouvrage est alors moins celle de se loger que celle de réduire au maximum le coût de constructions destinées en tout ou en partie à assurer des revenus. C'est dans ce type de quartiers que s'installent souvent les nouveaux venus à la ville, comme locataires, avant de partir en périphérie où, ayant 'attrapé' une parcelle et suffisamment épargné, ils deviendront eux-mêmes autopromoteurs et peut-être plus tard, à leur tour, propriétaires–bailleurs (Kinshasa). On peut ainsi faire le profil-type du constructeur:

(a) Il se situe dans la frange la moins défavorisée des plus démunis (il est 'en haut des en bas').

(b) Il a une activité et un revenu réguliers.

(c) Ses dépenses pour l'alimentation n'excèdent pas 75 pour cent de son budget de consommation.

(d) Il réside depuis au moins six ans dans la ville, ce qui lui permet de s'intégrer dans le circuit de distribution des matériaux, de trouver une parcelle en périphérie, des tâcherons et de négocier le contrat de construction.

En d'autres termes, on voudra bien admettre *la forte ambiguïté*, sinon l'inadéquation totale du qualificatif de 'spontané' pour caractériser ce processus de production de l'habitat et cet habitat lui-même. Il s'agit bien d'opérateurs ayant un projet, toutes les études récentes sont convergentes sur ce point. La difficulté, pour le chercheur comme pour le practicien, est d'opérer la sommation de cette multitude de 'projets' inhérents au processus d'autoproduction de la construction, en intégrant trois données complémentaires:

(a) La distorsion fréquente entre la taille du projet et les besoins effectifs du constructeur.

(b) La lenteur des chantiers.

(c) L'émergence d'une rente foncière, au fur et à mesure que s'étend l'agglomération et que sont implantés des équipements ou assurés des services.

Pour la clarté d'ultérieures analyses, on peut aussi réserver le terme d'autoproduction à la construction à usage personnel d'habitat et celui d'autopromotion à la construction destinée à d'autres usages que l'habitat familial du propriétaire constructeur occupant, l'autopromotion intégrant alors la dimension lucrative de la construction et donc la notion d'investissement.

Ce qu'il m'a été donné d'observer personnellement à Brazzaville en 1975 et en 1984 me conduit à penser qu'existent d'assez nettes similitudes dans les processus observables en Afrique Centrale francophone, par delà les différences de régimes politiques.

L'apport de *Construire la Ville Africaine*, entre autres éléments, a incité les responsables du programme REXCOOP à transformer l'essai en lançant un appel d'offre sur l'économie de la construction (mai 1984), avec pour objet d'éclairer les relations entre secteur formel et secteur informel de la production du cadre bâti, de mettre l'accent sur les aspects micro-économiques de la production de l'habitat, d'analyser les relations entre entreprises (modernes ou informelles) et les autres acteurs.

## UNE ETUDE DE CAS SIGNIFICATIVE: L'ECONOMIE DE LA CONSTRUCTION A LOME (TOGO)

C'est dans ce contexte qu'a travaillé l'équipe animée par D. Bouzy sur l'économie de la construction à Lomé, en bénéficiant du support du groupe RUPHUS[1] et de l'EAMAU[2].

Aux *hypothèses de base* énoncées dans l'appel d'offre (articulation entre secteurs formel et informel à trois niveaux: main d'oeuvre, matériaux de construction, concepteurs), le groupe RUPHUS en a ajouté trois autres:

(a) Le secteur informel est en cours de renforcement (baisse de la capacité du secteur formel à satisfaire les besoins dans le domaine de la construction urbaine).

(b) L'effritement du secteur formel s'accompagne de la naissance d'un secteur intermédiaire dont les caractéristiques sont empruntées aux deux secteurs.

(c) L'articulation entre les deux secteurs est principalement déterminée par la nature du maître d'ouvrage, indépendamment du niveau de ressources du promoteur.

La *méthode de travail* a reposé sur une enquête approfondie d'un échantillon représentatif d'une centaine de chantiers (sur cinq zones significatives), a partir d'une localisation préalable de tous les chantiers en cours au printemps 1985. L'enquête de terrain a duré douze semaines (avril–juin 1985); finalement soixante chantiers furent enquêtés, les autres s'étant révélés abandonnés, ou leurs propriétaires étant absents. Il s'agit donc d'une 'photographie du moment', qu'il faudrait pouvoir répéter; elle n'en a pas moins livré d'intéressantes indications sur les processus de construction actuels, qu'une simple mobilisation des informations et données statistiques accessibles usuellement n'aurait pas permis de caractériser valablement.

## LE CONTEXTE LOMEEN

Rappelons que Lomé, qui compte environ 450.000 habitants, a vu sa population croître de 190.000 à 390.000 habitants de 1970 à 1981 et sa superficie urbanisée, de 2.000 à plus de 6.000 ha. entre ces deux dates.

On assiste donc à une rapide urbanisation en périphérie et à une accentuation du contraste des densités (120 habitants ha. au centre, trente dans les quartiers périphériques les plus récents, où la plupart des lots ont 600 m$^2$), ce qui aggrave les problèmes de transports et d'infrastructures, l'assainissement étant le point le plus préoccupant. Des études récentes (Le Bris, 1984: Marie, 1984) montrent que ce mode d'extension relève plus d'un processus de promotion sociale, sans ségrégation spatiale, que d'un rejet des plus pauvres. L'acquisition d'un lot, pour y construire sa maison, n'est pas perçue comme une opération marchande et il n'y a pratiquement pas de spéculation foncière, y compris au centre, étonnamment stable (Diop, 1983: Marguerat, 1983; Felli, 1986): les deux tiers des parcelles n'y ont pas changé de propriétaire depuis 1914, phénomène révélant l'attachement des familles à leurs parcelles et à leur habitat (Adjamagbo, 1986).

L'Etat contrôle la situation par un plan d'urbanisme (approuvé en 1981) et par la réglementation des lotissements qui en découlent, les transactions restant libres avec les propriétaires fonciers coutumiers. Cela dit, la ville n'est pas exempte de *traumatismes fonciers*, du fait d'expropriations conduites par l'Etat:

(a) 275 ha. en 1968 pour l'université, sans indemnisation de la population rurale des ayant-droit.

(b) 1.000 ha. en 1974–75 pour la création du domaine de Lomé II, futur quartier de résidences aisées (les populations locales furent indemnisées par l'attribution d'autres terrains).

(c) Destruction du vieux Zongo (6 ha.) en 1977, à proximité du centre, pour faire place à la construction de banques, avec transfert des habitants à 15 km au nord (Agier, 1983).

(d) Déclaration d'utilité publique de 800 ha. dans la zone portuaire et industrielle (1982) sans indemnisation, avec 'déguerpissement' brutal de 6.000 à 7.000 personnes du domaine public de la zone industrielle en 1983, sans dédommagement.

Ces transplantations massives et autoritaires ont entraîné des bouleversements sociaux, notamment par l'éparpillement des réseaux de relation et de voisinage et accentué le processus d'étalement de Lomé en périphérie, où il faut reconnaître la relative facilité d'accès au sol, jouant un rôle de frein au développement de l'habitat précaire. Tous ces éléments confèrent à Lomé une certaine spécificité en Afrique de l'Ouest.

## LA MUTATION EN COURS DE L'APPAREIL DE PRODUCTION

Dans ses deux composantes majeures (formelle et informelle), l'appareil de production du logement à Lomé connaît actuellement un phénomène convergent de mutation. Les quelques données fiables remontant à 1978 (enquêtes du Bureau International du Travail (BIT), actualisées par Schwartz, 1982, mais à échelle non opératoire pour la présente recherche), c'est-à-dire juste au début des difficultés économiques graves ayant conduit le Togo à se soumettre aux exigences du Fond Monétaire International, c'est essentiellement à partir des enquêtes chantiers conduites en 1985 auprès des propriétaires–promoteurs et des maîtres d'oeuvre constructeurs qu'a pu être menée l'analyse de ces mutations, même s'il n'a pas toujours été possible de faire le partage entre caractères structurels et déterminants conjoncturels des articulations entre secteurs formel et informel.

(i) *Le secteur moderne est dans l'ensemble dépressif* Sur moins d'une quarantaine d'entreprises répertoriées en 1985, peu interviennent directement dans la production du logement à Lomé; elles se cantonnent surtout dans le second oeuvre et la maintenance de bâtiments existants. L'Etat ne finançant plus de logements, ces entreprises hésitent à s'engager sur des marchés privés, à faible garantie financière, dans un contexte de baisse du pouvoir d'achat et des capacités à investir. Depuis 1978 on constate une diminution de la taille de ces entreprises: seules trois entreprises, émanations de sociétés étrangères, ont un capital social supérieur à 100 millions de francs CFA; une trentaine d'entreprises ont un capital inférieur à six millions de francs CFA, dont une vingtaine ont été créées entre 1979 et 1984, période de crise économique avec fort taux de mobilité; la majorité de ces entreprises emploient moins de vingt salariés, aucune n'en a plus de soixante. Entre 1979 et 1982, les entreprises de plus de vingt salariés ont perdu plus de la moitié de leurs effectifs (contre 6 pour cent aux plus petites entreprises, qui n'ont toutefois qu'une durée de vie assez brève). Pour treize entreprises ayant répondu à un questionnaire détaillé, la masse des salaires versés a diminué de 50 pour cent entre 1981 et 1983.

Au total, le secteur moderne du Bâtiment et des Travaux Publics a perdu près de 53 pour cent de ses effectifs entre 1979 et 1982. Tout se passe comme s'il se restructurait par le bas, en petites unités, soit que les entreprises réduisent leur personnel, soit que des artisans du secteur informel accèdent au statut de la petite entreprise formelle. Il faut noter aussi que les petites entreprises adoptent les pratiques du secteur informel (devis d'entreprise concernant uniquement la main d'oeuvre, l'achat des matériaux étant à la charge du donneur d'ordre maître d'ouvrage, sous-traitance à des tâcherons). Rien d'étonnant dans ces conditions à ce que ce secteur ait vu son chiffre d'affaires baisser de 42 pour cent entre 1981 et 1983 et que la recherche de la compétitivité se fasse en s'adaptant à une micro-demande diversifiée et en minimisant les frais fixes de main d'oeuvre.

(ii) Dans ce contexte, on assiste à *un renforcement du secteur informel* sous deux aspects principaux:

(a) Renforcement sur le marché de la construction: 42 pour cent des tâcherons sont établis depuis moins de cinq ans et leur effectif global croît. Les enquêtes ont révélé la position quasi-hégémonique du secteur informel à Lomé en 1985. Les raisons en sont assez claires: prix moins élevés que dans le secteur moderne (faiblesse relative des rémunération des tâcherons, coûts réduits en capital fixe, coût social faible, système de formation–apprentissage sans rémunération ou à très faible rémunération, etc.).

(b) Apparition de certaines formes de structuration, soit d'origine interne au milieu, soit à l'initiative de l'administration (création de groupements–associations de tâcherons, formant des réseaux susceptibles d'intervenir sur plusieurs chantiers à la fois; structuration de tâcherons autour d'un ou de plusieurs concepteurs assurant la conduite de la maîtrise d'oeuvre, tels des dessinateurs, des métreurs, ces formes échappant au contrôle de l'administration). Par contre le GIPATO (Groupement Interprofessionnel des Artisans du Togo), créé en 1982 avec l'appui du Bureau International du Travail, est tout à fait officiel, avec ses huit comités de quartier regroupant 640 artisans (menuisiers, soudeurs, ferronniers, plus que maçons proprement dits).

De ces indications, il ressort que le secteur informel a par nature été plus apte à faire face à la crise. L'émergence de nouvelles formes de division du travail et de nouvelles spécialisations suggère que ce secteur connaît une phase de transition.

(iii) *Les articulations entre secteur formel et secteur informel* sont assez complexes et dépendent de la nature du maître d'ouvrage, du mode de financement, du type de produit et de son coût. On peut distinguer trois niveaux d'articulation:

(a) Pour *les matériaux*, dans la mesure où 90 pour cent de la production se fait en parpaings de ciment, le secteur moderne, qui a assuré la diffusion de ce matériau, conserve un rôle dominant dans l'approvisionnement du marché, mêmes remarques pour les autres produits industriels, importés ou non (fers à béton, tôles, plomberie, vitrerie, etc.). Le secteur informel n'intervient qu'en aval, au stade de la fabrication des parpaings, sur le chantier, ou par des artisans revendeurs, dont la présence dans les quartiers périphériques est révélatrice de l'existence ou de l'attente de chantiers. En bref, l'essor du secteur informel ne gêne nullement le secteur moderne (national ou étranger) de la production et de la commercialisation des matériaux de construction, bien au contraire.

(b) En ce qui concerne *les concepteurs*, ils sont tous issus du secteur formel (écoles ou entreprises). Architectes, ingénieurs, géomètres, topographes, ils savent tous adopter un comportement adapté au processus d'auto-production du logement, quand bien même ils continuent à exercer parallèlement leurs activités au sein du secteur formel, public ou privé. Selon les objectifs du promoteur, ils peuvent intervenir au stade de l'élaboration de la demande du permis de construire (25 pour cent des chantiers enquêtés), du dossier de demande de prêt bancaire (21 pour cent des cas) et donc à la fourniture d'un plan sommaire, sans suivi ultérieur. Mais si le promoteur souhaite une construction d'un certain standing, le concepteur peut jouer un rôle actif de coordination et de surveillance de l'équipe de tâcherons.

On ne s'étonnera donc pas de voir ces concepteurs véhiculer les modèles architecturaux et techniques importés alors qu'ils pourraient avoir une fonction innovatrice, en vulgarisant, par exemple, le recours à la terre stabilisée.

(c) Quant à *la main d'oeuvre*, le secteur informel dispose d'une autonomie certaine, assurant la reproduction du système. Le passage du secteur formel, où ils ont été formés, représente moins de 15 pour cent des tâcherons; ceci recoupe les observations du BIT signalant l'aspect largement positif de l'apprentissage dans le secteur informel. Quant à la mobilité et à l'alternance d'activités dans les deux secteurs, observées dans d'autres villes africaines, elle n'est pas repérable à Lomé en 1985, du fait même de la paralysie actuelle du secteur moderne. Cela dit, les entreprises du secteur moderne sous-traitent presque toutes des travaux à des tâcherons. C'est à ce niveau qu'on peut déceler les formes les plus fréquentes d'articulation entre secteur formel et secteur informel, la crise ayant eu pour effet d'accentuer ce phénomène.

Au total, les articulations entre les deux secteurs sont marquées. Facteur passif, s'agissant des matériaux, où la situation ne semble pas différer de ce qu'on peut observer dans d'autres pays, où le développement de l'autoproduction du logement va dans le sens des intérêts du capitalisme national et étranger; facteur actif, s'agissant des concepteurs, au point de donner au secteur informel de Lomé une réélle originalité dynamique aussi dans le domaine de la main d'oeuvre, avec l'extension de la sous-traitance et du recours aux tâcherons.

## LES FILIERES DE PRODUCTION DU LOGEMENT

C'est dans ce contexte, révélé ou confirmé par l'enquête, qu'ont pu être identifiées les principales filières de production des logements, selon cinq critères constitutifs (nature du promoteur, mode de financement, nature du constructeur, nature du concepteur et statut d'utilisation du logement). Leur analyse a permis d'identifier les types de blocage et les faiblesses de chacune d'entre elles au regard de l'environnement économique et institutionnel.

(a) La filière 'promotion publique', pratiquement absente au moment de l'enquête, ne peut offrir un produit habitation à moins de 30.000 francs CFA le $m^2$ bâti; seuls des ménages disposant d'un revenu mensuel d'au moins 90.000 francs CFA peuvent accéder à ce type de logement: s'en trouve exclue la majorité de la population. Il y a donc un net glissement de 'cible' pour ce type de logement pourtant qualifié de 'social', en accession à la propriété, correspondant à des opérations conduites de 1978 à 1984. Aucun programme de ce type n'a été engagé après cette date et, des 500 logements que la SITO (Société Immobilière du Togo) estimait devoir construire annuellement, seuls 120 ont été réalisés au cours des six dernières années! La crise économique et les mesures drastiques du FMI ont fait leur effet: l'arrêt est total.

(b) La filière 'promotion privée avec constructeur déclaré et concepteur agréé' n'était représenté, en 1985, que par quelques chantiers de maisons individuelles (5 pour cent de l'échantillon). Les entreprises semblent traverser la crise en position de 'veilleuses', ne cherchant à prendre aucun risque.

(c) La filière 'autopromotion de logements individuels' est actuellement dominante, le plus souvent sous le contrôle direct des propriétaires, qui recrutent eux-mêmes des tâcherons indépendants. Financement par épargne personnelle ou par prêts bancaires, ce qui implique alors une régularisation des titres fonciers et permis de construire (procédures longues et coûteuses). Le recours à de petits prêts échelonnés explique aussi qu'il peut s'écouler de neuf à dix ans entre l'achat d'une parcelle et l'achèvement de la construction, mais cela permet d'atteindre des coûts de production plus faibles que dans les filières (a) et (b), qu'il s'agisse de constructions de standing moyen ou élevé, ou de 'maisons-wagon' destinées à la location. Sans être exclues, les familles pauvres sont très minoritaires dans cette filière.

(d) Quant à la filière qui précisément concerne la population pauvre, elle n'était guère présente dans l'enquête. C'est pourtant selon cette filière (autoproduction populaire sans réglementation, sans infrastructures, par autofinancement) que s'était par exemple construit le quartier Akodessewa, sur la zone portuaire, déguerpi en 1983. Les anciens habitants sont devenus locataires dans les quartiers voisins, ou ont construit des baraques provisoires sur des terrains loués ou prêtés, en périphérie.

Il apparaît clairement, au total, que la population pauvre est exclue de fait, actuellement, du processus de production de l'habitat. D'autres expulsions n'étant pas impensables à terme, la question du logement des plus pauvres demeure posée à Lomé.

En conclusion, il convient d'être prudent sur l'interprétation à donner aux résultats de cette recherche sur Lomé. C'est une observation du moment, non un bilan. On notera cependant que l'hypothèse d'un mode de structuration original du secteur de la production du logement, empruntant aux deux secteurs, se trouve vérifiée. Il s'agit moins d'identifier un secteur intermédiaire que de caractériser un 'champ de production', lieu de convergence de deux tendances:

(a) Apparition, dans le secteur informel, d'une frange dynamique combinant un procès de travail se rapprochant du secteur formel *et* des formes d'organisation informelles.

(b) Réaction d'adaptation du secteur moderne, qui se traduit par la création de petites entreprises jouant le rôle de charnière dans la chaîne de sous-traitance.

Mais s'agit-il d'une réaction ponctuelle à la crise économique, ou de l'embryon d'un phénomène nouveau, appelé à se développer? Dans le premier cas, ce serait un phénomène essentiellement conjoncturel, sous forme de production transitionnelle et rentable; dans le second cas, ce pourrait être l'apparition, plus structurelle, d'un véritable secteur intermédiaire de la construction, appelé à durer. Il est trop tôt pour se prononcer et il serait souhaitable de confronter ces indications aux résultats recueillis simultanément dans d'autres villes inclues dans le même programme de recherches lancé par REXCOOP (Abidjan, Le Caire, Tunis, Nouakchott, Kinshasa . . .). La tâche se révèle ardue, tant chaques cas semble avoir sa spécificité, hors des normes connues.

## NOTES

1   Recherche Urbaine et Politiques d'Habitat et d'Urbanisme dans les pays du Sud (Research on Urban Policies and Human Underdeveloped Settlements), Laboratoire de Recherche de l'Institut d'Urbanisme de l'Université de Paris VIII, animé par M. Coquery et A. Osmont.

2   Ecole Africaine et Mauricienne d'Architecture et d'Urbanisme de Lomé. Dans le cadre de cet appel d'offres, d'autres équipes de recherche ont travaillé sur Hyderabad, Tunis, Le Caire et le Maroc.

## REFERENCES

Adjamagbo, K. 1986. 'Les Successions au Togo. Réalisme d'un Code. Réalités Loméennes'. Thèse inédit 3e cycle, Sciences Juridiques, Université de Paris I.

ADRET: (Canel, P. Delis, P., et Girard, C.) 1984. *Construre la ville africaine: histoire comparée de chantiers d'habitation autoproduits à Douala et à Kinshasa*. Paris: Plan Construction, REXCOOP.

ADRET/BEAU 1986. *Economie de la construction à Kinshasa*. Paris: Plan Construction, REXCOOP.

Agier, M. 1983. *Commerce et sociabilité: les négociants soudanais du quartier Zongo de Lomé (Togo)*. Paris: ORSTOM.

Arecchi, A. 1984. 'Autoconstruction in Africa: prospects and ambiguities', *Cities*, 1 (6), novembre, pp. 575–9.

Bryant, C. 1980. 'Squatters, collective action and participation: learning from Lusaka', *World Development*, 8, pp. 73–86.

Burgess, R. 1978. 'Petty commodity housing or dweller control? A critique of John Turner's views on housing policy', *World Development*, 6, pp. 1105–34.

—— 1982. 'Self-help housing advocacy: a curious form of radicalism?, in P. M. Ward (ed.), *Self-Help Housing: a critique*, pp. 55–59. London: P. Wilson.

CEA (*Cahiers d'Etudes Africaines*). 1973. 'Villes africaines', numéro spéciale, XIII (51).

—— 1981. 'Villes africaines au microscope', XXI (81–3).

CEGET/CNRS. 1972. *La croissance urbaine en Afrique noire et à Madagascar*. Colloque, Talence, septembre 1970. Paris: CNRS.

—— 1980. *La croissance périphérique des villes du Tiers-Monde: le rôle de la promotion foncière et immobilière*. Table ronde, Talence, 1977. Paris: CNRS.

Chrétien, M. *et al.*, 1985. *Pour un financement autocentré de l'habitat: de la Tontine à l'Epargne-Logement*. Paris: GRET/Plan Construction, REXCOOP.

Coquery, M. 1983. *La coopération face aux problèmes posés par l'urbanisation dans le Tiers-Monde*. Rapport au Ministre Délégué à la coopération, mai. (Voir également, sous un titre identique, 'Les pesanteurs d'un héritage', *Hérodote*, 31, 1983, pp. 148–58 et *Politique Africaine*, mars 1985, pp. 135–42.)

Diop, M. 1983. *Le centre-ville de Lomé: évolution de la situation foncière et de la trame urbaine*. Lomé: ORSTOM.

Dresch, J. 1950. 'Villes d'Afrique Occidentale', *Cahiers d'Outre-Mer*, juillet–septembre, pp. 200–30.

Durand, J. 1963. 'Quelques réflexions sur l'urbanisme et l'habitat en Afrique', *Industries et Travaux d'Outre-Mer*, avril, pp. 401–3.

Durand-Lasserve, A. 1984. 'Le logement, l'état et les pauvres dans les villes du Tiers-Monde', *Pratiques Urbaines*, 2.

—— —— 1985. 'Crise et évolution des modes de gestion des villes dans les P.E.D: quels nouveaux acteurs? Quelles nouvelles pratiques? Quelles dynamiques?', *Journées d'Etudes Marly-le-Roi, Réseau CEGET/CNRS*, janvier (communications multig.)

—— 1986. *L'Exclusion des pauvres dans les villes du Tiers-Monde*. Paris: L'Harmattan.

—— et Tribillon, J. F. 1983. 'La production foncière et immobilière dans les villes des pays en voie de développement', *Hérodote*, 31, pp. 9–37.

Dwyer, D. J. 1975. *People and Housing in Third World Cities: perspectives on the problem of spontaneous settlements*. London and New York: Longman.

Felli, D. 1986. 'Les pratiques foncières face à l'urbanisation dans la région maritime du Togo', dans B. Crousse, E. Le Bris et E. Le Roy (sous la direction de), *Espaces disputés en Afrique Noire: pratiques foncières locales*, pp. 41–9. Paris: Karthala.

Gilbert, A. et Gugler, J. 1982. *Cities, Poverty and Development: urbanization in the Third World*. Oxford: University Press.

GRAIN. 1984. *Chaînes de production et appropriation de l'habitat dans les P.E.D.* (Zimbabwe, Tunisie, Mozambique, Madagascar). Paris: REXCOOP.

Grimes O. F., Jr. 1976. *Housing for Low-income Urban Families: economics and policy in the developing world*. Washington DC: World Bank.

Gutkind, P. C. 1960. 'Congestion and overcrowding: an African urban problem', *Human Organisation*, (3).

—— 1968–70. 'The poor in urban Africa. A prologue to modernization, conflict and unfinished revolution', dans Bloomberg et W. Schmandt (eds.), *Urban Poverty its social and political dimension*, pp. 123–63. Beverly Hills: Sage.

Haeringer, P. 1969. 'Structures foncières et création urbaine à Abidjan', *Cahiers d'Etudes Africaines*, IX (2), pp. 219–70.

—— 1972. 'L'urbanisation de masse en question: quatre villes d'Afrique noire', dans Colloques internationaux du CNRS, *La croissance urbaine en Afrique noire et à Madagascar* (Talence, Sept. 1970), vol. 2, pp. 625–51. Paris: CNRS.

—— 1973. 'Propriété foncière et politiques urbaines à Douala', *Cahiers d'Etudes Africaines*, XIII (3), pp. 449–96.

—— 1985. 'Vingt-cinq ans de politique urbaine à Abidjan', *Politique Africaine*, 17 (mars), pp. 20–40.

Hugon, P. 1980. 'Secteur informel et petites activités marchandes dans les villes du Tiers Monde', *Tiers-Monde*, XXI, 82.

—— et Deblé, I. 1982. *Vivre et survivre dans les villes africaines*. Paris: PUF.

Lacoste, Y. (sous la direction de). 1970. 'L'habitat sous-intégré'. Colloque Université de Paris VIII/SMUH, publié in *Hérodote*, 19, décembre.

Le Bris, E. 1984. 'Usages d'espaces et dynamique du front d'urbanisation dans les quartiers périphériques de Lomé', dans E. Le Bris, A. Marie, A. Osmont et A. Sinou, *Anthropologie de l'espace habité des villes africaines*, pp. 189–268. Paris: Ministère de la Recherche. Aussi sous le titre *Familles et résidence dans les villes africaines*, Paris: Harmattan.

McAuslan, P. 1985. *Urban Land and Shelter for the Poor*. London: IIED and Washington: Earthscan paperback.

Manou Savina, A., Antoine, P. Dubresson, A. et Diahou, Y. 1985. 'Les en-haut des en-bas et les en-bas des en-haut: classes moyennes et urbanisation à Abidjan (Côte d'Ivoire)', *Tiers-Monde*, XXVI (101), janvier–mars, pp. 55–68.

Marguerat, Y. 1983. 'Le capitalisme perverti, ou cent ans de production de l'espace urbain à Lomé'. *Colloque International de St. Riquier/ORSTOM.*

—— 1984. 'L'armature urbaine du Togo', dans *Les villes du Togo: bilans et perspectives*, pp. 23–163. Lomé: Banque Mondiale/FAC/PNUD.

Marie, A. 1984. 'Espaces, structures et pratiques sociales dans les quartiers centraux de Lomé', dans E. Le Bris *et al.*, *Anthropologie de l'espace habité des villes africaines*, pp. 269–386. Paris: Ministère de la Recherche.

Maximy, R. de. 1984. 'Kinshasa, ville en suspens', Thèse d'Etat, Paris: ORSTOM.

Morrison, M. K. C. et Gutkind, P. C. (eds.) 1982. *Housing the Urban Poor in Africa.* Africa Colloquium 1980, Syracuse University, New York.

Osmont, A. 1980. 'Stratégies familiales, stratégies résidentielles en milieu urbain', *Cahiers d'Etudes Africaines*, 81–3, pp. 175–95.

—— 1984. 'Pratiques foncières locales à Rufisque (Sénégal)', *Pratiques Urbaines*, 1, pp. 81–96.

—— 1985. 'Du programme à la réalité: la réalisation d'une opération d'aménagement foncier à Dakar'. Colloque International *Stratégies urbaines dans le Tiers-Monde*, septembre, Paris: CNRS.

Pain, M. 1985. 'Kinshasa, Ecologie et Organisation'. Thèse d'Etat, Paris: ORSTOM.

Pasteur, D. 1979. *The Management of Squatter Upgrading: a case study of organisation, procedures and participation.* Farnborough: Saxon House.

Payne, G. F. (ed.). 1984. *Low-income Housing in the Developing World: the role of site and services and settlement upgrading.* Chichester: John Wiley.

Perlman, J. E. 1976. *The Myth of Marginality: urban poverty and politics in Rio de Janeiro.* Berkeley: University of California Press.

*Pratiques Urbaines*, 1, 1984. 'Terres des uns, villes des autres, questions foncières et pratiques urbaines en Afrique.' CEGET/CNRS.

Richards, P. J. et Thomson, A. M. 1984. *Basic Needs and the Urban Poor: the provision of communal services.* London: Croom Helm.

Sandbrook, R. 1982. *The Politics of Basic Needs: urban aspects of assaulting poverty in Africa.* London: Heinemann.

Schwartz, A. 1982. *Evolution de l'emploi dans les entreprises togolaises du secteur moderne de 1979 à 1982*, Lomé: ORSTOM (Mimeo).

Skinner, R. J. et Rodell, M. J. (eds.). 1983. *People, Poverty and Shelter: problems of self-help housing in the Third World.* London and New York: Methuen.

Spence, R. J. et Cook, D. J. 1983. *Building Materials in Developing Countries.* Chichester: John Wiley.

Stren, R. E. 1975. *Urban Inequality and Housing Policy in Tanzania: the problem of squatting.* Berkeley: University of California Institute of International Studies.

—— 1978. *Housing the Urban Poor in Africa: policy, politics and bureaucracy in Mombasa.* Berkeley: University of California Press.

—— 1986. 'Underdevelopment, urban squatting and the state bureacracy: a case study of Tanzania', *Canadian Journal of African Studies*, 16, pp. 67–91.

Stren, R. et Letemendia, C. 1986. *Coping with Rapid Urban Growth in Africa: an annoted bibliography. Aux prises avec l'urbanisation rapide en Afrique: bibliographie annotée.* Edition bilingue (traduction par C. Stren), Montreal: McGill University.

Tribillon, J. F. 1984. 'Problématique socio-foncière d'un projet de réhabilitation d'un quartier populaire (Fass Paillote, Dakar)'; 'La clientèle foncière de l'Etat'; 'Le cas de K . . . opposition entre la ville légale et la ville de fait'; et 'Le tiers-habitat africain: fait et politique', 4 des 6 articles, *Pratiques Urbaines*, 1.

Turner, J. F. C. 1969. 'Uncontrolled urban settlements: problems and solutions', in

G. Breese, (ed.), *The City in Newly Developing Countries*, pp. 507–34.
—— 1979. *Le Logement est votre affaire*. Paris: Le Seuil. (English edition, 1976, *Housing by People*. London: Marion Boyars.)
—— 1982. 'Issues in self-help and self-managed housing', in P. M. Ward (ed.), *Self-Help Housing: a critique*, pp. 99–114. London: Wilson.
—— 1986. 'Future directions in housing policies', *Habitat International*, 10 (3), pp. 7–25.
UNCHS. 1981. *The Residential Circumstances of the Urban Poor in Developing Countries*. New York: Praeger.
United Nations. 1965. *Housing in Africa*, septembre.
—— 1972. *Amélioration des taudis et des zones de peuplement non réglementé*. New York (English edition, New York, 1971).
Venard, J. L. 1985. *Vingt-cinq ans d'intervention française dans le secteur urbain en Afrique noire francophone*. Paris: Ministère de l'Urbanisme, du Logement et des Transports.
Vernière, M. 1973. 'Volontarisme d'Etat et Spontanéisme Populaire dans l'Urbanisation du Tiers-Monde. Formation et Evolution des Banlieues Dakaroises: le cas de Dagoudane Pikine', Thèse de 3e Cycle, EPHE/CNRS.
Ward, P. M. (ed.) 1982. *Self-Help Housing: a critique*. London: Wilson.

## SUMMARY

From the early 1960s onwards, most large urbanised areas have been under the pressure of rapid population growth (4 to 8 per cent per annum). During this time at least 80 per cent of the new urban-dwellers obtained shelter via self-help methods. Literature is prolific *and* controversial on the subject and it might be argued that there is no strict coincidence between self-help housing and poverty. In the early 1980s some French scholars and practitioners not interested in the pursuit of macro-economic approaches, in the fading context of theoretical debates on development, emphasised the very local urban issues through multidisciplinary surveys. They pointed out specific inhabitants' and users' strategies as referred to informal activities, urban mobility, land-use and tenure, self-help housing . . . From these researches it became obvious that the Western system of technical and cultural references, too often considered as universal, largely fails to express what is now happening in the African process of urbanisation. Most African governmental urban policies, more or less defined or reshaped after World Bank and other international aid standards, are also far from facing reality. After *Construire la ville africaine* was published (ADRET, 1984) it became clear, within French literature, that concepts and terms referring to actual practices had to be seriously redefined. What does 'marginality' mean when the largest part of the population is concerned? What do 'spontaneous' settlements mean when the largest part of the population is concerned? What do 'spontaneous' settlements mean when most families have to manage strategies for months and years to get plots to build and improve their shelter? What does 'self-help' (*autoconstruction* in French) itself mean when people are not actually building their own house but managing the whole process (finding and paying for the plots, the materials, and the skilled or unskilled craftsmen)? This chapter enlarges and exemplifies the topic with reference to a recent survey carried out in 1985–86 in Lomé, Togo.

# PART II
# CASE STUDIES IN HOUSING MARKETS: COMMERCIALISATION AND CHANGE

## 3 T. O. Okoye

# HISTORICAL DEVELOPMENT OF NIGERIAN HOUSING POLICIES WITH SPECIAL REFERENCE TO HOUSING THE URBAN POOR

Provision of appropriate housing for the urban population, particularly for the urban poor, has always been a major problem faced by most countries of Africa and the developing world in general (Abrams, 1964). Before the beginning of this century, it did not appear to be much of a problem in the towns of those areas that came to be known as Nigeria, because under the pre-industrial conditions at the time, houses were built completely of local materials and to the taste and specifications of the owners. Thus most of the urban poor, at least, had their own houses, even though the quality of the buildings, in the changing circumstances of the present century, is now considered sub-standard. The situation began to change from about the second decade of this century, and provision of adequate housing for the urban population, particularly the urban poor, came to be seen as a problem. By the end of the colonial period this problem had escalated and, after the Nigerian civil war, became an enormous and very pressing one.

This chapter, therefore, aims to examine closely, in historical perspective, the development of Nigerian housing policies and the extent to which they enabled the country to grapple with the problem of housing the urban population, particularly the urban poor.

The problem of housing the urban poor arose mainly as a result of a combination of several factors, including a rapid urbanisation rate, the setting of high building standards, the high cost of building materials, and high rents.

Changes in the economy brought about by colonial rule, increased mobility of individuals with the changing social and political conditions and with the introduction of new modes of transport (the motor vehicle and the railway) and, more particularly, the concentration of infrastructure and social amenities in the urban areas by the colonial administration, led to large-scale rural–urban migration. Table 3.1 shows that within the decade 1921–31, most of the old towns increased their population by over 50 per cent, with Kano almost doubling its population, while the towns founded during the colonial period, Enugu and Port Harcourt, for example, more

Table 3.1
Comparison of the population of selected Nigerian towns, 1921 and 1931 Censuses

| Town | Population | | Increase in the decade | % change |
|---|---|---|---|---|
| | 1921 | 1931 | | |
| 1 Ibadan | 238,094 | 387,133 | 149,039 | 63 |
| 2 Lagos | 99,690 | 126,108 | 26,418 | 27 |
| 3 Kano | 49,938 | 97,031 | 47,093 | 94 |
| 4 Abeokuta | 28,941 | 45,763 | 16,822 | 58 |
| 5 Enugu | 3,170 | 12,959 | 9,789 | 308 |
| 6 Port Harcourt | 7,185 | 15,201 | 8,016 | 112 |
| 7 Ilorin | 38,668 | 47,590 | 8,922 | 23 |
| 8 Ijebu Ode | 21,765 | 27,909 | 6,144 | 28 |
| 9 Onitsha | 10,319 | 18,084 | 7,765 | 75 |
| 10 Katsina | 17,489 | 22,620 | 5,131 | 29 |

*Source:* 1931 National Census of Nigeria.

than doubled their population, mainly through rural–urban migration.

The housing supply could not keep pace with the rapid growth of the urban population and so led to congestion and overcrowding, particularly of the urban poor, in the residential areas. As the physical development of the urban centres slowly responded to the fast population growth, the urban administration, in order to protect house-dwellers from the hazards of poorly-constructed homes and to improve the quality of housing, set up building regulations, which were such that most local building materials could no longer be used in the urban areas. The cost of house construction further worked to reduce the rate of housing supply in relation to the ever-increasing demand. House rents, which are a function of housing supply and demand, therefore, increased to the extent that the average urban worker preferred to rent just one or two rooms, while the urban poor could ill afford to rent even one room. Congestion became pronounced, especially in rooming-houses.

## MARGINAL GOVERNMENT PARTICIPATION IN HOUSING PROVISION

Throughout the colonial period and into the early period of independence, the government participated only marginally in housing provision. In the first three decades of the present century, what served as the government's policy on housing were the sections on housing as contained in Lugard's 'Instructions to Political and Other Officers on Subjects Chiefly Political and Administrative' (Lugard, 1906: 272) and in the Political Memoranda

(Lugard, 1918: 416–19). These sections merely gave guidelines for the laying-out of townships, the construction of houses and the maintenance of specified housing standards in the 'European Reservation' and the 'Native Quarters', forbidding the use of grass mats for walls or enclosures and encouraging the use of burnt bricks for walls, non-inflammable materials like sheet-iron and tiles for roofs, and angle-iron for ridge-poles and rafters.

It is not clear whether Lugard's government adopted the policy of regarding housing as a social utility which people could acquire in the open market according to their ability and willingness to pay for it, or that it had a commitment to provide housing for its citizens, particularly the underprivileged. This is because, while in the 'Government Reservation' the government built houses for its senior staff, mainly Europeans, in the other parts of the town house construction was left largely to private effort. Only in exceptional circumstances, where the government depended heavily on artisans or unskilled labour, were quarters for junior staff built. Thus the earliest participation of the government in provision of housing for the urban poor was the construction of junior staff quarters, like miners' quarters built in the Iva Valley, Enugu, by the Colliery Department in 1922, and the Artisan Quarters (China Town) built in Enugu in 1923 by the Railway Department for its junior staff (Onitsha Province, Annual Reports, 1922, 1923). Other government departments, like the Post and Telegraph Department, also established quarters for their junior workers in various other towns in the country.

In Lagos, the outbreak of bubonic plague between 1925 and 1928 led to the government taking action in the provision of public housing (Abiodun, 1985: 180; Fadahunsi, 1985: 106). The Lagos Executive Development Board (LEDB) was formed in 1928, charged with the duty of clearing the swampy areas to establish housing units.

There was no doubt that the instructions in the Political Memoranda, as they pertained to housing and township development, with time proved grossly inadequate to cope with the problems of the rapidly growing towns. Modifications were made as the need arose or completely new ideas were introduced. In 1922 a Town Planning Committee for the Southern Provinces was formed in Lagos, with sub-committees in the major towns. Its responsibility was to oversee the planning of all towns in the Southern Provinces and consider planning schemes submitted to it by the various Local Authorities. In Enugu, for example, the Town Planning Sub-committee was formed in 1923 (Onitsha Province, Annual Report, 1923). In 1924 a similar Town Planning Committee was formed for the Northern Provinces. The accomplishment of the Town Planning Committees in the area of housing lay in the development of new layouts with access and internal streets and the allocation of plots to private individuals who could afford to build houses to township specifications. As would be expected, most of the urban poor could not benefit from the programme. In January 1927 the Town Planning Committees were abolished. The establishment of Town Planning Authorities with the enactment of the Nigeria Town and Country Planning Ordinance of 1946 did not much improve the situation since, by the Ordinance, the function of the Planning Authorities with regard to housing lay only in estate development and building control (Uyanga, 1977: 7; Mabogunje, 1978: 11).

A later development was the introduction of the African Staff Housing Scheme by which housing loans were provided to African senior civil servants to enable them build their own houses. But owing to its restrictive nature, this scheme did not do much to increase the housing supply.

Towards the end of the colonial administration, with the adoption of the regional system of government in the country, housing was listed among the subjects vested in the regional governments (Okunnu, 1978: 4). Thus each region was free to formulate its own housing policy and carry out its own programmes. The main agency for the execution of regional governments' housing programmes was the Regional Housing Corporation (RHC), formed first in 1958. The duties of the RHC included (a) laying out housing estates with the necessary infrastructure and allocating the plots to those who could afford to build their own houses; (b) the construction of model houses with modern amenities for sale or renting and as examples of acceptable standards; and (c) the provision of loans to individuals to build their own houses. Because of the high prices of the houses built by the corporations and the difficulties of obtaining loans from them, only the high and middle-income groups benefited from their housing programmes. The total contribution of the RHCs to housing supply remained minimal.

The federal government, as the regional government of the federal territory of Lagos, continued to use the LEDB in the execution of its housing programmes for Lagos. Like the RHCs, the LEDB developed housing estates in Lagos (in Apapa, Victoria Island and Surulere), but mainly for the high and middle-income groups. Of significance for the urban poor in Lagos was the slum-clearance scheme of central Lagos started in 1955. The scheme was accompanied by government provision of housing units for the low-income group, that is, the Surulere Low-income Housing Scheme. About 1,300 housing units, comprising mainly one-bedroom and some two-bedroom apartments, were provided to serve as temporary relocation houses for the slum-dwellers. The rent was highly subsidised. Nevertheless, as observed by Marris (1961), many of the slum-dwellers refused to move into the housing units in Surulere but preferred to live with relations in other parts of the town. For those who moved into Surelere, the houses eventually became permanent residences, as they could not afford to return to the redeveloped site owing to the high repurchase price of the buildings in the redeveloped area.

In 1956, the Nigerian Building Society was established as an institution for financing private housing construction; it thus became the forerunner of the Nigerian Mortgage Bank.

## POST-INDEPENDENCE DEVELOPMENTS

The rapid growth of the urban centres, which began in the colonial period, continued after political independence in 1960. The fast rate was sustained and even further accelerated by such factors as (a) the political and social changes following the attainment of independence; (b) the free primary education introduced in some regions from 1955, which produced school-leavers unwilling to return to rural agricultural life and most of whom drifted into the urban centres in search of salaried jobs; (c) the oil boom of the 1970s which supported increased social and economic activities, particularly in the urban areas; and (d) the creation of states (twelve in 1967, rising to nineteen in 1976) and the consequent administrative decentralisation whereby several urban centres were raised to the status of state capital, and many others to the status of divisional, and later local government, headquarters. The population growth of the urban centres was due more to rural–urban migration than to natural increase. Table 3.2 shows that in the inter-censal period 1953–63 most of the urban centres grew at the rate of over 5 per cent per annum. Kaduna grew by as much as 11·3 per cent, Port Harcourt by 10·5 per cent and Warri by 9·8 per cent per annum.

In their areal expansion, most of the towns, particularly the larger ones like Lagos, Ibadan, Kano, Kaduna, Onitsha, Enugu, Benin, Port Harcourt and Calabar, extended beyond their previous administrative boundaries and encroached upon nearby rural settlements, some of which were later incorporated into the sprawling towns.

Table 3.2
Population growth of selected Nigerian towns, 1952/53–1963

| Town | 1952/53 Census | 1963 Census | Growth rate per annum |
|---|---|---|---|
| Lagos | 267,407 | 665,246 | 8·6 |
| Ibadan | 459,196 | 635,011 | 3·2 |
| Onitsha | 76,921 | 163,032 | 7·2 |
| Aba | 57,787 | 131,003 | 7·8 |
| Kaduna | 44,540 | 149,910 | 11·3 |
| Port Harcourt | 71,634 | 179,563 | 10·5 |
| Warri | 19,526 | 55,254 | 9·8 |
| Enugu | 62,764 | 138,457 | 7·5 |
| Jos | 38,527 | 94,451 | 8·6 |
| Benin | 53,753 | 100,694 | 5·9 |

*Sources:* 1953 and 1963 National Censuses of Nigeria

Since the private sector continued as the main source of housing supply, with the government playing only a marginal role, the housing shortage became particularly acute. More than 50 per cent of households in most urban centres lived in only one room. Table 3·3 clearly illustrates the dismal housing situation in most towns at this time. In Lagos, for example, as many as 72·5 per cent of households occupied only one room, with an average room occupancy ratio of 3·8, and only 43·5 per cent of the houses had a flush toilet. In Kano, 69·1 per cent of households lived in one room, with an average room occupancy ratio of 2·4; only 1·8 per cent of the houses had a flush toilet.

Table 3.3
Housing conditions in selected Nigerian towns, 1975

| Town | % of households occupying one room | Average number of persons per room | % of houses with tap water | % of houses with flush toilet | % of houses with electricity |
|---|---|---|---|---|---|
| Lagos | 72·5 | 3·8 | 71·7 | 43·5 | 93·2 |
| Port Harcourt | 51·5 | 2·4 | 75·0 | 18·6 | 81·4 |
| Benin | 48·0 | 2·2 | 24·9 | 4·0 | 59·3 |
| Warri | 59·9 | 2·6 | 62·4 | 10·9 | 89·7 |
| Kaduna | 63·9 | 2·1 | 40·3 | 14·1 | 53·3 |
| Kano | 69·1 | 2·4 | 26·1 | 1·8 | 69·1 |
| Ilorin | 23·9 | 1·6 | 30·7 | 10·3 | 28·4 |
| Ibadan | 47·3 | 2·1 | 33·4 | 25·2 | 56·1 |

Source: Third National Development Plan, 1975: 307.

Despite this deplorable housing situation during the 1960s and early 1970s, the government still contributed little to solving the housing problem. Housing remained the responsibility of the regional governments and, with the creation of states, that of the state governments. Each regional, or later state government pursued its independent policy so that there was no co-ordination of policies. During the period of the First National Development Plan (1962–68), for example, the federal government expressed its awareness of the fact that the people of Lagos, and several other major towns in the country, lived in crowded conditions, yet it had to limit its actions to Lagos federal territory alone. Within the period of the Plan it proposed to construct about 24,000 housing units in Lagos, about 60 per cent of which would be for the low-income group (with 30 per cent and 10 per cent for the middle and high-income groups respectively). It proposed a new approach to the provision of low-cost housing: the federal government would develop the land, turn out by mass production methods 'shell houses': two-roomed dwellings supplied with electricity and water services. The 'shell houses' would then be sold to low-income persons who would be required to finish the interior of the houses. The purchase price would be payable over twenty years at a monthly instalment lower than the current rent for similar houses at the time (First National Development Plan, 1962: 94). The programme, it was envisaged, would pay its way and would require no subsidies.

In effect, during the period of the Plan, the federal government was reviewing its policy on housing, with a view to eliminating subsidies as far as possible and placing the cost of housing programmes on the beneficiaries. Accordingly, the Nigerian Building Society was required henceforth to provide mortgage credit and credit from the African Staff Housing Fund at economic rates, so that these institutions could be self-supporting.

## HOUSING AS A NATIONAL ISSUE

The fact that housing remained a state matter militated against concerted national action and there was little co-ordination of state policies. The idea of a national housing policy was mooted in 1968, but it was not well received, particularly by the state governments, which feared erosion of their powers by the federal government (Okunnu, 1978: 5). The first successful attempt to give the housing issue a national focus was by the establishment in 1971 of the National Council on Housing, membership of which comprised commissioners responsible for housing in all the states of the federation. The achievements of the council include the fact that it brought home to various state governments the very poor state of housing in the country and the need for co-ordinated action. The council noted that a major problem of housing in the country was lack of funds, and so adopted the idea of a House Mortgage Bank (first proposed by the Association of Housing Corporations of Nigeria) and also suggested that the National Provident Fund, the insurance companies, and the commercial banks could be additional sources (Okunnu, 1978: 5).

The new national focus led to the establishment of a national housing programme in 1972. Although the programme was unscheduled, it aimed to construct 59,000 dwelling units all over the federation, with 15,000 in Lagos and 4,000 in each of the eleven states. In May of that year, a Federal Government Staff Housing Board was established to take over the African Staff Housing Scheme started in the colonial period. In the following year the Federal Housing Authority (FHA) was formed to oversee the national housing programme, and the federal government also acquired the Commonwealth Development Corporation's 60 per cent shares in the Nigerian Building Society, making its total shareholding 91 per cent. The aim was to make the Nigerian Building Society an instrument of government housing policy.

## GOVERNMENT INTERVENTION IN HOUSING PROVISION
## ON A LARGE SCALE

The new national focus and the increased government revenue as a result of the oil boom emboldened the federal government to declare that it 'now accepts it as a part of its social responsibility to participate actively in the provision of housing for all income groups and will therefore intervene on a large scale in this sector during the plan period' (Third National Development Plan, 1975: 308). The government proposed to accomplish the envisaged large-scale intervention by (a) direct construction of housing units by both federal and state governments for letting at subsidised rates; (b) increased construction of quarters for government officials; (c) expansion of credit facilities to enhance private construction of housing; (d) increased investment in the domestic production of cement, iron rods, and other essential building materials; (e) increased importation of these materials to supplement domestic production; (f) vigorous promotion of the use of local materials such as burnt bricks to minimise dependence on imported substitutes; and (g) assisting indigenous contractors to improve their skills.

During the Third National Development Plan (1975–80), therefore, the federal government proposed 60,000 housing units mainly for low and middle-income groups with the FHA as the executive agency. An allocation of 1·5 billion *naira* was made for the purpose. Later, in 1976, the housing programme was enlarged to a total of 202,000 housing units (8,000 units for each state capital and 12,000 and 46,000 units respectively for Kaduna and Lagos States – Fourth National Development Plan, 1981: 338). The government directed that, in setting up the housing units, attention would be paid to the provision of a basic infrastructure including the supply of water and electricity and such social amenities as schools, health centres, shopping centres and so on in order to establish viable communities.

In keeping with the government's policy of expanding credit facilities, in 1976 the Nigerian Building Society was converted into a Mortgage Bank with a capital of 150 million *naira* so that it would be able to lend, not only to individuals, but also to state government housing corporations and private real estate developers.

The federal government also encouraged companies having more than 500 workers to develop housing estates for their employees, and directed the commercial banks to set aside 10 per cent of their loanable funds for lending for housing purposes and to lend to the Federal Mortgage Bank any unused part of the 10 per cent.

Within the same plan period (1975–80), the various state governments had their proposals for increasing the housing units in their states. Table 3·4 summarises the state allocations on housing generally.

Table 3.4
Government allocations for housing in the Nigerian Third National Development
Plan, 1975–80

| States | Total estimated expenditure (N million) |
|---|---|
| Benue-Plateau | 5·00 |
| East-Central | 20·50 |
| Kano | 30·93 |
| Kwara | 8·00 |
| Lagos | 11·00 |
| Mid-Western | 30·00 |
| North-Central | 10·00 |
| North-Eastern | 18·00 |
| North-Western | 10·00 |
| Rivers | 10·00 |
| South-Eastern | 10·00 |
| Western | 24·00 |
| Total: All states | 187·43 |
| Federal government | 1,650·00 |
| Total: All governments | 1,837·43 |

*Source:* Third National Development Plan, 1975: H 311.

## LEVEL OF ACCOMPLISHMENT

There is, however, a wide gap between proposal and accomplishment. At the end of the period of the Third National Development Plan, in 1980, of the proposed 46,000 housing units to be built in the Lagos metropolis, directly handled by the FHA, only 8,616 housing units, or approximately 19 per cent of the proposed total, were completed. Of the 8,000 units proposed for each of the states, the average accomplishment was only about 13 per cent, ranging from 0·5 per cent in Benue to 32·3 per cent in Oyo State. Thus in 1980, less than one-fifth of the proposed 202,000 housing units was added to the existing housing stock. When the barracks building programme achievements of the Armed Forces and the Police Force, as well as the various staff quarters and state governments' programmes are taken into consideration, the overall amount added to the existing stock remained insignificant.

## FURTHER ATTEMPTS AT LARGE-SCALE GOVERNMENT INTERVENTION BY DIRECT CONSTRUCTION

Despite the colossal failure of direct construction recounted above, during the Fourth National Development Plan Period of 1981–85 the federal government proposed to construct 2,000 housing units in each state every year, comprising one-bedroom core houses expandable to three bedrooms and three-bedroom duplexes. For these the sum of 600 million *naira* was allocated. Another direct housing construction proposal, to be implemented by the FHA, involved building about 143,000 low-cost housing units in various parts of the country, including Lagos. In addition, the federal government would continue their provision of staff quarters and loans to enable staff to build their own houses (Fourth National Development Plan, 1981: 343). State governments had their own housing schemes for the period of the plan.

The schemes soon became caught up in the economic depression that subsequently afflicted the country. With the consequent cut-backs in budgets, the escalating costs of building materials, expensive contractual procedures and many other problems, these programmes fared no better than those of the preceding plan.

## THE NATIONAL HOUSING POLICY

In keeping with the now established national focus on housing, the civilian administration that took office in 1979, in initiating the Fourth National Development Plan (1981–85), produced a National Policy on Housing. The policy examined the housing situation in the country from the colonial period to 1980, discussed the housing need, demand and supply in the country, and the problems in the housing delivery system, and formulated policy objectives. The goal of the policy was 'to provide affordable housing to accommodate all Nigerian households in a livable environment'. Its specific objectives, nine in number, included:

(i) To increase and improve overall quantity and quality of housing by increasing substantially the rate of new housing production at the highest standard affordable at each income level, while at the same time upgrading service and living conditions in the existing deprived areas; (ii) to give priority to housing programme designed to benefit the low income groups . . .; (iii) to vigorously mobilise housing finance from all sources: public sector sources, private savings, and private sector investment; and (iv) to improve the quality of rural housing and rural environment, through integrated rural development programmes. (Federal Ministry of Housing and Environment, 1981: 11)

The policy then dwelt on methods of achieving the specified objectives, taking into consideration the major functional components of the housing delivery system. They include: (i) policy development and initiation; (ii) land provision; (iii) housing finance; (iv) infrastructure and service provision; (v) design, construction and building materials; (vi) rental accommodation and rent control policy; and (vii) institutional framework and roles.

## SITE AND SERVICE PROJECTS AND
## VILLAGE UPGRADING SCHEMES

New aspects of the national housing policy are the site and service projects and village upgrading schemes in which the federal government, the World Bank, and the state governments are co-operating. The underlying principle of the site and service schemes is that the authorities provide and service the land with the necessary infrastructure (roads, drainage channels, electricity, etc.) and social amenities (schools, health centres, markets, etc.), while the individuals who are allocated the housing plots proceed to build their houses in accordance with approved plans of their own choice. The beneficiaries are helped to obtain loans from the FMB, repayable over fifteen years at 6 per cent interest. They then build the core units under the supervision of the Project Implementation Unit. Each householder can later expand the core unit, adding additional rooms in accordance with his needs and financial capability. In Bauchi State, 2,100 residential plots and 1,850 infill plots in Makama, Bauchi, and in Imo State, 3,500 plots each in Owerri and Aba, and 6,500 plots in Umuahia are involved in the scheme.

The village upgrading scheme aims to conserve the existing low-income housing stock in relatively central locations to ensure residents' accessibility to their place of work and social amenities. The scheme includes the preparation and implementation of redevelopment plans, including the provision of an infrastructure, and the provision of loans to residents through the FMB to upgrade or renew their houses. In Bauchi, the scheme involves 140 ha. of Makama, and in Imo State the six core villages of Owerri.

The third aspect of the scheme are the increased employment opportunities owing to the development of small-scale industrial estates and the establishment of small-scale enterprises to improve the earning capacity of the low-income group.

## CONCLUDING COMMENTS

The National Housing Policy provides for the federal government's direct construction of housing on a large scale in order to help increase the supply of housing. The poor performance of the government in direct construction in both the Third and Fourth National Development Plans lends strong support to the view that government should not undertake direct housing construction.

The continuing difficulty of land acquisition in the urban areas in spite of the Land-use Act of 1978, and the escalating cost of building materials, even though most of the materials are now manufactured in Nigeria, pose important problems for the realisation of the policy objective.

The search for methods of providing really low-cost housing by using local materials and adapting the traditional methods of house construction, as experimented upon by the Western Nigeria Housing Corporation in 1975–76 (Onibokun, 1985b: 277–85) should be more vigorously pursued. A co-operative approach to low-cost housing as planned by Anambra State Housing Corporation may prove a good alternative to site and service schemes.

There is the need for an efficient administrative and management framework for translating policy and objectives into reality. Without such an efficient framework, the National Housing Policy, no matter how well conceived, may fail in its objective of improving the housing lot of the urban worker, particularly the urban poor.

## REFERENCES

Abiodun, J. O. 1985. 'The provision of housing and urban environmental problems in Nigeria', in J. O. Abiodun (ed.), *Urban and Regional Planning Problems in Nigeria*, pp. 174–91. Ile Ife: University of Ife Press.

Abrams, C. 1964. *Housing in the Modern World*. London: Faber & Faber.

Fadahunsi, S. O. 1985. 'Fifty years of housing in Nigeria', in P. Onibokun (ed.), *Housing in Nigeria: A Book of Readings*, pp. 105–32. Ibadan: Nigerian Institute of Social and Economic Research.

Federal Ministry of Housing and Environment. 1981. *National Housing Policy*. Lagos: Government Printer.

Lugard, F. D. 1906. *Instructions to Political Officers on Subjects chiefly Political and Administrative*. London: Waterlow & Sons.

—— 1918. *Political Memoranda: revision of instructions to political officers*. London: Waterlow & Sons.

Mabogunje, A. L. 1978. 'Towards an urban policy in Nigeria', in P. O. Sada and J. S. Oguntoyinbo (eds.), *Urbanization Processes and Problems in Nigeria*, pp. 7–20. Ibadan: University Press.

Marris, P. 1961. *Family and Social Change in African City: a study in rehousing in Lagos*. London: Routledge & Kegan Paul.

National Development Plans (1962, 1968, 1975 and 1981). Federal Government of Nigeria, Lagos.

Okunnu, F. 1978. 'Government policy on housing and urban development', in P. O. Sada and J. S. Oguntoyinbo (eds.), *Urbanization Processes and Problems in Nigeria*, pp. 3–6. Ibadan: University Press.

Onibokun, P. 1985. 'Low cost housing: an appraisal of an experiment in Nigeria', in P. Onibokun (ed.), *Housing in Nigeria: a book of readings*, pp. 277–86. Ibadan: Nigerian Institute of Social and Economic Research.

Onitsha Province, Annual Reports 1922 and 1923. Enugu: National Archives, UniProf.

Uyanga, J. 1977. 'Problems of institutional planning in urban Nigeria'. Paper presented at the seminar on Urban Planning and Management in Nigeria, Enugu: University of Nigeria Economic Development Institute.

# RESUME

Le logement, en particulier en ce qui concerne la population urbaine pauvre, n'est pas nécessairement devenu un problème au Nigéria avant les années 20, lorsque la rapide croissance des villes, dûe en grande partie à la migration rurale–urbaine, a créé une pénurie de logement en zone urbaine. Tout au long de la période coloniale et jusqu'en 1970, les logements ont été pour la plupart fournis par le secteur privé. Le gouvernement n'a joué qu'un rôle marginal et n'avait pas de véritable politique du logement. La régionalisation du gouvernement et plus tard la création d'états ont compensé le manque de coordination des politiques de logement car chaque région ou état a mené indépendamment sa propre politique. Grâce au rétablissement de l'attention nationale sur la question du logement au début des années 70, d'ambitieux programmes de logement nationaux ont été instaurés, et une politique nationale du logement a été formulée en 1981, qui a entraîné la construction d'habitations directement par le gouvernement, encourageant les tentatives privées et la création de logements de coût modeste par les programmes de site et de services. Tandis que la plupart des programmes directs gouvernementaux de construction d'habitations au cours des troisième et quatrième périodes d'expansion nationale ont échoué, les programmes de site, de services et de modernisation des villages constituent le meilleur moyen d'apporter des logements standards à la population urbaine pauvre.

# PETTY LANDLORDS AND POOR TENANTS IN A LOW-INCOME SETTLEMENT IN METROPOLITAN LAGOS, NIGERIA

## INTRODUCTION

The existence and pervasiveness of the housing crisis that has accompanied recent modern urbanisation, particularly in developing countries, is no longer subject to denial (Blitzer, Hardoy and Satterthwaite, 1981; Gilbert and Gugler, 1982; Lynn 1983; McAuslan, 1985). Its consequences have ranged from appalling housing conditions, a deficiency in or complete lack of essential services, continuing exploitation and/or domination of the urban poor in land and shelter matters, and the growth of deprived settlements to, in extreme cases, outright homelessness.

Nigeria has had its fair share of the problems of urban underdevelopment and housing crisis. This is evidenced by the rapid population growth in towns, the collapse of urban planning and administration, the decay and deterioration in the provision of services and infrastructures, and the proliferation and predominance of deprived shelter and settlements (Okpala, 1978, 1984a, 1984b; Abiodun, 1985; Ozo, 1986).

Responses to the problems posed by the housing crisis could be broadly classified as twofold. The first consist of the *elite-based responses* made up of responses that emerge from the state and those of minority elites who control it or possess advantageous strategic access to it. The set of responses, which may be called *popular responses*, are those that emerge from the majority of the people who have to live in, and make a living in the cities. These, in the main, are the urban poor. However, it is important to note that both sets of responses do not form isolated, distinct unrelated structures and processes; rather, they are closely articulated. Also it is important to note that between both sets of responses, there exist not only diversity but in certain cases, even inconsistencies. This is because these patterns of responses at any given time are themselves determined and influenced by a configuration of factors and forces. These include indigenous customs, practices inherited from colonial rule, the nature of the political economy, its history, current conditions, world economy, the impact of professionals, ideology and international institutions on domestic policy, and finally the internal balance of strategic domestic social forces and class interests. All of these, in terms of a delicate pattern of interaction, possess implications for the overall response to the housing crisis.

Thus the Nigerian State, in response to the crisis identified as far back as 1963 (UN Report on Metropolitan Lagos), has oscillated between neglect and waves of massive intervention that varied from the direct provision of housing to the aggressive demolition of unauthorised housing and settlements.[1]

Popular responses, on the other hand, have been more successful in providing the bulk of housing in Nigerian towns and cities. Official sources, in fact, have recognised and accepted this predominance for about 94 per cent of the housing stock.[2] However, what can be called *popular responses*, as we have noted above, vary extensively in terms of location, that is, whether in the city centre, the traditional town or the 'new towns' on the outskirts. They also vary in terms of orientation, namely provision of shelter for the owner alone, or for the owner and some tenants, or mainly for tenants. And finally, another source of variety within the popular responses has to do with the relative wealth or status of the provider of shelter and the gap between such a person and those, the majority, for whom shelter is provided. An understanding of these differences is important as it is central to the dynamics of the housing crisis, the type or variety of long-term trends that are emerging, if any, and their implications for policy, political action and general well-being.

## COMMERCIALISATION IN POPULAR RESPONSES

In terms of long-term trends, an emerging one that has been confirmed elsewhere is that of the commercialisation of housing (Moser, 1982; Edwards, 1982; Amis, 1984), meaning by this that part of the popular response to the housing crisis has been the provision of housing, or land for housing, in exchange for money. It has thus become a source of income or revenue, turning both land and shelter principally into commodities and thereby creating a rental housing and land market. It is this specific phenomenon that is creating both landlords and tenants within the context of housing the urban poor.

In the case of the city of Lagos, evidence of commercialisation dates as far back as the 1940s and the 1950s. Perhaps owing to the growth of the city, its economic and political position in Nigeria which in turn encouraged inward migration, and the spatial limitations imposed by its island situation and swampy terrain, commercialisation of both land and housing had occurred relatively early, with rental housing being the predominant form of housing, even for the hitherto traditional Yoruba family compounds

(Marris, 1961: 26–7). But the available facts go beyond the Lagos experience. The vast literature on the development of entrepreneurship in Nigeria had long recognised the importance of housing as a source of investment by indigenous entrepreneurs and had in fact criticised their preference for this rather 'non-productive' investment of profits.[3] Thus rent and landlordism have featured not only as legitimate sources of income and occupation but have also defined the basis of community power, and prestige in the urban context (Lloyd, 1974; Peace, 1979).[4]

But more recent urbanisation in Metropolitan Lagos has moved from being an inner-city phenomenon to the creation of newer forms of low-income settlements both on the outskirts of the city and in hitherto difficult terrain (such as the swamps and flooded plains) of the Lagos mainland. The nature of this development has led to the emergence of settlement types that can be characterised as 'shanty-towns' but which in our view are best described by the non-pejorative term 'popular settlements'.[5] The question is, to what extent is this phenomenon of commercialisation occurring in these settlements? What are its dynamics? What are its problems? And what are the implications for public policy, political action and collective well-being?

Providing an answer to these questions is the task of this chapter, which looks at the phenomenon of commercialisation of land and shelter, land-lordism, and landlord–tenant relations in one of such newly-emerging low-income settlements in metropolitan Lagos. In doing this, the rest of the chapter is structured into two main sections. The first one deals with the study – background and findings. Here we look at methodology, shelter and land conditions, landlord and tenant relations and interaction. The second and concluding part of the chapter draws certain implications for policy, political action and future developments from the trends discerned in the study.

## THE STUDY

### METHODOLOGY

The discussions in this paper are based on data from a study of two low-income settlements in Metropolitan Lagos. Although the overall sample for that study were 700 heads of households selected through systematic sampling, we are concerned here with the results based on the analysis of the material from 438 heads of households, which make up just one of the settlements. The data were collected through the use of (i) a 98-item interview-schedule; (ii) free interviews with strategic informants; (iii) life-histories; (iv) documentary analysis; and (v) a structured

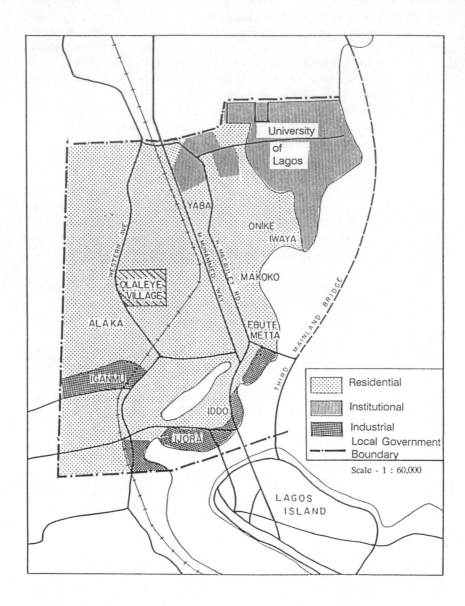

Figure 4.1  Lagos mainland and local government area, land use map
*Source: Lagos State Regional Plan, 1980–2000*

observation check-list. Data-gathering took six months, between mid-1984 and early 1985.

## BRIEF HISTORY OF SETTLEMENT STUDIED

The main settlement of study with which we are concerned here is Olaleye–Iponri Village. The title 'village' which accompanies its name is a reflection of the way in which Metropolitan Lagos has developed through engulfing the various outlying rural settlements, made up of agricultural and fishing villages. The nature of this development, however, need not detain us, as it has been well documented by others.[6]

Olaleye–Iponri Village, an outcome of this growth of the city, is located in the Lagos Mainland Local Government area (see Figure 4·1). Although it is now referred to and considered as one settlement, it was originally two communities, Olaleye and Iponri, which have gradually been merged over the years for administrative and political purposes. The data for the two communities are amalgamated in this chapter.

The settlements, located in terrain which consists of flooded depressions which slope into swampy land, were originally founded about 150 years ago (Olaleye Village around 1830, Iponri around 1878). The whole land area was initially owned by the Oloto Chieftaincy Family which gave it as grants to a few settlers who farmed and fished on it. It has, however been gradually sold over the years, so that effectively the largest concentration of plots is in the hands of between five and six Lagos families of Sierra-Leonean descent who bought them from the original settlers between the 1930s and 1950s.

The settlements' initial growth began with the construction of the various phases of the railway line, particularly the extension to Apapa around the 1940s and 1950s. It is with this that the first wave of migrants, who served as construction workers, labourers and staff of the railways, and the petty traders, came. Official figures of Olaleye Village showed the extent of this growth. In 1967, the Lagos Executive Development Board, in a survey, estimated the total population at approximately 2,500 persons. These lived in 279 buildings on 31·6 acres and consisted mainly of '. . . labourers, vagrants, and many people of the low income group'.[7]

The settlements have, however, grown since the end of the Nigerian Civil War in 1970 and the period of the economic boom occasioned by the revenue from petroleum exports. As of 1983, it was estimated in another survey conducted by government officials as containing over 20,090 inhabitants on a total land area of 35,316 ha.

## SOCIO-ECONOMIC CHARACTERISTICS OF RESIDENTS

The residents of Olaleye–Iponri are mainly migrants to Lagos. This is because residents of Lagos State make up less than five per cent of the sample. The majority of them, over half of the sample, are, however, people of Yoruba origin from the states adjacent to Lagos. Respondents of Igbo origin from Bendel and the eastern states account for another quarter, while the rest are mainly members of smaller Nigerian ethnic groupings.[8] The majority of the respondents can be described as long-term residents, with about three-fifths of them having lived in the settlement for over ten years, while another fifth had lived there for between five and ten years.

Large households are most common. Two-thirds of the sample consist of households of not less than five persons and in certain cases, these go up to eleven persons. The tendency also is to have large numbers of children; families with three or more children constitute a majority, while those with six or more children account for an important proportion. Most of the households, about 60 per cent, occupy just one room.

In terms of the ratio between the sexes, our sampling procedure of selecting heads of households only introduced a gender and age bias: only 12 per cent of our respondents are female, and a majority of the respondents, about 55 per cent, are between the ages of twenty-six and forty-five.

Economic life in the settlement is dominated by what has been called either the 'informal sector' or petty commodity production. It consists mainly of petty producers, petty services, petty artisans, craftsmen and workers. It is therefore mainly a settlement of the self-employed and workers. Those who are self-employed constitute almost 40 per cent of the respondents, making up the largest single category of source of employment. Formal employment accounts for the rest, but the civil service is the most important sector of this as it makes up about 30 per cent of the respondents. The rest of the respondents are divided between employment either in the private sector or in the parastatals. Residents in the sample are predominantly low-income earners, with about three out of every five earning less than N240 per month and at least four out of every five earning less than N300 per month.[9]

Tenants constitute the largest category, making up nearly three-quarters of the sample, while about 23 per cent are landlords. Residents who claim family compound or communal dwelling status come to about 4 per cent.

## LAND CONDITIONS IN THE SETTLEMENT

The development of landlordism, its extent, and the type, quality and cost of shelter it provides depends largely on access to land. In the case of the urban poor, this access refers in the main to buildable and affordable land located within a reasonable distance of main centres of relevant economic activities.

Access to land in Lagos is, however, governed by the limitations imposed by an island status, and a mainland with a predominantly flooded and swampy terrain. There are also the limitations of the structure of property relations. These, in terms of ownership and the norms and rules governing access to and transactions in land, are more complex and clearly the source of greater obstacles to housing the urban poor. Property relations in land are governed by norms and rules deriving from both customary law and modern legislation. The most recent modern legislation – the Land Use Decree of 1978 – has attempted what was perceived as a reform.[10] But the existence of a parallel system, loopholes in the law itself, and official connivance have all led to the perpetuation of old practices, failure of reform, and the continuous deprivation of the urban poor in terms of access to land. This blockage of access is however effected mainly through the pricing of urban land. For instance, the cost of public land, which is usually the most subsidised, rose from 12s 6d per square yard in 1959 to N9 in 1978, an increase of 620 per cent, using 1959 as the base year, (LSDPC, n.d. 16).

For the urban poor, therefore, access to land has been through customary or other informal means. But the use of customary law has not been inconsistent with commercialisation. And, in fact, evidence of commercialisation of land in Lagos dates as far back as the nineteenth century. By the middle of this century, commercial transactions in land and attendant litigations and disputes over land had become common.

In Olaleye-Iponri, available evidence points to the intense commercialisation of land. The original grant from the Oloto chieftaincy family to the Olaleye family has been subjected to extensive sale and lease to several others.

Landowners in Olaleye-Iponri form a minority, made up of two categories, consisting of the large landowners and the small landowners (the petty landlords). The large landowners are, however, even fewer, consisting of about five or six Lagos families of Sierra-Leonean descent, and descendants of the Olaleye family.[11]

On the whole, freehold titles of all types are held by just over one-fifth of the landlords, made up of about 17 per cent in Olaleye and about 28 per cent in Iponri. Short leases are most common. Such leases, particularly those of less than five years, account for over half of all responses in Olaleye-Iponri (about 53 per cent). Other short-term leases of between five and ten years account for about 6 per cent of the Olaleye-Iponri sample.

There are also medium-term leases of between eleven and fifty years which account for about 8 per cent of the responses, while long-term leases of between fifty-one and ninety-nine years represent just about 12 per cent of the sample. The prevalence of the very short leases in this sample requires some explanation, particularly when one realises that annual leaseholds for shelter or those of less than five years are not common in customary Yoruba land-tenure practice.

In the case of this settlement, they are a reflection of the pattern of ownership and control of the land, its commercialisation, the widespread phenomenon of sub-letting on the land and a certain uneasy feeling of insecurity of tenure in the settlement.

They are also a post-1970 phenomenon in terms of common occurrence. Part of it is due to the extensive sub-letting of the land, a phenomenon which accounts for a number of landlords not having any direct links with original landowners but paying their rents to co-landlords from whom they derive their access. Such arrangements involve the sharing-out of plots between two or even three persons for the construction of housing.

Another reason for the short-term leases concerns the role of certain large landowners. One particular family in this case, apart from being landlords, also let out vacant plots of land of about 60 ft. by 40 ft. on a monthly basis to those who are instructed not to construct any permanent structures on them. The result is a line of shanties and shacks built of corrugated iron sheets, zinc, wooden boards and planks. This represents part of the family's attempt at protecting their land from both government acquisition and squatting by keeping it occupied by tenants. It also ensures that the family can respond rapidly to speculative bids for their land through their capacity to give very short notice for repossession. This would not have been possible with more durable structures.

Short-term leasing is also related to a pervasive feeling of insecurity of tenure by many landowners. This has to do with the fact that Olaleye–Iponri has been the subject of threats of government acquisition since the 1950s. This intention was first raised by bureaucrats in the 1950s and was then shelved; it was reopened in the late 1960s and early 1970s, when the Abule-Nla Development Scheme was proposed by bureaucrats, and was shelved again, and in 1983 the whole question of redevelopment was again reopened.[12] It is obvious that all of these factors have implications for the construction of housing and the phenomenon of landlordism.

## LANDLORDS

Although landlords in Olaleye–Iponri account for about 23 per cent of the sample and possess certain similar characteristics, there are also important differences within the group. These latter have to do in particular with economic characteristics and the nature of property-holding.

In terms of broad similarity, the landlords in the sample are older; they are mainly over forty years of age. They also come predominantly from the Yoruba states of Kwara, Oyo and Ondo. Those of the landlords resident in the community tend to be long-term residents, with the predominant proportion having been there for over ten years, and none for less than seven years. Most of the landlords tend to be self-employed, either as businessmen, traders and contractors. Craftsmen and employees of formal organisations are very few. The latter often tend to be of supervisory rank, or have worked for several years. There are also a handful of pensioners among them, although these are involved in some kind of business or other.

The variety begins to emerge when one considers income, landholding, number of houses, and whether they are resident in the settlement or are absentee landlords. Starting with the last point, it was found that about 30 per cent of the sample claimed that their landlords lived on the premises. Thus a large proportion of the one thousand or slightly more houses in Olaleye–Iponri do not have resident landlords. Of the respondents who claimed to be resident landlords, about 55 per cent claimed ownership of one house only within the settlement. The remaining claimed ownership of more than one house; there are others who own three, four or five houses. And in one or two cases, apart from the major landowning families mentioned earlier, there are about three or four absentee landlords who own between seven to twelve houses in the settlement. It was found, too, that among the respondents over 80 per cent built with the intention of having tenants.

It should also be noted that of the sample, only about 7 per cent claimed to have recovered their costs of building, almost 68 per cent have not yet recovered building costs, and about a quarter could not yet say.

Some variety also occurs with regard not only to the number of houses, but the type in terms of structure, the size of the plots on which they are built and the type of tenure they have on the land. The average one-house landlord often builds on one standard plot of 40 ft. by 60 ft. – in certain cases, it could be less – and he is most probably on a short-term leasehold, or on a sub-let. Depending on the resources available to him and the conditions of the tenure, the house is built of more or less durable building materials. Also, he often lives in two or three rooms, and lets out the rest to tenants. His basic income, apart from the rent, tends not to be very different from that of his tenants. He is what can be described as the petty-landlord. This fact brings out the need to distinguish between petty-landlordism, which is the renting out of part of one's house to other tenants, and what Peace (1979: 32) has called 'entrepreneur–landlords', that is those for whom house-ownership is mainly a business from which income is derived, like in any other enterprise. In the case of Olaleye–Iponri, petty landlords are the more common category. The evidence therefore points to commercialisation, but the scale and organisation varies.

## TENANTS

Tenants, being the majority of the population of Olaleye–Iponri (about 74 per cent), tend to reflect more sharply the dominant characteristics that have been presented in the socio-economic and demographic profiles above. They are predominantly low-income, they constitute the majority of workers, many of them are self-employed, and they primarily occupy one room. They also reflect a wider cultural and ethnic mix, including virtually all the ethnic groups found in the sample.

Unlike the conditions of members of the elite in government, or those employed by formal organisations whose rents are paid by their employers, most of these low-income tenants, 94 per cent, pay their rents themselves. Rent payment by employers account for just about 1 per cent of the sample.

The rent paid is distributed as follows: about 72 per cent pay between N10–N25 per month. Just about 4 per cent of the sample pay over N50 per month. In a comparative sense, these amounts, particularly the N10–N25 category, seem quite low when they are compared with some of the other low-income settlements in the older parts of the metropolis where the average rent payable per room was, in 1984–85, between N30 and N80.

Although over 68 per cent of the respondents claim that their rents have been increased at least once since they moved into their present houses, only about 13 per cent claimed that this had been done within the six months preceding the interview (late 1984), while about 71 per cent claim that the last increase in rent was made between one and three years prior to the interview. These features of their tenancy perhaps account for the predominant assertion among respondents that the rent being paid is fair. About 56 per cent of the respondents hold this view, while about 41 per cent feel that the rent is unfair, while less than 2 per cent of them cannot judge. This evaluation of the extent to which their rent is fair is further reinforced by the fact that at least half of the respondents who are tenants categorically stated that they were not seeking alternative accommodation. Whatever the reason for this preference, this is a strong indication of the usefulness of their current accommodation.

## LANDLORD-TENANT RELATIONS

Landlord–tenant relations vary according to the type of living arrangements, i.e. whether the landlord is resident in the house, resident in the community, or completely absent. They also depend on who collects the rent, whether it is the landlord, a rent collector or a caretaker.

Generally, a predominant proportion of the tenants believe that their landlords, particularly the non-resident ones, do not care much for the houses. This is often reflected in the extent of deterioration, breakdown, or non-availability of facilities in the houses. Such absentee landlords are often the object of hostility if they collect their rents personally. The tenants are often resentful of the fact that various minor and/or major repairs that should have been carried out have not, and they often show this when they have to pay their rent, and which in some cases is directly to the landlord. In some other cases, tenants scarcely see their landlords or even know who they are. Rent in this case is collected by a paid rent-collector, caretaker, or some other intermediary.

With resident landlords, it was generally felt that services tended to be more available and repairs carried out more promptly. But the tenants complained in certain cases of segregation, whereby some landlords built kitchens, toilets and bathrooms for themselves and took good care of these, while what they provide for their tenants are rarely of similar standard or promptly repaired when they break down. The situation is therefore that of two sets of facilities, with the tenants using the worst ones.

On a more positive side, landlords in the settlements have been known to be sympathetic with their tenants when they encounter personal problems such as unemployment, illness, etc., and in such instances some landlords have allowed considerable arrears in rent or have even written them off. This applied more to the small-scale resident landlords.

On the negative side, landlords, and particularly those who use rent collectors, 'caretakers', and other such intermediaries, have resorted to all kinds of intimidatory tactics such as removal of windows, roofs and other fittings, and at times the use of threats of traditional magical spells, as a means of either collecting their rents or evicting tenants who are considered troublesome or in default of rent.

## CONCLUSIONS

So far, the major conclusion that emerges from the questions and issues raised at the beginning of this study is that the only seemingly effective response to the provision of housing for the poor is the popular one. However, as the study has shown, this response is being carried out under conditions of an ongoing commercialisation of housing and within the constraints of institutional obstacles posed by the state. What are the dangers that these pose for the effective housing of the urban poor and what can be done? We conclude with these considerations.

Perhaps the most obvious danger of commercialisation is the emerging trend of the commoditisation of shelter and the potential emergence of a stratum of 'landlord–capitalists' who will then not only exploit low-income tenants, but will also concentrate the ownership of shelter. This of course is the 'entrepreneur–landlord' phenomenon, which has been emerging in

Lagos for some time now. But as has been shown in the study, this seems to occur simultaneously with the phenomenon of 'petty landlordism'. The latter, it seems, is a major contribution to the resolution of the housing crisis, and as long as there is the encouragement of home-ownership among the poor, it is a phenomenon which cannot be halted. What might be a useful option here is to continue to encourage the provision of shelter in low-income settlements by enhancing the access of the ordinary low-income dweller to important resources such as land, affordable building materials, relevant and cheap skills and technology, and credit facilities for the building process. At the same time, low-income settlements must be protected from being taken over by speculators and 'entrepreneur-landlords', specifically through effective legislative action. This of course is a political question, and rests on the capacity to influence the state and its functionaries, the nature of emergent policies and the actual process of implementation.

Several means exist to guarantee this process of influencing or transforming the state towards a more people-orientated strategy for housing the urban poor. However, the choice of a specific or a combination of means is not the prerogative of an academic researcher, but will be rather a product of the unfolding action and interaction of the urban poor with themselves, their environment and their national elites.

## NOTES

1   The initial report was written by C. Abrams, *et al.* and an abridged version was published in 1980 as part of a tribute to Abrams. See Abrams, C. *et al.*, 1980.

2   See Lagos State Development and Property Corporation (n.d.), *50 Years of Housing in Lagos*.

3   Two very comprehensive discussions of entrepreneurial studies in Nigeria are Kilby, 1969 and Akeredolu-Ale, 1975.

4   Both Lloyd, 1974 and Peace, 1979 have grappled with the different features and meanings of power and prestige among the urban Yoruba, showing the significance of housing as an indicator of this.

5   For a fuller discussion see Chapter 1 of Aradeon and Aina, 1985.

6   See Ohadike, 1968; Ejiogu, 1975; Adalemo, 1981 and Fajana, 1984.

7   This was from an unpublished report of the Lagos Executive Development Board, *The Abule-Nla Redevelopment Scheme*, n.d.

8   There are about 250 ethnic groups in Nigeria, but most of these are small in population when compared with the three big groups, Yoruba, Igbo and Hausa.

9   At the time of study (1984–85) one *naira* (NI) was roughly equivalent to one US dollar (US $1.00). But with the beginning of devaluation from September 1986, the exchange rate has fluctuated between N3–N4 to US$1.00).

10   The Land Use Decree of 1978 was a major attempt at land reform which ceded all landownership in Nigeria to the government. On this see Omotola, 1980. It has however been breached endlessly by both the public and officials.

11   These are descendants of freed slaves who were settled in Freetown, Sierra

Leone, and who returned to Lagos in the late nineteenth century. Their offspring have featured prominently among the early educated Lagos elite.

12 This was the Olaleye–Iponri Upgrading Scheme set in motion by the Urban Planning Division of the Office of the Governor of Lagos State in 1983.

# REFERENCES

Abiodun, J. 1985. 'Housing problems in Nigerian cities', in P. Onibokun (ed.), *Housing In Nigeria: a book of readings*. Ibadan: Nigerian Institute of Social and Economic Research, pp. 49–63.

Abrams, C., Kobe, S., Koenigsberger, O., Shapiro, M., and Wheeler, M. 1980. 'Metropolitan Lagos', edited selection of the UN 1963 Report, *Habitat International*, 5 (1/2), pp. 55–83.

Adalemo, I. A. 1981. 'The physical growth of metropolitan Lagos and associated planning problems', in D. A. Oyeleye, (ed.), *Spatial and Concomitant Problems in the Lagos Metropolitan Area*. Department of Geography, University of Lagos.

Akeredolu-Ale, E. 1975. *The Underdevelopment of Indigenous Entrepreneurship in Nigeria*. Ibadan: University Press.

Amin, S. 1972. 'Underdevelopment and dependence in Black Africa – origins and contemporary forms', *Journal of Modern African Studies*, 10 (4), pp. 503–24.

Amis, P. 1984. 'Squatters or tenants: the commercialization of unauthorized housing in Nairobi', *World Development*, 12 (1), pp. 87–96.

Aradeon, D. 1983. 'Public learning and participation in the development process', *Habitat International*, 7 (5/6), pp. 385–94.

—— and Aina, O. A. 1985. 'Popular settlements in metropolitan Lagos'. Unpublished report, London: International Institute for Environment and Development.

Aribiah, O. 1972. 'Social aspects of urban rehousing in Lagos', *Lagos Notes and Records*, III (2), January, pp. 40–8.

Blitzer, S. Hardoy, J. E. and Satterthwaite, D. 1981. '"Shelter: peoples' needs and government response', *Ekistics*, 286, January/February, pp. 4–13.

Burgess, R. 1985. 'Problems in the classification of low-income neighbourhoods in Latin America', *Third World Planning Review*, 17, pp. 287–306.

Davis, K. 'The urbanization of the human population', in G. Brease (ed.), *The City in Newly Developing Countries*. New York: Prentice-Hall.

Edwards, M. 1982. 'Cities of tenants: renting among the urban poor in Latin America', in A. Gilbert *et al.* (eds.), *Urbanization in Contemporary Latin America*. New York: John Wiley.

Ejiogu, C. N. 1975. 'Metropolitanization: the growth of Lagos', in J. C. Caldwell, *Population Growth and Socio-Economic Change in West Africa*. New York: Columbia University Press.

Engels, F. 1969. *The condition of the Working Class in England*. London: Granada.

—— 1979. *The Housing Question*, Moscow: Progress Publishers.

Fajana, F. O. 1984. 'Socio-economic conditions of metropolitan Lagos', in A. A. Adeyemi (ed.), 'Report of the Nigerian team on administrative issues in ordinary crime prevention and control'. Unpublished report presented to UNAFEI TOKYO, May.

Fapohunda, J. *et al.* 1978. *Lagos: urban development and employment*. Geneva: International Labour Office (ILO).

Gilbert, A. and Gugler, J. 1982. *Cities, Poverty and Development: urbanization in the*

*Third World*. Oxford: University Press.

Hardoy, J. and Satterthwaite, D. 1982. 'Public housing programmes are not working', *The Courrier* (European Community – ACP Nations Magazine), July/August, pp. 76–8.

—— 1984a. *Shelter: need and response: housing, land and settlement policies in seventeen Third World nations*. Chichester: John Wiley.

—— 1984b. 'Third World cities and the environment of poverty', *Geoforum*, 15 (3), pp. 307–33.

—— 1986. 'Shelter, infrastructure and services in Third World cities', *Habitat International*, 10 (3), pp. 245–84.

Harrison, P. 1982. *Inside the Third World*. Harmondsworth: Penguin.

Home, R. K. 1976. 'Urban growth and urban government: contradictions in the colonial political economy', in Gavin Williams (ed.), *Nigeria: economy and society*. London: Rex Collings Ltd.

—— 1983. 'Town planning, segregation and indirect rule in colonial Nigeria', *Third World Planning Review*, 5 (2), May, pp. 165–76.

International Labour Office (ILO), 1981. *First Things First: meeting the basic needs of the people of Nigeria*. Addis Ababa: Jobs and Skills Programme for Africa.

Kilby, P. 1969. *Industrialization in an Open Economy: Nigeria 1945–1966*. London: Cambridge University Press.

Linn, J. F. 1983. *Cities in the Developing World*. New York: World Bank/Oxford University Press.

Lloyd, P. C. 1974. *Power and Independence: urban Africans' perception of social inequality*. London: Routledge & Kegan Paul.

—— 1980. *The 'Young Towns' of Lima: aspects of urbanisation in Peru*. Cambridge: University Press.

LSDPC/Lagos State Development and Property Corporation. n.d. *50 Years of Housing and Planning Development in Metropolitan Lagos: challenges of the eighties*. Lagos: LSDPC.

Mabogunje, A. L. 1968. *Urbanisation in Nigeria*. London: University Press.

—— 1977. *Cities and Social Order*. Inaugural Lectures Series, Ibadan: University Press.

—— 1980. *The Development Process: a spatial perspective*. London: Hutchinson University Library for Africa.

McAuslan, P. 1985. *Urban Land and Shelter for the Poor*. London: IIED and Washington: Earthscan Paperback.

Marris, P. 1961. *Family and Social Change in an African City: a study of rehousing in Lagos*. London: Routledge & Kegan Paul.

Megbolugbe, I. F. 1983. 'The hopes and failures of public housing in Nigeria', *Third World Planning Review*, 2 (4), November, pp. 350–69.

Moser, C. O. 1982 'A home of one's own: squatter housing strategies in Guayaquil, Ecuador', in A. Gilbert *et al.* (eds.), *Urbanisation in Contemporary Latin America*, New York: John Wiley.

Ohadike, P. O. 1968. 'Urbanisation: growth transitions and problems of a premier West African city (Lagos, Nigeria)', *Urban Affairs Quarterly*, 3 (4), June, pp. 69–86.

Okpala, D. 1978. 'Housing standards: a constraint on urban housing production in Nigeria', *Ekistics*, 270, June, pp. 249–57.

—— 1984a. *Managing Urbanisation in Nigeria: social pressures and the public policy dilemma*. Project Ecoville Working Paper No. 18, Institute for Environment Studies, University of Toronto, February, pp. 1–24.

—— 1984b. 'Urban planning and the control of urban physical growth in Nigeria', *Habitat International*, 8 (2), 73–94.

Olawoye, C. O. 1974. *Title to Land in Nigeria*. Lagos: Evans Brothers Ltd.

Omotola, J. A. (ed.) 1980. *The Land Use Act*. Lagos: University Press.

Ozo, A. O. 1986. 'Public housing policies and the urban poor in the Third World: a case study from Nigeria', *Third World Planning Review*, 8 (1), pp. 51–67.

Peace, A., 1979. 'Prestige, power and legitimacy in a modern Nigerian town', *Canadian Journal of African Studies*, 13 (1–2), pp. 26–51.

## RESUME

Il y a eu deux séries de réponses aux problèmes de l'habitat au Nigéria. Celles venant de l'élite n'ont pas réussi à construire des logements pour les gens à faibles revenus, tandis que les 'réponses populaires' venant des couches populaires sont responsables de plus de 90 pour cent des logements du pays. Ce chapitre représente une étude de deux régions de Lagos effectuée à partir de données provenant d'une enquête menée sur l'une d'elles. Les terres étaient à l'origine détenues par des groupes de souche locale selon des formes coûtumières de bail mais elles sont soumises à des ventes commerciales depuis le dix-neuvième siècle. Il existe peu de grands propriétaires mais la plupart possèdent quelques parcelles. Les trois quarts de la population locale actuelle sont locataires et un quart sont propriétaires; la forme de bail varie énormément, certaines locations étant de faible durée. La plupart des locataires sont des Yorubas qui vivent au Lagos depuis longtemps et qui font partie du secteur non officiel de l'économie. Il est clair que certains propriétaires visent à optimiser leurs revenus provenant de la location; certains jouent le rôle de protecteur envers leurs locataires. Mais en général, les propriétaires n'ont pas recouru à des majorations fréquentes et massives des loyers et la majorité des locataires jugent leurs loyers raisonnables.

# L'ARTICULATION DES DEUX CIRCUITS DE LA GESTION FONCIERE EN EGYPTE: LE CAS DU CAIRE

La prolifération des lotissements illégaux sur les terres agricoles de la région du Grand Caire menace de disparition la moitié de la superficie cultivée en l'an 2000. Ce développement rapide d'une urbanisation 'spontanée et informelle' s'articule à un développement planifié et public sur les terres désertiques. Le premier qui concerne le plus grand nombre comble les insuffisances du second qui ne concerne qu'une minorité. Le marché foncier illicite et spéculatif qui couvre des centaines d'hectares de bonnes terres cultivables tous les ans se déroule apparemment sans obstacles. Et s'il constitue la seule réponse aujourd'hui, aux besoins massifs en logements des dizaines de milliers d'habitants supplémentaires que compte la région du Grand Caire tous les ans, il est néanmoins révélateur d'une série de contradictions.

Ce qui surprend au premier abord, c'est la facilité avec laquelle les paysans propriétaires se désaisissent de leur unique moyen de production et de reproduction, la terre, abandonnant ainsi leur sol pour lequel eux et leurs ancêtres ont mené des luttes acharnées. Il n'y a pourtant pas si longtemps des expropriations nécessaires à la réalisation d'ouvrages d'utilité publique pouvaient engendrer des révoltes sanglantes.[1] Plus paradoxal encore est le rôle joué par ces petits propriétaires dans le processus de lotissement. Ils sont les premiers fournisseurs de terrains sur ce marché mais aussi les principaux lotisseurs! Il faut se souvenir de l'épopée d'Awad, ce petit paysan honni par tout son village pour avoir vendu son lopin de terre.[2] Ces pratiques sont révélatrices d'un bouleversement profond dans les rapports idéologiques, sociaux et économiques de la propriété foncière. Certes, la proximité du Caire donne à ces terres une valeur marchande supérieure à leur valeur d'usage ce qui les rend particulièrement vulnérables à l'urbanisation. Mais cette loi économique ne suffit pas à expliquer l'absence de résistance de la paysannerie des banlieues à la poussée des villes, du moins à terme. Dès lors il faut s'interroger sur les causes réélles qui ont transformé les exploitants agricoles en marchands de sol. Le deuxième paradoxe est l'acquisition de ces terres agricoles périurbaines par des couches sociales modestes et la perception de la rente par des acteurs sociaux, dans leur majorité, non intégrés au système dominant. Ces terres, évidemment plus convoitées que les terres désertiques, étant mieux désservies, plus proches des sources d'énergie, des moyens de transport ferroviaires, routiers et fluviaux, facilement constructibles, auraient pu être génératrices de surprofits pour le capital immobilier et industriel. Comment se fait-il que l'on ait laissé des pauvres construire des cités en dur sur des terrains situés quelquefois sur le front du Nil, à cinq kilomètres du centre de la capitale, créant ainsi un fait irréversible du moins à moyen terme?[3] On pourrait croire que la loi de 1966 prohibant le changement d'usage des terres agricoles a eu des effets dissuasifs sur le grand capital en quête de sol support pour ses investissements. Pourtant l'urbanisme dérogatoire est la règle dans ce pays: le dépassement du coefficient d'occupation du sol (COS) est couramment pratiqué par les promoteurs immobiliers; les constructions de l'Etat sur les terres agricoles et l'accaparement des domaines de l'Etat par les membres des conseils locaux sont des phénomènes courants. Le rôle de l'Etat en tant que planificateur et régulateur des rapports sociaux est des plus surprenants dans les situations évoquées ci-dessus. Ses interventions sont tardives, mal adaptées, sectorielles et sélectives.

Depuis deux décennies les actions concrètes des autorités publiques contredisent leur discours sur la nécessité de lutter contre l'urbanisation des terres agricoles et l'exode rural. Face à cette déperdition des terres agricoles l'Etat a entrepris, à des coûts exhorbitants, d'importants travaux de bonification de terres désertiques. Si cette initiative est nécessaire à l'accroissement de la superficie de terres cultivées dans un pays n'en possédant que 4 pour cent de sa surface, elle ne recompense pas la perte des bonnes terres de la vallée. L'un des moyens de cette préservation est l'encouragement du peuplement du désert. Or les villes nouvelles et satellites construites dans cette perspective ne sont pas destinées aux couches sociales démunies. Les New Settlements,[4] projetées à l'est du Caire, susceptibles de répondre aux besoins des catégories à bas et moyens revenus, constituent une bonne option, mais elle intervient très tardivement. De même que la concentration de la majorité de ces nouvelles zones de développement urbain dans la région du Grand Caire ne peut qu'accentuer le déséquilibre, déjà énorme, entre 'l'empire du Caire' et le reste du pays. La métropole devrait contenir 17 millions d'habitants en l'an 2000.

Simultanément, l'Etat applique une politique agraire discriminatoire vis-à-vis de petits et moyens exploitants qui constituent le gros de la population rurale, ce qui contribue à leur appauvrissement et conséquemment les contraint à abandonner l'agriculture, à vendre leurs terres et à émigrer ensuite vers les villes. D'autre part l'Etat tolère l'accaparement de ses domaines par les classes dominantes au moment où il réprime la population démunie qui s'y installe. Il l'oriente de la sorte vers les terres agricoles tout en forgeant des lois et des décrets qui pénalisent leur changement d'usage. Mais aussi d'autres lois régularisent a posteriori l'intégration définitive de ces terres à l'urbs. Reste à savoir comment l'Etat gère-t-il ces contradictions et comment parvient-il à maitriser l'espace urbain?

## L'ETAT ET LA MAITRISE DE L'URBANISATION

L'Etat possède 96 pour cent des terres de l'Egypte; il est donc, et de loin, le plus grand propriétaire foncier. Son droit juridique s'exerce sur des terres désertiques et incultes qui, une fois développées (urbanisées ou bonifiées), sont intégrées à la sphère marchande et vendues à des particuliers.

En outre, il agit à différents niveaux et ses interventions portent sur l'affectation et l'usage du sol. C'est lui qui prend des décisions en matière de planification, de définition des zones et des normes de lotissements, de la réalisation des équipements infrastructure et de l'implantation des équipements collectifs. Ces interventions ont donc des conséquences considérables sur la valorisation des terres. Les lois et règlements dont il s'est doté lui confèrent des compétences élargies notamment en ce qui concerne la libération du sol: expropriation pour causes d'utilité publique en vue de l'affectation du sol à des usages résidentiels, industriels et touristiques ou en vue de la protection d'un site historique.

Mais le recours à l'expropriation est une pratique rarissime en Egypte, particulièrement en milieu urbain. Elle dépend de la conjoncture, du rapport de force entre l'Etat et les propriétaires, de la place de ces derniers dans la hiérarchie sociale et de la nature du projet à réaliser.[5]

L'importance de la propriété foncière de l'Etat a nécessité la mise en place d'une structure institutionnelle de gestion s'appuyant sur douze organismes principaux pouvant être classés en trois catégories:

(a) Des organismes ayant exclusivement des fonctions de gestion foncière: sélection et appropriation du sol, affectation à différents usages, transfert ou vente aux individus, aux sociétés publiques et privées et aux différents ministères, (par exemple, les gouvernorats).

(b) Des organismes de gestion foncière et de promotion immobilière, tels que les sociétés concessionnaires. Ces dernières sont passées récemment sous le contrôle du gouvernorat du Caire. Les ministères de la défense et du tourisme peuvent être inclus dans cette catégorie.

(c) Des organismes de planification tel que le General Organisation for

Physical Planning (GOPP).

Chaque niveau de décision dispose de ses comités et conseils; le seule assemblée populaire de l'arrondissement ouest du Grand Caire dispose de douze commissions techniques spécialisées. De même qu'au niveau de l'urbanisme opérationnel tout est spécifié dans les moindres détails, la taille des parcelles, les COS, les redents, les hauteurs des bâtiments, les rapports entre les vides et les pleins. Tout est sujet à permis et chaque infraction est justiciable d'une amende. Quant à la procédure du changement d'usage d'un terrain agricole, elle nécessite l'approbation préalable d'un comité au niveau du gouvernorat, puis celle d'un autre comité comprenant des sous-secrétaires d'Etat chargés des ministères de l'agriculture, de l'industrie, de l'éducation, de la planification et du logement. Mais l'objectif de cet exposé n'est pas de démontrer l'inefficacité ou les carences du système de la gestion foncière au Caire. Si les lourdeurs administratives, les enchevêtrements des responsabilités et quelquefois les insuffisances techniques peuvent expliquer en partie le laisser-aller qui caractérise la gestion urbaine en Egypte, il n'en demeure pas moins que ces institutions existent, prennent des décisions et les éxécutent. Mais il faut surtout voir en faveur de qui elles interviennent et quels intérêts sont en jeu?

## A QUI PROFITE CE SYSTEME?

Deux logiques différentes ont prévalu au cours des vingt-cinq dernières années, appuyées sur un même cadre institutionnel de gestion foncière publique. A partir de 1961[6] et jusqu'au milieu des années 70, les terres désertiques développées et vendues par les sociétés concessionnaires publiques (Héliopolis, Maadi, Madinet Nasr), supportaient une marge bénificiaire réduite. Les prêts bonifiés par l'Etat offerts aux coopératives de construction et d'habitat permettaient l'accession à la propriété de ces terrains aux classes moyennes à salaires réguliers et sûrs capables de rembourser les prêts à long terme qui leur étaient octroyés. Les investisseurs immobiliers pouvaient également acheter ces terrains: les lois de contrôle des loyers réduisaient leur marge bénificiaire et constituaient une forme d'imposition sur les surprofits qu'ils étaient susceptibles de réaliser en intervenant sur les domaines équipés de l'Etat.

Le strict respect des spécifications contenues dans les cahiers de charges relatifs à chaque tranche de l'opération d'urbanisme était exigé des acquéreurs. A ces contraintes s'ajoutait l'engagement qui leur était imposé par la société de construire leurs lots dans un délai de trois ans à compter de la date d'achat, faute de quoi, la société récupérait le lot en remboursant à l'acquéreur les sommes versées déduction faite de 5 pour cent des frais de gestion. Si ce système a pu supprimer les lotisseurs privés et a permis de développer un marché foncier non spéculatif, il a été cependant incapable de répondre à la demande de larges couches sociales en matière de logements, et par conséquent n'a pas abouti à une maîtrise totale du processus d'urbanisation.

Les fortes subventions supportées par le budget de l'Etat pour la bonification des prêts aux coopérateurs limitaient les couches sociales susceptibles d'en bénificier. Les classes à bas revenus et celles ne pouvant pas justifier de salaires réguliers ou d'autres garanties furent exclues de cette production foncière publique, mais aussi de la production immobilière assurée par les sociétés concessionnaires. Le coût du foncier dans ces zones, la taille des parcelles, le respect des normes édictées par l'Etat en matièré de COS, de règlement sanitaire et de standing ne permettaient pas l'accession à la propriété d'un lot aux investisseurs détenteurs de petits capitaux patrimoniaux – ce sont eux que nous retrouverons comme acteurs dans les zones périurbaines 'informelles'.

Pour ne citer qu'un exemple; la taille des parcelles vendues par la société de Madinet Nasr variait entre 300, 600 et 1.000 m$^2$, et le prix du m$^2$ valait entre £E150 et £E300 (actuellement £E1.000). Il fallait donc disposer de £E30.000 pour acquérir une parcelle de 150 m$^2$, c'est à dire le salaire d'un ouvrier qualifié en cinquante ans de travail!

On peut se demander pourquoi l'Etat n'a pas mis sur pied une filière de lotissement adaptée aux capacités financières des couches à bas revenus. Plusieurs raisons expliquent, selon nous, ce manque d'initiative.

D'abord la réalisation de lotissements faiblement équipés supposait une révision en baisse des normes urbanistiques et constructives, ce qui pouvait être en contradiction avec une urbanisation reglementaire et 'moderne' et portait atteinte à l'image que se faisait l'Etat de la ville, de sa ville.

Une telle option allait ensuite à l'encontre d'une politique qui visait à la concentration et l'accumulation dans le secteur de la construction nationalisé à partir de 1961. Diffuser le lotissement faiblement équipé et permettre à la population de construire graduellement selon ses moyens pouvait mener à une dispersion dans ce secteur.

Soulignons qu'au cours de cette période l'Etat ne voulait pas que le sol joue le rôle du 'phagocite' de la petite épargne qu'il essayait de mobiliser et de drainer vers la participation au développement industriel. Il tablait sur le développement du système coopératif dans le cadre d'un système général amené à dépasser les contraintes qu'imposent les situations de sous-développement, perçues à l'époque comme transitoires et non structurelles.

L'Etat qui avait enfin comme objectif de fixer les paysans à la campagne et commença même à refouler les migrants ruraux en 1966 vers leurs villages d'origine n'allait pas créer les conditions de leur insertion en milieu urbain! Si les tentatives de maîtrise de l'urbanisation au Caire au cours de cette période ont produit des effets pervers: exclusion des couches sociales peu solvables de la ville 'légale' et développement des lotissements illicites sur les terres agricoles périurbaines, la gestion foncière en milieu rural n'en fut pas moins pervertie. La distribution des terres aux paysans en petits lots (1,2 à 2,1 ha.) a abouti à une extrême fragmentation du foncier rural accentuée par une forte explosion démographique. Le contrôle de la répartition et de l'accaparement du surplus agricole par l'Etat a contribué à l'appauvrissement des petits paysans. Rappelons que l'Etat exigeait de l'ensemble des agriculteurs la fourniture obligatoire d'un quota de leur récolte de blé, de coton, d'oignons et de riz. Il fixait des prix d'achat inférieurs aux prix des marchés locaux et internationaux. Cette politique défavorisait particulièrement les petits exploitants qui, après avoir rempli leurs obligations vis-à-vis de l'Etat, se trouvaient dans l'incapacité de subvenir à leurs besoins. Il ne leur restait souvent plus qu'à vendre leur terre.

A partir de 1973, la hausse vertigineuse des prix du foncier, la réouverture du Canal de Suez à la navigation internationale, la récupération des puits de pétrole du Sinaï et la découverte de nouveaux gisements en Mer Rouge, accentuées par l'augmentation du prix du brut et le changement de cap économique et social de l'Etat, allaient faire de l'Egypte un pays rentier, non comparable bien évidemment à ses voisins de la Péninsule Arabe. Dès lors le principe de base de l'économie égyptienne n'était plus la production mais la quête d'une rente, faisant du foncier urbain une source de rentes différentielles considérables pour l'Etat, qu'il pouvait s'approprier par la vente de terrains urbains et urbanisables et des sites archéologiques[7] aux capitaux internationaux et aux investisseurs locaux. Par ailleurs, la rente tirée de la location ou de la vente des domaines de l'Etat était supposée alimenter les fonds de logements populaires des gouvernorats. L'Etat voulait donc faire aussi du sol urbain l'instrument de sa politique sociale et économique.

Si cette politique semblait aller à l'encontre des intérêts de la classe dominante, la pratique n'allait nullement nuire à son enrichissement. Les sociétés concessionnaires publiques, qui ont charge de gestion de ce patrimoine foncier, vont le vendre à des promoteurs privés, certes au prix du marché, mais les surprofits qu'un promoteur peut tirer d'une terre en la construisant ne reviendront pas dans la poche de l'Etat. La rapidité d'action de ces promoteurs, dûe à la forte demande de logements des classes aisées bénificiaires des retombées de l'infitah[8] et de l'émigration, plus la pratique de la vente sur plan, vont diminuer l'immobilisation des capitaux investis et favoriser le renouvellement de ces coups; les disponibilités de terrains étant importantes. De plus, contrairement à la pratique habituelle, c'est l'Etat qui va prendre en charge les frais d'investissement des equipements collectifs. L'Etat devait par la suite récupérer une partie des surprofits, non par l'imposition des promoteurs mais par la taxation des acquéreurs.

D'autre part, le laxisme de l'Etat face à la rétention des terrains (en 1977, 50 pour cent des terrains acquis à Madinet Nasr étaient toujours vacants) traduisait un encouragement implicite à la spéculation foncière. Mais plus explicite encore fut la régularisation de la situation des accapareurs des domaines de l'Etat.[9] Il s'agit 'de notables, de parents d'actuels et d'anciens ministres, de gouverneurs, de députés de l'assemblée du peuple, de l'assemblée consultative et des conseils municipaux, des industriels, des commerçants et des membres notoires du parti au pouvoir' conclut un rapport d'enquête sur ce phénomène. L'exemple le plus frappant de ces situations est celui d'Alexandrie où 45 pour cent des terrains propriété du gouvernorat furent l'objet d'accaparements frauduleux grâce à la complicité de la municipalité dont soixante membres sur les soixante-cinq membres du conseil élu furent directement impliqués dans cette affaire.[10] Au Caire on a fait état de l'accaparement de plus de 1.400 ha. Ces pratiques privent bien évidemment les gouvernorats d'une des sources principales du financement du logement populaire, diminue la crédibilité de l'Etat et aboutit à des tendances de laisser-faire qui se diffusent à l'échelle de la société toute entière.

Quant aux coopératives de construction et d'habitat; sur les 1.400 existantes en 1980, seules trente pratiquaient les règles de la coopérative: les autres spéculaient sur les terrains qu'elles ont acquis de l'Etat à des prix symboliques en les revendant au prix du marché, et destinaient les logements qu'elles produisaient à la vente et non à l'usage des coopérants.[11] Elles se sont transformées de la sorte en promoteurs immobiliers tout en gardant la couverture de coopératives pour ne pas en perdre les avantages.

Dans ce contexte, le processus d'exclusion des couches sociales peu solvables ne pouvait que s'accélérer et s'élargir, touchant de larges strates des classes moyennes. Néanmoins, grâce à l'émigration temporaire vers les pays arabes producteurs de pétrole, ces classes moyennes accédaient à une augmentation de revenus et à des capacités d'épargne leur permettant l'acquisition de logements décents. Mais l'inflation galopante des coûts du foncier et des prix des appartements, tant sur le marché public que privé; ont opéré une sélection dans les rangs de ces candidats. Les plus nantis furent intégrés dans la ville légale, les autres qui sont de loin les plus nombreux furent exclus vers les zones périurbaines. C'est ainsi que le rêve urbain des classes moyennes fut balayé; elles n'auront d'autres moyens de s'assurer un logement qu'en profitant des possibilités offertes en dehors du circuit officiel.

## LE PROCESSUS D'URBANISATION DES TERRES AGRICOLES

Le dépôt d'une couche de limon dû à la crue annuelle du Nil a permis pendant des millénaires la fabrication de briques de terre crue ou cuite. La construction du Haut Barrage qui supprima la crue a rendu cette pratique inacceptable pour l'agriculture égyptienne. Entre 1972 et 1982, 35 millions m³ de terres vont passer par les usines de brique et stériliser 17.000 feddans (7.140 ha.).[12] En 1985 on compte 12.000 usines de brique fournissant 90 pour cent des besoins du marché de la construction. Il était donc devenu indispensable de substituer d'autres matériaux à la brique rouge, ce que l'Etat fit tardivement sans réussir à couvrir les besoins du marché de la construction par la brique d'argile ou le parpaing. Mais la démolition brutale et spectaculaire de nombreuses usines de brique rouge dans la vallée du Nil en 1985 n'a pas mis fin à une production qui en demeure indispensable. Un an plus tard, la fumée se dégageait de nouveau des fours à briques. La stérilisation des terres agricoles se poursuit. Les producteurs de la brique rouge offrent £E5.000 par feddan. Voilà une proposition irrésistible qui incite les paysans pauvres à vendre leurs terres. Mais cette transaction illégale fait encourir au paysan une sanction d'un an de prison plus le paiement d'une amende de £E1.000 Le ministère de l'agriculture saisi de l'affaire a le droit de confisquer la terre du contrevenant en ordonnant son expulsion. Seulement ces mesures sont rarement appliquées grâce à la complaisance des autorités locales. Les fonctionnaires des coopératives agricoles, les notaires, ingénieurs agronomes, inspecteurs, etc., ceux qui exploitaient déjà le paysan et qui sont pour une part responsables de son endettement et son appauvrissement, trouveront ici de nouvelles occasions d'extorsion.

A chaque étape du processus de transformation des terres agricoles en terrains constructibles, ils perçoivent un 'backchich'. L'inspecteur établit un procès verbal à la suite du refus de l'agriculteur de reçevoir les engrais et les pesticides et lui fait payer une amende. L'ingénieur agronome déclare ensuite le terrain incultivable pour des raisons techniques: obstruction des canaux de draînage et d'irrigation, augmentation du degré de salinité du sol dûe à la hausse du niveau des eaux mal draînées, etc. Le notaire intervient enfin pour faciliter la transaction entre le paysan propriétaire et les producteurs de la brique. Il doit intervenir une seconde fois au moment du transfert de la propriété.

Dépouillée de sa couche arable et des contraintes qui frappaient son changement d'usage, la terre devient ainsi prête à être lotie et vendue.

## LE LOTISSEMENT

Le processus de lotissement (libération du sol de son rapport de propriété antérieur, sa subdivision et sa commercialisation) met en présence une multitude d'acteurs, des intérêts et des logiques divergents, des modes et des types de lotissements différents. Cette diversité témoigne de l'existence d'un marché foncier hiérarchisé et différencié, capable de s'adapter à la demande provenant de différentes catégories de revenus.

Nous distinguons trois formes de lotissements: (i) le lotissement type 'parcelle agricole' où la configuration des lots se superpose au parcellaire agricole; (ii) le lotissement constitué de vingt-quatre lots égaux de 175m$^2$, chacun qui sont les fractions du feddan;[13] (iii) le lotissement libre.

La première forme de lotissement a comme acteurs de petits paysans propriétaires dont la limite de la propriété se situe à 1 feddan (0,42 ha.). Ils peuvent être des paysans pauvres obligés de vendre leur moyen de production, des propriétaires absents vivant en ville et exerçant un autre métier ou des hériters d'agriculteurs urbanisés ne désirant pas poursuivre le métier des parents. La logique des uns et des autres est différente. Tandis que les exploitants vendent immédiatement leur terre à la suite de son dépouillement par les producteurs de briques, les seconds attendent que la zone soit urbanisée pour vendre au meilleur prix. Ces agents lotisseurs s'adressent en général à une population modeste, nouveaux migrants ruraux venant de la campagne ayant un petit pécule tiré de la vente de leur bétail ou même de leur lopin de terre, concierges des immeubles cossus du centre, petits commerçants et artisans, etc. Les tailles des parcelles vendues varient entre 40 et 80m$^2$; le remboursement se fait à crédit selon les capacités des acquéreurs; il peut s'étaler sur six ans.

Lorsque le propriétaire a vendu son avant-dernier lot, il peut se trouver souvent dans l'incapacité de financer la construction du lot qu'il s'est réservé. On peut identifier trois types de comportements:

(a) D'une part un propriétaire d'une parcelle fait construire par un maçon une maison en rez-de-chaussée pièce par pièce, il en occupera une et louera les autres. Après des années d'épargne il fera construire un deuxième niveau – ce processus durera de huit à douze ans pour construire trois étages.

(b) D'autre part, un propriétaire ayant émigré dans un pays arabe producteur de pétrole pourra disposer de la totalité du capital nécessaire à la construction d'un immeuble de plusieurs étages – il occupera un appartement et louera les autres.

(c) Enfin, un propriétaire n'ayant pas émigré lui-même fera financer la construction de son immeuble par des candidats au logement ayant émigrés. Dans ce système c'est le futur locataire qui paie comptant la construction avant même de l'habiter, et n'obtient en échange qu'un usufruit temporaire correspondant aux investissements initiaux et en fonction du montant des loyers.

Ces trois types de comportement peuvent se recouper ou avoir un seul acteur. Ainsi l'ancien paysan bénificiaire de la réforme agraire devient propriétaire rentier d'un immeuble de plusieurs niveaux dans la région du Grand Caire après avoir vendu sa terre. Certains auront des commerces au rez-de-chaussée; d'autres achèteront une petite camionnette ou un taxi; d'autres enfin deviendront des courtiers au service des sociétés de lotissement ou des lotisseurs professionnels.

Les lotisseurs professionnels sont les agents support de la deuxième forme de lotissement. Ils sont à l'origine de petits exploitants possédant des superficies agricoles supérieures à 1 feddan. Le but de l'opération de lotissement qu'ils engagent sur leur propre terrain est d'en financer d'autres sur des terrains avoisinants et les sommes tirées de la vente des premiers lots seront affectées à l'achat de nouvelles parcelles. Ces marchands de gros et vendeurs de détail, puisqu'ils achètent en feddan (4.224 m$^2$) et vendent des mètres carrés, sont capables de réaliser des profits de 200 pour cent. La population cible visée par leur intervention est plus aisée que celle s'adressant aux propriétaires lotisseurs; il s'agit d'une main d'oeuvre émigrée moyennement qualifiée, travailleurs dans le secteur du bâtiment, divers artisans, etc. Contrairement aux précédents dont la commercialisation se fait de bouche à oreille, ils font une publicité par voie d'affichage sur le lieu de lotissement. Les modalites de paiement qu'ils adoptent se rapprochent de celles des propriétaires lotisseurs, mais ils perçoivent une avance des acquéreurs égale à 30 pour cent du prix du lot. Ces agents lotisseurs sont très mobiles, l'accumulation rapide de l'argent que leur assure leur activité leur permettant de passer à d'autres secteurs d'activité dont la promotion immobilière et la construction. Nous pouvons citer le cas d'un lotisseur qui intervenait à Boulaq El Dakrour et Embaba,[14] devenu entrepreneur promoteur, réalisant des logements 'clés en main' dans les zones périurbaines. Un autre s'est converti dans la production du mobilier d'intérieur et possédait un salon d'exposition à Héliopolis! Mais plus diversifiée encore est l'activité des sociétés de lotissements.

## LES SOCIETES DE LOTISSEMENTS

Selon le fichier du Gouvernorat du Caire, jusqu'en 1973 il n'existait que neuf sociétés de lotissements ayant un registre de commerce. En 1982, nous avons pu en recenser trente-cinq d'après les annonces publicitaires passées dans la presse. Parmi ces sociétés, trente possèdent un registre de commerce et exercent une autre activité que le lotissement:

import–export, activité de courtage, vente de matériaux de construction, ou interviennent comme entreprise de bâtiment. La création de la majorité de ces sociétés (80 pour cent) date de la période post-73.[15] Leur apparition est à mettre en relation avec l'Infitah et l'émigration, ayant entraîné l'essor d'une demande de terrains urbains parmi les catégories sociales à moyens revenus.

La situation juridique de ces sociétés est très ambigüe. Sur les trente-cinq sociétés étudiées, neuf seulement ont chacune un lotissement approuvé. Les autres n'ont aucun dossier de demande d'approbation de lotissement dans les trois gouvernorats composant le Grand Caire. Alors qu'elles ont pignon sur rue, passent quotidiennement des annonces publicitaires dans les trois plus importants quotidiens du pays, annonces comportant leur adresse, numéro de téléphone, localisation du lotissement, taille des parcelles, prix au mètre carré, dates et heures de visites de l'opération par des 'micro-bus' de la société, etc., contre ces annonces publicitaires les gouverneurs des gouvernorats où sont situés ces lotissements passent des contre-annonces publicitaires dénonçant l'activité de ces sociétés et mettent en cause les services de presse pour non vérification de la fiabilité de ces lotissements, car 'aucun permis ne leur a été accordé par les autorités. Mais ces sociétés intensifient leur campagne publicitaire en adressant à l'occasion, des remerciements à leur aimable clientèle pour la confiance qu'elle leur accorde'!

L'analyse d'un échantillon de 425 lotissements[16] montre que les petits exploitants lotisseurs viennent en tête avec 89, 8 pour cent des lotissements. Ils sont suivis par les lotisseurs professionnels (6 pour cent) et les sociétés de lotissements (4,2 pour cent). Mais l'importance de ces sociétés et leur poids sur le marché foncier périurbain ne se mesure pas au nombre de lotissements mais par la taille de leurs opérations et par leur capacité financière.

Le nombre de lots par opération varie entre 50 et 300, allant de 150 m² pour les plus petits à 300m² pour les plus grands. La largeur de la voierie y est de 8 m et le prix de £E6 à £E30 le mètre carré, selon la distance du lotissement par rapport au centre, aux secteurs urbains avoisinants et la qualité des travaux de viabilisation (terrassement, tracé des voies, etc.). Les sociétés de lotissements offrent des crédits remboursables en vingt-quatre mois à un taux d'intérêt de 4 pour cent et exigent une avance de 50 pour cent du prix du lot. Leurs opérations sont concentrées dans leur majorité au nord-est du Caire (Mataréyah), au nord (Choubrah Al Kheima) et à l'ouest (Ghuizah). Elles se répartissent de la façon que montre le tableau 5.1.

Au fur et à mesure que la société s'aggrandit elle étend son activité à d'autres villes comme il apparaît dans le tableau 5.1. La différenciation entre les sociétés de lotissement s'appuie donc sur leur puissance

Tableau 5.1 La carte de lotissements sociétés

|  | No. de lotissements | % |
|---|---|---|
| Mataréyah | 45 | 57,6 |
| Choubrah Al Kheīma | 3 | 3,8 |
| Qualioubéyah (ville de Qualioub) | 6 | 7,7 |
| Guizah (Avenue des Pyramides) | 14 | 17,9 |
| Alexandrie | 4 | 5,3 |
| Autres | 6 | 7,7 |
| *Total* | 78 | 100 |

*Note:* La carte des lotissements sociétés se superpose avec celle de la croissance de la population et de la surface bâtie. Mataréyah se trouve être l'un des secteurs ayant enregistré le plus fort taux de croissance au cours des dix dernières années.

financière pouvant se mesurer par la taille de leurs opérations, leur nombre et l'extension territoriale de leur activité. En nous appuyant sur ces critères nous pouvons distinguer deux types de société:

(a) Les sociétés ayant réalisé un minimum de trois lotissements concentrés dans le même secteur. La société El Sawah peut être un cas représentatif. Créée en 1979 par un entrepreneur privé et un fonctionnaire du gouvernorat du Caire, la société débuta son activité par une opération de 1,26 ha., la deuxième porta sur un terrain de 2,1 ha. et la troisième fut de 3,78 ha. La société acheta le feddan (0,42 ha.) à £E30.000 et vendit le mètre carré à £E15, réalisant ainsi un taux de profit de l'ordre de 200 pour cent. Ce bénéfice peut être plus important dans le cas d'une circulation rapide des lots, car si le temps nécessaire à la vente de 100 lots (1 ha.) se situe autour de trente-cinq mois, pendant la période du retour annuel des émigrés, un mois peut suffire. La contenance des superficies acquises par ce type de sociétés demeure très faible; leur stratégie consiste à réaliser des surprofits avec une faible mise et d'offrir une marchandise en rapport à la solvabilité d'une population cible déterminée dès le départ. Leur intervention a un caractère occasionnel, car elles continuent à exercer d'autres activités telles que la vente des matériaux de construction et l'importation de biens de consommation, ce qui laisse supposer qu'elles pourraient se retirer du marché si celui-ci devenait moins rentable.

(b) Le deuxième type de société comprend celles qui interviennent en tant que promoteurs fonciers et immobiliers et qui ont réalisé plus de trois opérations dans la région du Grand Caire et dans d'autres villes. Il s'agit de la société Al Nasr pour le commerce et le lotissement (quatre opérations dont une est á Alexandrie), la société Al Dawleya pour le lotissement et le courtage (quatre opérations dont deux ont une superficie de 32 ha.) et le groupe Abou El Ezz, comprenant cinq sociétés. Ce groupe concentre 26 pour cent des opérations de lotissement recensées (21 sur 78). Il s'agit d'un groupe familial géré par quatre frères dont un est ingénieur, un est avocat et deux sont comptables. En 1961 seule la société Ramsès de Mohamed Abou El Ezz était créée. En 1981, le groupe comportait cinq sociétés parmi lesquelles était une société de promotion foncière et immobilière qui fait construire des villas sur la côte d'Alexandrie.

Cette catégorie de sociétés réalise des lotissements très divers avec plus ou moins d'équipements, des parcelles de superficies différentes et offrent des prix allant de £E9 à £E40 le mètre carré. En s'addressant à différentes tranches de revenus, elles ont tendance à monopoliser le marché de terrains périurbain et illicite. Mais leur nature parasitaire et affairiste a déjà fixé les limites de leur intervention dans ce domaine. Car au fur et à mesure de la réduction de la demande provenant des émigrés en raison du ralentissement de l'émigration, les unes, après avoir suffisamment accumulé, retrouveront leur activité initiale; les autres passeront à la promotion immobilière ou s'orienteront vers des secteurs plus lucratifs et qui présentent moins de risques.

L'analyse du processus de lotissement des terres agricoles a mis en évidence le rôle joué par le foncier comme moyen d'enrichissement et d'accumulation pour certains groupes sociaux d'une part, et comme réceptacle de l'épargne des émigrés et même des couches sociales modestes de l'autre. Ces différentes fonctions du foncier semblent avoir fortement contribué à assurer une certaine paix sociale au cours des dix dernières années. Certes, les mécanismes d'appropriation et de redistribution des terrains et la spéculation foncière qui les accompagne reproduisent sans cesse une spirale d'exclusion des plus pauvres, ce qui risque d'exacerber les tensions sociales. Mais la diversité des capacités d'accueil dans cette métropole qui ne connait pas le phénomène des bidonvilles et où presque personne ne dort dans la rue, empêche toujours que ces situations débouchent sur une catastrophe.

Quant à la filière du lotissement informel, elle apparait dans son ensemble assez structurée malgré les divergences des intérêts et des stratégies de ses agents support. Elle se présente et s'impose comme un véritable sous-secteur de promotion foncière et immobilière populaire. Il semble de plus en plus évident que dans les zones d'habitat spontané se trouvent rassemblés des ingrédients permettant de répondre aux besoins et aux pratiques spécifiques de chaque groupe social selon ses origines et ses capacités financières. Si l'on en juge par les récentes interventions de l'Etat, il y'a lieu de s'inspirer fortement de ces processus pour définir les futures politiques d'urbanisme et d'habitat pour le plus grand nombre. Ceci nous amène à nous interroger sur le devenir de l'urbanisation des terres agricoles. Serait-elle freinée par l'imminente mise en chantier des New

Settlements où il est prévu un abaissement préalable des normes urbanistiques et constructives et la mise en place d'une offre de terrains adaptée aux couches sociales à bas revenus? Ou va-t-on assister encore une fois au détournement de cette offre au profit d'une clientèle plus aisée? On pourrait enfin s'interroger sur le bien fondé de ces New Settlements et des villes satellites lorsque les premiers résultats du recensement de 1987 nous révèlent l'existence de près de deux millions de logements vacants en Egypte, dont la moitié serait concentrée au Caire!

## NOTES

1   A ce sujet voir *La Terre*, nouvelle d'Abd El Rahman el Charqawi, publiée en 1956.

2   De nombreuses épopées folkloriques faisant partie du patrimoine culturel de la campagne égyptienne tournent autour de la terre, de la dépossession des paysans par la force, de l'attachement millénaire du paysan égyptien à sa terre, etc.

3   Il s'agit d'Embaba, quartier populaire sur la rive ouest et de Dar Es Salaam au sud du Caire, sur la route de Maadi.

4   Les New Settlements sont des nouveaux quartiers projetés à l'est du Caire sur des terres désertiques. Elles sont conçues pour recevoir deux millions d'habitants nouveaux.

5   Les autorités publiques ont mis dix ans pour convaincre les habitants d'Echech el Tourgomane, un secteur sité au centre du Caire, de déménager dans les nouveaux logements construits pour les accueillir. Si l'Etat a pu contraindre de nombreux habitants à partir, la majorité des artisans et des commerçants n'ont toujours pas obtempéré.

6   1961 est la date où l'Etat nationalisa totalement toutes les compagnies privées du secteur de la construction et de la promotion immobilière et foncière.

7   Il s'agit de l'affaire de la vente du plateau des pyramides à une société étrangère en vue de la réalisation d'un projet touristique en 1977. Les très nombreuses protestations que ce projet a soulevés ont porté échec à sa réalisation.

8   Terme désignant la politique de libéralisation économique instaurée à partir de 1973.

9   En 1981, le premier ministre émet un décret régularisant la situation des accapareurs des domaines de l'Etat et il fut entériné par la suite par l'assemblée du peuple.

10   Rapport du comité d'enquête du conseil municipal d'Alexandrie publié dans l'hebdomadaire *El Mossawar*, n° 2987, 8 janvier 1982.

11   Cf. *Al Ahram*, 12 mars 1980 et *Al Ahram el Iqtisadi*, 16 avril 1980.

12   Cf. *Al Ahram*, 24 mai 1982.

13   Un feddan égale 4,224m$^2$. Il se subdivise en vingt-quatre unités, appellées *Karate*, de 175m$^2$.

14   Quartiers spontanés de la région du Grand Caire situés respectivement à l'ouest et au sud de Madinet El Mohandessines, sur la rive ouest.

15   L'étude de l'activité des sociétés de lotissements fut menée en 1982 dans le cadre d'une thèse de docteur ingénieur sur 'l'urbanisation spontanée au Caire' soutenue en 1983 à l'Institut d'Urbanisme de Paris par l'auteur. Elle s'appuya sur le dépouillement du fichier des lotissements dans les trois gouvernorats composant le

Grand Caire et sur des enquêtes non-directives menées auprès des sociétés.

16   Il s'agit de lotissements rejetés par les gouvernorats pour non-conformité aux normes urbanistiques. Ils ont pourtant été réalisés.

**Annexe**

Tableau 5.2

Localisation des opérations des sociétés du lotissement, Le Caire

| Nom de la société | Nom du projet No. de lotissements | Prix au $m^2$ du terrain (£E) | Localisation du projet | Remarques |
|---|---|---|---|---|
| 1 Sté Wadi Al Nil de lotissement. Abd Allah Chawrawi & Co. | Zahret Al Lotus Zahret Al Madaen | | Malawi Menya Env. de Hélipolis | |
| 2 Al Moassassa Al Arabyah pour le commerce et la construction et le lotissement. Abd El Salam Abou El Ezz | Madinat Al Ahlam Madinat Al Riviera Madinat Al Nasr Madinat Al Salam Madinat Abou El Ezz Villas au Hanoville Al Khanka Ezbet El Nakl El Marg | 22 14 à 22 | Mataréyah Pyramides Pyramides Pyramides Alexandrie Qualioubéyah Mataréyah Mataréyah | Surface des lots 200 à 400 |
| 3 Abd Al Mohsen Solayman | Madinat Omal Moïménine Al Kalag | 20 à 30 | Mataréyah | |
| 4 Moassassat Gosn Al Zeïtoun | Madinat Aly Ben Abi Taleb | | Mataréyah | |
| 5 Sté Al Guizah Arabe | Madinat Al Nozha Al Marg et Ezbet Al Nakl | | Mataréyah | |
| 6 Al Salam pour la bonification et le lotissement des terres. Mohamed Ebeïd & Co. | Qualioub | 22 | Qualioubéyah | |

| Nom de la société | Nom du projet / No. de lotissements | Prix au m² du terrain (£E) | Localisation du projet | Remarques |
|---|---|---|---|---|
| 7 Al Moassassa Al Masreya pour le commerce et le lotissement | Al Marg<br>Env. d'Helipolis<br>Moassassat Al Zakat | | Mataréyah<br>Mataréyah<br>Mataréyah | Crédit 40 mois |
| 8 Sté Hagag pour le commerce et le lotissement | Al Chorafa<br>Hagag<br>Al Wafaa<br>Al Amal | A partir de 9 | Qualioubéyah<br>Mataréyah<br>Mataréyah | |
| 9 Sté d'ingénierie pour le commerce, le lotissement et la construction | 1 N.D.<br>2 N.D.<br>3 N.D. | A partir de 5 | Mataréyah<br>Mataréyah<br>Mataréyah | Mohamed Abou El Ezz (direct.) |
| 10 Moassassat Al Nasr pour le commerce, le lotissement et la construction | | | | |
| 11 Sté Al Kahéra pour le commerce et le lotissement | Ezbet Al Nakl<br>Al Aham | 5 | Mataréyah<br>Pyramides | |
| 12 Abd El Salam. Abou El Ezz | Madinat Al Moonib | | Pyramides | |
| 13 Al Wedi pour le commerce et le lotissement. Ingénieur Farouk Abou El Ezz | 1<br>2<br>3 | 9<br>12<br>40 | Mataréyah<br>Mataréyah<br>Alexandrie | |
| 14 Sté studio Misr d'ingeniérie pour le commerce et le lotissement | Madinat Al Samar<br>Madinat al Riviera | A partir de 14 | Pyramides<br>Pyramides | |
| 15 Albahi foncière pour l'investissement | Mataryah | | | |
| 16 Abdel Mohsen | Madinat Al Hanan<br>Madinat Al Djihad<br>Madinat Moubarak | | Qualioubéyah<br>Mataréyah<br>Qualioubéyah | |

Tableau 5.2 suite

Localisation des opérations des sociétés du lotissement, Le Caire

| Nom de la société | Nom du projet / No. de lotissements | Prix au m² du terrain (£E) | Localisation du projet | Remarques |
|---|---|---|---|---|
| 17 Al Maktab Al Arabi pour travaux d'entreprises générales et le lotissement | Le Caire et ses environs / 5 lotissements | | Mataréyah / Mataréyah / Mataréyah / Mataréyah / Le Caire/Alexandrie | |
| 18 Sté Awlad Amer pour le commerce et le lotissement | Madinat Al Salam | A partir de 7 | Mataréyah | |
| | Madinat Al Zakat | A partir de 6 | Pyramides | |
| 19 Sté Internationale de courtage et de lotissement | 1 / 2 | | Mataréyah / Mataréyah | |
| 20 Al Guizah Unie pour le lotissement | 1 / 2 | | Pyramides / Pyramides | |
| 21 Al Salam | 1 | | Qualioubéyah | |
| 22 Al Nil pour le lotissement | 1 / 2 | | Pyramides / Pyramides | |
| 23 Al Mansoura pour le commerce, la construction et le lotissement | 1 | | Helwan | |
| 24 Al Guizah Al Arabya pour le lotissement | 1 / 2 / 3 | | Mataréyah / Mataréyah / Mataréyah | |
| 25 Masr pour le commerce et le lotissement | Rue Ahmed Esmat / Madinat Al Gamaa / Madinat Al Chorafa / Madinat Al Nabila | | Mataréyah / Mataréyah / Mataréyah / Mataréyah | |

| Nom de la société | Nom du projet / No. de lotissements | Prix au m² du terrain (£E) | Localisation du projet | Remarques |
|---|---|---|---|---|
| 26 Zahret Aïn Chams pour le commerce, la construction et le lotissement | Madinat Wadi Al Dahab<br>Madinat Wadi Al Rabi<br>Madinat Omar Makram<br>Madinat Al Khossous | | Mataréyah<br>Mataréyah<br>Qualioubéyah<br>Mataréyah | |
| 27 Itihad Al Arabi pour le commerce, la construction et le lotissement. Salim Al Zocla | Madinat Al Fajr Al Djadid<br>Madinat Al Taof<br>Madinat Al Ahlam | A partir de 5 | V.N. 10 Ramadan<br>Mataréyah<br>Mataréyah | |
| 28 Qalioub pour le commerce, le construction, et le lotissement. I. Métry Sergah | Madinat Al Wahda<br>Madinat Al Mostakbal | | Qualioubéyah<br>Mataréyah | |
| 29 Al Nasr pour le commerce, l'import–export, la construction et le lotissement | Madinat Al Nozha<br>Madinat Al Naïm<br>Madinat Al Saada<br>Madinat Al Ahlam | | Mataréyah<br>Mataréyah<br>Qualioubéyah<br>Alexandrie | |
| 30 Al Dawleya pour le courtage et le lotissement | 25 Fedd. au 10 Ramadan<br>52 Fedd. sur la route Le Caire/Alexandrie | | V.N. 10 Ramadan<br>Le Caire/Alexandrie | |
| 31 Al Moutahida | 1 | A partir de 5 | Mataréyah | |
| 32 Al Samah | 1 | | Mataréyah | |

## SUMMARY

The absence of government provision of land with basic amenities appropriate to the needs of the poorer social classes has given rise to the birth of an
illicit and speculative channel of land management in Egypt. Although
these speculators may have been able to keep the lid on the housing crisis,
thereby guaranteeing a degree of social peace, they have also generated
adverse effects. The proliferation of informal development plots on agricultural land around the towns threatens to halve the area of land available for
cultivation in the region of Greater Cairo by the year 2000. The mechanisms
of appropriation and redistribution of land and the corresponding increase
in land speculation create an endless spiral which excludes the poorest
sections of the population and threatens to exacerbate social tensions.

The question of access to the land for the greatest number has led us to
analyse the logic and practices of public and private land management
agents and to discuss the role they have played during the past two decades.

# CHANGING HOUSING STRATEGIES AND PATTERNS AMONG THE CAIRO POOR, 1950–85

Housing is a major factor determining the life and welfare of the urban poor, but it is never an isolated issue. Housing is but one of a whole number of key existential concerns – to eat, to sleep, to be appropriately dressed, to obtain help in times of sickness, care and affection in times of need, and the livelihood to provide the necessities of life are basic preoccupations of the poor everywhere as well as of those who are better off. This means that when studying housing the 'problem' must be placed within a larger contextual framework. Housing must be seen as being integrated with other aspects of life and as contingent on a number of factors at both the macro and micro level. The larger context comprises factors of both supply and demand, the economics and technicalities of house renting, building and buying, and also such more elusive factors as the values and priorities people have in life. What *they* judge to be at stake, in the choice between better lodgings and other priorities they also value, is essential knowledge for any planner who seeks to make people beneficiaries in a housing project, whether in an active or passive role.

Housing is important for several reasons: (i) it provides the necessary facility for intimate relations, family care and social development: (ii) it is a major and inescapable item of the household budget, and thus affects all other expenditure on material consumption; (iii) it determines a person's location in relation to workplace and other activities, and thus limits options and social networks; and (iv) it is a major factor determining time use.

Under each of these headings it is important to recognise that people's standards and needs are culturally and sub-culturally determined. We are dealing here not with a prototype human or African – apt in any case to be a product of Western imagination – but with Kenyans and Tanzanians, Nigerians and Egyptians. And even within the large metropolises that are the capitals of their native countries, standards may differ, for their populations are heterogeneous in culture and background: housing standards, even for the poor, are not an objective given, something that may be set once and for all in terms of internationally fashioned catalogues of human needs.

Culture affects, even determines this. The value of a house, its size, location, physical and aesthetic properties will take on a different meaning in cultures where people are judged by the places they live in (e.g. Oman, Norway) than in places where clothes (e.g. Egypt) or feasts (e.g. Indonesia) matter more as sources of social respect. But beyond such basic value-considerations perceptions of space and the use of it also differ significantly across cultures. There are people who like, even evaluate positively, being cramped together and sleeping several people to a bed (e.g. the Cairo poor), others whose ideas of privacy and silence are hyper-developed (e.g. Omanis). Without underestimating the role of objective factors in planning for housing among the urban poor, such as health and health hazards, hygiene, public policy and development, etc., it is essential to recognise that the appropriateness and physical quality of housing facilities can only be meaningfully judged in terms of culturally constructed standards. Particularly under the three headings listed above, cultural considerations are paramount.

In the following, then, I shall seek first to describe the actual housing patterns that have obtained among the Cairo poor over the past twenty-five years, which is the period my data covers.[1] Secondly, I shall seek to identify the factors that have constrained their options and decisions by placing housing within their larger matrix of values and also within a socio-economic context that they have perceived and reacted to in specific ways. Even the 'facts' of sheer material forces are regarded through cultural lenses in terms of which they derive their meaning and importance for people. Thirdly, I divide the senior generation of my sample (people now in their early forties and late fifties) between those who had education aspirations for their children and those who did not, and trace the implications of this variable. It was in fact the latter, the poorest among the poor, who did best in the way of housing because, paradoxically, they could better afford it. Their resources were not frozen elsewhere. Fourthly, I compare the young generation now about to establish themselves with their parents' generation and show the significantly different opportunity situation in which they find themselves. As regards housing, the young face a predicament that no one had envisaged. How they will cope, what the repercussions will be on their marital relations, family life and care-seeking in times of crisis, remains to be seen. But some of their likely prospects may be sketched out.

I start from the premise that we need to be both precise and sensitive in analysing the many ways in which culturally defined standards enter into the human facts which indices such as the standard of living, in which housing is a central element, purport to measure (Wikan, 1985). Every assessment must take the *style* of living into account and measure life in terms of the priorities that people have for themselves. As regards the Cairo poor it is important to note that housing had, until the early to mid-1980s,

not been regarded as an indication of a particular family's rank or achievements. Housing was seen as a given constraint that could be modified only
by excessive expenditure. There was a kind of tacit agreement among the
poor not to let it reflect on their social selves or their social prestige. Thus in
this fiercely competitive environment, where people constantly vie with
each other in acquiring and exhibiting material goods of value as sources of
prestige, efforts were directed at *other* valued goals, notably clothes and
certain kinds of household equipment (see Wikan, 1985: 12–14). The gross
parameters of class and neighbourhood were of course acknowledged as
indices of social status, but mainly *vis-à-vis* outsiders. Drastic government
regulation of rents had created an immobilised housing market for tenants
where personal history and economic advancement could not be reflected in
changes in tenancy and location.

Where this population, as I shall show, *has* succeeded in improving its
standard of housing, this reflects the effects of saving rather than directly
planning improved housing. In the course of the fifteen years during which
I have been studying them, the families – and particularly their women –
have shown an impressive drive, foresightedness and commitment to 'make
a future for the children' (*yiᶜ mil mustaqbal lil ᶜayyal*) that have resulted in
considerable improvement of their standard of living and, in many cases,
beneficial effects on their housing. Having now satisfied what they saw as
the primary needs, improved housing is emerging as a new goal for their
persistent efforts, and thus is beginning to reflect on the people themselves.
But these are still only vague trends, not clear or consistent developments.
Moreover, the value of a dwelling is as much determined by its location and
rent as by its physical appearance or size. At the same time these initial
struggles for improved housing have also been associated with a number of
unsought and partly negative effects on neighbourhood structure, social
networks and life options. These are important mechanisms that deeply
affect the lives of the urban poor, yet are not often visible to powerful
developers and reformers. It therefore seems worthwhile to uncover the set
of factors that interact in this complex situation.

As a background for the reader, I need to emphasise Cairo's characteristics as a Middle Eastern society and culture, in some respects different from
most other regions of Africa. Cairo is not only an ancient city, it is also part
of a civilisation primarily shaped by cities. Thus the consciousness even of
the new rural migrant to Cairo is already shaped by urban ideas and
standards. What is more, city life is the culturally valued way of life in the
native traditions of the population and rural migrants have come to the city
with a view to staying there, as a desired and meaningful advance in their
lives. Thus, although Cairo has grown swiftly over recent years, its population is profoundly adapted to urban living.

My data on the urban poor in Cairo come from an area of Giza – a poor district historically ante-dating even Cairo itself. Since I began my first fieldwork there in 1969, I have maintained intimate and comprehensive contact with the members of a score of households, participating as a frequent visitor in their trials and tribulations. Over the years, I have thus developed detailed longitudinal data on seventeen couples, and their friends, neighbours, acquaintances and even enemies. In addition, I have been able to study fifteen children from these seventeen households as they have matured, entered into betrothals and marriage, and progressively established themselves as a second generation of households. What this material lacks in gross numbers, it compensates for in intimacy, depth and continuity. It should provide an adequate basis for describing cultural standards, priorities, and praxis in coping with life in a poor quarter, with special reference to household economy, the domestic cycle, marriage, family planning, and the concerned persons' subjective personal histories.

The families live in the back streets of Giza, and share their low class and economic position with millions of other Cairo citizens. They range from the unskilled and under-employed poorest to the better employed – teachers, clerks, etc. – with lower middle-class aspirations. Housing varies from windowless basement rooms – one to a family – and flimsy sheds on roofs to three-room apartments on upper floors with plastered walls, proper windows, and a balcony. Most buildings have three to four floors, and are equipped with electric light, with a water tap and a hole-in-the-floor toilet in most apartments. Waste disposal is generally unavailable and the sewage system blocks and floods regularly, but the buildings are substantial and each proper apartment has its front door that can be closed upon the world.

Most residents are tenants, but practically all housing is locally owned. Thus there is generally a house-owner occupying one apartment and renting out the six to seven others. Only in few cases will a home-owner own more than one building. It is indicative of the upward movement of this population that whereas in 1969 only one in seventeen families was a house-owner, in 1985 four of the thirteen families remaining of the original sample of seventeen owned a house, whereas one owned a quarter, and three, one-eighth each. Characteristically, most of the new house-owners are women.

But before exploring some of the institutions that have made possible such self-help and self-improvement, we should investigate some of the locally valid cultural premises and preferences that constrain housing and lodging in Cairo.

It is a striking indicator of the force of these premises that Cairo shows few of the overt signs of abject poverty so frequently exhibited by the large, overcrowded cities of the world. There are few street-dwellers and few settlements resembling shanty towns. People can generally count on a place to stay and a roof over their head. Whole families will crowd in with their kin (and kin being counted bilaterally, most people have many) rather than set themselves up in culturally degrading circumstances. The flat is seen as 'belonging' to the woman and women cannot refuse to take in kinspersons in need, while men are legally obliged to materially provide for destitute kin. Female friends are also culturally obliged to provide lodging for each other in time of need, and often do. Even strangers who let it be known that they have no place to go can count on if not a bed, at least a mat on the floor, plus food, plus clean clothes while their own are being washed (for two cases, see Wikan, 1983: 207, 209).

Over the years, every one of my families has housed kin, in-laws, friends and even strangers for weeks and months on end – at considerable cost to themselves. Though a concept of overcrowding exists, it is likely to be resorted to only when the run on one's *expendable* material resources seems excessive (for a case, see Wikan, 1983: 188): to feed an extra mouth day after day detracts from scarce resources that are needed to feed one's own family and keep up one's appearances in the world. But to share one's home and comfort adds to one's self-perception as honourable and hospitable.

Of importance too is a culturally shared perception that every human being *needs* a home, as a provider of warmth and comfort, and also as a private place in which to prepare one's entry into the world. 'What matters is not what you are, but what you appear to be', goes an oft-quoted Egyptian saying. This appearance is orchestrated in the home: the contrast between untidiness and even squalor in private, and the spotless, smart public appearance attests to a culturally conceived need for a private refuge. This goes some way to explain why wage-earning sons are never forced out of the home, even when, as is commonly the case, they do not contribute a piastre to the household and are derided for their selfishness and callousness. Yet they may remain at home even when, as in a case I know, hearts have grown so bitter that for five years mother and sisters have not been on speaking terms with their son/brother. They share 5 sq. m. between them.

Another cultural value which affects housing decisions is the premium put on nuclear living. Extended family living is considered undesirable, particularly if it must be with the husband's kin. Enmity between mother-in-law and daughter-in-law is not only the expectation but the rule. Lodging with the wife's parents is much more acceptable, but still uncommon, due to congestion. In the one case that I know, a mother took her daughter and son-in-law in when they had struggled through the seven years of their engagement to find a flat. In cases of joint living a couple is always allotted a separate room, no matter how miniscule, and if they live with the man's parents, they will also cook separately. Joint living is culturally believed to interfere with a couple's independence and bargaining position *vis-à-vis* each other. Visiting among female kin, on the other hand, is highly desired and frequent, and one may easily form the impression that the wife's mother and sisters are living in the house when really they are only constant visitors. As a widow, however, a mother will expect, and be expected to, move in with a married daughter.

The aggregate result of these cultural premises, combined with poverty, is extreme congestion. My early counts from 1969 indicated gross densities of one person per 2 sq. m. to be common (Wikan, 1980: 21), while on an average the families had nearly two persons per single sleeping place: people slept *under* beds as well as on top, three adults or up to seven children to a double bed, etc. At the same time, such crowding is considered a hardship, and there are strong pressures to maintain a minimal separation of the sexes and privacy. Ideally, children aged four and over should sleep in a separate room from their parents; from puberty, brothers and sisters should sleep in separate rooms; unrelated male guests should be received in a room which does not serve as a bedroom for women; and each family should have a kitchen (with a primus stove only) protected from the prying eyes of visitors. But again, it is characteristic of the hospitality and generosity of these people that I have never come across a case of kin being turned away, no matter how severe the congestion. Standards are sacrificed, bitter feelings are kept in check. Thus when I was in Cairo in September 1986 I was surprised to find that a son, who had been bitterly chided for his selfishness and scorn, and who made his siblings and his mother rejoice when he finally married and moved out, had moved back in again, with his (unbeloved) wife and (beloved) young son. He was in need, so there was no question other than to help. Seven adults had to vacate one room of their flat, 30 sq. m. in area and were left with one double bed and a couch.

Some external parameters have also been provided. All rents have been frozen by government decree since 1948 in the sense that the original tenant, or his/her heir, pays the monthly rent originally fixed. If the apartment is vacated, on the other hand, the house-owner is allowed to set the rent at current market rates. The average rent paid constituted, in the early 1970s one-sixth (or 17 per cent) of the average income of heads of household employed in the public sector. This proportion has declined over time, and now may be no more than 2 to 5 per cent. As a result of these regulations, families with old contracts pay as little as £E4 per month for apartments of average standard whereas the current monthly rent when such an apartment exceptionally becomes available on the open market would be £E65–£E100, with a down-payment of £E5,000–£E6,000 demanded as 'key money' (*xilawil*). From the latter half the monthly rent is deducted until it is 'repaid'.

The disadvantage of these regulations, from the owner's point of view, makes the shrewdest of them resort to various techniques to make life so unpleasant for the tenants that they are eventually forced out: throwing dirty water from the upper floors, picking quarrels, forbidding tenants to

Table 6.1
The development of rents and down-payments with reference to the second
generation, Cairo, 1974–86

| Year acquired | Distance from child-hood home (mins.) | Rent (£E) | Deposit (£E) | Size of rooms (sq. m.) | Piped water |
|---|---|---|---|---|---|
| 1974 | 40 | 5 | 0 | 2 | Yes |
| 1979 | 40 | 15 | 700 | 2 | Yes |
| 1979 | 30 | 20 | 900 | 2 | Yes |
| 1981 | 120 | 35 | 1,000[a] | 3 | No |
| 1982 | 20 | 35 | 2,300[b] | 3 | Yes |
| 1983 | 10 | 60 | 3,000 | 4 | Yes |
| 1983 | 10 | 15 | 1,000[c] | 2 | Yes |
| 1983 | 75 | 30 | 1,300 | 2 | No |
| 1983 | 40 | 35 | 1,250[d] | 3 | Yes |
| 1983 | 40 | 25 | 2,500 | 2 | Yes |
| 1984 | 120 | 45 | 500 | 2 | No |
| 1984 | 120 | 25 | 1,000 | 2 | No |
| 1985 | 30 | 45 | 20,000 | 2 | Yes |
| 1985 | 40 | 65 | 30,000 | 3 | Yes |
| 1986 | 120 | 65 | 2,000 | 3 | No |

Notes
(a)  Plastering and painting by tenant for £E1,000. Public housing.
(b)  For £E1,500.
(c)  Very cheap, because believed to be haunted by ghosts (afrit) after two women
     committed suicide in the flat.
(d)  Very low deposit, because vacated another flat that could be rented out at five
     times the earlier rent plus deposit of £E2,500. New flat plastered and painted by
     tenant for approximately £E1,200.

keep pigeons and rabbits on their balconies (an issue where they have, in
fact, the backing of the law). But on the whole, relations between owner and
tenant are calm, even amiable, especially in the old established quarters.

The second generation, however, cannot hope to find lodgings in these
old established quarters – unless they are lucky heirs to the occupancy of an
old flat. The very central location of these quarters, with their closeness to
public transport, markets and other public facilities, has made them, over
the past ten years, appear extremely attractive, and rents have risen accordingly. The new generation is therefore forced to settle on the city margins,
year by year further away from the relatively central parts of Giza where
they were born and raised. There is a free market for property, including
building sites, in Cairo. But the part of town where my sample lives is
densely built up so new building land is located increasingly further away.
Building is, however, extremely active, and new apartments may be rented
before they are built. An apartment on the city margins, without piped
water and twenty minutes' walk from public transport costs approximately

£E30–£E45 with a down-payment of £E2,000 for a two-room flat and £E50–£E65 with £E3,000 down payment for a three-room flat. On average, the monthly rent thus constitutes 50 to 75 per cent of an average income in a household head's main job, compared to the 2 to 5 per cent of the income of a man established fifteen to twenty years ago.

In the old quarter, most of the families have lived in their present flat since their marriage. However, a third of my original sample have moved due to enmity with neighbours or kin. At that time, new lodgings could be found within walking distance of the old – this was of importance to keep up contact with allies and kin who are called on in times of crisis or conflict. In the generation of forty to sixty-year-olds, it was common for all members of a sibling group to live within easy walking distance – in extreme contrast to the pattern that is emerging among young families today, as we shall shortly see.

Intended to aid the poor and undoubtedly serving their interests in the essential respect of keeping rents low and preventing exploitation, this policy of freezing rents is increasingly immobilising the established population, locking them into the particular apartment where they happen to be, and making them unable to move away from neighbours with whom they may fall out. But the chances of falling out – for some peculiarly cultural reasons (Wikan, 1980: Ch. 7) – are much less once the children are grown, and for this reason the immobility strikes young families particularly hard. The newly-established families, moreover, are given no governmental support in their efforts to find a home. There is no public housing available to the poor, except as replacement for houses that actually collapse or are so derelict that the owner can obtain permission to tear them down. For such evicted tenants only are there special replacement housing projects on the city periphery in subsidised government housing – with the result that derelict flats are tenaciously occupied until they are condemned. It is not uncommon for people to be wounded or even killed as such houses collapse. When a girl I knew was killed in such an accident her parents and her marrying brother were provided with inexpensive government flats (opposite each other, to the daily detriment of relations between in-laws).

Another background factor of profound importance over the seventeen years I have followed these families is, of course, the level of consumer prices, economic activity and employment as these affect the urban poor. Very briefly, a highly regulated and stagnant economy under Nasser meant a low level of wages and employment. A new economic policy under Sadat created an economic boom in the late 1970s, especially for unskilled labour, which coincided with an increasing flow of labour migrants from the Giza poor to Libya and Saudi Arabia, creating opportunities for higher material consumption. Though there has been a slow-down under the present

Mubarak regime, there is still an atmosphere of optimism, and clear opportunities for improvement, especially in the sectors of building and transport. As all men in my sample have secondary jobs – from which they may derive their main income – as unskilled labourers in these sectors, all are in some measure beneficiaries of the employment boom.[2]

Under the depressed conditions of poverty, and with the slightly improved opportunities of recent years, what are the priorities and decisions whereby the Cairo poor shape their own lives and their networks and neighbourhood through decisions that affect housing?

We might first consider the senior generation of households in my sample. Despite ubiquitous difficulties in reaching agreement in marriage negotiations and piloting the parties through the betrothal period to a completed marriage, the average age of spouses in the senior generation was fifteen for women and twenty for men. In the early 1960s conditions were roughly similar; approximately eighteen for women and twenty-three for men. Housing was found through friends and kin, and new couples established themselves close to their place of birth. Thus, in the forty to sixty age range, sibling groups are found scattered within a fairly small radius, a walking distance of around five to ten minutes, and when these households were established the parental generation likewise lived close by.

But this does not make for particularly well integrated neighbourhoods. Beyond one's own back streets most neighbours are strangers, and especially when the children are small, some are enemies, due to conflicts and quarrels between them in which mother is culturally bound to stand up for *her* child. Women form the main structure of neighbourhoods, since men's lives revolve largely around places of work outside the neighbourhood and public cafés which may be located at any convenient place. These women generally establish a relationship of 'best friend', however temporary and brittle, with one or two similarly placed women within accessible distance, and maintain the self-confirming conception of a rather hostile neighbourhood in which gossip and ill-will are rife. The value of neighbourhood stability has thus been that of securing physical access to close kin, not a particularly improved ambience of the neighbourhood as a community.

As I have documented elsewhere, it is characteristic of most of the seventeen households of my original sample that they have undergone a considerable transformation and improvement through their own effort and management (Wikan, 1985). This has been effected primarily by the wives. Among the Cairo poor, gender roles are such that women, though having no employment or income, have still been the family's household managers: the wives are the planners, savers and investors. Men are seen as irresponsible, without either the ability or incentive to economise and plan. Thus the wives have set the economic priorities in these households. They differed in what their first priority has been; and this has significantly affected their opportunities for better housing.

Two out of three chose education for their children – an ambition that necessitated massive economic investment. School uniforms, books, private tuition and all the fees required have been expended, at great hardship, year after year, to pilot their children through schools and exams. In this, perhaps the mothers were motivated by a dream: to become the proud grandmother in the pleasant home of a successful middle-class child. But above all, the dream has been to see their own beloved children successful and happy, where the parents had failed.

A third of the households failed to attempt this characteristically Egyptian direction of aspiration and improvement, and let their children remain uneducated and unskilled. As things have turned out, there has been an unexpected reversal of fortunes or rewards. Lower middle-class aspirations have been hard to realise, salaries for clerks and schoolteachers have remained depressed, and the employment market for poorly-educated persons has been flooded, whereas with the boom in building and infrastructure there has been a great improvement in salaries for the unskilled, combined with great opportunities for labour. This has affected housing options for the second generation, as we shall shortly see.

The mothers with middle-class aspirations for their children had yet another dream: a house of their own – far away from the noise and conflict of the back-street environment. As tangible evidence of this, some bought a plot of land, located on the outskirts of Cairo by the Pyramid Road in what was at the time (the early to mid-1960s) a peaceful, clean, and calm environment. Land could be bought for £E3 per square metre, with a small down-payment of one-sixth paid as cash and the rest as monthly instalments over four to five years. One-third of the mothers in my sample bought such plots, usually of 60 sq. m., whilst one bought 100 sq. m. – as a real concrete step in reaching for the dream. But to build was beyond the reach of those who simultaneously sought education for their children.

Options were different, as we shall shortly see, for those who did not have education as their first priority. But for all, an impressive economic institution of the poor quarter provided the foundation for down-payments and investments of every kind, and must be spelled out. A financial system exists on the folk level where, by common conventions, down-payments and debts alike are interest-free; it is only a matter of current saving and progressive paying-off of instalments. A prototype for this are the popular, female-run savings-clubs (*gamᶜiyyat*) in which all members pay weekly, bi-weekly or monthly contributions which are all pooled, each member appropriating the whole amount once, by turns. By organising such a savings-club (and thereby being allowed first turn to receive the pooled result), the more forceful or foresighted women are able to raise capital for down-payments on plots. Others in need are helped when others organise such clubs on their behalf. This social organisation for saving, and the interest-free character of loans, deposits and instalments, prove powerful tools for saving and investment in the hands of even the most economically marginal households. In periods of economic expansion, they may be quite successful.

The dream of a house of one's own has been a woman's dream, and I think it is essential to recognise its character as a dream, rather than as a pragmatic step towards improving one's life situation. Confined to the back streets with the noise, turmoil and neighbourly interference, the desire for *peace* is one constantly expressed by poor women, and is embodied in such dreams. Thus Umm Ali, the first of my sample to act, made a *gamʿiyya* for a first deposit of £E50 in 1963. For years the matter remained most precarious, with postponements of further instalments, physical violence in the family when her husband tried to steal and cash the deed during the family's recurring economic crises, etc. Yet others followed, and by 1985, five out of twelve families in my sample had obtained such plots as well as three out of fifteen children (see Table 6·1). Umm Ali's plot of 100 sq. m., bought for £E300 through the years 1963–70, is now valued at £E22,000.

In no case has any of these slightly better-off women, with middle-class aspirations, actually been able to make such a move themselves. By the time they have accumulated enough money to build, they regard themselves as too old and settled actually to make the move. Interestingly, it was the poorest families who proved the most persistent, and successful, in succeeding in the project. They had the added incentive of needing desperately to escape the burden of their low, frozen rent of £E2·5 to £E3 per month. So they bought the cheapest plot, furthest out – indeed in what was still a village – and as soon as the plot was theirs, they moved out to an unfinished building consisting of walls only, with a mud floor and open to the sky, with neither water nor electricity and fifteen minutes' scramble over undeveloped countryside to the nearest public transport. As they conceived of it, what mattered was to place oneself in a kind of forced savings situation where every available piastre went into the house project rather than being spent on a host of other dire necessities. Progressively, they have added a roof, a floor and further storeys until they are now the owners of buildings three or four storeys high, valued at approximately £E40,000 each. (Some have even bought a neighbouring plot on which to build as an investment.) Relieved of the expense of education, they could afford such an investment.

For the less desperate, however, who had chosen to give first priority to education for their children, the dream of a house of their own has turned into one of a place to accommodate their children. But the dream has overlooked some cultural constraints. One woman whom I know has, through sheer saving and persistence (she was reputed not even to let her children eat properly), managed to build a five-storey house – to house her five sons, or so she thought. But only one of them, the most destitute, has agreed to live there with his wife. All the others, more favourably positioned – for she also ruled their education with an iron hand – have heeded their wives and chosen independence above the imminent conflicts in the relationship between mother and daughter-in-law. Indeed, had she housed her own sons, she might not have been able to build so well. Key money from tenants has been an essential part of the capital.[3]

The second generation have had a very different fate. With what the poor in Giza have experienced as a swiftly rising housing crisis over the past ten years, both their options and their strategies have changed profoundly. New apartments can only be obtained at a considerable distance, on the periphery of town, far away from parents and siblings, because, with the accelerating rents, a flat that is within reach of a sibling marrying one year will be beyond the one who marries in the next, assuming they are on approximately the same level. Indeed, we find a pattern of sibling groups being ever more widely dispersed with the first-marrying one being located in a better, more centrally-located apartment whereas later-marrying ones are ever more disfavourably placed. A mechanism in this is the dramatic rate of rent increases per year. With annual increases of approximately 30 per cent (not including the increase in 'key money'), a flat that rents for £E25 per month one year is likely to cost double three to four years later, while the down-payments, say of £E2,000, also doubles. In the same interval, wages are likely to rise by a maximum of 40 per cent only. One factor actually pressing rents up is the rent freeze. Prohibited to change the rent in the foreseeable future, owners are naturally out to get the most they can obtain in a market where the demand far exceeds the supply and where a particular flat may also be occupied for generations by a tenant and his descendants – at no rise in cost.

The cost and difficulty of obtaining lodging has been a major factor behind the sharp increase in the average marriage age over the past ten to fifteen years. Whereas their mothers married at about fifteen, and their fathers at twenty, brides nowadays are more likely to be over twenty-five and grooms about thirty. Indeed, it is not at all unusual to find brides of thirty and even thirty-five – an age when their grandmothers would indeed have been grandmothers.

Marriage negotiations and proceedings have changed to accommodate the new situation. Previously the *mahr* (bride price) – an old, venerated institution inseparably bound up with marriage – was paid in gold jewellery from groom to bride and money to help her parents provide the furnishings. Nowadays the *mahr* is about to disappear, to be replaced by a concept of 'preparing or making things ready together' (*yitgahhiz sawa*) – acknowledging the joint, persistent efforts that must be met by bride and groom and the bride's family to enable a couple to set up a house. Gold jewellery is now a luxury that few can afford. The *mahr* has become an anomaly – due to the impressive adaptability of the population to changing economic circumstances. The first priority is given to a home, and the groom and bride's family must pool all available resources to produce 'key money' for a flat and furnishings to go with it.

Furnishings must be elaborate. Newly-married couples must be prepared to have their flat inspected by numerous house guests who are less than discreet if the appearance is not up to standard. The shame inflicted when house guests spread the 'dark secrets of the house' (*yigib sirr ilbet*) is intensely felt, and the fear of such disclosure is a powerful incitement to invest in household equipment. Consequently, by the culture of the Cairo poor, considerations concerning flat rental are closely linked, with a view as to how the particular flat is to be furnished. To rent a three-room flat and furnish only two rooms would be shameful, whereas expensive furnishings may in part compensate for a discreditable location of a flat. Interestingly, the option of renting a cheap flat now to save for a better one later is precluded, due to the rent freeze. It is better to exceed the maximum of what one can manage, from the start, furnish it accordingly – through loans and instalment-buying – even though, as everyone knows, the furnishings must soon be sold to make room for beds for a growing family. One's self-respect and social position, however, demand that appearances are put right from the start.

For the second generation, with rising costs and the requirements of 'key money', simply obtaining an apartment to rent has been the main problem. Characteristically, the children of mothers who did not invest in education have had a distinct advantage in obtaining housing. They married earlier, when the rent was lower, and work as unskilled labourers in relatively well-paid jobs. The most extreme example in my sample is a man, originating from one of the poorest families, who married a girl who was equally poor. He had four years at elementary school, she had none. Working as the driver of a horse and cart when they married in 1974, he now (1986) owns a lorry (bought for £E15,000 cash) plus two houses, valued at £E50,000 and £E35,000. His average monthly income is estimated at £E1,500 to £E2,000. Though clearly unusual, his case shows what possibilities are within reach for the enterprising ones of the second generation.

By contrast, the two male children of my sample who managed to finish university education, and now work as engineers, earn approximately £E150 per month in their main job. One of them occupies a small room in his wife's mother's flat. A man who works as a teacher earns £E75 per month, whereas from his afternoon work as an unskilled labourer (painter) he earns an additional £E100 per month. He lives with his wife and son in a tiny room in his mother's flat. It goes without saying that housing options will differ significantly where there are such a range of incomes.

To pay for lodgings and furnishings, a pattern has crystallised among the educated whereby the wife, as well as the husband, must seek paid work. Generally speaking, the poor estimate that one (woman's) income as clerk or factory worker will cover the monthly expense of the flat. This need for two incomes has put the premium on wage-earning brides higher, especially among educated low-paid men, and pressured men to pressure wives to keep on working after marriage. (This was unheard of in the previous generation, where men said they would rather throw themselves into the Nile than have their wife working.) It is a paradoxical situation in that some of these same men objected violently to their fiancée's continued schooling and in many instances forced the girl to quit for fear that she would end up in a higher position than he. In one case I know a man compelled his extremely education-motivated fiancée to quit, but gave in, two years later, when she relentlessly pressed the point. By then she was too old to continue at a government school and had to enter a private secondary school, at great expense to her family. But when, five months ago, she became pregnant with their first child, the husband became so angry at the prospects of lost income, that he maltreated her until she poured kerosene over herself and tried to set herself on fire. Whereas young couples, among the educated, tend to agree that a wife must carry on working, even though her own dream may be to be 'wife of the house' (sitt ilbet), they are also under cross-pressures from a cultural belief that does not permit family planning in connection with the first child. As few of the second generation have close kin nearby to tend their babies there is often no option for the wife but to stay at home once the first child arrives. The man is then forced to work even harder to make ends meet.

This new absence of kinsfolk, particularly mothers and sisters, in the neighbourhood, has a number of implications. On the one hand, it may force the young spouses together in an enhanced solidarity. On the other hand it creates a situation of isolation and considerable hardship for them, particularly for the woman. Thus one young woman, now pregnant, sees a situation arising where she must get up at 4.30 a.m. in the morning to travel on two buses to deliver the child to her mother before she proceeds, on another two buses, to get to work, from where she will return at 3 p.m. Fetching the child on her way back, she may get home at about 5.30 p.m.[4] Another, who is not working but has four young children under eight, lives isolated from all her kin and has no one to help her intervene in her husband's constant maltreatment. Her own mother, when she was in a simular situation, had a mother next door to appeal to, besides brothers and other kin – with the result that her husband and her kin were not on speaking terms for twenty-five years! The mother credits her kin's presence with the fact that her life turned out as good as it did.

The situation that is emerging for this, the second generation, is thus a rather confused one, with many contrary forces and trends, and certainly very different from that of the previous generation. The most salient features are the reduction of kinship relations as effective supports, dispersal to less central areas, and isolation in these relative anomic new locations. The households in question are furthermore established with a higher age at marriage, an expectation of a wage-earning career for wives, based in part on some intermediate, though poor-standard education. Families are smaller because of fairly successful planning, and family earnings have clearly been improving.

On the other hand, there have been soaring costs, particularly in the field of housing, where prices are confusingly uneven and the market imperfect and constantly changing. Yet through these developments, poor housing retains its character as private and self-financed, based mainly on tenants and single-house-owner landlords.

The culture of the persons coping with this situation shows some very characteristic features, decisive for reproducing major features of the situation. The most important are gender role and the organisation of these poor household economies, where dominant and enterprising women have tended to manage the household economy and struggle with considerable skill and persistence to economise, save and plan with a view to upward mobility for their children, and for the household as a whole. An essential feature of this culture is the near-absence of wealth-destruction in connection with feasting (very different from Indonesia where I now work) and great emphasis on the accumulation of material objects as a source of prestige. Wives have been aided in these efforts by traditional savings-clubs and by very active information networks apprising them of market costs, options and possible strategies, and enabling them, despite their very weak economic base, to participate in various forms of accumulation, including private housing development along the fringes of an expanding Cairo. There is some question, however, of the extent to which these co-operative and supportive aspects of otherwise divided and hostile neighbourhoods can be retained and reproduced in the new neighbourhoods which are now forming under new conditions.

## NOTES

1   I use 'Cairo poor' as a shorthand for the actual families I studied in a certain area of Cairo. Though I have intimate data on only these families, knowledge about a wider circle of kin and acquaintances in other parts of Cairo indicate that the genealisations I draw may have wide applicability.

2   Conditions have changed since the time when this was written in 1986/87.

When I last visited the families in December 1988, employment opportunities and wage levels for the unskilled had declined markedly.

3   The strategy, though of a kind practiced by 'all', backfired. The landlady committed the mistake of giving tenants a receipt for the key money, when they asked for it. Thye used this to file a court case on the grounds that key money is illegal. She will probably have to sell the house, and at drastic loss.

4   The strain of such practice turned out to be too much. She now leaves the child at her mother's five days a week, going there daily after work to see him. The child is sickly and unhappy and the mother beside herself with concern. But she sees no other alternative.

## REFERENCES

Wikan, U. 1980. *Life Among the Poor in Cairo*. London: Tavistock.
—— 1983. *Tomorrow, God Willing*. Oslo: Norwegian University Press (in Norwegian).
—— 1985. 'Living conditions among Cairo's poor – a view from below', *The Middle East Journal*, 39 (1), pp. 7–26.

## RESUME

Le logement doit être considéré dans un vaste contexte culturel dans lequel les besoins sont vécus et exprimés et les stratégies développées. Le Caire est une ancienne cité aux traditions urbaines longuement établies; la plupart de la population pauvre habite des taudis dans les zones urbaines plutôt que des bidonvilles périphériques. Ce chapitre décrit une telle région et un exemple de ses habitants. La vie et le sort de dix-sept familles ont été suivis de près pendant vingt-cinq ans. L'étude montre les stratégies opposées employées par les membres de l'ancienne génération et les perspectives très différentes offertes à la jeune génération d'aujourd'hui comparées à celles de leurs parents.

Au début de l'étude, la plupart des familles servant d'exemples étaient des locataires vivant dans des conditions très exigües. Mais dans cette culture, le logement des membres moins favorisés de la famille était obligatoire et le style de logement a peu contribué à l'évolution du statut social parmi la population urbaine pauvre. Comme les loyers ne pouvaient être augmentés que par un changement de locataires, toute motivation est restée stationnaire. Les familles plus aisées avaient tendance à investir dans l'éducation, pensant qu'elle offrirait à leurs enfants de meilleures perspectives professionnelles; bien que beaucoup achetaient des parcelles de terrains, leur développement faisait l'objet d'une faible priorité. Cependant, les familles plus pauvres étaient obligées de placer toutes leurs économies dans la terre et le logement afin d'éviter de payer des loyers élevés. Au cours des années, ce sont ces familles pauvres qui ont gagné le plus; elles ont accumulé d'importants avoirs fonciers. Cependant, l'éducation a permis aux enfants d'accéder à des postes à salaires médiocres; ils recherchent un mode de vie plus privé et leur statut est lié au mobilier de la maison. Il n'est plus possible d'acheter une parcelle de terrain bon marché. Les jeunes couples repoussent leur mariage pour économiser ensemble afin d'établir un chez soi; la jeune femme continue de travailler et repousse ainsi sa maternité. De nouveaux styles et de nouvelles valeurs culturelles apparaissent.

# TUNIS: CRISE DU LOGEMENT ET REHABILI-TATION URBAINE

La crise urbaine que connaît le Maghreb aujourd'hui est sans précédent dans son histoire: elle est l'expression d'une crise structurelle profonde de son économie et de sa société.

Le syndrome d'une telle crise s'exprime en dernière analyse par une involution urbaine[1] évidente, expression elle-même de déséquilibres structurels globaux qui plongent leurs racines dans la période coloniale et qui s'aggravent aujourd'hui. L'extraversion croissante de l'économie et l'aliénation de la société opèrent simultanément dans un sens d'approfondissement de tels déséquilibres.

Les intérêts des classes hégémoniques en formation et leur tendance à adopter des stratégies conventionnelles de développement excluent toute perspective de résorption de la crise. A défaut d'alternatives globales de développement démocratique et populaire, rien n'indique que la crise ne s'approfondirait davantage à l'avenir mettant en péril jusqu'à l'existence même des Etats–nations concernées.

Notre propos dans ce travail est d'aborder la crise urbaine à partir de l'un de ses paliers les plus critiques, celui de l'habitat populaire, et en centrant l'analyse sur un cas, celui de la ville de Tunis.

Nous montrerons que la politique de l'habitat en Tunisie, au niveau du discours et parfois même des réalisations, cherche à prendre en charge le logement des néo-citadins; elle se heurte en fait à des blocages structurels induits par la nature de classe de l'Etat et un mode conventionnel de développement et qui précipitent inévitablement l'échec d'une telle politique.

Il est vrai que la tentative officielle de prise en charge partielle du logement des masses populaires urbaines renvoie à la reconnaissance par l'Etat de ces masses en tant qu'acteur urbain nouveau et virtuellement menaçant. La stratégie actuelle de l'Etat vis-à-vis des néo-citadins et en articulation avec le capital international (Banque Mondiale) correspond en fait aux exigences de l'étape actuelle de la division internationale du travail.

Il s'agit en sorte d'organiser et de désamorcer la violence de la force de travail que représente la masse des néo-citadins en les faisant servir la nouvelle étape d'industrialisation par import–substitution, qui correspond à la fois aux intérêts du capital international à ceux de la nouvelle bourgeoisie locale en formation.

Dans cette perspective il est impératif, comme nous le montrerons plus loin, de satisfaire certains besoins essentiels pour que la force de travail puisse être reproduite dans des conditions de disponibilité et de mobilité adéquates (logement et transport), sans perdre de vue que le secteur de l'habitat peut constituer une nouvelle source de profit capitaliste à un moment où les secteurs classiques de profit affrontent une grave crise générale.

L'Etat, en tant qu'Etat–nation et Etat–parti, à travers son processus de contrôle d'une *société assistée*, procède alternativement par répression–concession, cherchant à globaliser les demandes émanant des différents acteurs ou forces sociales. Il y répond généralement de manière sélective selon à la fois l'équilibre des forces qui dominent l'appareil politique et les pressions venues de la base. Il tente de satisfaire les demandes essentielles selon des modalités parfois manipulatives dans un souci d'équilibre global, aussi précaire soit-il.

Cependant, le caractère conventionnel du modèle de développement dépendant et l'influence – dans le cas particulier de la politique de l'habitat populaire – de la stratégie techno-bureaucratique et néo-libérale de la Banque Mondiale, en focalisant uniquement sur des 'enclaves' populaires qui sont les plus directement utiles au système productif dominant, évacuent de ce fait de larges secteurs de la pauvreté urbaine de toute intégration à la dynamique générale de développement; ils créent à leur insu les forces antagonistes qui risquent de mettre en péril le système qui les a engendrées.

D'où les contradictions insurmontables d'un tel modèle de développement dans une société dépendante et à croissance économique limitée.

Nous nous proposons dans ce travail de montrer l'ampleur de la crise du logement et notamment de l'habitat populaire dans une ville qui se développe à un taux d'urbanisation excessif. Puis nous essaierons de caractériser la politique officielle de l'habitat populaire et d'identifier le sens et l'efficacité des interventions de la Banque Mondiale dans ce secteur. Enfin nous focaliserons l'analyse sur les acteurs qui occupent le 'centre urbain de la pauvreté' pour diagnostiquer leur véritable identité de classe ainsi que l'origine et les modalités de leur confrontation à l'Etat.

## LES ORIGINES DE LA CRISE DU LOGEMENT ET DE L'EXPLOSION DE L'HABITAT 'SPONTANE' A TUNIS

A grands traits, la Tunisie est l'un des pays en développement les plus urbanisés du bassin méditerranéen. Sur une population totale de 6,6 millions, la population urbaine représente 55 pour cent de la population totale. Le sixième plan national de développement (1982–86) projette une population urbaine de 4,9 millions, soit 64 pour cent du total de la population.

La macrocéphalie du grand Tunis est frappante. Avec une population de 1,2 million elle s'accroit à un taux de 6,9 pour cent par an et représente 34,3 pour cent de la population urbaine totale et plus de la moitié de la population des vingt plus grandes villes du pays. De plus, sa consommation annuelle par tête est de 80 pour cent plus élevée que la moyenne nationale. A elle seule elle monopolise 32 pour cent de tous les investissements industriels réalisés depuis 1973 et offre en 1980 plus du quart des emplois industriels et de services (Collectif, 1980: 230).

Cette hyper-urbanisation de la ville de Tunis, maintes fois décrite, est l'expression éclatante d'un mode de développement global fortement dépendant et résolument tourné vers les régions côtières les plus anciennement dotées d'une base infrastructurelle avancée. Et c'est ce modèle de développement qui est à l'origine des déséquilibres de toutes sortes que connait la ville de Tunis aujourd'hui ainsi d'ailleurs que toutes les capitales du Maghreb.

C'est sur cette toile de fond que s'inscrit la crise du logement à Tunis et singulièrement celle du logement populaire.

## LA CRISE DU LOGEMENT A TUNIS

Le parc immobilier de Tunis représente 150.000 logements pour une population de 170.000 ménages regroupant 1,2 million d'habitants. Le taux de cohabitation est de 1,2 ménage–logement, celui d'occupation de 6,7 personnes–logement. Ce dernier atteint même huit et jusqu'à onze personnes dans les quartiers d'habitat dit spontané où un tiers des ménages au moins vivent en cohabitation.

L'exiguité du logement constitue un indice supplémentaire de la crise aiguë qui caractérise le secteur de l'habitat à Tunis. En effet, près de la moitié des logements sont constitués d'une ou deux pièces au maximum, avec une détérioration croissante de la situation puisque la proportion des familles qui vivent dans une seule pièce est passée de 17 pour cent en 1975 à 26 pour cent en 1980.

De plus, ce patrimoine immobilier particulièrement exigu est anormalement sous-équipé en services, puisqu'il est à 40 pour cent privé d'eau courante, à 22 pour cent d'électricité et à 35 pour cent de connection à l'égoût. Et dans ce domaine aussi la situation continue à se détériorer par rapport à ce qu'elle était en 1975 (BIRD, 1982: 22).

En dépit de ces conditions défectueuses du logement de près de la moitié de la population, le niveau des loyers est tel qu'il exige un taux mensuel d'effort très élevé puisque 27 pour cent du revenu des ménages y est consacré. En outre, certaines pratiques illégales (pas de porte, cautionnement élevé, sous-location) contribuent à la sur-occupation et à la cohabitation.

D'autre part, la spéculation foncière galopante, jointe à l'insuffisance de la réserve foncière publique et à une augmentation spectaculaire des prix de matériaux de construction,[2] ont imposé des coûts prohibitifs de production du logement et ont de ce fait privé deux tiers de la population de leur droit au logement. D'où l'aggravation de la crise du logement particulièrement pour les familles à faible revenu. D'où aussi la tension, le malaise et la violence parfois avec lesquels s'accompagnent les revendications en matière de logement.

La seule issue laissée à la population sous-logée du fait de l'incapacité de l'Etat à prendre en charge correctement le logement des masses populaires consiste pour ces dernières à envahir littéralement l'espace urbain et à défier ainsi toute la symbolique légale de l'Etat. D'où l'explosion récente de l'habitat dit spontané comme réaction à une politique conventionnelle techno-bureaucratique dans le secteur de l'habitat.

## L'EXPLOSION DE L'HABITAT 'SPONTANE'

L'incapacité de la politique conventionnelle à satisfaire le besoin de logement du plus grand nombre des populations de la ville de Tunis s'est traduit par une explosion récente de nouveaux quartiers spontanés, construits clandestinement sur des terrains envahis ou même délapidés au patrimoine foncier public.

Le recensement officiel de 1975 devait dénombrer 40.000 logements et 300.000 habitants environ dans le secteur d'habitat dit spontané soit un tiers du parc immobilier et de la population de la ville. Entre 1975 et 1980 l'habitat spontané se serait accru de 50 pour cent en cinq ans. Et rien n'indique à l'avenir un fléchissement de cette tendance, bien au contraire.

En effet, la photo aérienne de mai 1980 a permis de constater que sur 1,570 ha. totalement urbanisés et 1.450 ha. en cours d'urbanisation pour l'habitat, ce sont respectivement 770 et 775 qui le sont par l'habitat spontané. De sorte qu' en tablant sur des densités basses de vingt logements à l'hectare et sur un taux de réalisation de 30 pour cent seulement pour les sites en cours d'urbanisation, on peut estimer le nombre de logements construits entre 1975 et 1980 à 15.000 (soit un tiers des logements légalement réalisés), abritant 18.000 familles et 100.000 habitants, soit les deux tiers de la population supplémentaire entre 1975 et 1980 (Morched, 1976, 1978; Bellalouna, 1980).

L'exemple du quartier appelé Ettadhamen au Nord-Ouest de Tunis et dont s'est saisie la presse locale récemment[3] est typique de cette urbanisation par envahissement. Il s'agit d'un quartier qui ne comptait guère plus de 7.000 habitants en 1975 et qui devait passer à 28.000 en 1979 et 65.000 en 1983. En somme, un quartier aussi peuplé que la fameuse ville de Kairouan et qui se classe tout juste après les sept plus grandes villes de la Tunisie. Curieusement, sur le plan juridique il s'agit d'un quartier pirate, un hors-la-loi, car il ne fait pas partie du périmètre communal de la ville de Tunis.

On doit se rendre à l'évidence et admettre qu'entre 1975 et 1980 la moitié environ de l'urbanisation nouvelle est le fait de l'habitat qualifié officiellement d'illégal. Symbole d'un changement sociologique important, ce mode de production de logement est le fait d'une population fixée depuis relativement longtemps à Tunis (dans une proportion de deux-tiers dans le cas du quartier Ettadhamen et disposant de revenus appréciables par contraste avec les premières vagues d'immigrés des premiers bidonvilles.

Ce système d'habitat 'illégal' contemporain de la décennie 80 vient ainsi renforcer et aggraver la situation de l'habitat 'anarchique et non codifié' hérité de la période coloniale et qui devait s'accroître de façon démesurée au cours des décennes 60 et 70, formant la première ceinture des bidonvilles de Tunis (Mellassine, Saïda Manoubia, Djebel Lahmar, etc.) (Stambouli, 1977). Une deuxième ceinture, encore plus périphérique, vient de s'ajouter à la première, symbole de l'extraordinaire vitalité de l'habitat spontané, qui loin de représenter un phénomène social marginal (une simple séquelle de l'ère coloniale) constitue au contraire, aujourd'hui, le système principal de production d'habitat des masses populaires urbaines.

## L'ETAT, LA BANQUE MONDIALE ET LA QUESTION DE L'HABITAT POPULAIRE

Devant l'ampleur sans précédent de la crise urbaine, l'acuité dramatique de la question du logement populaire et la violence incontrôlable des populations promptes à remettre en cause et éventuellement à détruire le modèle de société qui les marginalise, un début de politique urbaine a pu petit à petit voir le jour avec le soutien effectif de la Banque Mondiale et dont l'objectif est de mieux contrôler le contexte urbain global et de désamorcer les foyers les plus effervescents de tension sociale.

On sait que l'intérêt porté par la Banque Mondiale pour la Reconstruction et Développement (BIRD) à la question urbaine est relativement récent et témoigne d'une inflexion de ses préoccupations antérieures.

L'explosion urbaine dans la plupart des pays du Tiers-Monde et les risques croissants de confrontation sociale et politique (pas uniquement sous forme de mouvements sociaux urbains) qu'elle induit ont progressivement amené les responsables de la BIRD à faire porter leurs efforts non plus seulement sur des investissements considérés par eux comme susceptibles de favoriser la croissance *stricto sensu*, mais aussi d'opérer des actions ponctuelles en milieu urbain capables à la fois d'améliorer l'environnement général de la croissance et de prévenir l'irruption de la violence.

D'ailleurs il s'agit moins de modifier réellement les conditions socio-économiques et politiques qui induisent les déséquilibres urbains, comme par exemple l'irrationalité des politiques d'aménagement du territoire que de définir des politiques sectorielles (logement, équipements collectifs, transports) et ponctuelles dont l'objectif est d'atténuer les aspects les plus visibles de la pauvreté urbaine et les formes imprévues de la violence.

## LES PROJETS DE LA BANQUE MONDIALE A TUNIS

C'est ainsi que la BIRD a tenté à Tunis une expérience pilote qui mérite d'être analysée. Cette expérience a privilégié deux secteurs sensibles d'intervention: les transports et l'habitat au sens large incluant l'infrastructure foncière, l'aménagement et les équipements collectifs. Elle s'est effectuée en trois temps: (a) premier projet urbain: transports (1973–75); (b) deuxième projet urbain: habitat (1979–81); et (c) troisième projet urbain: habitat et rénovation urbaine (1981–83).

*Premier projet: transports* Il s'agit d'un projet financé par la BIRD et destiné à décongestionner la ville de Tunis en allégeant les contraintes induites par les problèmes de transport et de circulation d'une métropole millionnaire dont la population dépassera 2 millions à l'horizon 2000. Un service moderne d'autobus a été mis en place ainsi qu'une ligne TGM reliant la cité à sa banlieue nord. Quelques années plus tard le réseau est dépassé, ce qui a poussé les autorités à penser à un projet de métro léger reliant le centre à ses banlieues ouvrières et qui est actuellement en cours de réalisation.

*Deuxième projet: l'habitat populaire du centre de Tunis* Le deuxième projet, qui a porté sur l'amélioration des conditions d'habitat des quartiers pauvres proches du centre ville, a été précédé par une opération vigoureuse d'institutionalisation urbaine qui a donné naissance à de très nombreuses institutions destinées à concrétiser la nouvelle politique urbaine (Ministère de l'Habitat, direction de l'aménagement du territoire, district de Tunis, Agence Foncière d'Habitation, Caisse Nationale d'Epargne–Logement, Caisse de Prêts et de Soutien des Collectivités Locales, Office National d'Assainissement, Agence de Réhabilitation et de Rénovation Urbaine, etc.).

Dans sa partie 'logement' le deuxième projet comprend en effet une composante appelée 'aide à la production de logements sociaux évolutifs et auto-construits' et qui consiste à fournir des parcelles viabilisées d'une superficie allant de 70 à 108 m$^2$ branchées aux réseaux d'eau potable et d'égoûts et comportant une pièce, un WC et la clôture entière. Un crédit d'extension du logement est prévu.

On a visualisé 2.000 parcelles après un travail important de législation foncière. Djebel Lahmar, Saïda Manoubia et Mellassine sont les quartiers bénéficiaires. On a distribué 300 logements.

Rappelons que ce deuxième projet urbain a nécessité un investissement important de l'ordre de 12 milliards d'anciens francs.

*Troisième projet: l'habitat populaire à la périphérie de Tunis* Le troisième projet urbain qui démarra à la fin de 1983 a pour objectifs essentiels, selon les experts de la BIRD: (a) Concevoir et concrétiser de nouveaux projets de logement populaire tout en eméliorant les services urbains au profit des population à faible revenu. (b) Renforcer les institutions impliquées dans le secteur de l'habitat populaire. (c) Aider le gouvernement à mieux coordonner les activités des différentes institutions intéressées au secteur en vue d'encourager la mise en place d'une véritable formulation nationale de la politique de l'habitat.

Ce dernier projet concentre ses actions cette fois sur le quartier périphérique Ettadhamen dont la population double chaque année, et sur la rénovation de la médina de Tunis.

A la lecture de ces trois projets urbains parrainés et partiellement financés par la BIRD nous pouvons déduire que les préoccupations principales de la Banque à travers sa politique urbaine visent essentiellement un double objectif:

(a) Mobiliser et rendre aisément disponible la partie de la force de travail la plus directement articulée à la phase actuelle de l'industrialisation par substitution aux importations.

(b) Désamorcer les foyers de violence les plus proches du centre stratégique de la cité et mettre cette dernière à l'abri des actions qui peuvent bloquer son fonctionnement normal.

## BILAN DE LA POLITIQUE D'HABITAT POPULAIRE A TUNIS

Le bilan de cette politique urbaine conseillée par la BIRD et appuyée par sa finance[4] s'est soldé par un échec évident. C'est ce qui ressort des conclusions des experts de la Banque eux-mêmes dans un rapport officiel rédigé en Juin 1982: '98% de ceux qui ont bénéficié des investissements publics dans le secteur de l'habitat appartiennent aux classes supérieures et moyennes et aux fonctionnaires de l'Etat.' Et les experts ajoutent: 'Les programmes publics sont incapables de toucher de manière significative les familles à faible revenu. 75% des programmes de logement subventionnés par l'Etat entre 1975 et 1980 n'ont pas bénéficié à de telles familles' (BIRD, 1982).

Les raisons de l'échec de cette politique sont nombreuses. Les plus révélatrices sont à notre avis les suivantes.

Le statut de la propriété du sol urbain et de la rente foncière constituent des freins décisifs à une politique urbaine équilibrée. En effet les coûts prohibitifs du sol urbain et corrélativement l'insuffisance de lotissements viables pour la construction à l'intérieur des périmètres communaux bloquent les chances des masses populaires de se loger.

Cet argument est démontré *a contrario* par l'ampleur des investissements privés entre 1975 et 1980 à l'extérieur des périmètres communaux et qui représentent 60 pour cent des investissements globaux dans le secteur du logement. Et il est significatif que la moitié environ de cet espace bâti en dehors des programmes gouvernementaux soit situé dans les quartiers populaires frappés d'illégalité.

Ce sont donc bien des raisons structurelles qui poussent tous ceux que les programmes publics n'arrivent pas à toucher, à construire eux-mêmes 'clandestinement' et 'anarchiquement'. Les experts de la BIRD n'ont pas manqué de noter d'ailleurs que 'Plus de 52% des logements construits entre 1975 et 1980 le furent en dehors et contre la règlementation communale tant la demande de logement a dépassé amplement les possibilités de l'Etat à contrôler l'urbanisation.'

Le quartier périphérique Ettadhamen cité plus haut est un exemple éclatant de cette urbanisation incontrôlée que les experts de la Banque perçoivent comme un facteur de 'détérioration des villes'.

D'autre part, les coûts de production du logement par les programmes publics sont trop élevés et dépassent de loin les possibilités financières des masses populaires. Il est significatif à ce sujet que la Caisse Nationale d'Épargne–Logement, défiée par le taux élevé de l'inflation et un accroissement continu des matériaux de construction, a décidé d'abandonner son programme de logements dits économiques, ce qui implique l'élimination de tous ceux dont le revenu est inférieur à 90 dinars tunisiens par mois, environ deux-tiers des ménages.

Les coûts de production du logement sont d'autant plus élevés que les matériaux sont inadaptés (intégrant des inputs couteux) et les densités relativement basses.

De même la réalisation de ces programmes est souvent confiée à des entreprises de type capitaliste qui grèvent encore davantage les prix de revient. Il est absurde, par exemple, que les programmes de logement des cités populaires de Mellassine et de Djebel Lahmar aient été confiés à une grande entreprise comme Al Iskan. De ce fait il n'est pas surprenant que les coûts de logement populaire (terrain et infrastructure inclus) varient de 850 à 7.000 dinars tandis que l'autoconstruction permet d'abaisser ces coûts de moitié.

En plus de ces causes structurelles, les experts de la BIRD imputent l'échec de la politique du logement populaire à Tunis à des facteurs d'ordre institutionnel, comme le manque de coordination entre les organismes étatiques spécialisés ainsi que l'ambiguité du rôle dévolu aux municipalités qui n'ont jamais pu agir de manière efficace pour 'stopper la croissance du secteur de l'habitat informel'.

## LES NOUVELLES RECOMMENDATIONS DE LA BIRD

Devant cet échec évident de la politique du logement populaire à Tunis, il est intéressant de commenter les recommandations des experts de la BIRD qui cherchent à 'imaginer' une issue à la crise.

Après avoir conseillé l'abandon de la politique de logements clefs en main, ils adressent un programme en quatre points:

(a) Orienter les programmes publics d'habitat dans un sens d'équité surtout en ce qui concerne les familles à faible revenu.

(b) La politique de prêt de la Banque doit s'articuler aux institutions existantes et les renforcer lorsque c'est nécessaire.

(c) Veiller à ce que les bénéficiaires payent régulièrement leurs dettes. Dans ce sens il serait plus raisonnable d'encourager les demandeurs éventuels de logement à contracter un prêt-logement et à construire eux-mêmes leur logement ou à le confier à un petit tâcheron.

(d) Enfin à long terme les experts estiment que l'amélioration des conditions urbaines est une tâche qui doit revenir aux villes elles-mêmes, contrairement à la politique suivie par la Tunisie qui a privilégié des organismes centralisés chargés d'entreprendre des tâches d'utilité publique à une échelle nationale.

L'idéologie néo-libérale sous-jacente à cet ensemble de recommandations est claire. L'ambiguité et les contradictions qui les recouvrent parfois ne sont qu'apparentes.

Comment peut-on en effet faire preuve d'équité envers les démunis et en même temps leur conseiller de recourir au crédit et de rembourser régulièrement leurs dettes afin d'alléger les charges de l'Etat? D'autre part, que veut dire qu'à long terme ce sont les villes elles-mêmes qui doivent gérer la crise urbaine et non l'Etat? Autant dire que seule la libre entreprise est capable de loger les sans-abris!

La contradiction est évidente. En effet il est révélateur que le style techno-bureaucratique de la BIRD s'accomode mal par exemple de tout modèle associatif et d'organisation autonome des populations concernées, puisque ses experts recommandent le renforcement des institutions publiques existantes, celles-là même dont ils critiquaient le centralisme et l'hégémonisme.

## POUR UNE POLITIQUE ALTERNATIVE DE L'HABITAT POPULAIRE

En fait, nous croyons qu'il est grand temps de repenser la politique de l'habitat populaire et de concevoir un modèle alternatif d'habitat inspiré des considérations fondamentales suivantes:

(a) Dans un pays non développé et à urbanisation trop rapide, le besoin de logement des néo-citadins ne peut pas être satisfait par le marché officiel, de sorte que l'habitat dit spontané s'impose comme un mode d'accession normal et inévitable au logement par la grande majorité des populations urbaines. Il ne doit pas être considéré comme une production spatiale illégale et pathologique.

(b) Il est admis à présent qu'il est important de tirer profit de l'initiative féconde des populations urbaines pauvres qui consiste à améliorer leur cadre de vie, et d'encourager une telle initiative en la mettant au service de la réhabilitation des quartiers d'habitat spontané. L'Etat devrait pouvoir résoudre en leur faveur et en priorité le problème foncier et améliorer l'infrastructure générale. Il devrait encourager la population à s'associer et à renouer avec ses traditions culturelles qui exaltent l'autoconstruction individuelle ou collective.

(c) Pour aborder correctement le problème du logement populaire, il faut abandonner la logique économique conventionnelle qui a été à l'origine de tant de déboires et qui a conduit à l'impasse, comme nous l'avions montré dans ce travail.

On le sait, dans le cadre de cette logique le problème du logement social était posé en termes de besoins définis à partir de normes de construction préétablies (souvent inspirées d'un système normatif étranger), et de coûts de construction dérivés du marché officiel de la promotion publique ou privée. Ces besoins définis de manière aliénée se révélaient évidemment inadéquats avec la solvabilité des ménages car ils induisaient des coûts insupportables même par l'Etat.

Nous proposons au contraire d'inverser la logique conventionnelle; de partir des revenus des ménages en tant que contrainte et de la culture nationale en tant qu'identité et matrice de modèles pour déterminer ainsi des profils de logement adaptés aux populations concernées.

(d) Un programme d'habitat populaire viable est indissociable d'un modèle de développement populaire. Il est impératif, par exemple, que les programmes de logement social dans les quartiers pauvres soient articulés en même temps à la promotion du petit commerce, des petites entreprises locales et de la main-d'oeuvre local prioritairement.

Or, malheureusement l'expérience montre que ces programmes sont souvent réalisés à travers des appels d'offre internationaux, impliquant de ce fait des garanties financières élevées, des cautions bancaires, une inscription sur les registres de commerce, etc., autant de garanties que les petits tâcherons locaux ne possèdent pas. Ce qui induit des coûts de production trop élevés et éloignent les chances d'un développement local intégré.

(e) Pour être viables et constituer des instruments efficaces d'équilibre social général, l'aménagement urbain et la planification urbaine devraient prendre en charge et intégrer l'habitat spontané dans la dynamique de développement urbain global.

Il est vrai que l'habitat spontané est apparu jusqu'ici comme un facteur de distorsion des plans officiels d'aménagement urbain. Une telle distorsion n'est pas accidentelle; elle est au contraire due au fait que l'habitat spontané considéré par les techno-bureaucrates comme illégal a été de ce fait exclu de l'urbanisation institutionnelle ou planifiée. Il existe ainsi comme une contradiction ou une incompatibilité structurelle entre ce type d'habitat et la planification urbaine conventionnelle.

Nous pensons qu'il est grand temps de dépasser cette contradiction en surmontant la *dichotomie ville-légale* et *ville réelle* et de reconnaître à tous les citoyens *le droit à la ville*.

Dans cette perspective nous pensons que seule une politique associative, communale et autogestionnaire peut constituer une stratégie alternative de promotion de l'habitat populaire, expression d'un modèle global de développement populaire.

C'est-à-dire qu'aujourd'hui la *rive sud de la Méditerranée* a autant besoin sinon plus d'imagination politique que la rive nord pour concevoir une véritable renaissance des formes de développement.

## L'ETAT ET LES MASSES URBAINES DEFAVORISEES: UN DIAGNOSTIC POLITIQUE

Qui sont en fait ces néo-citadins? Comment se définissent-ils, et quelle est la nature profonde de leurs revendications? D'autre part, comment l'Etat les définit-il lui-même, et quelle est la finalité de sa stratégie à leur égard?

On sait que la recherche urbaine est dominée par deux tendances théoriques principales, celle qui réduit la question urbaine à une dimension écologique et à une mécanique de fonctions et d'organisations intégratrices, par contraste avec l'école néo-Marxiste qui soutient que les acteurs sociaux urbains défavorisés et leurs mouvements sociaux s'inscrivent essentiellement dans le champ politique et sont de ce fait irréductibles à une réalité écologique (Castells, 1971; Roberts, 1978).

En fait les appellations euphémiques comme celles d'habitat spontané ou illégal, établissements humains marginaux ou encore secteur d'habitat informel, cherchent à occulter le véritable problème, celui de l'existence au coeur même de la cité et à ses alentours immédiats, de larges masses populaires plus ou moins récemment urbanisés vivant dans des conditions de misère évidente et constituant virtuellement des forces sociales et politiques capables de peser sur le système social dans son ensemble et de le remettre en cause de façon chronique.

## LES ORIGINES DE LA RENCONTRE ENTRE LES APPAREILS D'ETAT ET LES MASSES URBAINES DEFAVORISEES

Aussi est-il important de cerner de façon pertinente l'état de la question urbaine et d'évaluer sa gravité et sa signification socio-politique profonde dans des sociétés en transition comme la Tunisie.

Le point de départ consiste à recueillir les éléments essentiels qui sont à l'origine de 'l'illégalité' de tels établissements humains et à partir desquels se structurent des mouvements sociaux urbains. Les adjectifs euphémiques signalés plus haut et destinés à désigner ces populations occultent en réalité les dénominations données par ces populations elles-mêmes aux lieux qu'ils occupent et que l'on peut synthétiser par l'expression 'enclave urbaine de pauvreté'.

L'adjectif 'illégal' pour désigner ce type d'habitat est certainement le plus révélateur. Il nous place d'emblées au coeur du statut du sol urbain et de son appropriation privée. Il désigne l'importance de la rente foncière dans le mode de production capitaliste. La possession privative du sol urbain s'inscrit à la base d'un ensemble de contradictions, expression des revendications des populations (logement, services, etc.) en conflit avec les 'hauteurs rigides' de l'Etat.

De sorte qu'à partir du statut privé de l'appropriation du sol urbain ces populations sont confrontées sur un mode conflictuel ou réel à l'Etat. C'est l'origine de la rencontre Etat–masses urbaines défavorisées. En effet l'appareil étatique est ce à quoi, au sens strict du terme, s'affrontent ces populations dès l'origine de leur implantation à la périphérie de la cité.

Les fonctions économiques et idéologico-politiques de l'Etat en font le garant du système social total. Sa fonction économique oblige l'Etat à garantir l'inviolabilité des lois qui régissent l'occupation du sol urbain (étatique ou privé) et qui garantissent le loyer capitaliste. D'autre part, la fonction idéologico-politique de l'Etat en fait le garant de l'unité et de la cohésion du 'tout social'. L'Etat cherche de plus en plus à encadrer une population perçue comme pouvant remettre en cause non seulement 'l'ordre urbain', mais aussi et surtout l'équilibre social défié par une population 'envahisseuse' qui, pour satisfaire ses revendications se met, tantôt passivement tantôt sous forme d'affrontement, en marge des principes juridiques établis.

## QUI SONT LES MASSES URBAINES DEFAVORISEES?

Après avoir établi que les masses néo-citadines occupaient le 'centre urbain de la pauvreté' et étaient considérées comme des 'envahisseuses illégales', essayons à présent d'évaluer les chances qui permettraient à ces 'masses' de constituer une véritable force politique.

Peut-on affirmer que les mouvements sociaux urbains sont l'expression de contradictions secondaires nées de revendications spatio-matérielles (secteur de la consommation de logement, de services, etc.) et de ce fait ne peuvent en aucun cas mettre en cause ni le modèle de développement dont ils sont l'expression ni la domination de classes ou fractions hégémoniques qui contrôlent un tel modèle?

Ou bien au contraire, de tels mouvements qui s'enracinent dans des revendications 'urbaines' finissent-ils par accèder à un 'niveau de généralité des objectifs et de potentialités politiques qui peuvent virtuellement modifier les relations de pouvoir' (Nun *et al.*, 1972; Ikonitoff et Sigal, 1983).

En fait, le profil des revendications dépend de plusieurs variables: forme d'organisation des populations, forme d'articulation au procès de production et degré de qualification, type d'alliance au noyau ouvrier organisé, degré de maturité politique. . . L'aptitude de l'Etat à provoquer, accepter ou réprimer de telles revendications est elle-même fonction des formes de lutte en même temps que de contradictions internes à la classe dirigeante.

Il s'en faut cependant pour que ces masses néo-citadines accèdent au statut politique et acquièrent une identité de classe univoque.

Au fond la revendication commune à tous ceux qui occupent la périphérie urbaine (en dehors de l'emploi) est une revendication de consommation (logement, équipement collectif, transport, etc.). Or la sphère de la consommation dans un mode de production capitaliste périphérique divise plus qu'elle n'unifie, elle effrite plus qu'elle ne rassemble car dans 'les rapports de production capitaliste l'individu est l'unité par excellence et la concurrence la forme de rapport de base' (Poulantzas, 1972).

D'autre part, étant donné que dans une économie d'enclave le processus d'industrialisation reste limité, les tendances à l'effritement et à la désagrégation des masses néo-citadines ne sont même pas compensées par la socialisation que les grandes unités de production industrielles induisent généralement.

De sorte que pendant longtemps encore les masses récemment urbanisées et insuffisamment intégrées à l'appareil de production avancé risquent de s'identifier négativement par rapport à l'Etat, à travers la précarité de leurs conditions générales et par contraste avec les privilégiés et leur consommation ostentatoire.

A défaut d'être socialisées au contact de la technologie avancée porteuse d'une nouvelle symbolique sociale et culturelle, elles le seront à travers les circuits économiques 'traditionnels' et seront logiquement pris en charge par la symbolique 'traditionnelle' même à l'état résiduel et dégradé. De ce fait elles constituent volontiers la base d'appui des idéologies adverses à l'idéologie dominante.

Et la 'retraditionalisation' peut constituer à l'avenir une arme de défense – retrograde et passéiste – des 'exclus' du développement périphérique et dépendant (Stambouli, 1980)!

## NOTES

1   McGee, 1968. La notion d'involution urbaine est employée ici dans le sens d'une pseudo-urbanisation qui n'est pas l'expression d'un développement économique soutenu et équilibré.

2   Les matériaux de construction et la force de travail ont augmenté d'un indice 100 en 1973 à 246 au début de 1981, soit un accroissement annuel de 13,76 pour cent. Signalons aussi que le taux des loyers est trop élevé en dépit du blocage officiel des loyers depuis les années 70 à ce jour.

3   'La cité populaire Ettadhamen ou la ruée vers l'Ouest', L'Avenir, 30 juillet 1983.

4   Le montant global des prêts de la BIRD dans le secteur de la réhabilitation urbaine est de 125 millions de dollars.

## REFERENCES

Bellalouna, R. 1980. L'habitat spontané et les formules alternatives de production du logement social. District de Tunis.

BIRD. 1982. Tunisia: housing sector review. World Bank, June.

Castells, M. 1971. La question urbaine. Paris: Maspero.

COLLECTIF. 1980. Tunis: evolution et fonctionnement de l'espace urbain. Paris et Tours.

GROUPE HUIT. 1973a. Les villes en Tunisie. Tunis: Ministère de l'équipement.

—— 1973b. Villes et développement: armature urbaine Tunisienne.

—— 1978. Réhabilitation des quartiers de Jebel Lahmar et Saïda Manoubia.

Hardoy, J. E. and Satterthwaite, D. 1986. 'Urban change in the Third World', Habitat International, 10(3), pp. 33–52.

Ikoncoff, M. et Sigal, S. 1983. 'Armée de réserve, marginalité et secteur

informel: le rôle de l'Etat', dans *Emerging Development Patterns*. Vienna: EADI.
Institut National de la Statistique. 1975. *Recensement général de la population et des logements*. Volume II. Tunis.
—— 1980. *Enquête population-emploi 1980: les conditions d'habitat en Tunisie*: Tunis: Directions.
McGee, T. 1968. 'A theory of urban involution', *Civilisations*, 3.
Morched, C. 1976. *Population, revenus et systèmes d'habitat à Tunis*. District de Tunis.
—— 1978. 'Evolution et croissance du grand Tunis', *Art, Architecture et Aménagement*, 1.
Municipalité de Tunis. 1978. *Réhabilitation de Mellassine: enquêtes socio-économiques*. Tunis.
Nun, J., Quijano, A. et Singer, P. 1972. *Urbanisation, dépendence et marginalité en Amérique latine*. São Paulo: CEBRAP.
Roberts, B. R. 1978. *Cities of Peasants*. London: Edward Arnold.
Stambouli, F. 1977. 'Urbanisation difforme et émergence d'une nouvelle société urbaine au Maghreb', *Les Temps Modernes*, octobre.
—— 1980. 'Aspects of urban immigrant society in the Maghreb', dans H. A. B. Rivlin et K. Kelmer (eds.), *The Changing Middle Eastern City*. Binghamton: State University of New York Press.
USAID. 1979a. *Programme d'aménagement intégré pour les quartiers de Mellasine à Tunis*. Préparé par Louis Berger International.
—— 1979b. *Tunisia Shelter Sector Analysis*.
—— 1980. *Shelter Upgrading Seminar*. Tunis.
Waltz, S. 1982. *Women and Shelter in Tunisia: report to Resources for Action*. USAID.

## SUMMARY

This chapter focuses on the issue of housing the urban poor in the city of Tunis. After a historical overview of the context in which the urbanisation process of Tunis city took place, delineating the 'dependent' character of such an urbanisation profile, which has led to an acute urban crisis, the chapter analyses national housing policy and its limitations on the issue of housing the urban poor. The study shows that 40 per cent of the total housing production in Tunis has an 'underground' or 'informal' character. This is a vivid expression of the widening gap between housing offer and demand, whereby 75 per cent of state-aided housing construction is not affordable in low-income households.

# RESIDENTIAL URBAN LAND MARKETS IN KENYA

An African who wishes to build a house can hope to obtain a piece of land in an urban area has four routes open to him. He can approach the local chief or king's representative for allocation of a plot from communal reserves, he can take advantage of government schemes to distribute serviced land for housing purposes, he can buy or lease the land in the open market, or he can build illegally on someone else's land, be it public or private. These methods all apply in varying degrees of relevance to most African countries. In Azera and Mbabane, for instance, all four methods described are valid modes of operation. And where there would be no chief and land is state-owned in Addis Ababa or Dar es Salaam, private transactions still take place and squatters prosper.

All four methods cater for the rich as well as the poor. In fact it is easier for the rich to squat than the poor. The likelihood of success in securing a plot is therefore dependent only partly on the ability to pay and largely on social connections, daring, and allegiance to the right leaders. It is necessary to understand this situation when analysing urban land markets. In this chapter I shall examine the conditions prevailing in a particular African country, Kenya, with a view to identifying the various arenas in which market activity takes place and the major trends of which one should take note. Kenya is one of the many African countries where there is a mixture of public, private and communal ownership of land. Within these three broad categories there are numerous combinations, permutations and deviations into unorthodox forms of tenure. Transactions in land rights take place over the whole spectrum.

## RESIDENTIAL LAND MARKETS IN KENYA

About 9,300 residential sites or plots are created annually. Of these only a tenth are plots allocated by the Commissioner of Lands, the National Housing Corporation, Nairobi City Council and other local authorities. The remainder are the result of private-sector efforts, much of them (2,300 plots) illegal, in the form of squatting and unlawful sub-division. That is, the private sector manages to find something like 4,000 plots a year through the sub-division of land already in private hands.[1] This land falls into two major categories. First there are the peri-urban tracts of agricultural land which are being converted to urban use. And secondly one finds 'infill' schemes in the suburbs of the larger cities where the authorities have re-zoned the land to higher densities. For example, the latter method has been a major source of new legal plots over the last few years, with re-zoning of most of the high-income neighbourhoods in the western part of the city. Private-sector sub-divisions create only a few new plots at a time. For example in 1980, less than 10 per cent (20 out of 230) of the sub-division applications approved by Nairobi City Council created ten sub-plots or more. Two-fifths of new private plots were created in the outer western suburbs such as Langata, Karen, Dagoretti and Riruta.

The processes of zoning more residential land and of approving sub-divisions are therefore important in making land available to private developers. In both cases there are severe bottlenecks both at local and national level which encourage squatting and illegal sub-division. (The Kenyan requirements for urban residential land are shown in Table 8.1.) That is, nearly 5,000 ha. of land will have been converted to residential use in the period 1980–85, much of it illegally. The figures also show that the government is not doing enough to release land for private development. Either too much land is allocated to a few individuals as has been the case in Nairobi in recent years, and those individuals 'sit on it' for speculative purposes without any beneficial development taking place, or too little is made available in some towns. In other words, there is no land development programme or project pipeline aimed at releasing adequate land in the right locations over a period of time. There are six main reasons for this deficiency:

(a) The Lands Department is very well endowed to deal with the legal,

Table 8.1
Annual residential land requirements, Kenya, 1982–86

| | Kenya | | Nairobi | |
|---|---|---|---|---|
| | DUs | Land (ha.) | DUs | Land (ha.) |
| Government, parastatals, local authorities | 3,000 | 75 | 2,000 | 50 |
| Private authorised | 4,000 | 400 | 2,500 | 250 |
| Private unauthorised | 2,300 | 460 | 1,000 | 200 |
| Total | | 935 | | 500 |

Source: Author's estimates.

valuation and administrative aspects of land; it is not designed to cope with the problems of long-term planning and land budgeting, or with the complexities of land-use forecasting. That function is the province of the Physical Planning Department, where it is very low on the list of departmental priorities. In the sense that the Housing Department in the central government has its own housing planners, it is also necessary for the Lands Department to have in-house planning expertise.

(b) Because of the institutional difficulties described above there is a methodological blind spot in that the general feeling among experts is that land data do not exist or are hard to come by, whereas in fact there is an untapped wealth of information in the valuation rolls, land registers, land control board minutes, local authority minutes, planning reports and other official sources which could be used to form the basis of reliable forecasts.

(c) The vagaries of the government's budgeting process make both the Lands Department and the local authorities reluctant to formulate a long-term land development programme when they are not certain whether the money to purchase and service land will be forthcoming or not.

(d) Any long-term plans have to be synchronised with the wishes of the local authority and the government has no power to make a local authority co-operate if it does not want to. Ordinarily the initiative comes from local councils which are inundated with applications for plots and are threatened by illegal development.

The failure of the Lands Department to formulate a nation-wide land allocation programme is also partly a reflection of the Commissioner of Lands's traditional role as the custodian of government land, of which there used to be plenty, and which he used to 'alienate' as and when needed for the public good. Virgin land used to be alienated to settlers for development. The normal method is to advertise the plots in the *Kenya Gazette* and invite applications from eligible candidates. Special requests for large blocks of land may, however, be made direct to the Commissioner, and these are considered on their merit. That is how large-scale residential developers sometimes obtain land.

(e) It has proved difficult for the Lands Department and local authorities to enforce the development covenant which requires the lessees to develop the land within a stipulated time period, usually two years. Repossession is a tedious and politically sensitive process, and plots change hands at market prices which are considerably higher than that paid to the government.

(f) Plots are sometimes allocated but the government then takes a long time to lay on any services, largely owing to financial constraints. This has happened on several sites for high-cost housing in Nairobi.

Table 8.2

Urban plots allocated by the Commissioner of Lands, Kenya, July 1977 – June 1980

| Period | Total | Residential | Business/Residential | Industrial | Educational | Religious | Other |
|---|---|---|---|---|---|---|---|
| July 1977 – June 1978 | 1,069 | 548 | 332 | 141 | 14 | 9 | 25 |
|  | 100% | 51·3% | 31·1% | 13·2% | 1·3% | 0·8% | 2·3% |
| July 1978 – June 1979 | 1,225 | 761 | 135 | 280 | 18 | 12 | 19 |
|  | 100% | 62·1% | 11·0% | 22·9% | 1·5% | 1·0% | 1·5% |
| July 1979 – June 1980 | 2,379[a] | 1,711 | 369 | 222 | 22 | 28 | 45 |
|  | 100% | 71·4% | 15·4% | 9·3% | 0·9% | 1·2% | 1·8% |
| 3-year total | 4,691 | 3,020 | 836 | 643 | 54 | 49 | 89 |
|  | 100% | 64·4% | 17·8% | 13·7% | 1·2% | 1·0% | 1·9% |

Source: Commissioner of Lands' monthly reports.
Note (a) includes 1,176 plots allocated at Dandora.

The Commissioner of Lands is therefore not only seriously constrained by the dwindling sources of government land, but also by lack of financial resources. This is where the private sector could assist. Land could be released in large blocks to individuals or groups who would then be required to plan, service and distribute it in a mutually agreed manner. Private resources would be used to finance the servicing of the land. That is, some of the powers now enjoyed by the Commissioner of Lands, the Director of Physical Planning and the local authorities would be devolved to private citizens and professionals. There is sufficient development control expertise in the country to make it possible for the market, mainly through the well-established leasehold system, to relieve the government of much of the routine work involved in land management.

The Commissioner of Lands estimates that there are about 20,000 acres of uncommitted public land in urban areas. Although this is not much, if nurtured carefully it may go a long way towards easing the problems that are likely to arise within the next decade.

The majority of plots allocated by the Commissioner of Lands are residential; about four-fifths of the plots allocated in the three-year period from July 1977 to June 1980 were residential or mixed commercial and residential (see Table 8·2). Mixed-use plots are more predominant in the smaller towns than in Nairobi, for no apparent reason. In terms of area the figures in Table 8·3 also indicate that the amount of land allocated for housing is relatively

Table 8.3

Urban plots released for development by the Commissioner of Lands, Kenya, January 1980 – April 1982

| Year | Residential | Commercial | Industrial | Others | Total |
|------|-------------|------------|------------|--------|-------|
| 1980 | 43·85 | 9·51 | 14·62 | 3·59 | 71·93 |
| 1981 | 34·97 | 6·25 | 8·43 | 2·20 | 51·85 |
| 1982 | 48·85 | 14·50 | 14·95 | 8·50 | 86·80 |
| Total | 127·67 | 30·26 | 38·0 | 14·65 | 210·58 |

| Percentage of total plots released | | | |
|---|---|---|---|
| | 1980 | 1981 | 1982 |
| Residential | 60·90 | 67·44 | 56·27 |
| Commercial | 13·22 | 12·05 | 16·70 |
| Industrial | 20·32 | 16·25 | 17·22 |
| Others | 5·49 | 4·24 | 9·79 |
| Total | 100 | 100 | 100 |

*Source: Kenya Gazette.*

insignificant, for example 34·97 ha. in 1981 as compared to the estimated need of 860 ha.!

In addition to its slow pace and weak impact the alienation process is encumbered by the following disadvantages:

(a) The plots are allocated on terms that are too favourable from the purchaser's point of view. The plot premium and annual land rent are calculated on the basis of actual cost to the government. Typically, the premium would be a fifth of the total cost and the rest would be amortised over twenty years (i.e. at 5 per cent). There is certainly potential here for raising extra revenue for the state.

(b) The prospect of obtaining a cheap plot from the government results in intense competition for the plots whenever they are advertised. Competition and irregularities are therefore unavoidable. The government ruled in 1980 that all land allocation committees should be chaired by the District/Provincial Commissioner.[2] The confidence and credibility of the officials traditionally responsible for land allocation have been severely shaken.

## ARENAS

The alienation of government land, the adjudication of communal lands, and the granting of sub-division approval to private landowners help to bring more·plots on to the market and increase the pool of plots available to dealers – landowners, tenants, lenders, brokers and so on. This is important because it is necessary to maintain a balance between the volume of money invested in real estate and the quantity of available plots. Mortgages are tied to particular identified sites. An expansion of the pool of plots therefore not only creates new opportunities for investment of private funds, but it also increases the number of landlords, developers and entrepreneurs. Their activities are sustained by the enhanced access to credit that their title gives them, and by the promise of huge profits through capital appreciation. We know that investors are prepared to accept low yields to start with in expectation of rapid increases in capital value. That expectation is based on recent experience. Between the late sixties and 1981, for example, land prices in Nairobi rose on average by 20 per cent a year. The post-independence recovery began in 1968, since when land and house prices have risen steadily. A 5,000 sq. m. plot in Eastleigh that sold for 15,000s now changes hands at 100,000s. The price of serviced land in selected locations in Nairobi is shown in Table 8·4. (The same data are presented differently in Figure 8·1.) It is quite clear that land in the poorer eastern neighbourhoods is not necessarily cheaper than in the richer ones. On the contrary, some of the exclusive neighbourhoods show lower figures per unit area because of lower densities. For large portions of the city the price per residential site –

Table 8.4
Price of serviced land in selected locations in Nairobi, March 1982

| Location | Price ('000s per acre) |
| --- | --- |
| Dandora | 240 |
| Umoja | 200 |
| Buru Buru | 300 |
| Karen/Langata | 86 |
| Ngei | 350 |
| Dagoretti | 140 |
| Kangemi | 110 |
| Loresho | 580 |
| Lower Kabete | 600 |
| Westlands | 580–740 |
| Lavington | 600 |
| Parklands | 1,200 |
| Kitisuru | 600 |
| Ridgeways | 400 |
| Ruaraka | 200 |

irrespective of size – tends to be constant, since the zoning laws are very strict in limiting the number of dwellings that can be erected on a plot.

Indicative figures of land values in the smaller towns are given in Table 8·5.

It seems that the critical determinants of what a developer is prepared to pay for a piece of land are location, type of zoning, and quality of services. Characteristics such as soil type, slope and view are marginal. In the peri-urban areas the possible, rather than would-be, development is an important consideration, and huge sums are paid for agricultural land in anticipation of urban development and capital appreciation. Thus agricultural land in the rural–urban fringe outside the bigger towns would sell at anything up to 20,000s per acre.

The main sub-markets for urban residential land can be categorised as follows:

(a) Smallholdings at the edge of town which are accessible to individuals for occupation and/or speculation.

(b) Shares in a large farm bought by a co-operative or land company for the benefit of its members, who are not necessarily farmers. Examples abound in the main towns.

(c) The right to build on somebody else's land, which confers on the developer the right to own the building but not the land. Such transactions are common in Mombasa and other coastal towns. For example in Kisauni one can purchase a site for 3,000s and a monthly ground rent of 10s. This is a traditional arrangement which is even more efficient than site and service schemes.

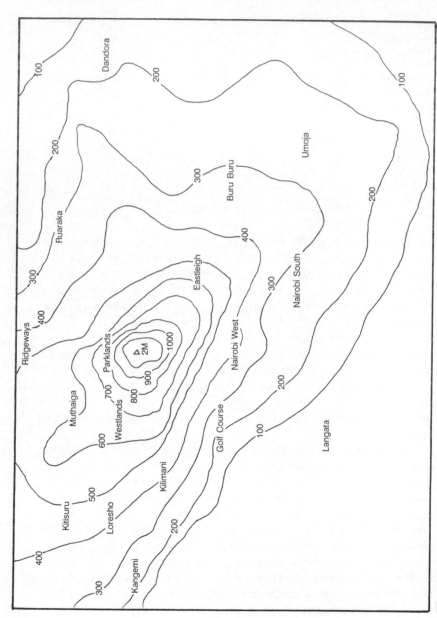

Figure 8.1 Land values in Nairobi, mid-1982 (*'000s* per acre)

Table 8.5
Selective average land values, Kenyan townships, 1982

| Location | Use | Value ('000s per acre) | Remarks |
|---|---|---|---|
| Embu | Commercial | 500 | |
| | Agricultural | 8 | |
| Tithunguri | Agricultural | 20 | Kiambu District |
| Kiambu | Residential | 100 | Municipality Area |
| Kiambaa | Residential | 200 | Kiambu District |
| Kiambu | Agricultural | 70 | |
| Nanyuki | Residential | 65 | |
| Nakuru | Residential | 150 | Nakuru West |
| | Residential | 100 | Milimani |
| | Agricultural | 12 | Lanet |
| Nyandarua | Agricultural | 7 | |
| Ngong | Residential | 120 | Township |
| Ongata-Rongai | Residential | 96 | |
| Thika | Residential | 300 | |
| | Industrial | 20 | |
| Sigona | Residential | 120 | |
| Londiani | Residential | 10 | |
| Malindi | Residential | 200 | Beach plot |
| Msambweni | Residential | 180 | Beach plot |
| Diani | Residential | 90 | Beach plot |
| Kilifi | Residential | 80 | Beach plot |
| Kwale | Agricultural | 26 | |
| Chuka (Meru) | Agricultural | 3 | |
| Meru | Residential | 140 | Municipality |

(d) Site and service schemes which do not really constitute a market since the participants are carefully pre-selected and their choices as to how they should develop the plots are also restricted. Nonetheless, because of the volume of transactions and the presence of clandestine resales of plots, it is a factor to be reckoned with.

(e) Official sub-divisions by the Commissioner of Lands and local authorities for medium and low-density development. As we have already seen, this is a token measure which has no real impact on the demand for urban plots.

(f) Inner-city infill plots and redevelopment sites where a developer sees the opportunity of putting up a few additional units either by utilising an existing vacant plot, sub-dividing an already developed plot, or demolishing an old house and rebuilding at a higher density. Such plots are generally small, very expensive and hard to come by.

Transactions in large tracts of urban land for private development by corporate developers are the exception rather than the rule. Such developers have found it more profitable to utilise government land.

Lack of space prohibits us from discussing in greater detail the operations of each of the above markets and who operates where. However it is worthwhile examining the prevalent modes of land development and the possible areas in which the private and public sectors could co-operate.

## ALTERNATIVE LAND DEVELOPMENT STEPS

The *de facto* sub-division, servicing and distribution of land is carried out much more quickly by the private sector than by the public, in spite of the vast array of controls imposed by planning, building and title regulations. This is the one lesson that can be learned from the many settlements springing up on the periphery of the main towns. The reason for the speed is not only the urge to settle and build, but also the ability on the part of these developers to devise short-cuts and simple solutions that evade or short-circuit the official procedures.

In the private sector, an important phenomenon is the voluntary collectivisation of land development efforts in the form of limited liability companies and landowning co-operatives on prime land in the squatter colonies and rural urban fringes. This situation is discernible in many large and medium-sized towns in the scheduled areas (i.e. Nakuru and Eldoret in the former white highlands) where there are no small-holdings, and the only way an ordinary Kenyan can own a farm is to join with colleagues to form a co-operative or limited liability company.

In Nairobi such companies abound in Mathare Valley, Kariobangi, Kasarani and other areas. A recent survey in Mathare has shown that 45 per cent of the landowners in the valley are either companies or co-operatives; the latter control 62 ha. of the 152 ha. of registered land in the valley.

Although the majority of the members of land development groups are simple folk, the leaders are invariably influential and well-informed politicians or businessmen who have access to sophisticated professional services – legal, planning, valuation and accounting – in Nairobi and other major towns. Whereas this development makes life more difficult for the authorities, say, in land acquisition, it does make for order and rationality in land conversion and development. Landowning companies have from time to time used reputable planning and architectural firms for subdivision and the preparation of development plans.

The companies and co-operatives proliferated in the late 1960s and early in the subsequent decade when the departing white settlers and Asians were selling their land and the government was encouraging indigenous Kenyans to buy these farms. Since there were few Africans who could raise sufficient capital to purchase one of these large farms, and subdivision was restricted by law, it was a good opportunity for *ad hoc* groups to be formed specifically for this purpose. Enterprising politicians saw this as an opportunity to mobilise support, since company membership can vary from a few dozen to several thousand shareholders. Some of them, like the Nakuru-based Mutukanio–Ngwataniro Farmers' Co. Ltd, have grown into conglomerates owning numerous farms in various parts of the country.

Both models, i.e. the limited liability company and the co-operative, have their inherent merits and demerits. For instance, companies have a much wider scope for commercial activity than co-operatives, which are kept under close surveillance by the Ministry of Cooperative Development under the Cooperative Act. Limited liability is an added advantage, while access to credit is easier. Tax laws are, however, more favourably inclined towards co-operatives. Whereas both companies and co-operatives are engaged in farming activities, in the urban areas companies tend to predominate.

It is not known how much land in the country is controlled by such incorporated bodies. However cases of fraud are worrying the government. When addressing a co-operative society in Kiambu in June 1981 an Assistant Minister for Urban Development and Housing requested directors and committee members of land-buying companies not to collect money before acquiring the land. There had been many cases in the past of ordinary folk being swindled by company directors and leaders.[3] Similar sentiments had earlier been expressed by the President at a fund-raising meeting in aid of a church at Kikuyu.[4]

The actual process of transferring land-occupancy rights from the company/co-operative to the individual member will not be discussed here. What ought to be regarded as an issue is the emergence of a large number of individuals who have a valid claim on a piece of land by virtue of being members of a particular co-operative company, but have no specific title to the land they occupy and develop. There is clearly room here for alternative types of tenure to develop. For instance condominium-type titles evolved in North America, Australia and other countries under similar circumstances where it became necessary to distinguish between the rights of the individual and those of the group to which he belongs. Within Kenya the Sectional Titles Act has recently been passed to fill that gap.

## COLLECTIVE ACTION

The companies and co-operatives epitomise private initiative which exhibits the following positive qualities as opposed to official site and service efforts:

(a) Quick execution, in that the landowning company or individual wastes very little time in deciding on layout, siting of buildings, choice of advisers and contractor, assembly of materials and commencement of

construction.
(b) Flexibility in the development process; for example one can build before laying on services; occupy the building before completion; transfer before surveying; plan and sub-divide after some structures have already been erected.
(c) Variability in the standard of services provided; the quality of infrastructure can be improved gradually as resources permit rather than as the law requires.
(e) Community involvement in the choice of affordable and possible alternatives.
(f) Political strength deriving from sheer numbers; this enables effective negotiation with the local authority on various matters affecting their development proposals.
(g) Commercial identity resulting from incorporation; this not only improves access to financial markets but also makes it possible, given efficient organisation and competent leadership, for the group to raise more funds internally, disburse loans, collect repayments and perform other routine functions.

The landowning companies and co-operatives assist the public sector by not only releasing more plots at reasonable cost but also by supervising the development carried out by the members. Professional advice is available in the market and often used. In fact there are several firms of planners, architects and surveyors which specialise in this type of work. However, more expertise is needed, and a technical assistance programme prepared by the government and/or local authorities would be welcome.

Examples of such companies may be found in many towns. For instance in the Rift Valley there are several such companies. Typically a group will have purchased a large farm from a settler on a 999-year lease. The farm is then sub-divided illegally into individual plots ranging in size from $21 \times 45$ m. to $55 \times 65$ m. The members build houses and occupy them, or some may be non-resident and allow tenants to build on their plots. Some build houses and let them out themselves to tenants. The major problems encountered by such groups are:
(a) Difficulty in obtaining sub-division and change of use approval from the Commissioner of Lands and local authority. The Commissioner of Lands is trying to deal with this problem by allowing as many sub-division applications as possible. He reports that about 200 applicants are considered every quarter.[5]
(b) Poor leadership, resulting in bad organisation and loss of funds through mismanagement.

## LAND USE CONTROLS

The legal and administrative hurdles that hinder private initiatives are briefly as follows:

(a) Zoning as practised by the planning departments and the central government Physical Planning Department. There is a development plan for each town which specifies the land uses, plot sizes and development densities.
(b) The building code, which regulates plot sizes, setbacks, wayleaves, etc.
(c) Sub-division control as required by not only planning legislation but also by the Land Control Act, which restricts change of use and transfers in agricultural land.
(d) Restrictive covenants that apply to leasehold land and restrict such matters as sale, change of use, development, sub-letting, extensions and renovations, and so on.

Nonetheless a well-run control mechanism can be advantageous to the private sector. These advantages include:

(a) Stability in the land market.
(b) Certainty by the investor that the quality of the surroundings will be maintained.
(c) The ability to forecast movement in land prices.
(d) Efficiency in the management of land use and complimentarity of functions.
(e) The preservation of resources and the environment, from which the private sector stands to benefit, e.g. fresh water, clean air, open spaces, etc.
(f) The control of squatting in specific areas.

Thus land-use controls should be used to assist the private sector and not hinder its growth.

The urban planning process is an important aspect of urban land policy in that it introduces a reasonably stable environment in which land-use decisions and market transactions can take place. The development plan or structure plan attempts to ensure that each parcel of land is used or reserved for the best use in the community's interest. The local authorities can also programme their investment in infrastructure with some degree of certainty. On the other hand, however, stability, accurate data and reliable forecasts encourage land speculation.

Planning also makes land acquisition more difficult, although it must be remembered that land acquisition is a mere tool, not a goal in itself.

## LAND ACQUISITION

Public land acquisition is an important tool for regulating the supply of residential land. Land acquisition legislation in Kenya is clear and specific. The government has often used it to acquire land for public purposes. Indeed the one major obstacle, as far as the private sector is concerned, is that the Land Acquisition Act defines public purpose in a very precise manner, which does not include the acquisition of land so as to give it someone else to develop, while the Constitution is quite specific in its provisions safeguarding the right to property. There have been several controversial cases recently where land was allegedly acquired for one purpose but was subsequently used for another. If there were no such controls the possibilities for abuse of the land acquisition powers would increase.

In any case housing has never featured as a major beneficiary of the Commissioner of Lands' powers to acquire land compulsorily for the government as well as for the local authorities. Over the period 1980–83 only 23,727 ha. were acquired for housing, representing 0·1 per cent of all land acquired during that period. However in the six-year period 1974–79, about 7,931 ha. had been acquired for housing[6]. The drastic reduction in the acreage acquired indicates the difficulties being experienced by the Kenyan government, especially in the form of popular opposition to acquisition resettlement problems, and budgetary constraints.

Although it is unlikely that the Kenyan government will acquire land for private development of housing on a large scale – apart from the site and service schemes – it can play an important role in providing land for public facilities such as schools, clinics and open spaces which support housing development.

It is apparent therefore that the Lands Department and local authorities will have to take new initiatives in putting together development schemes in partnership with private landowners.


## PROPERTY TAXES

All landowners in urban areas, including the government, have to pay rates, which are based on the market value of unimproved land. That is, only the land is taxed, not the buildings, although to the property owner this distinction is academic. Nairobi and Mombasa prepare their own valuation rolls (assessment lists) and the Commissioner of Lands does so for the smaller towns.

Landowners have protested vehemently against the new valuation rolls introduced in 1980–83 for Nairobi and Mombasa, both of which have resulted in numerous increases in assessments. The Nairobi roll has finally been adopted, after a long and acrimonious debate both with the government and in the media. Approval of the Mombasa roll took a long time; in the meantime local property-owners, the business community and parliamentarians made repeated representations to the Kenyan government to get the roll annulled. Both valuation rolls came at a rather difficult time when the councils desperately needed additional revenue, but property-owners themselves were experiencing financial difficulties in a harsh economic climate, with rents remaining stagnant, development credit scarce and expensive, and construction costs rising relatively fast. The immediate impact of the new rates was therefore dramatic, but over time there is no doubt that the market will be able to absorb these increases quite easily.

Rates are deductible against income tax as an expense. To that extent, then, property-owners enjoy some relief. Nonetheless additional relief could be given by exempting new development from rates during construction and the first two years of occupation. Such a relief would help the developer and new house-owner to reduce costs.

## CONCLUSION

The above discussion highlights the need for some policy and administrative reforms in a number of areas, not only in Kenya but in other African countries where similar situations occur. First the planning machinery and methodologies need to be improved so that they keep pace with actual developments on the ground and with the demand for urban land. Secondly it is important that not only more land is zoned for residential development but that the very concept of zoning is more flexible, especially in relation to standards and plot sizes. It must be recognised that there are areas where development control in the traditional sense is impossible and some functions have to be devolved to the private sector, i.e. the landowners, be they individuals, incorporated bodies or community groups. Thirdly, tenurial changes are necessary to cater for the needs of group members who have an interest either in a piece of land or part of a building. Further, central governments and the local authorities have to devise means of going into partnership with private developers.

The call for innovative tenures which meet social as well as economic objectives is justified on the grounds that existing forms are either ideologically too rigid, pander too much to the dictates of finance houses and donor agencies, or adhere uncompromisingly to the ancient laws and customs of the major African monarchies and chiefdoms. The rampant commercialisation of urban land found in, say, Kenya or Nigeria needs as much restraint as the fierce protection of stool lands (i.e. communal lands administered by chiefs) in Ghana or Swazi Nation Land in Swaziland. Novel solutions will not only guarantee security but also expand the mortgage market, which is now in many countries constrained not so much by the shortage of funds as by the paucity of mortgageable interests. Credit schemes that will finance low-value land transactions between poor people are scarce. Because of the high risks involved such schemes have either to be guaranteed by the government or carry exceedingly high interest rates. Owing to the lack of space it has not been possible to deal with the mortgage market and its relationship, say, with the demand for marketable titles as opposed to land as such.

Also, we have not discussed the resilience of the land market to social and political upheavals such as those experienced in recent years in, say, Uganda, Ghana, Ethiopia and Mozambique. Conditions of social strife and political instability are accompanied by varied responses in the land market. The small and low-priced plots are the most resilient. The demand and supply of building land for the poor are the least sensitive to changes in government or exchange-rate fluctuations.

Market information is pitifully scarce in most African countries. Only a fraction of the transactions are documented and registered. A great deal of revenue is therefore lost. At the same time urban land inventories do not exist. This makes it difficult to forecast with any degree of accuracy future demands for land, nor does it facilitate the largely futile attempts made by various African governments to control land prices and land transactions. Another sensitive point in market operations is the role of the various intermediaries such as land agents, lawyers, valuers, mortgage brokers, surveyors and the phethora of consultants who thrive on the large amounts of money changing hands in property transactions. Some of these intermediaries belong to strong professional institutions protected by statute, and it is often difficult for governments to intervene directly on behalf of the poorer sections of its citizens.

## NOTES

1   These figures are estimates based on the Commissioner of Lands' monthly reports, approved sub-division statistics, Nairobi City Council monthly minutes and National Housing Corporation statistics.

2   This was announced in Parliament by the Hon. G. G. Kariuki on 17 June 1980. The news was greeted with applause by members (*The Standard*, 18 June 1980).

3   *Daily Nation*, 9 June 1981.

4   *The Standard*, 9 February 1981.

5   The President ruled in 1982 that chairmen of farming companies should divide the farms and give plots to their members immediately (*The Nairobi Times*, 27 November 1982).

6   Details of each plot acquired, i.e. date, place and purpose, are available.

## RESUME

Ce chapitre analyse différents types de transactions qui sont pratiquées sur les marchés fonciers résidentiels en Afrique, et tout particulièrement la situation au Kenya. L'histoire, les coutumes, le commerce et la cupidité se mêlent pour produire de nouvelles forces qui risquent de saper les principes fondamentaux sur lesquels reposent les politiques foncières et les pratiques de planification existantes. La planification et les mesures de division de zone se sont avérées totalement inadéquates, à la fois en tant qu'instruments de développement et instruments de contrôle.

Bien que les pauvres jouent un rôle prépondérant dans le marché, ils représentent principalement des consommateurs d'espace urbain qui est fourni soit par les plus affluents ou par les corporations sous la forme de sociétés d'achat foncier ou de coopératives. Ces dernières constituent un puissant groupe de pression qui pourrait menacer les autorités. Les gouvernements trouvent qu'il est plus facile de traiter avec les chefs et autres dirigeants traditionnels qu'avec des groupes bien organisés de locataires, de squatters ou de petits propriétaires. Il est donc probable que les formes traditionnelles de bail foncier fondées sur la propriété communale se perpétuent pendant encore longtemps et de nouvelles techniques de financement devront être développées pour satisfaire ce secteur du marché.

Finalement, le chapitre met en lumière le besoin de voir les querelles sociales, les troubles sociaux et les turbulences économiques comme des évènements réels et fréquents plutôt que comme des phénomènes passagers et intermittents; il rejette brièvement la résistance des marchés fonciers résidentiels à ces conditions.

# SQUATTER LANDLORDS IN NAIROBI:
# A CASE STUDY OF KOROGOCHO

## BACKGROUND

This chapter explores some of the ways in which unplanned urban settlements form and grow in relation to formal and informal systems of land allocation. A general discussion is supported by some limited data gathered in 1980 on Korogocho, a large settlement which grew rapidly at the eastern edge of Nairobi from 1979 onwards.

The rate of population growth in Kenya is the highest in the world, 4 per cent, while the amount of productive land is limited to only one-third of the total. Rural population densities in some high potential areas of Kenya are also extremely high, and equivalent to urban densities. Pressures on rural land under the present system of ownership and methods of production contribute to one of the highest rates of urban growth as well. As in most African countries, after independence there was a flood of migration to the towns as restrictions on population movement were eased. This growth has continued unabated owing to pressure on rural land. The large majority of the population rely on a combination of subsistence agriculture and cash income from limited employment sources.

Urban growth results in the mushrooming of squatter settlements at the edges of towns or on marginal and under-utilised land within towns. This has been a bitter pill for young post-independence governments to swallow. It is hard to adjust to the severe disparity between jobs available and the number of workers, and the urban population's reliance on subsistence and petty commodity production for survival. In the absence of enough national resources to provide urban services, these often get channelled to a privileged few.

African governments, consisting of educated middle-class people, want everybody to have a decent quality of life. But this aspiration emerges as a restriction on low-standard accommodation. At its worst, it leads to demolition of the dwellings of the urban poor while high-standard houses go to the officials themselves. Similarly, governments may harass or at least discourage petty commodity production (otherwise known as the informal sector) because it does not conform with the ideals of the formal private capitalist sector or with state socialism. Nevertheless, poor urban populations continue to support themselves through a combination of subsistence food production, petty commodity production, petty landlordism, and wage-income distribution through kinship networks.

In Nairobi, as in many places, there is a combination of official low-income, urban settlement schemes together with widespread unplanned squatter areas. The site and service approach was officially adopted in the 1970s in Kenya. Upgrading of existing squatter settlements was initiated, with the legalisation of tenure and bringing of services to Kawangware settlement in Nairobi in 1978, but later efforts at upgrading in the capital were aborted. A large effort was made with the Dandora site and service scheme in Nairobi in the period 1976–82. However, in providing accommodation for about 2,500 households per annum during its life, this major project only coped with about a quarter of the annual demand, and production of site and service plots has since slowed down. A large number of households continue to live in unplanned areas, and the size of these grows as Nairobi grows.

## TENANTS IN SQUATTER SETTLEMENTS

The image of the squatter as independent self-builder has tended to obscure the fact that this type of settlement usually has more tenants than owners. Generally, the older the settlement, the higher the ratio of tenants to owners. This is true irrespective of whether there is a private land market or nationalised land; it has to do with the number of buildings and the number of people looking for accommodation. Many poor people who need to move around in search of work prefer to rent rooms. Those who own a structure provide space for others and may continue extending in order to gain more rental income.

Sub-letting in squatter settlements may be particularly widespread where there is a shortage of older housing stock which can be used for rented accommodation. It has been pointed out that squatter settlements grow more rapidly in cities with an absence of an older housing stock (Perlman, 1976). It seems obvious that the pressures towards entrepreneurial growth, and even the creation of completely entrepreneur-built, 'squatter' settlements are great under the same conditions, and in the absence of a policy of legal access to land by low-income groups.

Entrepreneurial activity in squatter settlements is much more widespread than was commonly recognised a decade ago. As has been shown by work in Latin America and by a study of Kibera squatter settlement in

Nairobi (Amis, 1984), the image of the squatter settlement as the home of the self-help builder/owner–occupier needs revision. This image is based on the initial start of the settlement and not on its process of growth and change. In a free land market the original squatters rely on this process of growth through entrepreneurism for their economic improvement while other owners of capital from outside the settlement may also use it as a source of revenue.

The case of Korogocho in Nairobi illustrates this. Githaa, the extension of Korogocho described below, is an example of a completely entrepreneur-built 'squatter' area. Nairobi is a useful case to examine because its present conditions give rise to extensive entrepreneural activity by the private sector in low-income housing. The following case study illustrates some of the processes of formation and growth of an unplanned settlement in a free land market. The operation of informal allocations is also elucidated by the description of landlords and tenants. The material was gathered in 1980, while Korogocho was growing rapidly.

## KOROGOCHO IN THE CONTEXT OF NAIROBI

It is estimated that 30 to 40 per cent of Nairobi's population live in squatter settlements. The largest and best known of these is Mathare Valley, in eastern Nairobi. It pre-dates independence and grew explosively during the late 1960s and early 1970s to house about 100,000 people, although opinions vary on this estimate. Kibera and Kawangware in the south and west also grew rapidly in the 1970s. The population of Kibera was estimated to be 64,000 in 1979. There are numerous small pockets of illegal squatter housing around the city and, depending upon conditions, some of them may become the focus of future rapid expansion of the type seen in Mathare, Kibera and Kawangware. The growth in urban population continues, shifting from place to place as one area becomes full up, and as new areas are identified as having the potential for growth. They may be so identified by squatters, the authorities, and/or entrepreneurs.

In the late 1970s, Korogocho became the focus for expansion. Like Mathare Valley it is in the eastern part of the city, but further out on the periphery of growth. Its growth had much to do with the dynamics of Mathare, where the landowners were interested in investing in more permanent and lucrative housing. It is located on government land between two rivers in the part of the city planned for extension, particularly through industry and low and middle-income housing. The area to the south of Korogocho is occupied by two World Bank-funded site and service projects, two USAID-funded core-house and site and service projects, and a middle-income housing project aided by the Commonwealth Development

Corporation.

A new industrial area is also planned to the south, and some industries are located to the north. Korogocho merges into an area of equally densely-built villages near these industries. Some of these are more permanently built. One, Baba Dogo, was due for formal upgrading by Nairobi City Council, but the project was aborted.

The first of the site and service projects consists of 6,000 plots in Dandora, with an estimated final population of 60,000. The first phase, 1,000 plots, was carried out and occupied during the period 1976–79. Korogocho is immediately adjacent and parallel to this first phase, and grew at the same time, although at a faster pace.

## THE STUDY AREA

The area studied actually consists of seven villages, only one of which is called Korogocho, but the whole area is also sometimes so called, and the only Village Committee is located there. The oldest villages are Korogocho and Ngomongo; they originated with a few residents as much as twenty years ago. The more recent villages started with relocations of squatters from other areas by the authorities; Highridge and Gitathuru in the early seventies and Grogan in 1978. Githaa is an entirely speculative village, built by entrepreneurs for rental from 1980. The whole area has mainly grown and densified in the late 1970s through 1980s. Before the 1979 general elections, many people were given plots in the various villages by prospective members of parliament or their agents, in return for election support. At the time of the survey in late 1980 there was a great deal of construction going on in all areas, but particularly in Githaa and Gitathuru.

In late 1977 and early 1978 the government and Nairobi City Council cleared a large squatter settlement in the centre of the city, near Nairobi river. This was an old settlement from pre-independence days. In 1971 it housed a few very poor people, some of whom had lived there for up to eleven or more years. Many were female-headed households relying on hawking and other informal sector activities in the city centre. Because of the sensitivity of their location, they would camouflage their dwellings or take them down in the morning and re-erect them at night. In the mid-1970s the number of very poor-quality shelters grew dramatically until they were cleared. The families from this settlement who were officially resettled by the City Council formed the basis of the village called Grogan in Korogocho.

The 1980 survey showed that Grogan had the poorest quality houses in the whole Korogocho area, mostly one-room shacks of plastic or cardboard; most of the household heads were women and there was no business activity there. Ngunyumu on the other hand had many stone houses and appeared the most permanent part of the settlement, though with a mainly tenant population. Ngomongo had mainly mud houses of quite poor quality. Although close to a quarry and covered in dust, making it an unpleasant place to live, there were many tenants and quite a lot of commercial activity. Gitathuru similarly had mainly mud houses with corrugated metal roofs, each building having between two and six rooms. Highridge had houses of about the same size but many were also built of timber and were of a better quality. Korogocho again had mud houses with corrugated metal roofs. Houses in Githaa were very large, consisting of rows of mud-walled rooms with metal roofs.

Water was available in Korogocho from a pipe brought in by the City Council, one of the achievements of the Village Committee. Various people in Korogocho had concessions to sell water, which was bought at 15c per *debe* (a four-gallon tin) by people from most of the other villages. This was cheap compared to the 25c or 35c charged in Kibera, but was above the City Council's 10c maximum. However, from the middle of 1980 water was supplied free, following a cholera scare in Nairobi. Pit-latrines were dug adjacent to some dwellings, and at the end of each row of dwellings in Githaa, but these were generally inadequate. Many people used either the bush or unfinished buildings.

## SURVEY METHOD

The information presented here is based on a quick questionnaire survey of 101 respondents in Korogocho, Highridge, Gitathuru and Githaa villages in September 1980. Information was also gathered through participant observation in the same four villages, and a building count was taken of all seven villages.

Although there is much variation between the villages, each one has a characteristic size and type of structure. For the four villages surveyed, the numbers of rooms, families and persons were counted for every tenth structure. For the other three villages the number of persons per structure was assumed by comparing the typical structure, size and occupation with one of the four villages surveyed, in order to derive an estimate of the total population.

The one-page questionnaire was applied to any household in every tenth structure. The whole survey took one interviewer only one month, since time was not spent looking for a specific respondent. There are drawbacks to such a 'quick and dirty' method, but it does reveal the overall pattern of population and building ownership. Where there were mostly absentee landlords, as in Githaa, this led to a high proportion of 'don't know' responses to questions on where the landlord lived and worked. Also, very few tenants knew whether the landlords owned plots in Dandora, the adjoining site and service scheme. Participant observation, including free-ranging discussions with building owners, revealed that a far higher proportion owned such plots than was indicated by the tenants. The data from this survey is compared with similar data from Dandora where it seems useful to illustrate patterns of settlement formation and entrepreneurism.

## KOROGOCHO COMPARED TO THE SITE AND SERVICE SCHEME

There were an estimated 26,300 people living in the seven villages around Korogocho in September 1980, based on the above survey method. The population of the four villages surveyed more accurately was estimated as follows: Korogocho: 5,870 in 512 structures; Highridge: 3,250 in 289 structures; Gitathuru: 6,720 in 563 structures; Githaa: 2,380 in 88 structures. The total was 18,220 people in 1,952 structures. By comparison, the population of the first phase of the adjacent site and service area was estimated to be approximately 10,000 on 1,032 plots at the same time. That is, the squatter settlement was housing twice as many people under much poorer conditions.

Two-thirds of the population of the site and service area and 87 per cent in the squatter area were tenants. Occupants of the site and service scheme had more public open space, a flush toilet and one or two water taps on every plot, access to roads with street lighting, a community centre, three nursery schools and a primary school. The squatter settlement, as already mentioned, was under-supplied with pit-latrines and water had to be carried from a few water points. There were nursery schools in three of the villages. Residents walked to Kariobangi for bus transport, which was also poor in the site and service scheme. Both groups of residents had to pay a high price ($K. Sh. 2 \cdot 60$) for transport to town. Transport accounted for 13 per cent of the income of the site and service area residents, whose average income was $K.Sh.833$ in 1978. Incomes in the squatter area were obviously much lower, although no data were collected.

Rents in the site and service area were about $K.Sh.150$–250 per room with water in 1977–78 and $K.Sh.250$–350 in 1980. In Korogocho rents were $K.Sh.70$ in 1980, plus water, although some rooms in Githaa cost $K.Sh.120$. It cost $K.Sh.3,600$ to build a permanent room in Dandora in 1977, so with plot and water charges and some maintenance the crude return on an investment in three rooms was 55 per cent in the first year. Three mud and wattle rooms could be built in Githaa for $K.Sh.4,500$ in 1980, so the crude return on investment was 88 per cent in the first year, at $K.Sh.120$ rent per room.

Table 9.1
Where landlords live, Nairobi, 1980

| Area | Same building | | Another building in Korogocho | | In adjoining site and service scheme | | Elsewhere in the city | | Not known | | Total | |
|---|---|---|---|---|---|---|---|---|---|---|---|---|
| | No. | % | No. | % | No. | % | No. | % | No. | % | No. | % |
| Korogocho | 26 | 51 | 9 | 18 | 3 | 6 | 8 | 15 | 5 | 10 | 51 | 100 |
| Highridge | 22 | 71 | 0 | 0 | 1 | 3 | 4 | 13 | 4 | 13 | 31 | 100 |
| Gitathuru | 5 | 45 | 1 | 9 | 0 | 0 | 5 | 45 | 0 | 0 | 11 | 100 |
| Githaa | 0 | 0 | 5 | 63 | 0 | 0 | 1 | 12 | 2 | 25 | 8 | 100 |
| Total | 53 | 53 | 15 | 15 | 4 | 4 | 18 | 17 | 11 | 11 | 101 | 100 |

## WHO ARE THE LANDLORDS?

The two settlements were very similar in the pattern of landlord occupation. Exactly half the owners in both Korogocho and Dandora occupied their dwellings, the rest being absentee landlords. It is important to point out that in both cases the majority of the landlords were not part of the high-income group. Although half the landlords in Korogocho were absentees, the pattern varied from village to village. In Highridge three-quarters of the owners lived in their dwellings, but in Githaa there were only absentee landlords (see Table 9·1).

One-tenth of the people questioned did not know where their landlords lived and a third did not know where they worked. Most of the known absentee landlords lived in other low-income areas of Nairobi, many of them nearby. Fifteen per cent lived elsewhere in Korogocho. One-third of the known landlords were unemployed, almost another third worked in the settlement or were itinerant workers, and the remainder worked in the industrial area or other parts of the city. One was a government official. Since the characteristics of landlords varied from village to village the data collected is presented below in some detail.

## KOROGOCHO

Half of the fifty-one owners of buildings surveyed in Korogocho proper were absentee landlords and half owner–occupiers, mainly men in both cases. Only four owners did not sub-let. The twenty-two residents who did included fourteen men and eight women. Four of the men and one woman had been successful applicants for the Dandora site and service scheme and two of the men were skilled masons who earned their living in the nearby site and service scheme. Another man worked as a carpenter in the squatter settlement. The others were four men and five women self-employed in the informal sector, an unskilled employee of the City Council, and six unemployed women. Most of the unemployed had applied unsuccessfully for site and service plots. They sub-let an average of six rooms each. The self-employed women all sold charcoal, as well as vegetables and sometimes water, while the men ran food kiosks or sold charcoal. Several of those who were unemployed used to have informal businesses or jobs, but now lived on rents alone.

There were twenty-five absentee landlords, twenty-two men and three women. Eight of the men were virtually unknown to their tenants though two were known to be employed. Eight landlords lived elsewhere in the settlement and owned more than one structure; they included two self-employed and four unemployed men, an unskilled male worker, and an unemployed woman member of the Village Committee. Nine landlords lived elsewhere and owned several structures. They included three men self-employed in the informal sector, two unemployed men, two women living in City Council houses elsewhere (one of them in Dandora) and two men with houses in Dandora (one a skilled mason, the other a government employee who came to collect rents from many structures using an official car). The houses owned by absentees and owner–occupiers were not different in size. In-depth discussions with several plot owners revealed that some had obtained their plots as election favours.

## HIGHRIDGE

The majority of those who owned the thirty-one buildings surveyed in Highridge were male owner–occupiers. One-third did not sub-let, and these included a very old woman living with a family of sixteen and a woman working as a toilet-cleaner in another squatter settlement; three of the men worked in the informal sector and five were unskilled workers. The twelve owner–occupiers who also sub-let included only one aged woman who earned a living by sub-letting to two families. The rest were men, with a similar pattern of employment to those who did not sub-let.

Almost all the absentee landlords owned structures of six to eleven rooms as opposed to the owner–occupiers, who owned structures of one to six rooms. The nine absentee landlords were all male; two were completely unknown to the tenants questioned. Four were known to live outside the settlement and own other buildings they sub-let. The others included a shop-owner, a District Officer, and someone who had also illegally purchased a site and service plot. Several plot-owners who had in-depth discussions with the interviewer told that they had been allocated their plots on being moved from other areas and been given permission to build six-room temporary shelters by government officials. One said he had paid for the plot and also had permission to build a permanent stone house. Some had been promised serviced plots and were disappointed with the lack of services in Highridge.

## GITATHURU

The owners of the eleven buildings surveyed were mostly women. There were five female owner–occupiers, four of them selling vegetables and charcoal, while the other was unemployed. Two were waiting to occupy site and service plots they had been allocated. Of the six absentee landlords, only one was female. One of the male landlords both worked for the City Council and lived in a City Council house. The four others owned multiple structures, and included a *matatu* vehicle operator, an owner of an informal sector clothing business, and another City Council employee. One of the women owner–occupiers had no tenants, and the other owners sub-let to between three and seven families, with little difference between the structures owned by absentee landlords and owner–occupiers. Several plot-owners said they were allocated their plots and promised site and service plots afterwards, whereas only a few had in fact been successful in the official plot ballot. They were also told they could build six-room temporary structures in Gitathuru.

## GITHAA

Owners of all the eight buildings surveyed in Githaa were absentee landlords. Of the six who were known, five lived in other parts of the settlement, and all were said to own many structures. One, in addition, operated a water point, worked in town and owned a car, one was a shopkeeper, another was an unemployed member of the Village Committee, and another was a plot-owner in the site and service scheme. All were men. The largest structure had twenty rooms and a population of fifty-seven, though two rooms were unoccupied and one was a shop where only one person slept. In-depth discussions were held with several other plot-owners when they came to collect rent. They were all well-off men from other areas than Korogocho. They explained that formal applications for plots were processed by the Village Committee and government officials who allowed them to build temporary structures of a specified type: ten rooms of 14 sq. m. each; they were also instructed to paint the corrugated metal roofs black in order to create the impression of poverty. It may be imagined that the additional cost of painting was included in tenants' rent, despite the fact that it created a hot and unpleasant environment for them.

## FORMAL AND INFORMAL LAND ALLOCATIONS

It is useful to compare the process of allocation of plots and absentee landlordism in Korogocho with Dandora, the adjoining site and service scheme. The City Council controlled the allocation of plots there through a carefully organised system of screening applicants in interviews, followed by a random ballot. Applicants had to be low-income heads of households with no other properties in the city, and had to have lived in the city for two years. On the whole it was successful, the large majority of allottees fulfilling the conditions, despite efforts by some officials to operate the more usual informal networks.

The scheme relied on sub-letting of rooms by low-income plot-owners for its economic viability. This was successful in that 95 per cent of the owners had a low income, did sub-let rooms and were able to pay for their plots.

However, half of the owners also became absentee landlords, sub-letting their dwellings completely, although this was against the terms of their lease. It seems some of them at least chose to live in Korogocho, or other squatter areas, while recouping their investment in construction. They let rooms in the site and service area to families with a slightly higher and steadier source of income. Tenants in the site and service scheme were more often wage-earning male heads of households with smaller families than the plot-owners, who included more females and self-employed people with larger families (Senga Ndeti Associates, 1979).

Korogocho settlement was established by poor people coming from various parts of the city who brought their problems to local or central government officials or the Village Committee and were given a place to build. Often they had been evicted from their previous place by the authorities. These people established their foothold in Korogocho through influence or mutual favours with various people in power. Often these were opposing groups or individuals, as was the case between two candidates standing for election in the same area, or between central and local government officials. Some obtained plots through their connections with City Hall by virtue of being city employees. Other people used the same networks of influence to acquire plots even though they lived elsewhere.

Although the building owners in the Korogocho area all perceived their allocation of land as official, it is clear that such actions by central or local government officials were mostly taken unofficially, and often without reference to each other. For example, officials of the local government surveyed and allocated sites in Gitathuru prior to the elections and central government officials later came to try and stop construction and gave notice to vacate.

Korogocho residents are represented by the Village Committee, which wields some influence. Some building owners were of the opinion that the Village Committee was more powerful than the local politicians, and that successful access to land was through this committee and central government officials. The fact that the land was government-owned reinforced their perception. However, many residents, including some plot-owners in villages other than Korogocho itself, were unaware of the Village Committee, and dealt direct with the District Officer when they had problems.

Once they had plots, the majority of squatters were able to increase their income through sub-letting to the extent that some gave up their other sources of income. Many more men than women became absentee landlords. Two-thirds of the landlords were the original squatters expanding their interests; one-third from outside. In either case, they had access to sites in the squatter settlement as favours from influential people, in return for political support, or from connections through their employment or other place of residence. The officials also gave themselves plots in some cases.

The survey of Korogocho did not include questions on the ethnic origin of owners and tenants. However, it is likely that the networks of influence described are through contacts of the same tribe. (In November 1980 there was a riot in Korogocho over selective allocation of plots to people of one tribe.) A similar study of Kibera states that it is likely, contrary to previous work on rural–urban migration, that landlords prefer tenants from a different tribe than their own, since the relationship is a purely economic one (Amis 1980). A pattern of landlords of one tribe and tenants of another could easily conflate a class conflict with an ethnic one.

## CONCLUSIONS

According to African tradition, land allocation was decided communally, more recently by chiefs or leaders. These systems continue to operate today alongside, and sometimes incorporated into, formal systems of land allocation. Plots for farming or building are allocated by chiefs and Village Committees, sometimes in collaboration with party officials and other elected representatives. Formal systems of land tenure are growing more widespread even in rural areas. But urban squatter areas continue to operate under an adapted form of the older system.

There are several points of contact between the two systems. Elected officials such as councillors, ward representatives or members of the national legislature intervene in the semi-traditional allocation system, as well as being the representatives of the formal system. They may be the advocates of community interests in gaining access to land for either temporary or formal occupation. They may represent conflicting interests of different communities or formal versus informal landholders. They may mediate between the community and the bureaucracy. On the other hand, they may use their positions of access and authority to accumulate land. They may exacerbate land shortages in order to retain their control over it, and over the communities which form their power base.

These generalisations, based on observation of the dynamics of land-use and allocation in several African countries, are supported by this case study of Korogocho in Nairobi. It is suggested that similar dynamics may operate for other developing African countries, regardless of their overt political ideology, or the nationalisation of land, even though the motivation of leaders to put private gain above community needs will be greater in a free land market, where opportunities for profit are greater.

It is in the interests of the ruling elite to continue to prevent easy access to land by the urban poor because controlling access to land as a scarce resource provides a source of cash income and political support. It is also apparent that maintaining control over informal systems of land allocation is easier and more rewarding for individuals within a ruling elite than formal systems of land allocation to the poor. These interests are likely to continue to reinforce the official ideology of maintaining urban standards and ensuring that petty commodity production (including that of buildings) is kept under informal, and not formal control.

Finally, entrepreneurial activity in squatter settlements (and site and service schemes) benefits the low-income producers of housing. Under informal systems of land allocation the benefits of this market in housing tend to accrue to high and middle-income producers of housing as well as to the original low-income occupants.

## REFERENCES

Amis, P. 1980. 'The operation of the private sector in the low-cost housing market: a case study from Nairobi'. Draft paper presented to EDI/HABITAT training workshop, Nairobi.
—— 1984. 'Squatters or tenants: the commercialization of unauthorized housing in Nairobi', *World Development*, 12(1), pp. 87–96.
Perlman, J. 1976. *The Myth of Marginality: urban poverty and politics in Rio de Janeiro*. Berkeley: University of California Press.
Senga Ndeti Associates. 1979. *Monitoring and Evaluation Study of Dandora Community Development Project. MEDIS Reports 5 and 7. Nairobi.*

## RESUME

Cette étude de cas examine l'esprit d'entreprise dans une colonie non planifiée dans les quartiers orientaux de Nairobi. Les propriétaires absents détiennent souvent des positions d'influence, possèdent plus de moyens et sont souvent des hommes qui sont occupants – propriétaires. La colonie non planifiée est comparée à un programme voisin de site et de services pour démontrer comment les systèmes officiels et non officiels de distribution des terres fonctionnent entre eux. La zone non officielle était utilisée comme zone d'attente en vue du programme officiel. Mais la première pouvait être plus facilement manipulée que la seconde. L'esprit d'entreprise a été utilisé avec de bons résultats comme stratégie pour loger les gens de faibles revenus dans le programme de site et de services. L'esprit d'entreprise dans la colonie non planifiée s'est avéré être à la fois une stratégie de survie utilisée par les pauvres et une source de profit pour les gens ayant une influence dans les milieux politiques et administratifs. On a suggéré que ces gens exerçant cette influence seront plus incités à promouvoir les systèmes non officiels que les systèmes officiels de distribution de terres aux pauvres.

# THE GROWTH OF SMALL-SCALE RENTING IN LOW-INCOME URBAN HOUSING IN MALAWI

## INTRODUCTION

Discussions of housing for the urban poor in the Third World have tended to concentrate on the virtuous case (often with reference to John Turner's bridgeheader-consolidator-status-seeker model – see Kliest and Scheffer, 1981) or the vicious circle as in Amis's (1984) discussion of the commercialisation of unauthorised housing in Nairobi by large-scale landlords charging exorbitant rents. Yet, as Michael Edwards argues in chapter 14 of this volume, these two polar cases do not resemble closely one of the most common housing situations for the urban poor – renting from small-scale local landlords. In Malawi the majority of the urban poor live under this form of tenure. The main purpose of this chapter is to examine developments in this small-scale rented sector, with special reference to site and service housing areas in Lilongwe, the new capital of Malawi. It is suggested that throughout the late 1970s there occurred a sequence of events that turned something of a virtuous case into something of a vicious circle.

The particular configurations of Malawian political economy were crucial in determining the course and possible outcome of the process that has taken place. Nevertheless, the developments have much in common with those occurring elsewhere and there is much to be learned from the kind of comparative perspective presented by Michael Edwards. The core of this chapter may be seen as a case study in the interaction through a particular time (the 1970s) and space (Lilongwe) of factors governing the housing market and, more specifically, tenure profiles. Edwards identifies a number of such factors, including city size, situation and growth rates, housing preferences, migration motives, household incomes and housing prices, and government policy. In this account particular stress is laid on government policy and on an additional factor – the capital market and the relative attractiveness to potential landlords of investment in site and service housing.

The chapter contains three main sections. The first presents a brief history of low-income housing in Malawi, with emphasis on the development of site and service housing, which now provides accommodation for the majority of the urban population. The second contains a discussion of the history of small-scale renting and the characteristics of owner–occupiers, tenants and landlords. The third section is a case study of the development of site and service housing in Lilongwe in the 1970s, when a hiatus in the development of site and service areas affected the market for rented housing by both restricting supply and increasing demand.

## LOW-INCOME URBAN HOUSING IN MALAWI: THE ROLE OF SITE AND SERVICE SCHEMES

Urban housing patterns in Malawi continue to reflect those established in the colonial era when the towns were laid out on the racially segregated lines familiar elsewhere (King, 1977; McMaster, 1970; Pennant, 1983b; Sanyal, 1981). Housing for Europeans was typically rented from an employer – most commonly the state, with some owner-occupation or private renting for longer-term residents. Housing for Asians was typically owner-occupied or provided by an employer (Dotson and Dotson, 1968). Africans living within the official urban boundaries were regarded as temporary residents and provided with housing tied to employment – in servants' quarters or the 'lines' of government departments, local authorities or private companies.

Much of the African urban population lived outside the narrowly drawn official boundaries, but still within a few minutes' walk of the town centres. Bettison (1958, 1961) and Norwood (1972, 1975) draw a contrast between the relatively liberal attitude to peri-urban settlement in Malawi up to the late 1960s and the much tighter controls exercised in Kenya and the Rhodesias in the colonial era. From the 1930s there were extensive discussions within the colonial administration of whether or not to incorporate wider areas into the towns (Pennant 1983b). The peri-urban fringe was potentially affected by innovations in housing policy on site and service principles which were made in the 1930s at about the same time as in Zambia (cf. Tipple, 1981). But these remained at a token level until the 1950s when more substantial urbanisation coupled with political changes made housing questions more pressing.

Within the colonial administration there were throughout the 1950s two schools of thought about low-income housing – one favouring government/employer/local-authority provision of permanent housing rented to Africans in urban employment who were to be regarded as temporary urban residents, the other favouring self-built, semi-permanent or temporary owner–occupier housing for individuals who were to be regarded as permanent urban residents. Despite a preference for the former on the part of most members of the administration it was the latter which received the greater emphasis from 1957 (Pennant 1983b: 8–9). Similarly both before and after independence the Malawi Congress Party (MCP) contained supporters of both forms – permanent and site and service. Again policy has emphasised site and service housing as the main provision for low-income urban dwellers, though the Malawi Housing Corporation has devoted most of its funds to permanent housing. Thus Malawi has had a continuous emphasis over three decades on site and service housing – in contrast to neighbouring anglophone countries (Sanyal, 1981; Stren, 1979).

Site and service areas ('Temporary', after independence 'Traditional Housing Areas' (THAs)) have been established on the edges of the towns. A parallel policy has incorporated the peri-urban fringe within town boundaries and planning controls. Upgrading of existing unplanned settlement has been confined to a few long-established areas in Blantyre which have politically influential owner–occupiers and landlords (Norwood, 1972, Schumer, 1973). Most of the peri-urban population, as we shall see in more detail in the case of Lilongwe, has been resettled on to site and service plots, if classified as 'urban' or in – often remote – villages, if classified as 'rural'.

Site and service has been a consistently emphasised policy more because of (financial) constraints than through (political) choice. Before independence there were some in the colonial administration who saw the site and service principle as a way of co-opting African owner–occupiers to the colonial and federal systems (Pennant, 1983b). After independence it has been seen as a way of stabilising the urban population politically. But the main reason for choosing it has been that it was the best available means of housing a low-waged urban labour force. Colonial officials were quite explicit in acknowledging this as a priority, as did the Officer in charge of Resettlement in Blantyre in 1959: 'The basic reason for these admittedly low (minimum building) standards must not be lost sight of; it is that the Minimum Wage is also extremely low. It is government's policy to attract to the townships a permanent labour force housed in self-owned houses' (MNA, 1959: 11).

Low wages for urban workers have been attractive for obvious reasons to urban employers – a government with a very restricted revenue base, commercial and manufacturing firms operating in an economy in which costs other than those of labour and locally-produced raw materials are high. There have been few counterweights to this low wage policy. Trade unions have been weak or outlawed (see Iliffe, 1985: 276). Urban dwellers' interests have been relatively weakly represented in the MCP, particularly after the Cabinet crisis of 1964, when Dr Banda consolidated his power-base among the (predominantly rural) conservative elements in the party. Aid donors, notably the World Bank and the IMF, have applauded a policy which has restricted rural–urban migration. Urban landlords, though often having some local political power, have not been a strong enough pressure group to rewrite the rules of the game overwhelmingly in favour of themselves. Unlike Nairobi, as described by Amis (1984) and others, landlordism in Malawi remains on a small scale and has offered lower returns on capital than some other forms of activity, notably tobacco-farming. There is more evidence of political weight being applied to the gaining of land, farming capital, crop production quota allocations, etc. (See Kydd, 1985: 326–8), than to the acquisition of urban land and building capital. Exchange-rate and other policies, including those encouraged by the World Bank in the 1980s, have favoured agricultural producers of export crops rather than low-income urban dwellers, who have relatively little disposable income for landlords to squeeze.

The major source of capital for site and service infrastructure has been foreign aid donors. By and large these have endorsed the site and service policy as a non-zero sum game, a rational organisation of collective consumption benefiting employers by providing cheap housing for workers near places of work, residents by providing cheap but hygienic living conditions and better housing opportunities than those in unplanned squatter areas, and the government by contributing to political order. Until recently donors have emphasised the importance of owner–occupation in site and service areas. This emphasis has been echoed in public statements by Malawian officials and it has been taken for granted that the great majority of site and service area residents belonged to the household of the plot-holder. As we shall see in the next section, the majority of them actually belong to tenant households.

## SMALL-SCALE RENTING: A HISTORY AND DESCRIPTION

Within the 'formal' housing sector in Malawi there is little evidence of the extensive sub-letting reported in Kenya by Amis (1984) and others, though there is some sub-letting of the servants' quarters provided both before and after independence for all but the lowest grades of government housing. In site and service areas, however, sub-letting by plotholders has become the most common form of tenure. The origins of this practice were to be found in the peri-urban settlements which preceded site and service areas. The best source of information on these is the series of publications by D. G. Bettison (1958, 1961, etc.) based on the Rhodes-Livingstone Institute study of peri-urban Blantyre in the late 1950s which he headed. Bettison distinguished three types of resident. The dominant one was identified as living in 'a traditional type of social composition' with a 'central structure . . . [of] a sibling group, headed usually by a man and containing his female dependents and unmarried brothers'. But 'in addition most villages contained groups of varied composition unrelated to this central structure' (Bettison and Rigby, 1959: vii). These consisted of both families and individuals – the second and third type of resident, described as 'accretions'. Bettison suggests that people in these last two categories were frequently paying rent to people in the first category, over and above the by then customary once-and-for-all fee or 'present' due to a village headman for permission to settle in his area (see Norwood, 1972). In some 'villages' the 'central lineage' was less dominant and it would seem that commerciali- sation had proceeded a stage further, with something like a notion of individual ownership of plots as well as of buildings. Bettison's study was carried out at a time of acute political tension and questions directed to this topic were unwelcome – the official line being that village headmen, guided since 1949 by the Town Planning Department, were responsible for con- trolling settlement. In the largest village the research was called off because of hostility to interviewers, but 'it is suspected on strong, but hearsay evidence, that the village contained numerous accretions resident on a landlord–tenant relationship to persons in the village' (Bettison, 1958: 8).

After Bettison's research there is little published evidence on small-scale renting for some years. Some data on the extent of renting is provided by income and expenditure surveys carried out by the National Statistical Office (1967, 1970). These do not distinguish small-scale renting from large-scale, formal-sector renting, but indicate that the proportion of different categories of low urban incomes spent on rent was between 1 and 3 per cent compared with between 10 and 22 per cent in Lilongwe THAs in 1980. This growth reflects an increase in the proportion of people paying rent rather than an increase in rent levels. In real terms, rents per room seem to have fallen slightly, at least through the 1970s, probably reflecting a similar, slight fall in real incomes, which has accelerated in the 1980s (Pennant, 1983a: 153–9; see also National Statistical Office, 1983). Two surveys of THAs were carried out in the early 1970s. The first, covering Blantyre (Schumer 1973), was primarily a physical survey and ignored sub-letting altogether. In the second, covering Lilongwe (Town Planning Department, 1972), tenure profiles were a subsidiary interest but it pro- vides information that may be used in conjunction with the findings of two later surveys, of THAs in Blantyre and Mzuzu in 1979 (Mhango, 1979) and in Lilongwe in 1980 (Pennant, 1983a).

## OWNER–OCCUPIERS AND TENANTS

By 1980 tenants formed the bulk of the THA population in Lilongwe. 67·6 per cent of the THA population, and 75·7 per cent of economically active individuals living in the THAs were members of tenant, as opposed to owner–occupier households. In relation to the population of the whole city, this represented some 39 per cent of the total and about 44 per cent of the economically active (Pennant, 1983a: 33, 104, 199). Proportions for Blantyre in 1979 seem to have been broadly similar (Mhango, 1979: 19; Pennant, 1983a: 88).

Owner–occupiers and tenants differed in a range of characteristics. Owners were older than tenants. In Blantyre in 1979 and Lilongwe in 1980 more than 90 per cent of owner–occupier heads of household were aged thirty or over, 33 per cent (Blantyre) and 20 per cent (Lilongwe) were over fifty, while nearly 50 per cent (Lilongwe) of tenant heads of household were aged less than thirty, and more than 80 per cent (Blantyre) aged less than forty (Mhango, 1979: 14–20; Pennant, 1983a: 145). Most of the differences between Blantyre and Lilongwe may be accounted for by the fact that Lilongwe's growth is more recent and most settlers in the city have been there for less time.

Their greater age than tenants is reflected in other characteristics of owner–occupiers. They are less well-educated (Pennant, 1983a: 73–4, 217) and more likely to have been abroad as labour migrants, external migration having declined since 1974 (pp. 56–7). Owner–occupiers had been resident in town for longer than tenants. Ninety per cent of tenant heads of households had been resident for less than ten years compared with 40 per cent of owner–occupiers (p. 87) who less commonly had rural gardens (49·5 per cent against 63·6 per cent for tenant heads of household) (p. 53).

The greater age of owner–occupiers was associated with larger household size, an average of 6·6 persons as compared with 3·7 for tenant households (p. 28). Generally speaking, tenant households were at an earlier stage in the typical cycle of family formation. Thirty-one per cent contained only one or two persons and 22 per cent consisted of single adults living alone or sharing accommodation (p. 147). Neither owner–occupier nor tenant households in town bore much resemblance to the type of extended family found by Bettison in peri-urban Blantyre in the 1950s. Eighty-four per cent of owner–occupier and 80 per cent of tenant household members in Lilongwe THAs in 1980 belonged to nuclear family categories of family membership (head of household accompanied by spouse or child) (p. 33).

In terms of occupations owner–occupiers and tenants were broadly similar, though tenants' higher educational qualifications were reflected in more frequent employment in clerical occupations. Employment status differed more substantially. Owner–occupiers were much more likely to be self-employed or not in employment and much less likely to be employed by private firms (Pennant, 1983a; 86–8; Mhango, 1979: 19).

In Lilongwe THAs there were wide variations in income levels between different owner–occupier households and different tenant households. Many of the former received rent in addition to other sources of income. The generous plot sizes (roughly one-eighth of an acre) and the favourable location of most THAs made them attractive to some individuals with relatively high incomes prepared to build substantial burnt-brick houses. Such people might be self-employed or otherwise not provided with housing by an employer, including those retired or preparing to retire. Both tenant and owner–occupier groups contained households with more than one earner; where two or more earners had secondary education this was associated with especially high income. But despite these wide income variations between and within the two groups, there were some overall similarities. Average individual occupational incomes were much the same. So too were per capita incomes after payment and receipt of rent, owner–occupier households having typically a larger number of dependants. One important difference in the pattern of incomes was the greater dependence of tenant households on the occupational income of the head of household. For tenant households nearly 80 per cent of reported income from all sources consisted of the occupational income of heads of households, compared with just over 50 per cent for owner-occupiers (Pennant, 1983a: 101–4).

## LANDLORDS

Landlords may be divided into two categories: resident and non-resident. In 1980 most belonged to both categories, since the majority of absentee landlords lived elsewhere in the THAs, proximity (or supervision by a resident agent, often a relative) being a prerequisite of effective management. Of every ten plots four had tenant households only, two resident plot-holder households only and four resident plot-holders with tenants, often housed in a separate building at the back of the plot. Between a quarter and a third of plots were owned by people (illegally) in possession of more than one plot. On average these owned 2·6 plots each, with 70 per cent of multiple plot-holders holding two plots. Some 6 per cent of multiple plot-holders owned between five and ten plots, accounting for about 10 per cent of total plots. Only two plot-holders, in a survey covering nearly 500 plots, were reported to own more than six plots.

The small owner–occupier landlords who dominate this picture were not unrepresentative of owner–occupiers as a whole. Sub-letting provides a steady and diversified income for small businessmen, an income supplement and pension for wage and salary earners, and can be combined with the provision of a retirement house for people provided with housing by an employer (Pennant, 1983a: 131–40).

## SITE AND SERVICE HOUSING DEVELOPMENT IN LILONGWE IN THE 1970s

Between the 1966 and 1977 censuses the population of Lilongwe grew from 19,425 to 102,924. Part of this increase was the consequence of a huge extension of the administrative boundaries, but the major factor was im-migration. Growth rates were high because the city became the national capital in 1975 and is the main service centre for the Central Region, which underwent economic transformation in the late 1960s and 1970s, with a major World Bank-funded programme for smallholder agriculture and a spectacular expansion of estate tobacco production after UDI in Zimbabwe (Kydd, 1985). By 1977 57·6 per cent of the city's population was housed on 8,427 plots in six site and service areas (THAs). The development of the THAs had occurred mainly in three phases: pre-independence (funded by the Colonial Development and Welfare Fund), the late 1960s and early 1970s (funded by the South African government as part of their support for the new capital city) and the mid-1970s (funded by the UK).

From 1977 a hiatus occurred in the THA development programme, occasioned above all by the views of President Kamuzu Banda, and in particular by his 1976 instruction, implemented from 1977 on, that one THA (Lilongwe Planning Area 47) be upgraded from site and service to medium-density permanent housing. This involved demolishing buildings on 1959 plots (23·2 per cent of THA plots ready by 1977), compensating plot-holders, and resettling the 5,970 people living in the area at the time of the 1977 census. (Without resettlement the area would have grown rapidly in population to 15,000 – 20,000 by the end of the decade.)

Speculation about President Banda's reasons for this decision has been extensive in Malawi, frequently centring on the nearby location of private housing belonging to relatives of prominent members of his entourage. It can, however, be explained in terms of a conflict between his own mon-umental conception of the new capital and the more utilitarian concerns of planners and officials. The new capital has been very much a personal project of and monument to the President (cf. Potts, 1985: 188). It is planned on a massive scale, stretching north from the old colonial district and regional centre through three further growth-poles of a city centre of prestige offices, embassies and public buildings, a heavy industrial area and the new international airport, a distance of some 30 km. from south to north. To planners Area 47 was well placed, like the first THAs, to enable workers to walk to work in the main existing area of employment – the old town, as well as to the new city centre where employment was expanding most rapidly. In a more monumental conception Area 47 encroached on the new city centre and it was more appropriate to develop areas designated as THAs further north and more peripheral.

Whatever President Banda's motives, they have been interpreted by officials as antipathy to houses not constructed of at least semi-permanent materials (sun-dried brick, corrugated iron roof). In the aftermath of the instruction to upgrade Area 47 officials even went to the lengths of disguising squatter houses visible from planned presidential routes by putting iron sheets and whitewash on top of wattle and daub and thatch, removing the iron sheets after the presidential motorcade had passed. Through the early 1970s building standards in Traditional (sic) Housing Areas were raised to exclude 'traditional' materials (thatch, wattle and daub), still commonly used in the unregulated peri-urban areas. In 1967 33 per cent of 'African housing units' in Lilongwe and 68 per cent in peri-urban Blantyre had been made of wattle and daub and thatch (National Statistical Office, 1967). Extensive tree-planting on THA perimeters and the designation of plots along major roads and on perimeters as suitable only for permanent housing were designed further to screen from view the semi-permanent buildings that constitute the bulk of THA housing (and, ironically, may be considered a major achievement of the new capital, providing a higher standard of housing than that available to people with similar income levels in most of urban Africa).

Up to the reclassification of Area 47 the establishment of the Lilongwe THAs was proceeding without fundamental hitches, and might be considered in some respects a model for such developments. New plots were allocated to applicants on a waiting list or to people being resettled with compensation from established peri-urban settlements cleared as part of the development of the new capital. Subsequently they could be transferred by purchase or inheritance.

From 1969 the THAs were administered by the Capital City Development Corporation (CCDC), whose files provided information on allocation and transfers through the 1970s. In early 1970 the waiting time for applicants was relatively short, but by later in the year applicants had to wait for three to four years, a waiting time that continued to apply through 1971 for people who were allocated plots in Area 47. This kind of time frame provided considerable scope for low-income settlers in the city to establish and consolidate a housing foothold. Centrally located rented accommodation and some temporary peri-urban areas were available for short-term circular migrants (including many building workers involved in the construction of the city) and younger individuals with few dependants, many of whom lodge with friends or relatives on first arrival. Those remaining in the city could obtain a plot after a few years and gradually expand the accommodation on it, beginning with a cheap temporary building (see Town Planning Department, 1972: 30). Some plot-holders were able to supplement their income by sub-letting accommodation. For many this has been a way of investing at relatively affluent stages of the life cycle to avoid deprivation at the stages most threatened by poverty – first, when a growing number of dependants require more food and shelter from a single income and secondly, following retirement (Bettison, 1960; Iliffe, 1985; Pennant, 1985).

Several factors, including above all the upgrading of Area 47 and its consequences, changed this picture of a relatively virtuous case of low-income housing development into one which showed some, if not all, of the characteristics of a vicious circle. The resettlement of Area 47 plot-holders and some tenants on plots in other THAs required nearly all the plots that became available between 1977 and 1980 and beyond, since aid donors were unwilling to make up the deficit (rather, they postponed or rejected proposals they might otherwise have accepted), and the Malawi government itself made virtually no financial provision for increasing the availability of plots. This meant that 1,972 applicants had to wait ten years or more for plots. In turn this meant that the waiting list became only tenuously related to housing need, since those best able to maintain their name on the list at the periodic updatings were those with the most stable (employment) addresses, who often had access to other housing resources and retained their interest because they were sufficiently well-established to contemplate landlordism (Pennant, 1983a: 167–8).

As the allocation of plots to waiting-list applicants declined the transfer of plots by purchase became more widespread. Officially, all transfers of plots required authorisation from CCDC, but from the mid-1970s unauthorised purchase became common for a time, much of it during a period of acute political tension when the relatively strict adherence to bureaucratic procedures usually maintained in Malawi was partially suspended for a time. Twenty-four per cent of 1980 plot-holders had acquired their plots by authorised purchase and a further 6 per cent or more by unauthorised purchase (Pennant, 1983a: 131). The growth of purchase as the main means of acquiring a plot was a natural development with the passage of time (in the older THAs over half the plots had been acquired by purchase), but it was clearly associated with the commercialisation of sub-tenure arrangements and the growth of absentee landlordism. Even if only authorised transfers are counted, absentee landlords were significantly more likely to have acquired their plots by purchase than were resident plotholders (Pennant, 1983a: 131–3).

A further aspect of commercialisation was the construction of housing designed for multiple sub-letting. The normal arrangement of buildings on plots in THAs draws its inspiration from the 'bungalow-compound' complex (King, 1977). A squarish front house with one main entrance and a verandah stands in front of a row of rooms with separate doors, which might be for servants or tenants. By 1980 some plots had rooms with separate doors arranged either in blocks or in rows on both the front and back of the plot.

The nature of changes through the 1970s in tenants' conditions and prospects can be shown by comparing data from the 1972 (Town Planning Department, 1972) and 1980 (Pennant, 1983a) surveys of Lilongwe THAs. A number of developments stand out:

(a) Between 1972 and 1980 the average number of people per plot nearly doubled, from 6·3 to 12·5. Whereas in 1972 72·8 per cent of plots, with 53·9 per cent of all THA inhabitants, had fewer than eight residents, in 1980 only 25·5 per cent with 10·2 per cent of inhabitants, had fewer than eight. In 1980 over 50 per cent of the THA population were living on plots with more than fourteen residents. Investment by plot-holders in buildings had nearly kept up with this, so that density per area of houses had not increased much (Pennant, 1983a: 10, 35).

(b) The 1972 survey design included the assumption that each plot contained one core household, with occasional individual lodgers. By 1980 such an assumption, probably misleading in 1972, was quite untenable. Seventy per cent of plots had more than one household, involving 89·6 per cent of households and 84·2 per cent of people (Pennant, 1983a: 36).

(c) Tenancy in the years before 1972 had been a transitional status for most; by 1980 it looked increasingly a permanent status for many. Of THA heads of household resident in the city for between five and nine years 89 per cent were plot-holders in 1972 and 23 per cent in 1980 (Pennant, 1983a: 161; Town Planning Department, 1972: 22).

(d) A much greater proportion of tenant households in 1980 had reached stages of family formation where children resident with their parents in the city outnumbered adults. Some of these households, especially those with higher incomes, who sometimes had their rent paid by an employer, might have chosen to remain as tenants. But many would in the past have taken advantage of the greater scope there had been for becoming owner–occupiers in unplanned peri-urban areas for the THAs. By 1980 67 per cent of members of tenant households were in households with four or more members and 48 per cent in households with five or more members. Children in tenant households heavily outnumbered children of plotholders and made up nearly 40 per cent of the tenant population (Pennant, 1983a: 30, 201). Thus a much higher proportion of tenants were facing increasing demands for food and rent on one wage-earner's income maintained at a level sufficient to support one or two people.

These developments cannot be attributed solely to the upgrading of Area 47 and its ramifications. Upward housing mobility for those established in a city undergoing rapid growth cannot be repeated for subsequent gener-ations. Plot densities were bound to grow as plots were developed and as the families of young urban settlers grow larger. Nevertheless, it is clear that the consequences of the decision to upgrade Area 47 accelerated processes of change in the low-income housing market to such an extent that qualitative changes occurred, as when tenancy became a near-permanent rather than transitional status for the majority of THA residents. This is not to say, however, that the processes result from the operation of an irreversible iron law. Nineteenth and twentieth-century Britain provides an example of a low-income urban housing market dominated by small landlords whose economic and political weakness has contributed to their near extinction. Their future in Malawi may or may not be a rosy one.

# REFERENCES

Amis. P. 1984. 'Squatters or tenants: the commercialisation of unauthorized housing in Nairobi', *World Development*, 12(1), pp. 87–96.

Bettison, D. G. 1958. *The Social and Economic Structure of Seventeen Villages, Blantyre-Limbe, Nyasaland*. Lusaka: Rhodes-Livingstone Institute.

—— 1960. 'The poverty datum line in Central Africa', *Human Relations in British Central Africa*, 27, pp. 1–40.

—— 1961. 'Changes in the composition and status of kin groups in Nyasaland and Northern Rhodesia', in A. W. Southall (ed.), *Social Change in Modern Africa*, pp. 273–85. London: Oxford University Press for the International African Institute.

—— and Rigby, P. J. 1959. *Patterns of Income and Expenditure, Blantyre-Limbe, Nyasaland*. Lusaka: Rhodes-Livingstone Institute.

Dotson, F. and Dotson, L. O. 1968. *The Indian Minority of Zambia, Rhodesia and Malawi*. New Haven: Yale University Press.

Iliffe, J. 1985. 'The poor in the modern history of Malawi', in C. J. Fyfe (ed.), *Malawi: an alternative pattern of development*, pp. 243–92. Edinburgh: Edinburgh University Centre of African Studies.

King, A. D. 1977. *Colonial Urban Development: culture, social power and development*. London: Routledge & Kegan Paul.

Kliest, T. J. and Scheffer, H. R. 1981. 'John Turner's theory of intra-urban mobility and the African reality', *TESG*, 72 (5), pp. 258–65.

Kydd, J. G. 1985. 'Malawi in the 1970s: development policies and economic change', in C. J. Fyfe (ed.), *Malawi: an alternative pattern of development*, pp. 293–380. Edinburgh: Edinburgh University Centre of African Studies.

McMaster, D. N. 1970. 'The colonial district town in Uganda', in R. P. Beckinsale and J. M. Houston (eds.), *Urbanisation and Its Problems*, pp. 330–51. Oxford: Blackwell.

Mhango, G. L. 1979. *The Housing Situation in the Traditional Housing Areas of Blantyre and Mzuzu*. Blantyre: Malawi Housing Corporation.

MNA/Malawi National Archives, 1959. 'Minimum building standards and health regulations: peri-urban housing areas.' URB/P/25.

National Statistical Office, 1967. *Housing-Income Survey for Major Urban Areas*. Zomba: National Statistical Office.

—— 1970. *Household Income and Expenditure Survey for Urban Areas and Agricultural Estates*. Zomba: National Statistical Office.

—— 1983. *Urban Household Expenditure Survey, 1979/80*. Zomba: National Statistical Office.

Norwood, H. C. 1972. 'Ndirande, a squatter colony in Malawi', *Town Planning Review*, 43, pp. 135–150.

—— 1975. 'Squatters compared', *African Urban Notes*, Series B, No. 2 pp. 119–32.

Pennant, T. G. E. 1983a. *Report on a Study of Traditional (Site and Service) Housing Areas and Squatter Areas in and around Lilongwe City.* Zomba: Centre for Social Research.
—— 1983b. 'Housing the urban labour force in Malawi: an historical overview, 1930–80', *African Urban Studies*, 16, pp. 1–22.
—— 1985. 'Housing the urban labour force in Malawi', in C. J. Fyfe (ed.), *Malawi: an alternative pattern of development*, pp. 547–83. Edinburgh: Edinburgh University Centre of African Studies.
Potts, D. 1985, 'Capital relocation in Africa: the case of Lilongwe in Malawi', *Geographical Journal*, 151 (2), pp. 182–96.
Sanyal, B. 1981. 'Who gets what, where, why and how: a critical look at the housing subsidies in Zambia', *Development and Change*, 12, pp. 409–40.
Schumer, M. 1973. *The Strategy of Planned Traditional Housing: prospects of the South Lunzu traditional housing programme in Blantyre.* Berlin: German Development Institute.
Stren, R. E. 1979. 'Urban policy', in J. Barkan and J. Okumu (eds.), *Politics and Public Policy in Kenya and Tanzania*, pp. 179–208. New York: Praeger.
—— 1982. 'Underdevelopment, urban squatting and the state bureaucracy: a case study of Tanzania', *Canadian Journal of African Studies*, 16 (1), pp. 67–91.
Tipple, A. G. 1981. 'Colonial housing policy and the "African Towns" of the Copperbelt: the beginnings of self-help', *African Urban Studies*, 11, pp. 65–85.
Town Planning Department. 1972. *Lilongwe THA Social Survey.* Lilongwe: Town Planning Department.

## RESUME

Ce chapitre comprend trois sections principales. La première présente un bref historique du logement de la population de faibles revenus au Malawi et met en lumière le développement du logement de site et de services qui fournit maintenant des habitations pour la majorité de la population urbaine. La seconde section contient une discussion sur la croissance de la location à petite échelle et les caractéristiques des occupants–propriétaires, des locataires et des propriétaires. La troisième section représente une étude de cas du développement dans les années 70 du logement de site et de services à Lilongwe, capitale depuis 1975 lorsqu'un contretemps dans le développement des zones de site et de services a affecté le marché immobilier en réduisant à la fois l'offre et en augmentant la demande, ce qui a diminué les chances des locataires de devenir propriétaires–occupants.

# PART III
# HOUSING PROJECTS AND POLICY OPTIONS

# 11  John Campbell

## WORLD BANK URBAN SHELTER PROJECTS IN EAST AFRICA: MATCHING NEEDS WITH APPROPRIATE RESPONSES?

The major concern of this chapter is to examine, from a broad urban policy perspective, the experience of the World Bank-sponsored urban shelter programmes initiated in East Africa since 1974. I am not specifically concerned here with a detailed analysis of the implementation of site and services schemes and squatter upgrading *per se* since such evaluations are gradually being made.[1] Instead I am concerned with somewhat broader questions concerning the degree to which such projects have met the shelter needs of the urban poor, and whether it is really desirable to replicate these types of shelter projects.

The need for an independent assessment of World Bank African projects is long overdue since such urban shelter schemes are now well into their second decade of existence and, not surprisingly, the Bank is making large claims concerning their viability and usefulness (World Bank, 1983, Mayo with Gross, 1985) Indeed, the Bank may be somewhat modest in claiming that only thirty-five developing countries were, by 1982, implementing urban policies among the lines that it suggests. The urban lending programme began in 1972 and, by the end of 1981, sixty-two projects will have absorbed approximately US $2,018 million (4·1% per cent of Bank finance). These include shelter projects (squatter upgrading and site and service schemes), urban transport projects, integrated urban projects, and regional development projects.

According to the Bank, some 1·9 million households, or about 11·4 million people benefited from its shelter projects between 1972 and 1981, and during the 1982–86 period a further ninety urban projects were under consideration for loans totalling US $4 billion (World Bank, 1983:2)! Whatever concerns or possible doubts the Bank may have entertained about such projects, the average size of such projects and of Bank loans has steadily increased to approximately twice that of initial projects (World Bank, 1983:17). Clearly there are vested internal interests within the Bank to maintain its current pattern of investments, and just as clearly there builds up over time a network of vested local interests in the states which collaborate with the Bank as well as within the communities provided with urban services and shelter.

Bank activities in East Africa have been more modest than in other regions. Only ten projects, all concerned with urban shelter, have been financed with loans of US $153·5 million. The bulk of these projects have been located in Kenya where considerable work on promoting shelter in secondary cities has continued; Tanzania has had two projects, and Zambia one.

The Bank's own evaluation of its urban lending programme has emphasised its achievements through examining, in an aggregate fashion, statistics on rates of physical implementation. Attention has also quite rightly focused on issues relating to accessibility of project benefits to the 'target population', on measuring improvement in urban housing, access to services, project contributions to generating employment and incomes, and finally to an analysis of the project's wider impact on urban housing and urban policies in general.

All of these criteria are without doubt important in an assessment of urban shelter programmes, but it seems to me that none adequately address the central issue: namely do large-scale shelter projects represent the most effective way of meeting the need for shelter of the urban poor? At no point have Bank evaluations asked this question, despite its obvious importance in relation to the problems the Bank identifies.

By the Bank's definition cost recovery in East Africa appears to be the most serious drawback in its projects. But on closer inspection, the issue is not cost recovery *per se* but the failure of urban management, and behind that of central governments, to apply sanctions against beneficiaries in order to collect revenue (World Bank, 1983: 24ff.; Bamberger *et al.*, 1982: 139ff.) Cost recovery has become a shorthand term for a complex range of government functions which are perceived to undermine shelter projects. More importantly, 'cost recovery' is implicitly about Bank assumptions concerning the desirability of promoting market-related urban programmes and the role which the Bank would like to see East African states assume.

A satisfactory understanding of how urban shelter programmes have worked requires an in-depth look at the evolution of urban policy in East Africa. In what follows I will focus upon the Tanzanian case. It is necessary to state at the outset that the Tanzanian case is not seen as representative of how all Bank projects have worked. However, as I hope references to projects elsewhere in East Africa will show, Bank policy has not varied greatly between countries in the region and *in principle* the major problems encountered in Tanzania were also met in Zambia and Kenya (though their resolutions may have differed).

## TANZANIAN URBAN PROGRAMMES IN THE 1970s

The adoption of *ujamaa* as a radical approach to rural development in the late 1960s substantially altered forms of bureaucratic management and state planning in the urban as well as in the rural areas. One important result of *ujamaa* was the major dislocation of the rural population it occasioned together with an attendant sharp decline in rural food and export production. Between 1968 and 1976, the extremely high capital costs of *ujamaa*, including the growing costs of importing food and oil (made worse by drought), exhausted Tanzania's foreign exchange reserves (Migot-Adholla, 1979).

Another less discussed problem was an apparent exacerbation of rural–urban migration (related in part to stagnating rural incomes and to rural perceptions of urban opportunities). Statistics show that after a small decline in the level of migration in the period following independence (from 7·4 per cent per annum in 1948–57, to 6·5 per cent per annum in 1957–67), rural–urban migration substantially increased at a rate of 9·2 per cent per annum between 1967 and 1978 (Barnum and Sabot, 1976).

The extent of these problems was not lost on the government, which reacted by renewing the emphasis on agricultural production (of food and cash-crops), together with increased political controls over population movement that were to be achieved by reducing unproductive elements of the urban population through: (a) repatriation to *ujamaa* villages; (b) round-ups of urban vagrants, and more importantly; (c) by making access to basic government services and rationed food dependent on registration with local party ten-cell leaders.

More significantly, a broad urban strategy was elaborated in the second Five-Year Development Plan (following the Arusha declaration) which outlined an approach aimed at containing uncontrolled urban development by linking it to a programme of decentralisation which, it was hoped, would stimulate regional growth-poles. Simultaneously, the needs of legitimate urban residents were to be met by adopting a housing and minimum service programme focused on the low-income population. In essence, urban policy was envisaged as an adjunct of a broad strategy of local agricultural capital accumulation that would enable Tanzania to attain a degree of autonomy within the world economy.

At a time when the exodus of peasants into the towns was increasing, urban local government was experiencing increased tension with central government and the Party which led to a government *decentralisation* in 1974. The effect of this move was *not* a devolution of power and responsibility to the regions and districts, but a de-concentration of government offices out of Dar es Salaam (Rweyemamu, 1974); it was also the death knell of urban administration as the locus of decision-making shifted to Regional

Councils where concerns for broader development issues ended even the maintainance of basic urban programmes (water supplies, sewage, roads and works, etc.) (Saduka, 1981). At the same time, local government staff were reallocated and funds for urban programmes diverted, with the result that substantial levels of unplanned 'shanty-town' development occurred. This situation remained in effect throughout the decade even though legislation was hurriedly passed in 1978 to reinstate local government.

If the absence of urban administration caused a deterioration in the level of basic services, it also predictably failed to ensure that settlement corresponded to the basic urban plan. Squatting escalated sharply to an average of 5,000 dwelling units per year between 1969 and 1972, declining to perhaps 3,000 units per year in the late 1970s. In effect, by the mid-1970s approximately 44 per cent of Dar es Salaam's population were squatters and by 1979 '11 persons lived in every squatter house compared to only about 8 persons per house in 1972, a rise in the occupancy rate of 40%' (Stren, 1982:80).

At the same time, the 1970s were marked by a decline in the availability of urban wage work (from 24 per cent of Dar es Salaam's population in 1967 to 17 per cent in 1978) and a compression of urban incomes (despite an 11 per cent increase in the size of the informal sector). By 1978 the *de facto* urban poverty line was estimated to have grown to include at least 60 per cent of the urban population (Tanzania, 1982: 9–17)! Finally, the rapidly expanding unserviced areas in which many of the poor were settling were being incorporated into an urban agglomeration which had neither the organisation nor the finance to develop and administer them.

Urban policy took on an active but very one-sided role in the state's attempt to counter the failure of market-oriented strategies to reach the poor, particularly with respect to the need for shelter. Following the nationalisation of urban land in the mid-1960s, the government nationalised all rental property with a value of over £5,000 (in 1971), and created a registrar of buildings to administer the 2,900 buildings it had acquired (valued at over £32 million). At least part of the rationale for this nationalisation derived from an attempt to break the monopoly enjoyed by the Asian landlord class in the urban housing market, but once achieved, the government made little attempt to maintain or expand public housing (the programme of public housing construction peaked in 1969 and was sharply cut back).

At about the same time the National Executive of the Party adopted a policy which was intended to redevelop the squatter areas. The 1972 Cabinet-level decision arose as a response to the rapid expansion of squatting, but its timing and enlarged scale (four years after it was set out in the Five-Year Plan) indicated a desire to defuse growing worker militancy in the squatter areas. As this decision coincided with the shift to a nationally

co-ordinated *ujamaa* policy with its attendant economic costs, the government looked to external sources to secure necessary finance.

Funding was eventually secured in 1974 from the World Bank after
nearly two years of negotiations, but once secured finance proved of
secondary importance to the direction of urban development and the key
issue came to be the dominant policy position assumed by the World Bank.
In general terms, this situation led to four basic problems which can be
grouped under: (a) issues relating to the basic planning conception of the
projects; (b) issues relating to the problem of scale; (c) problems arising out
of cost overruns, etc.; and (d) indirect 'costs' which affected urban planning
and development capability.

First, the form of the housing, indeed of 'community', which underlay
the Bank's *conception* of sites and services and squatter upgrading was
essentially derived from a model based on North American suburbs, i.e.
large well laid-out communities of single-family housing units serviced by a
high level of amenities (water, electricity, sewage, roads, etc.). Like the
North American model, this form of development required large levels of
investment in land and infrastructure (inevitably subsidised; in North
America by urban government but in East Africa by central government).
Additionally, its extensive nature required a well co-ordinated and carefully
planned approach to development. However, the method devised was a
complex, detailed and inflexible programme which made too many assumptions about the ease with which such innovatory projects could be implemented (Materu, 1986: 130); unlike the situation in Zambia, for instance.
Its inflexibility necessarily meant that implementation encountered many
difficulties of effective co-ordination and development which extended the
work schedule and contributed to overall project difficulties in terms of
completion and cost overruns, etc.

Second, derived from problems of conception was the problem of scale.
Some idea of the scope of the scheme can be gained from Bank estimates
that in the period 1974–83 nearly 1,400 ha. of urban land were to have been
redeveloped for upgrading while at the same time nearly 30,000 new sites
and services were to be built which were to have benefited 475,000 people
(73 per cent of the urban squatter population in Tanzania). In addition,
each 'community' was to have been provided with a minimum of facilities
(schools, health and nutrition centres, and markets). Though laudable in
intent, its very size – which made no concession to local conditions, needs or
geography[2] – complicated the project by requiring a level of planning skill
and expertise which only the Bank and its expatriate consultants could
provide. At the close of the second phase many of the physical components
originally envisaged were substantially revised, cut back and/or left
incomplete (indefinitely): this was particularly the case with community
facilities (in Tanzania only 24 per cent of those called for in Phase II were

complete in early 1985; while in Zambia only eight of twenty schools, six of seventeen markets, and seven of seventeen community centres were completed; Bamberger *et al.*, 1982: 89).

At the same time, and though ostensibly designed to allow for local replication, the project had built into it a high level of technical and managerial dependence. In addition to the site and services office set up in the parent ministry (and partially staffed by expatriate officers), outside consultants were called in to evaluate project performance (especially concerning cost recovery). Unlike other international and bilateral urban development assistance, Bank projects actually contained specific provisions intended to assist local manpower training (including upgrading local training institutions). Even so, not only was little real assistance received, but key proposals intended to integrate Tanzanian planners, etc., into the shelter projects were never implemented (Hayuma, 1979a: 123–4). The result has been that in addition to having been excluded from key policy-making positions, Tanzanian training institutions are unable to provide sufficient numbers of trained planners, architects, engineers, surveyors, or even trained artisans to man existing projects and ministries. This situation has inevitably meant that Tanzanians will continue to be marginal to major urban policy decisions and will be unable to assume much responsibility for management (Hayuma, 1979b).

Third, the Bank did not take into account the international economic climate of recession and its likely impact in delaying project implementation. The second and expanded phase was signed in 1977 when it should already have been clear that Tanzania's balance of payments position, together with the world recession, would result in significant inflation. Not surprisingly, by 1984/85 local cost overruns exceeded estimates by 56 per cent or T.Sh. 105 million (approximately $700,000); this in addition to the IDA project loan of $20·5 million (Sadashiva, 1985).[3] It should be clear that cost overruns of the scale indicated were bound to cause budgeting and balance of payments difficulties that in turn would have serious implications for government ability to maintain, much less replicate, shelter programmes with such high capital costs.[4]

Finally, a not unrelated 'cost' of the site and service project was the *dislocation caused in urban planning* capability by the distorting impact of the Bank-dominated programme. This can be observed at several levels. To begin with, the site and service project was designed and monitored by consultants with minimal local participation and, it appears, without being evaluated for its wider impact on the urban (or rural) sector. Additionally, rising local costs utilised subsidiary funding which effectively denied support for two other shelter programmes (Tanzania, 1982: 10), co-operative house production and provision of 5,000 building plots for middle-income recipients, which undoubtedly led to a much higher degree of upper and middle-income poaching of housing/plots made available by site and service projects.

'Poaching' or 'leakage' is a euphemism for the failure of shelter to reach the 'urban poor', the much vaunted target of Bank urban projects. Available evidence indicates that from 25 to 60 per cent of site and service plots in Tanzania were allocated, regardless of the income of the recipients (with additional plots and upgraded units being illegally transferred through sale after allocation) (Kulaba, 1985: 21ff.). Experience in Zambia and Kenya suggests a similar experience with about one-fifth of the plots going to the population originally targeted (not 50 per cent) in the former (Bamberger *et al.*, 1982: 17), while approximately one-half of occupied plots in the first phase of the Kenya Dandora project were rented out to low-income tenants (in some cases the entire house and/or plot was let illegally; Chana, 1984: 32).

There are at least two major factors responsible for leakage, neither of which are addressed by the Bank. The most important problem derives from the limitations of the key concept 'urban poor', for at no point has the Bank or host governments in East Africa gone further than defining poverty in statistical terms, i.e. those in a specific percentile of the urban income distribution. The minimum required of such an approach, were it really intended to be made operationally useful, would require coming to terms with mechanisms of income distribution rather than setting arbitrary standards, in short, of grasping the social relations which underpin and maintain urban poverty (Sandbrook, 1981: chs. 1–2). In such an ahistorical, asocial approach, reaching the poor becomes little more than a statement of intent, and large-scale urban shelter programmes become little more than directionless attempts to meet the vast public demand for shelter. Which brings us to the second factor responsible for leakage, the administrative/institutional components of such projects.

Available data on completed/consolidated housing under the sites and services and squatter upgrading schemes is presented in Table 11.1.

Apart from the issue of scale and the associated problem of effectively

Table 11.1
Shelter delivery in World Bank urban projects, Tanzania & Zambia

|  | Tanzania | | Zambia | |
|---|---|---|---|---|
|  | *No.* | *% of original estimate* | *No.* | *% of original estimate* |
| Site and service units | 14,944 | 50 | 11,439 | 101 |
| Squatter up-graded units | 38,445 | 126 | 19,916 | 118 |

*Sources:* Sadashiva, 1985:4; Bamberger *et al.* 1982: 17.

co-ordinating and implementing such a huge programme, it is fair to say that the allocation of housing and plots became a time-consuming bureaucratic business, with ever more complex procedures created to determine eligibility and to sort through the thousands of applicants. Unequivocal criteria on applicant and/or household incomes, overcrowding, family size, security of present tenure, present standards of housing, etc., came to dominate the allocation process for a total number of units far short of that needed to meet demand. Inevitably, other administrative and socio-political criteria crept into the allocation process. Administratively, it became the practice to emphasise project applicants' ability to pay charges and meet building costs, which meant in turn that minimum income levels for the 'low-income' group had constantly to be revised upwards in line with rising building costs (caused by delays in construction and rising inflation). Socio-political 'criteria'[5] in the form of special consideration/ access based on class and ethnicity also became important 'criteria' for allocation. The end result was that administrative convenience in conjunction with class/ ethnic considerations (Stren, 1982) resulted in short-cuts in allocation procedures with fewer benefits reaching the 'poor'. Not surprisingly, Bank evaluations have come to emphasise physical completion of the projects (e.g. numbers of units completed, roads made, land redeveloped), and have reduced the emphasis given to meeting the shelter needs of the 'urban poor'.

The central role of the bureaucracy in this process underlines two further issues arising directly out of large-scale shelter provision, namely the cost of individual units which is passed on to recipients and the overall role of institutions in the entire scheme. While lowered building standards undoubtedly reduced average urban construction costs, and vetting procedures attempted to ensure that beneficiaries could afford the units, evidence suggests that poorer beneficiaries still experienced problems in meeting housing costs. This problem is likely to have one of two results: either recipients will rent out part of their dwelling space (thereby negating direct improvements in their living conditions), and/or they will sell out entirely to wealthier strata (Bamberger et al., 1982: 150ff.; Chana, 1984: 29ff; Kulaba, 1985: 23).

The Bank's position on these problems has been to minimise their importance and more recently to reverse the terms of the argument by stressing the supposed income generating effects of improved housing (which allows beneficiaries to increase household incomes through renting). However, this side-steps the issue and prevents any serious discussion of costs and standards! Even if accepted, such a reply does not address the issue of the poor opting out of the scheme by surreptitiously selling their plots. The underlying issue here is that even the reduced housing costs realised by the project are too expensive for poor households, because their ability to generate sufficient capital to meet long-term payments, construct dwellings to minimum standards *and* meet household needs are more likely to decrease or remain static.[6] In the end, the limited income opportunities open to poor households, many of whom are headed by females, will ensure that either they will be removed from project sites through the market for urban land housing, or that they will choose to realise the value tied up in their property by selling out.[7]

The obverse side of large-scale projects is that they require considerably more in the way of management skills than many host governments possess. The Bank's term for this issue is 'institutional development', which tends to be a rubric for a variety of problems, the most important being the proliferation of institutions with cross-cutting responsibilities in urban areas. This problem is compounded through the creation – by the Bank and other aid agencies – of new bureaucracies and institutions designed to cut across existing institutional relations. Halfani, who has reviewed the operation of site and service schemes in Kenya, Senegal and Tanzania, aptly points out that the problems of bureaucratic instability and fragmented responsibilities are a manifestation of the 'politics of development management' in which

The urban administrative system was designed to perform sectoral tasks; since the SS project involves integrated functions, the system fails to operate smoothly. On the other hand, lack of coordination was a reflection of a reluctance to disrupt the existing authority relationships within the overall administrative system. For one organ to coordinate the activities of the others it entailed the subordination of the authority of the latter to the former. This would have disrupted the local balance of power. (n.d.: 20)

Halfani argues that external agencies, particularly monetarist institutions like the Bank who are interested in returns on investment, have a limited role to play in reshaping existing institutions (p. 24). I would go a step further. It seems to me that the Bank, more than most development agencies, has strengthened the role of the state and its institutions over local classes by channelling capital and resources through government. Indeed, Bank projects appear to have called forth, if not a proliferation, then an expansion of bureaucracy as new and more complicated regulations are required to administer the scale and type of projects it sponsors. The result has been to reinforce the power and patronage of the state over the poor.

In this view, implementation problems laid at the door of institutions who fail to maintain projects and to collect revenue – in the Bank's words, 'the absence of political will' – are wilfully shortsighted. Such problems must surely be seen as part and parcel of the very nature and size of the project being sponsored and not as a failure to adequately address 'the administrative challenge' of working with poorly staffed and badly co-ordinated institutions. In short, large-scale investment projects of this type compound administrative problems.

The fourth basic problem associated with Bank urban shelter programmes in Tanzania concerns their cost. Shortly after beginning phase II
in 1978 it was belatedly realised that rapidly rising local costs (fuelled by
inflation[8] associated with implementation delays) would entail a reduction
in the scope of the project. This led to a number of elements being eliminated (including support for an experimental employment creation through
small-scale industry) and, most importantly, to a devolution of project
responsibility to local government. It should be recalled that only that year
had local government been brought back into existence by legislation
following decentralisation. Needless to say, local government had neither
adequate finances nor experienced staff to deal with normal urban administration, much less with complex, large-scale shelter schemes. The foregone
outcome of the above problems was that the Bank shelter scheme, even in its
truncated and incomplete form, came to be a substitute for a coherent urban
policy package with the result that considerable chaos and poorly co-ordinated urban development occurred.

## WIDER IMPLICATIONS OF THE BANK PROJECT FOR URBAN DEVELOPMENT

Apart from the above unforeseen implications arising out of the Bank
shelter scheme, there were a number of important urban policy areas over
which Tanzania and the Bank differed sharply, and in which the former
should have anticipated difficulties. The most important of these policy
disagreements concerned *land and rent control*.[9] In the 1960s all freehold
land in urban areas was converted into government leasehold, with the
occupant obliged to pay ground rent. This created a legislative basis for
both effective urban development and for preventing land speculation
(which pushed up property values and pushed out the poor who would be
unable to afford escalating rents).

The unequivocal link between land control and rent levels built into the
above legislation was further reinforced by two additional laws: continu-
ation of colonial rent controls, and adoption of a sliding scale of rent
subsidies (based on a set percentage of salary) paid to government
employees living in public housing. Various opinions exist as to the effect
which government rent control had. While the obvious attempt was to
legislate a system of fair and reasonable rent, it seems clear that controls
probably helped to depress construction without effectively curbing
abusive and/or illegal landlord practices. At the same time, the policy of
supporting a small percentage of government employees in public housing
was highly inequitable and costly (in terms of the growing hidden subsidy
and in its encouragement to costly construction).[10]

The World Bank was very clear in its determination to sever the link between land and rent control. In its estimation this legislation had led to a grossly distorted rental market which prevented adequate returns on investment in housing which unnecessarily restricted construction. For several years the government and the Bank argued over the appropriate fiscal policies that would be both socially equitable and provide for the adequate recovery of urban and infrastructural project costs. In the end basic urban maintenance problems together with Bank arguments for a more effective method of cost-recovery (direct from users) was perceived by the government to be necessary, even though it was in clear contradiction not only with decentralisation but also with existing land and rent legislation. This did not mean that the offending legislation was dropped, rather a new tax was devised which progressively broke the link between land and rent in all squatter areas. The mechanism of cost recovery consisted of a complete house registration exercise coupled with the regularisation of land tenure that would allow efficient tax collection. Since squatter areas constitute a very large proportion of the urban land market, and because a process of sustained 'poaching' of plots was occurring, the effect of this decision was to render previous legislation redundant. The result was that land and housing prices escalated.

The overall effect of this decision on the housing market is uncertain. At one level it is apparent that despite the partially completed Bank project, a tremendous amount of private housing construction began to take place by the end of the decade which was financed from private sources. Much of this housing has been built to extremely high standards (at least in Dar es Salaam), thus indicating very high rents. As such it offers no solution to the housing needs of the majority of the urban population.

Rising land and property values have also meant that the poor who gained access to serviced plots under the upgrading programme have been under considerable pressure to sell and relocate elsewhere, though it is not clear to what extent this is occurring. In the sites and services component there has taken place an alarming (though probably not universal) overcrowding as unauthorised houses have been hurriedly constructed in these areas well in excess of available services (Chana, 1984: 28; Magembe, 1985: 5). At the same time, there is solid evidence that the recipient population is facing deteriorating housing and community conditions as a result of a much heavier usage than was planned for and which is exacerbated by the adoption of lower construction standards (Kamulali, 1985; Bamberger et al., 1982: 62ff.).

Clearly then, while private housing construction has increased in recent years, the housing market remains as fragmented as ever. More luxury housing is not going to offer any solution to the poor who compose 60 per cent or more of the rapidly growing urban population. In such conditions a rise in the level of squatter construction and further deterioration of squatter housing is more than likely. The only effective relief to the poor will come from enabling them to earn adequate, sustainable household incomes through employment opportunities (not from renting out their dwellings).

While the state had become very active in intervening in the housing market, very little was accomplished outside the sites and services scheme. For instance, all urban areas experienced a severe running-down of physical infrastructure that matched dilapidated housing conditions. As the former squatter areas were being transformed into new 'suburbs', the original infrastructural system proved utterly inadequate in meeting basic requirements.

Though the 1960s and 1970s witnessed large investments in urban infrastructure, the logic of urban development ensured that the bulk of investment would go into opening up new land for settlement. In either case, construction occurred as an extension of the original system developed during the colonial period for a far smaller urban population. The predictable result was the gradual collapse of basic services and urban infrastructure. Roads fell into disrepair; sources of clean water were exhausted; the entire sewage system packed up, creating growing problems with pollution; large areas were completely without electricity while other areas experienced frequent black-outs; finally, the system of public transport gradually broke down. In a situation of urban 'crisis' with large unmet demands on available finances and limited manpower resources, it should not have surprised the Bank that problems of urban maintainance and management became severe.

With planned urban expansion and the opening up of an (illegal) land and housing market, the displacement of the urban population out of the central and more developed areas has been given a renewed impetus. This has been the case especially for the poorer and migrant households as a corollary to their search for sources of cash income and for an area on which to erect shelter and establish a subsistence plot (Tanzania, 1975). The rationale behind this population movement has apparently been dictated, at least indirectly, by the location and nature of particular state programmes such as land development, public transport routes, the location of industries, etc., as well as by their own changing perceptions of the city (Yahya, 1969).

The effect of this movement, and specifically of site and service development, has been to fragment the underlying social fabric of the towns. The consequence of the slum-clearance schemes of the 1960s, of developing new neighbourhoods, of redeveloping squatter areas, and of the growing displacement of individuals through market forces, has had the effect of breaking up established communities and dispersing many of the poorer households to very marginal areas remote from social services. Simultaneously, with the expansion of the bureaucracy and the extension of its authority over all aspects of urban development, there are clear indications of continued marginalisation of the poor from political and economic decisions.

Against this observation it is possible, as the Bank has argued, that the shelter programmes did initially 'integrate' some of the urban poor into the political system through the selection and upgrading process. However, it also seems to have been the case that over the long term poor households are likely to be pushed out of the projects through their inability to afford the cost of improved shelter and meet basic household needs.

## CONCLUSION

The central question that needs to be asked of these large-scale, capital-intensive and bureaucracy-dominated urban shelter projects is whether they represent appropriate forms of development assistance to the low-income urban populations. Based on their performance in East Africa, it should be clear that there are serious doubts on several grounds.

The overriding issue must certainly be whether the low-income popu-lation can realistically be helped by such projects. This is because the scale of the projects (even with lower standards of construction) impose high costs relative to the incomes of the poor; and because a large percentage of the resources put into the programmes do not go out in the form of benefits to users, but are consumed by contractors, equipment and material suppliers, and as administration overheads (including consultants' fees).

In addition, rising financial costs strongly suggest that such large-scale programmes are not replicable without continued reliance on external finance and direction. Equally important, and given their capital-intensive and import-dependent nature, very little is known of the long-term financial cost of maintaining such projects.

At the same time, Bank projects have called for a high level of technical and managerial competence which it has found lacking. The scale and complexity of the projects have put excessive demands on local administrations both to implement and manage. Physical implementation has consistently overrun operating budgets, met with unexpected delays and resulted in incomplete programmes; while management problems have never been adequately resolved in spite of continuous monitoring and direction by the Bank.

But apart from technical and financial questions, there remain a number of issues which seem to indicate that such programmes may not be desirable for reasons of equity. Available evidence appears to indicate that an increasing percentage of shelter provided under the projects may be prone to 'leakage' and/or may be lost by the low-income population due to the low and irregular nature of household incomes. Alternatively, significant numbers of the low income population may prefer to rent rather than own urban housing, which would render such shelter programmes redundant for their purposes (though such schemes may be ideal for creating a class of landlords; Muwonge 1982: 74ff.).

As Lea (1979: 52–3) has observed in a slightly different context, the importance of regional and local variations in both national economic conditions (crucial to the consolidation of low-income housing projects) and in the shelter needs of different urban (migrant) groups all strongly suggest that there are distinct limits on the 'international transferability of housing strategies and instruments' to developing countries.

A propos of the latter issue, Lea has suggested that in sub-Saharan Africa, where strong rural links prevail, migrants may be much less willing to invest in an urban house or to upgrade their shelter. The necessity of addressing this particular issue and its special relevance for the success or failure of site and service schemes had been noted by Nelson:

The [SS] approach outlines that settlers will be both able and willing not only to build an initial shanty but also to improve their housing gradually. Where most migrants are permanent, 'sites and services' is a practical way to assist groups too poor to afford so-called conventional housing. But where the bulk of migrants are temporary, or are so committed to return eventually to their homeplaces that they give priority to investments there, then sites and service programmes are likely to produce shanty towns with a heavily tenant population. (Nelson, 1976: 746, quoted in Lea, 1979: 53)

Equally important, large amounts of capital are being expended into shelter schemes in which, for the most part, there has been a minimal input by potential beneficiaries concerning the nature of their needs. Zambia has gone the furthest to bring urban residents into the project, but despite their achievements virtually no local residents were consulted prior to implementation about what they wanted or needed (Jere, 1984: 64). The effort has been to utilise self-help as a technique to lower housing production costs and not as an end in itself, and consequently project beneficiaries often do not perceive of themselves as having responsibility for maintainance and upkeep, much less an obligation to pay charges. Instead, the project is seen as the responsibility of the government which planned and constructed it.

Clearly there is a need for caution in pursuing such large-scale programmes as well as for further detailed research into more cost-efficient and equitable forms of shelter. From the above observations, viable alternatives will have to give much greater attention not only to employment generation for the low-income population, but also to widely varying regional and local conditions. Without generating sustainable forms of local employment it may well prove impossible to support shelter schemes which do not have a large element of subsidy. Viable alternative programmes will also need to be of a much smaller scale and be based on strategies which combine grass-roots participation (Shah, 1984) with innovatory approaches to land development (Ward, 1984) that will reduce long-term shelter costs. Fortunately, such urban 'programmes' are being developed and pursued, principally by NGOs. While their experience to date has been limited to a small number of community self-help projects, results indicate that effective 'solutions' are possible but that they depend on recognising that there are no 'technical' answers to what are essentially socio-economic and political problems.

## NOTES

1   For Kenya see Chana, 1984. For material on Tanzania see Materu, 1986; Sadashiva, 1985; Siebolds and Steinberg, 1982; and Campbell, 1988. For material on Zambia see Jere, 1984; Bamberger et al., 1982; and Keare and Parris, 1982.

2   For example, a 'hasty' selection of sites in Morogoro led to the selection of an area subject to periodic flooding in which 13 per cent of sites were eliminated (Materu, 1986: 129); while in Dar es Salaam, over 100 site and service plots were unable to be developed due to the alignment of a water main, with a further 350 left undeveloped owing to unforeseen technical problems. Similarly, Site 6 in Lusaka was found to be subject to flooding which eliminated 530 of a planned 930 plots, resulting in substantially increased development costs (Bamberger et al., 1982: 51). Experience in Kenya has been much the same where selection of a site on cheap, swampy ground resulted in a 600 per cent increase in the cost of serviced plots (Peattie, 1982: 135).

3   Significantly, Tanzania's external debt was growing rapidly during this period, with approximately US $720 million owed to the Bank/IDA alone by 1981 (Bank of Tanzania, 1984: 227).

4   Hayuma (1979a: 128) correctly observes that the initial shortage of skilled local personnel means not only that most design work is carried out by expatriates and consultants, but also that there are few large-scale local building contractors capable of assuming project work. This has necessitated allowing multinational firms, whose techniques rely overwhelmingly on imported materials, to carry out the work.

5   See Bamberger et al. 1982, ch. 6, and Keare and Parris, 1982: 71.

6   While the Bank has argued that recipients of project housing have not been unduly affected by project costs, their data are unconvincing. For example, their figures for Lusaka indicate that an extremely high percentage of beneficiaries are, unusually for the urban poor, wage-earners (over 90 per cent)! Furthermore, for the lower-income area (George) nearly 26 per cent of household income is derived from rent and 'donations' (the latter from family or friends; Bamberger et al. 1982: pt. IV)! On the other hand, Jere indicates that repayments 'are beyond the reach of many households' (1984: 67). This is certainly the case in Kenya where average rents charged to tenants of site and service plots (at Ks. 150–200 per month per room; Chana, 1984: 32) are twice the average rents squatters pay near Mathare Valley (Kabagambe and Moughtin, 1983:241). Mgullu's analysis of the Dar es Salaam site and service scheme is equally clear that due to the irregular incomes of the self-employed and their exclusion from access to housing finance, project benefits will go to the better-off (1978: 83–124; see also Siebolds and Steinberg, 1982: 120). Peattie

provides an excellent discussion of the probable impact of site and service schemes on the poor (1982: 134ff.).

7   Interestingly, the Lusaka data indicate that project recipients who were female heads of household were much more likely to depend on rental incomes than were households headed by males (Bamberger *et al*, 1982: 151). A similar conclusion seems also to have been reached by the Bank's comparative study of site and service schemes in El Salvador, the Philippines, Senegal, and Zambia (Keare and Parris, 1982: 37).

8   Local inflation tends to heighten the effect of so called 'hidden' or unintended subsidies in Bank schemes, which are a result of being costed at below their real market value and which are extremely difficult to estimate. There is apparently some evidence to indicate that, at least for the early projects, this 'subsidy' was so high as to induce low-income groups to enter the project with the result that they may have 'consumed' more shelter than they could presumably afford over the long term. The net result would be for the low income population to opt out of the project, and for such subsidies to be passed on to upper-income groups.

9   The Bank was initially supportive of similar Zambian legislation (the Land Acquisition Act of 1969, etc.) until it determined that government acquisition was too slow for their purposes (Bamberger *et al.*, 1982: ch. 5). Mwita (1978: 138ff.) discusses Tanzanian rent-control legislation.

10   The Tanzania Ministry of Lands has not calculated this subsidy which covers only 7 per cent of public employees and probably amounts to government payment of at least two-thirds of the economic rent of its employees (Tanzania, 1980: 10). Similar subsidies in Zambia were analysed and were found to be prohibitive (e.g., approximately Kwacha 95·6 million, or roughly the entire budget of the Third National Development Plan; Sanyal, 1981: 426ff.).

# REFERENCES

Bamberger, M., Sanyal, B and Valverde, N. 1982. *Evaluation of Sites and Services Projects: the experience from Lusaka, Zambia*. World Bank Staff Working Paper No. 548, Washington DC.

Bank of Tanzania. 1984. *Tanzania: twenty years of independence (1961–81): a review of political and economic performance*. Dar es Salaam.

Barnum, H. N. and Sabot, R. H. 1976. *Migration, Education and Urban Surplus Labour: the case of Tanzania*. Development Centre Studies, Employment Series No. 13, Paris, OECD.

Campbell, J. 1988. 'Tanzania and the World Bank urban shelter projects: ideology and international finance', *Review of African Political Economy*, vol. 42, pp. 15–18.

Chana, T. S. 1984. 'Nairobi: Dandora and other projects' in G. K. Payne (ed.), *Low Income Housing in The Developing World: the role of sites and services and settlement upgrading*, pp. 17–37. Chichester: John Wiley.

Halfani, M. S. n.d. *The challenge of replicability: towards strengthening institutional capacities for the implementation of sites and services projects in Kenya, Senegal, and Tanzania*. Project Ecoville Working Paper No. 36, Institute for Environment Studies, University of Toronto.

Hayuma, A. M. 1979a. 'Training programmes for the improvement of slums and squatter areas in Tanzania', *Habitat International*, 4(1), pp. 119–29.

—— 1979b. 'A review and assessment of the contribution of international and bilateral aid to urban development policies in Tanzania', *Ekistics*, 279, November/December, pp. 349–61.

Jere, H. 1984. 'Lusaka: local participation in planning and decision-making' in G. Payne (ed.), *Low Income Housing in the Developing World*, pp. 55–69. Chichester: John Wiley.

Kabagambe, D. and Moughtin, C. 1983. 'Housing the poor, a case study in Nairobi', *Third World Planning Review*, 5 (3), pp. 227–48.

Kamulali, T. 1985. 'The management of the sites and services programme in Tanzania: case study of Nyakato in Mwanza municipality'. Paper given to the *International Conference on the Management of Sites and Services and Squatter Upgrading Housing Areas* (ICMSSSU), Arusha International Conference Centre, February.

Keare, D. H. and Parris, S. 1982. *Evaluation of Shelter Programs for the Urban Poor: principal findings*. World Bank Staff Working Paper No. 547, Washington DC.

Kulaba, S. M. 1985. 'Managing rapid urban growth through sites and services and squatter upgrading housing in Tanzania: lessons of experience'. Paper given to the ICMSSSU, Arusha.

Lea, J. 1979. 'Self-help and autonomy in housing: theoretical critics and empirical investigators', in H. S. Murison and J. Lea (eds.), *Housing In Third World Countries: perspectives on policy and practice*, pp. 49–54. London: Macmillan.

Magembe, M. J. A. 1985. 'Towards effective management and consolidation of squatter upgrading areas: the case of Mwanjelwa squatter settlement, Mbeya, Tanzania'. Paper given to the ICMSSSU, Arusha.

Materu, J. 1986. 'Sites and services projects in Tanzania, a case study of implementation', *Third World Planning Review*, 8(2), pp. 121–38.

Mayo, S. K., with Gross D. J. 1985. *Sites and Services – and Subsidies: the economies of low-cost housing in developing countries*. Development Studies Programme Working Paper No. B13, University of Toronto, April.

Mgullu, F. P. 1978. 'Housing: a study of Tanzania's national sites and services schemes.' Unpublished LLM thesis, University of Dar es Salaam.

Migot-Adholla, S. E. 1979. 'Rural development policy and equality', in J. D. Barkan with J. J. Okumu (eds.), *Politics and Public Policy in Kenya and Tanzania*, pp. 154–79. Nairobi: Heinemann and New York: Praeger.

Muwonge, J. W. 1982. 'Intra-urban mobility and low income housing: the case of Nairobi, Kenya', in M. K. C. Morrison and P. C. Gutkind (eds.), *Housing the Urban Poor in Africa*, pp. 57–80. Maxwell School of Citizenship and Public Affairs, Syracuse University.

Mwita, D. M. 1978. 'Urban Landlordism and the Acquisition of Buildings Act'. Unpublished LLM thesis, University of Dar es Salaam.

Nelson, J. 1976. 'Sojourners versus new urbanites: causes and consequences of temporary versus permanent cityward migration in developing countries', *Economic Development and Cultural Change*, 24, pp. 721–57.

Payne, G. K. (ed.) 1984. *Low Income Housing in the Developing World: the role of sites and services and settlement upgrading*. Chichester: John Wiley.

Peattie, L. R. 1982. 'Some second thoughts on sites-and-services', *Habitat International*, 6 (1–2), pp. 131–9.

Rweyemamu, A. H. 1974. 'Some reflections on decentralization in Tanzania', in A. H. Rweyemamu and B. U. Mwansasu (eds.), *Planning in Tanzania: background to decentralization*, pp. 121–31. Dar es Salaam; East Africa Literature Bureau.

Sadashiva, S. S. 1985. 'Financial management of the national sites and services and squatter upgrading project in Tanzania'. Paper given to the ICMSSSU, Arusha.

Saduka, P. N. 1981. 'Local government administration and urban development in Tanzania'. Paper given to the *Conference on Plan Implementation and Human Settlements Administration in Tanzania*, Ardhi Institute, Dar es Salaam, September.

Sandbrook. R. 1981. *The Politics of Basic Needs: urban aspects of assaulting poverty in Africa*. London: Heinemann.

Sanyal, B. 1981. 'Who gets what, where, why and how: a critical look at the housing subsidies in Zambia', *Development and Change*, 12, pp. 409–40.

Shah, K. 1984. 'People's participation in housing action: meaning, scope and strategy', in G. Payne (ed.), *Low Income Housing in the Developing World*, pp. 199–208. Chichester: John Wiley.

Siebolds, P. and Steinberg F. 1982. 'Tanzania: sites and services', *Habitat International*, 6 (1/2), pp. 109–30.

Stren, R. E. 1982. 'Underdevelopment, urban squatting and the state bureaucracy: a case study of Tanzania', *Canadian Journal of African Studies*, 16 (1), pp. 67–91.

Tanzania. 1975. 'Manzese Social Survey'. Mimeo, Dar es Salaam: Ministry of Lands, Housing and Urban Development.

—— 1980. *National Housing Development Policy*. Unofficial English translation, Dar es Salaam: Ministry of Land, Housing and Urban Development.

—— 1982. 'Proposal for the Third National Sites and Services Project: national sites and services project'. Mimeo. Dar es Salaam: Ministry of Land, Housing and Urban Development.

Ward, P. M. 1984. 'Mexico: beyond sites and services', in G. Payne (ed.), *Low Income Housing in the Developing World*, pp. 149–60. Chichester: John Wiley.

World Bank. 1977. *Tanzania: the second national sites and services project*. Washington, DC: Urban Projects Department, June.

—— 1983. *Learning By Doing: World Bank lending for urban development, 1972–82*. Washington DC: World Bank.

Yahya, S. 1969. 'Urban transportation and land use in Tanzania', *Ekistics*, 27 (159), pp. 144–7.

## RESUME

Ce chapitre examine les programmes d'abri urbain de la Banque Mondiale en Tanzanie, en Zambie et au Kenya et tente de mettre en valeur certains problèmes et certaines questions posés par les programmes à grande échelle à fort investissement de capitaux et dominés par la bureaucratie. La question primordiale est de savoir si de tels programmes d'abri conviennent aux besoins de la population urbaine pauvre d'Afrique orientale et s'ils devraient effectivement servir de modèles.

Le projet de site et de services en Tanzanie est examiné en profondeur et quatre questions fondamentales sont posées, à savoir si ces programmes sont appropriés en ce qui concerne: (1) les questions de conception fondamentale de planification; (2) les problèmes d'échelle; (3) les problèmes de coût; et (4) les 'coûts' indirects politiques et socio-économiques.

Ce chapitre conclut que les preuves actuelles suggèrent fortement que de tels programmes ne sont pas appropriés aux besoins de la population urbaine pauvre pour diverses raisons, essentiellement parce qu'ils coûtent trop cher et représentent une solution sans souplesse à ce qui s'avère être pour les pauvres une vaste gamme de besoins et, par conséquent, il faut établir des solutions plus appropriées qui diffèrent radicalement des projets de la Banque Mondiale.

# CONTRADICTIONS AND DILEMMAS IN THE PROVISION OF LOW-INCOME HOUSING: THE CASE OF HARARE

## THE CONTEXT

The intention of this chapter is to examine recent changes in housing policies in Zimbabwe, paying particular attention to aided self-help schemes. In this context the implicit contradictions between ownership and low-cost solutions are examined. The specific example of Harare will be used as it best exemplifies recent trends in policy in Zimbabwe.

Before any consideration is given to the specific problems faced in the provision of low-cost housing in the capital, some comment is needed on the form of settler–colonial provision of housing in the pre-independence era.

The most important changes taking place in housing policy can be traced back to the late 1970s. At this stage the Zimbabwean state began to move from a collectivised form of housing provision for the black population to one fundamentally based upon privatised provision, which later included recommodification policies. Hence by the late 1970s, freehold tenure was made available to all blacks in urban areas, at least to those successful via the housing waiting list. The late 1970s saw a changing political climate and an increased need to provide low-cost housing (Ministry of Finance, 1979); along with this one saw the development of self-help policies and a shift towards the provision of housing on a home-ownership basis. It was increasingly felt that where an individual was responsible for development then they should receive the benefit in the form of ownership. This can clearly be seen in a wider context as the need to create a stable, black, property-owning middle class. Consequently during this period one also saw the shift towards policies designed to privatise existing rental housing as dwellings were sold to residents at considerable discounts.

At this stage there were three important strands in central and local state policies. Firstly there was a shift in attitudes regarding styles of housing provision, secondly, a change in attitudes to tenure, and thirdly, superimposed upon these, was a rethinking of views regarding town planning, and the overall position of blacks in the urban economy.

During this period two contrasting groups were attempting to direct these strategies. Amongst the conservative element within the RF government was a feeling that the reforms regarding ownership, such as those proposed by the Quenet Commission into Racial Discrimination (1976), were beginning to undermine the philosophical underpinnings of separate development for the races.[1] Hence, rather than wishing to accept that 'Africans' should be considered a permanent part of the urban economy, they wished to see European domination of urban areas reasserted. For example, it was proposed that in order to achieve this the major centres, notably Salisbury, should see the development of new urban areas located in Tribal Trust Lands (TTLs), which would be exclusively for African development. These were seen as being ultimately self-sufficient (semi-)autonomous bodies generating their own incomes and economic structure. Within such a structure it was envisaged that African rights could mirror those of Europeans in urban areas. Such a strategy would ensure that higher-income Africans would be able to benefit from freehold tenure in an urban context, whilst still remaining technically in the TTLs. As a consequence one saw the development of Chitungwiza on the outskirts of Salisbury. Increasingly, however, it was acknowledged that the link with Salisbury would be maintained, and that Chitungwiza Urban Council would essentially be a dormitory town rather than an effective self-sustaining satellite. This conservative element had previously also called for the repossession of some 'African' areas within Salisbury.[2]

Other elements within the Rhodesian state, notably those middle-class blacks in Parliament, were calling for a housing policy to satisfy the needs of black middle-class groups.

This was clearly as much to stem the tide of black unrest as it was to improve housing facilities. Indeed it was proposed that only middle-class blacks should have access to freehold tenure, and again most whites objected. Home-ownership during the mid-1970s was therefore to be restricted to middle and higher-incomes groups, and it was specifically stated by the then Housing Minister, William Irving, that it was not a facility which would be available to low-income groups.[3]

Given the nature of this concern, at a national level a sub-plot began to develop between the local state in Salisbury and central state agencies in 1977, as the former attempted to cope with the waiting list (16,384 households in October 1977), with the proposal that housing provision should shift towards site and service facilities. Irving, however, was not prepared to sanction ownership on such low-income schemes. Salisbury City Council felt this to be an essential incentive to self-building.[4] This specific issue was not resolved until after a change in government and the installation of joint ministers in the transitional government of Muzorewa.

At this stage home-ownership was seen increasingly as an important ideological factor in the establishment of a black middle class. However, Salisbury City Council saw it also as an important element in the developing policy of aided self-help-style provision, which showed its concern for low-income groups and also ensured a minimum financial outlay in dealing with the growing problems of population increase in urban areas.

The ultimate result of this newly-defined policy (given the change of government) was the development of schemes at Glen View in 1979 and later the development of Ultra-Low-Cost cores at Seke in the outlying dormitory town of Chitungwiza. The former (considered in this paper) was a site and service scheme initially nicknamed 'Toilet Town', due to the initial construction of concrete toilet/shower units on 200 sq. m. plots. The plots were then to be developed by the beneficiary – allocated from the waiting list.

Seke was somewhat different in that it provided a very basic mortar mesh core (later refined into a breeze block construction). This was seen as providing at least some basic shelter at the rear of the plot which residents could later improve upon. The latter scheme was seen as being the basis of a National Five Year Low-Cost Housing Programme (Government of Zimbabwe, 1980) and was intended to provide 61 per cent of all publicly-provided housing. However, this was shelved by Eddison Zvobgo, the first Minister of Local Government and Housing in the Mugabe government.

During the early stages of the new government both the above approaches were rejected. Both schemes were criticised: Glen View as it provided no initial dwelling unit on site, and Seke because of the poor quality of the core.

Ultimately Zimbabwe saw a return to those policies used at Glen View. It should be noted here that for several years since the mid–1970s, Harare (formerly Salisbury) City Council had advocated a shift towards aided self-help policies and so was particularly pleased by the shift in government strategy. As a result all newly instituted housing policies have followed this model, specifically of providing a 200/300 sq. m. plot which residents were then expected to develop.

Glen View itself has seen substantial development and has been described by a World Bank official as 'one of the best examples of an aided-self-help scheme in the world' (DCS, 1983b).

## THE CASE OF GLEN VIEW

I will look initially at the development of Glen View in the context of Harare City Council's attitude towards housing strategies. From the outset Glen View was seen as a scheme which aimed to provide a housing solution for low-income groups. It was initially allocated to people on the waiting list with monthly incomes of between Z$40 and Z$150.

Glen View's establishment was based therefore on a changing attitude towards ownership, a strategy of self-help and, at the level of low-income policy, one based upon rather crude 'affordability' criteria. For the first time the waiting list was used as a filter, not simply to ensure priority for those who had been on the waiting list for the longest period, but amongst these to find specific income cohorts. It was used therefore as a specific tool for restricting access to a minimum and maximum income group. Hence it was clearly aimed at a targeted population identified as being low-income (although it appears that no preliminary research was undertaken to effectively ascertain who these groups were). Salisbury City Council's criteria seem to have been based on fairly arbitrary assumptions. Glen View therefore represented the first attempt within Salisbury to integrate both home-ownership and self-help strategies, and to be specifically aimed at targeted low-income groups.

Salisbury City Council therefore has had a clearly stated policy regarding the initial allocation of plots and dwellings within its jurisdiction. Having chosen the beneficiaries, fairly stringent conditions were imposed by the local authority. These were encapsulated in the Agreement of Sale. Whilst facilitating eventual accession to full freehold tenure (within thirty years), it also placed obligations upon beneficiaries in which they were required to construct a six-roomed (minimum) complete dwelling within ten years (to a value of at least Z$1,500). It also required the development of at least one room within three years. However, the bringing together of two radical approaches to housing provision has resulted in profound dilemmas in their operation. They have brought to the fore basic contradictory forces which the local state has not satisfactorily resolved or come to terms with, specifically the combination of self-help and home-ownership.

## TENURE AND HOME-OWNERSHIP

One of the major problems has revolved around the provision of housing on a home-ownership basis. The period before the mid-1970s saw disapproval of home-ownership as a policy for black housing, both by local and central government.

During the preceding three or four decades virtually all housing in urban areas was provided on a rental basis. This was in the form of central or local state provision or in the form of company-tied housing units. Consequently there was virtually no private ownership of housing by blacks in urban areas, and by extension, no housing market. Hence all housing was in a collectivised form. Except for small-scale squatter settlements and some illegal overcrowding, housing was almost completely in the hands of the local authority or the central state.

The changes in tenure policy resulted in major dilemmas for the local authority by the 1980s, however, because previously the latter had been able to control both the access to housing and the future tenure patterns.

The granting of freehold has led to the undermining of the local authority's ability to govern access to such housing. In the specific case of Glen View the Agreement of Sale represented the only way in which the local authority could maintain any influence upon both the physical development of the plot and its actual ownership. Until the conditions of this Agreement had been complied with, control of tenure lay, technically, in the hands of Salisbury City Council. Once the requirements of the agreement had been fulfilled then freehold could be granted in the form of a Certificate of Occupation, along with all the rights which that conferred upon the owner.

It was therefore theoretically possible for the local authority to prevent any plot from changing hands until such time as a Certificate of Occupation was granted. The only way in which a plot could legitimately transfer was if the stand and the Agreement of Sale were exchanged (locally known as a 'cession'). In this way the new resident had to agree to comply with the existing requirements already formulated. However, the Department of Community Services maintained the power to repossess and reallocate the plot, from the waiting list, if all the conditions had not been fully undertaken, and hence prevent the cession. In practice, however, such a policy was not carried through, for both pragmatic and political reasons.

It should be noted here that whilst the Agreement of Sale did not actually specify under what conditions Harare City Council could repossess the plot, it did specify that the authority's written permission would first of all have to be granted. There was clearly an inherent contradiction in this, in as much as the ability of blacks to put a plot on to the open market would undermine local authority attempts to ensure accommodation was restricted to a clearly-defined group.

From the outset the local authority did not perceive that cession would cause any serious problems, because of the newly-adopted policy which accepted home-ownership. However, by 1983 there was an increasing realisation that failure to control cessions could undermine site and service (and self-help) strategies as a 'solution', at least for low-income groups. Hence, there were increasing suspicions that some individuals were acquiring more than one plot either within Glen View itself or in other high-density areas, although by its very nature it was difficult to find clear evidence of this.

A much more serious problem, in terms of its consequences for the scheme itself and the philosophy behind it, was the growing belief that plots were filtering up to higher-income groups. Specifically this was seen as involving people who would not be eligible for allocation to Glen View in accordance with the Council's waiting-list criteria.

The local authority (DCS, 1983a) noted that in the period January to April 1983 cessionaries (those taking over plots with local authority permission) had average monthly incomes of Z$264. This would preclude these individuals from being allocated plots on to newly developing 'low-income'/low-cost schemes. This was not seen as a major problem in the case of Glen View. Prior to this the Ministry of Housing had made proposals aimed at restricting cessions. It was suggested, for example, that cession should be banned for a period of thirty years. The Director of Community Services at Harare City Council rejected this because of its likely retarding effect upon the self-building process.

Since the inception of the scheme and indeed prior to it, it had been argued that given the fact that responsibility for construction was shifted on to the shoulders of beneficiaries they should in turn have access to ownership – if for no other reason than construction would be unlikely to take place if the benefits accrued directly to the local authority in the form of rental payments.

It was felt that if residents were not free to dispose of dwellings which they had developed, the whole policy of aided self-help would be threatened. Indeed, given the circumstances, it is apparent that the policy of aided self-help could not have worked without the acceptance of home-ownership, at least not while a differential housing market persisted.

Having created a low-cost/low-income scheme the dilemma Harare City Council had to face was how to prevent low-income groups being ousted from a project intended for their benefit. At the same time however, Harare City Council was strongly in favour of residents disposing of dwellings in which the latter had invested time and money.

Cessions, however, have represented a problem for the City Council. Given the completion of a dwelling and the payment of the required costs to the local authority a Certificate of Occupation could be granted, freehold would accrue and beneficiaries could dispose of the plot as and when they chose. It had been anticipated that for the vast majority this would be unlikely to occur until the thirty-year period had elapsed, given the nature of the population who were initially allocated plots. Equally, there were perceived to be no problems in dealing with those beneficiaries who had undertaken no development at all. Rather than permitting a cession, the plot could simply be repossessed and reallocated to someone else on the waiting list, as no capital outlay had been made on the plot. However, problems did arise if development had been carried out beyond the level of a concrete slab. As a result, Harare City Council had to decide what should be the minimum amount of development which would have to have been carried out before the cession could be sanctioned. For example, the local authority had to decide whether cessions should be allowed where only one or two rooms had been completed.

## PROFITEERING

A second problem was the fact that when cession took place money was frequently exchanged, and hence to all intents and purposes the plot was 'sold'. Initially it was the authority's view that if money changed hands then it should only be the equivalent of the actual cost of the developments themselves.

The local authority had two basic policies, one to repossess the plot if nothing or very little had been carried out, and a second which involved attempts to prevent or at least restrict profiteering. The latter policy represented the most intractable problem in that the local authority itself acknowledged that to be able to maintain absolute control it would have to have a huge pool of financial resources in order to repurchase plots (DCS, 1983a). This would reduce the whole policy of aided self-help to a farce. It is clear that the local authority could not conceivably repossess plots without any form of compensation, if only because of the political implications, and indeed this idea was never given any serious consideration. It would at any rate have totally undermined the overall policy, as I have already indicated.

Having said this, however, the City Council could not sanction profiteering on what had begun as a local authority-inspired (and financed) scheme. The procedure followed was one which attempted to persuade cedants not to ask unreasonable prices for plots; consequently residents were brought into the local office to justify any given sale price. However, such informal persuasion collapsed if cedants chose to dig in their heels and insist on any given 'sale' price.

There was also at this time a certain amount of confusion in as much as the local authority could not itself assess what a reasonable sale price was. Indeed it had no resources for estimating house values and was not therefore really capable of making a reasoned judgement. This was highlighted by one official who identified five possible values that could be used, i.e. replacement value, rateable value, insurance value, market value, or the original price of the plot.[5] It soon became clear that the only acceptable one was that of the market value. Once again it should be reiterated that given the nature of the Agreement of Sale it would have been very difficult for the local authority to disallow such mutual agreements.

There were however, suggestions put forward which aimed to restrict such transfers, if belatedly, as the local authority began to realise the problems which could result (DCS, 1983a). The proposed restrictions included the imposition of a cession fee of Z$50 in order to attempt to prevent speculation, though this was not proposed to apply on a deceased's estate. It was suggested that cessions should be restricted for three years (and not for thirty years, as proposed by the Ministry). Cessions were to be prevented unless permission of the spouse had been gained, in order to protect the tenurial rights of divorced women. It was also intended that cessions should be restricted to cessionaries who would be eligible for housing in their own right according to waiting list criteria. Lastly it was proposed that cessions should not be sanctioned on vacant/unoccupied stands. These were formally accepted as local authority policy. However, they have largely proved ineffective in their stated intentions of preventing filtering to higher-income groups and in stemming profiteering.

As a consequence cessions continued unhindered by local authority intervention.


## CESSIONS AT GLEN VIEW

The transfer of plots at Glen View in the early months of the scheme occurred mainly as a result of repossession. During this period 'hundreds' of plots were reallocated as initial beneficiaries realised that they were not capable of fulfilling the requirements of the scheme. Harare City Council kept no record of the total numbers but as noted, they were sizeable, according to one official.[6] Whilst such transfers were, during the first few months, carried out through repossession, even then mutually agreed cessions did take place. And in the early stages of the scheme cessions were taking place for the same reasons repossessions were enforced. Consequently residents during this period clearly found it difficult to maintain plots and hence ceded agreements.

As Glen View was considered to be a model project its development was closely monitored. Hence detailed records were kept of cessions taking place, and information was collected on who was acquiring the plot and the reason why the plot was being ceded.

During the period from 1979 (the year of the initial allocation of the scheme) until April 1984, 1,059 cessions (i.e. 14.4 per cent of the 7,347 stands) were sanctioned by Harare City Council. This period saw a marked change in the reasons given for each cession.


## CESSIONS RESULTING FROM FINANCIAL DIFFICULTY

In the years 1980 and 1981 the primary reasons given related to the economic difficulty of maintaining the plot, or carrying out improvements on it. Hence in 1980, of the 174 cessions carried out 51·7 per cent were claimed to be a result of financial difficulties of one kind or another.

However, by 1983 such reasons only accounted for 22.6 per cent of cessions.

Such reasoning is reflected in the actual development which was carried out by this group. Over the period to April 1984 25·2 per cent of these particular cedants had undertaken no improvements at all and a further 16 per cent had only developed a concrete slab. This obviously represents a large proportion of those initially allocated when one considers that it was anticipated that all beneficiaries should have been capable of developing the plot. It is also clearly significant that the City Council rapidly abandoned its policy of repossession of undeveloped plots. Allocation had intended to select closely-defined income groups.

Within this group of cedants there were however substantial numbers who had undertaken improvement to the dwelling. Hence 47·5 per cent had carried out some development in that they had constructed one room or more, although only 13·4 per cent of this group had completed dwellings, i.e. six or more rooms on their plot.

This gives some indication of the problem that the local authority had to face in terms of controlling cessions and the filtering-up process. Whilst it was clear that this group could be viewed as 'failures' in terms of self-help they had not failed absolutely. This heightened the local authority dilemma, in that whilst technically plots could be repossessed it was simply not politically possible to do so, because about 60 per cent had gone beyond the foundation stage.

It should be noted that in the case of 12.9 per cent of those ceding due to financial hardship, development had actually been carried out by the cessionary. More specifically, in the instances where five rooms or more had been completed 42·3 per cent had been carried out by this person.

Clearly original residents began with great enthusiasm in the early years, but in the first eighteen months or so of the scheme realised that they had taken on too much. Hence where only one, two or three rooms had been developed prior to the cession then on the whole it had been undertaken by the initial beneficiary.

A sizeable amount of development therefore has been carried out by 'outsiders'. These individuals have often later acquired the dwelling through the cession procedure, but without going through the waiting list (even if, strictly speaking, they may have been eligible to do so).

At the same time those acquiring the plots have represented a higher-income group, not only in terms of eligibility for allocation to Glen View, but also for more recent schemes where the cut-off figure was Z$175. The average monthly income of all cessionaries in 1982 was Z$243, in 1983 it was Z$269·7 and for the first four months of 1984 the mean figure had risen to Z$339·8. In 1982 the figure of Z$175 was determined as being the maximum monthly income allowable for allocation to the new scheme of Kuwadzana.

## CESSIONS AS A RESULT OF ACQUISITION OF ANOTHER DWELLING

In the later time-period residents increasingly ceded dwellings because they had acquired other dwellings in other high-density areas (formerly African Townships) and also in low-density (formerly European) areas. By 1983 42·6 per cent of those moving were doing so because they had acquired another dwelling.

This group had, by this stage, built up a level of collateral which enabled them to move into a different area of the housing market. Thus they had developed plots to a much higher degree than the group moving owing to financial difficulties. Of the group moving into a different part of the housing market 34·3 per cent had completed dwellings on the plot at the time of the cession. On the whole improvements had been made by the cedants themselves: only 4·9 per cent of the whole of this group had improvements carried out by cessionaries.

In order to acquire these dwellings substantial amounts of money were needed (regardless of local authority policy to cessions). Approximately 19 per cent of seven-roomed dwellings sold were exchanged for more than Z$6,000, although it has to be said that the local authority has not been as effective in collecting information with regard to selling prices, and consequently it is suggested the figure of 19 per cent is probably an underestimate. The figure of Z$6,000 was crucial at the time in the local housing market because it was the level below which building societies considered housing to be 'low-cost' and therefore not eligible for mortgages. Hence, housing is beginning to move outside the realm of the poor.

The development of Glen View has been as much influenced by the indecision of the local authority (about what exactly it was trying to achieve) as it has been a direct product of the upgrading undertaken by beneficiaries on the scheme itself.

There was a clear failure to fully consider the implications of introducing a low-income housing strategy based upon home-ownership policies. This in turn has been a by-product of the general shift towards aided self-help styles of provision. From the outset it was apparent that there was no preconception that the acquisition of plots by higher-income groups could threaten the scheme, and as a consequence no measures were enshrined in the initial agreement to deal adequately with such a possibility. Given the existence (or creation) of a differentiated 'black' housing market it may be seen as inevitable that the part of the market it would penetrate would be the low-income part. By the same token development of this form of aided self-help was unlikely to take place without the ideological spur of home-ownership.

Clearly the introduction of aided self-help strategies and access to freehold tenure has not prevented the acquisition of this accommodation by higher-income groups, and indeed, despite the shift towards limiting cessions to those eligible on the waiting list (based on a maximum income of Z$450), the local authority did establish what it termed a 'special waiting list'. There appears to have been no apparent rationale determined for this; however it did enable people of any income to acquire plots and effectively saw the collapse of all restrictions on acquiring plots at Glen View, hence in a number of cases cessionaries revealed their monthly incomes to be in excess of Z$1,000.

At the same time Glen View is clearly changing in terms of the access which higher-income groups are gaining to plots there. The internal social structure is also increasingly becoming differentiated as an internal housing market is developing. This is clearly being expressed by the extent to which sub-letting ('lodging') has developed.

## SUB-LETTING

On the whole Harare City Council has been even less concerned with the development of sub-letting than it has with problems associated with cessions. Sub-letting has long been acknowledged as an expression of the housing shortage in Harare. However, its implications for the efficacy of self-help have not on the whole been challenged. It has been seen as being of benefit to allottees if they can bring in others to help defray costs of upgrading although sub-letting was never specifically seen as being part of the initial rationale of the project whereby beneficiaries were expected to be capable of developing plots from their own resources.

Harare City Council did not seek to enforce legislation which required lodgers to be registered with the local authority and ensure rents were not above Z$8 per month. It should be noted however, that the Agreement of Sale specifically stated that plots were not to be occupied by more than one residential household without the express written consent of the City Council.

In a survey conducted in January 1984 by the author at Glen View, it was found that 72·4 per cent of plots surveyed had one or more lodger households living on the stands, and indeed of the total population found to be living in the surveyed households 39 per cent were lodgers or their families. Lodgers obviously represent an important sub-group of the population at Glen View. Indeed as development of plots has progressed, so the importance of lodgers has increased. Hence 65·1 per cent of lodger households were found in dwellings which had more than six rooms completed on site. Lodgers have not been restricted to completed houses, which suggests that they have been brought in at early stages of development and have therefore aided upgrading of the plot itself; hence 25 per cent of lodgers were found in dwellings where four rooms or less had been completed. This is compounded by the fact that dwellings are not necessarily restricted to only one lodger household, hence 35·5 per cent of those having lodgers had more than three lodger households (predominantly in dwellings of six or more rooms, as would be expected). With regard to rents, on the whole these have averaged almost twice the stipulated level of Z$8 per month. (The average figure being Z$15·6 where there was one lodger household.) In dwellings where five lodger households lived, as much as Z$80 per month (in one specific instance) was obtained in total rental payments.

## CONCLUSION

Two important threads, therefore, have developed in the Glen View example which have profound implications for the schemes. The dilemmas originate in the shift towards aided self-help style policies and in the move from collectivised forms of tenure with no differentiated housing market to policies incorporating home-ownership. Both elements have counteracted each other in the sense of being able to effectively provide low-income housing. The policies can then be reformulated in terms of the shift of the costs of reproduction on to the shoulders of labour both as a political/ideological response and also in terms of the need to reduce production costs.

The ideological involvement of ownership has effectively allowed the differentiation of housing (formerly collectively consumed) and this in turn is gradually being penetrated by higher-income groups. It remains to be seen to what extent institutional capital will become involved in the form of building society finance, as the value of constructed dwellings effectively places them outside the reach of low-income groups to gain access to them. To date local authorities have proved powerless to prevent the housing market developing and in many senses have been part and parcel of its creation.

Neither the local or central state have shown any real inclination to prevent the development of such a housing market, and have clearly been predominantly concerned to ensure that the schemes work and, specifically, that construction takes place. This was later reinforced with the development of a scheme supported by USAID at Kuwadzana, in which the construction requirements in the Agreement of Sale were tightened up to the extent that beneficiaries were expected to construct four rooms within eighteen months (with a further six months' grace). Consequently there was less of a concern with providing low-income groups with housing that they were capable of developing, in the sense of 'self-help', than the physical provision itself. Hence no real effort was made to ensure that low-income groups did not lose out, either in the short or long term, to higher-income groups who would be likely to penetrate such schemes and then further differentiate the housing market by the introduction of lodgers. There has also been strong suspicion of the development of an absentee landlord class, despite the political rhetoric of 'one man (sic), one house'. There have been no concerted attempts to prevent landlordism or to bring it under effective control.

The low-income housing sector in Harare has therefore seen the under-mining of what had previously been a collectivised form of provision. This has been marked by the penetration of schemes by higher-income groups, who have ensured physical development of stands but have at the same time propagated the development of an increasingly sophisticated housing market in which the poorest are relegated to the lodging sector.

## NOTES

1   Noted in a memorandum by the Secretary for Local Government and Housing to Salisbury City Council Town Clerk, 5 June 1974.

2   In a paper submitted by Cllr Langley (29 July 1973) he called for the demo-lition of all single men's hostels at Harari and for the development of accommodation at St Mary's and Seki (later incorporated as part of Chitungwiza Urban Council).

3   Expressed in notes taken at a meeting between officials of the Ministry of Local Government and Housing and a delegation from Salisbury City Council, 11 February 1977.

4   Identified for example in a memorandum from Salisbury City Engineer to the Town Clerk, 22 August 1977.

5   Interview with J. Gibson, housing official at the Department of Community Services, 10 April 1984.

6   *Ibid.*

## REFERENCES

Department of Community Services (DCS). 1983a. Memorandum to the Town clerk, Re; Cessions of Agreements.
—— 1983b. *Glen View: an example of aided-self-help in Zimbabwe.*
Government of Rhodesia. 1976. *Report of the Commission of Inquiry on Racial Discrimination.* Salisbury: Government Printer.
Government of Zimbabwe. 1980. *Zimbabwe Five Year Low-Income Housing Plan, 1980–1985.* Harare: Government Printer.
Ministry of Finance. 1979. *Urban Development in the Main Centres.* Salisbury: Government Printer.

## RESUME

Ce chapitre prend comme étude de cas un programme de site et de services à Harare. Il est clair que malgré la distribution initiale à des groupes particuliers à revenus modestes, les groupes à revenus plus élevés ont réussi à posséder des logements prévus initialement pour ces groupes pauvres et on a constaté le développment d'un marché immobilier différencié qui laisse peu de place aux plus démunis qui sont condamnés à louer leurs habitats. Le programme a en même temps vu la mise en place d'une volorisation substantielle mais qui a été fréquemment consolidée après la création d'un groupe secondaire interne, par exemple les locataires.

# LAND FOR HOUSING THE URBAN POOR IN AFRICA – SOME POLICY OPTIONS

## INTRODUCTION

The housing situation in Africa is caught in two worlds. On the one hand, there is the traditional society with its dictates and strictures expecting all developments and innovations not only to maintain but to perpetuate traditional cultural values. On the other hand, there is the modern society with its sets of values determined in response to European acculturation, economic, industrial and political institutions. Such values are mainly at variance with the traditional values. For example, while notions of over-crowding are of little relevance in the African tradition, because the neces-sity to accommodate one's kith and kin must override all other considera-tions, the one-family housing unit is predominant in the modern society and people are sensitive to living in crowded conditions.

The result of this dilemma is a plethora of values, precepts and standards that must be recognised and served by the planner in Africa.

By whatever criteria one views housing in the continent, issues of the quality of urban housing and the urban environment, standards regarding space requirements, housing provision and the level and quality of urban services cannot be ignored. These issues cut across African cultural barriers.

Also of importance is the poverty dimension of housing which is accen-tuated by spatial disparities between the 'grass roots' and the rich and the educated elite. These have not developed merely by accident but through the formulation of policies that have often favoured the educated elite and the rich, perhaps because they are the policy-makers, to the disadvantage of the urban poor. The result has been an almost total unavailability of resources for housing provision, through the conventional means, to the urban poor. Resources such as housing land, housing finance, building materials and amenities are unavailable to the urban poor while the rich and the educated elite often take them for granted. The poor have had to content themselves with living in slums and squatter settlements in what are often very squalid conditions, devoid of urban services and amenities, while the rich and educated elite have well laid-out estates with all the amenities conductive to the enjoyment of their housing (Asiama, 1985). Such is the paradox of housing in Africa.

It appears, however, that the urban housing problem will continue to get worse unless some solution is found to the population problem. Population growth, particularly in urban locations (Acquaye and Asiama, 1986: 128) far exceeds economic growth and the result is inability on the part of African governments to provide the resources, such as housing, for a decent standard of living.

It is necessary that African governments develop, concurrently with any policies aimed at helping these urban poor, effective and workable regional planning policies to restrict, in a positive way, the continuing tide of migrants from the rural to the urban environment.

Otto Koenigsberger is reputed to have observed: 'if government is to improve a low-income majority's housing conditions then it must not build houses' (quoted in Turner, 1983: 210). John Turner (1983) has also commented:

The lesson for all contexts in the experience of direct action by the millions of ordinary people housing themselves, especially those on the peripheries of cities in rapidly urbanising countries, is at last beginning to be understood; in spite of all the constraints imposed, sometimes violently by police actions, and despite the consequent distortions of forms and procedures, the poor have done far more for themselves, in absolute terms, than the better off have done for them; and relatively, they have done vastly more in proportion to the resources used. (Turner, 1983: 213)

If housing policies in Africa are to be of any meaning then the people must be enabled to do something for themselves. Government policies must be geared towards the development of institutions to facilitate the urban poor to provide themselves with housing. A start could be made through land provision.

There is little doubt that of all the ingredients of housing the land factor is of paramount importance. This is because without land on which to build, accessibility to housing finance, labour and building materials become of little practical value. On the other hand it has been proved everywhere in the Third World that where land has been made available, even the urban poor have been able to provide themselves with housing. The ubiquity of squatter settlements and the progress of site and service schemes in many parts of the Third World provide evidence of this. If housing delivery for the urban poor is to meet with any success, therefore, the issue of accessibility to land must be given considerable attention.

African governments have had policies aimed at providing building land cheaply for the urban poor. Such policies have included site and service schemes and unserviced site schemes. One fundamental problem that has dogged all these schemes is how governments can obtain land for redistribution to the urban poor within the constraints imposed by the socio-political conditions of land and the limited budget of the urban poor.

In this chapter, an attempt is made to show the important place land has in housing the urban poor. I begin with a discussion of land tenure in Africa and attempt an overview of the traditional, political and socio-economic influences on land tenure. The attempts made by government to influence these traditional structures are then discussed. The impact of the combined effect of the traditional arrangements and government influence are discussed in relation to housing, particularly with respect to accessibility to land for the urban poor. Some policy options which could enable African governments to make land available to the urban poor for their housing, at prices they could afford, are then discussed. The chapter concentrates on sub-Saharan Africa because the influence of Islam on land tenure relations in the north of the continent introduced an important dimension that cannot be adequately examined here. Again, the lack of relevant data on housing in the Republic of South Africa has necessitated the exclusion of that country from this discussion.

## LAND TENURE IN AFRICA

Land tenure in Africa is characterised by traditional notions that are often in conflict with efficient and economic use of land. As these notions have a tremendous effect on land provision for housing they will be briefly discussed here.

Perhaps the most important of these traditional notions is the belief that land is not just a physical entity but also has spiritual characteristics. Among the Ashanti of Ghana, Busia (1951:42) has observed that land is a supernatural feminine spirit which can be helpful if propitiated and harmful if neglected. The belief is so strong that before an Ashanti farmer cultivates a new farm he offers a sacrifice of mashed yam, eggs and a fowl to the spirit of the earth to propitiate her to ensure him safety and a good harvest while he works on the land (Siriboe II, 1975). Among the Bete and the Dida of the Côte d'Ivoire land is owned by the ancestors who settled there after asking permission of a powerful local spirit, considered to be the owner of men, whether alive or dead (Chubb, 1961:7). Elias (1956:162) has observed that in West Africa generally land belongs to a community defined as a 'vast family of which many are dead, few are living, and countless members are unborn'.

Another traditional notion in Africa is the relationship between land-ownership and social and political status. In West Africa, while land is believed to be owned by spirits and departed ancestors, the administration is vested in the chief, the traditional political overlord (Asiama, 1981). Among the Buganda of Uganda, the Kabaka (the traditional ruler) was the ultimate owner of all land in the state, the other landowners holding their land rights through him. Land tenure among the Amhara of Ethiopia, before the Ethiopian Revolution, was closely related to social status and political authority and differences among social classes corresponded to differences in the type of land rights potentially available to its members (Hoben, 1973:7). While racial differences have exerted some influence on landownership structures in southern Africa, the landownership structures of the indigenous Africans have tended to be bound up with their political authorities. This is exemplified by the Xhosa of South Africa.

These traditional notions have been influenced by modernisation and its concomitants. In Ghana and some West African countries, the introduction of the cocoa industry has had some important effects on tenurial arrangements (Asante, 1975). The pattern of traditional ownership rights is under strain.

## GOVERNMENT INFLUENCE

Governments in Africa have made attempts to influence the ownership structures to bring them in line with the dictates of the modern economic and social conditions they find themselves in. In Ghana, the government has reserved for itself wide powers of compulsory acquisition of land though it has used such powers sparingly and only when 'the public interest' so dictated. In Nigeria, the Land Use Decree (1978) has vested all land in the state governments in trust for the people, because it is deemed in the public interest that 'the rights of all Nigerians to use and enjoy land in Nigeria . . . should be assured, protected and preserved'.

One of the fundamental results of the Ethiopian Revolution was the nationalisation of all urban land without compensation under the Government Ownership of Urban Land and Extra Houses Proclamation (No. 47 of 1975). This was to correct inequities in the Ethiopian urban land market. Marian (1970:28) reports that in 1966 an estimated 5 per cent of the population in Addis Ababa owned 95 per cent of the privately-owned land in the city.

In the new Republic of Zimbabwe, the government has pledged itself to seek the transformation of the land system by ensuring, among other things, 'an acceptable and fair distribution of land ownership and use'.

Under the Land Reform Decree of 1975 all land in Uganda was declared to be publicly owned and all tenures greater than leaseholds were abolished. All freeholds and absolute ownerships were converted into leaseholds and customary occupation of such public land was declared to be 'only under sufferance'. A lease of any such land could be granted to any person, including the holder of the tenure.

Under its policy of socialism, the Tanzanian government has adopted a utilitarian concept of landownership and has declared, in accordance with the Arusha Declaration of 1967, that land belongs not to individuals but to society.

## EFFECTS ON HOUSING LAND

It is apparent from the foregoing that African governments have a tremendous influence on landownership structures and hence could make substantial amounts of land available for housing. Unfortunately the reality does not support this view. Three reasons may be adduced for this state of affairs. First, African governments have historically been preoccupied with the provision of housing units for their populations. Secondly, the governments have been unwilling to extensively utilise the legislated powers available to them in disturbing land tenure relations. This is because of the important place land occupies in the traditional regime in the continent. The various traditional social and political institutions constitute formidable vested interests opposing government policies (Oram, 1979). Thirdly, the agencies established by governments to oversee the implementation of these policies have lacked the required level of commitment to the success of these programmes, perhaps, because, having their roots in the traditional regime, they feel averse to tampering with their institutions and arrangements. Or perhaps, being policy-makers, they have better access to the facilities that enable them to obtain either building land or the houses that their policies dictate to their governments to build.

## ACCESSIBILITY TO THE URBAN POOR

In spite of the influences that African governments have on the landownership structures in their countries, the persistence of the traditional institutions has created a dual land market in many of the countries.

In the traditional sector, acquisition of land for housing, and for any other purpose, is controlled by the traditional authorities. Frequently, they determine who is to receive land grants, how much is to be charged for the land, and how much land is to be offered for sale. The choice of recipients of land grants may not only depend upon a person's ability to pay the purchase price but also on his social and political influence in the society. Land prices are high and are often not directly determined by purely market conditions; the landowner's judgement of how 'beneficial' a prospective purchaser could be may outweigh market considerations (Asiama, 1984). In these circumstances the urban poor are at a disadvantage because they lack the social and political influence that landowners so often seek. They also lack the ultimate weapon, money, with which to participate in the market. In terms of accessibility to building land, therefore, this sector is closed to them.

In many countries in the continent, a market also exists in public lands for housing purposes. The aim of this sector is generally to eliminate some of the problems posed by the market in the traditional sector. In practical terms, this market has also not served to make accessibility of land to the urban poor any better, but rather, has often benefited the already privileged urban dwellers.

This market is often characterised by low land prices, ease of entry (at least conceptually), well-defined and secure titles and the provision of the services needed for the enjoyment of building land.

In Kenya and Uganda, Kanyeihamba (1973) reports that public policy towards housing has tended to favour civil servants in high positions who have been able to obtain loans on the strength either of their high salaries or the influence they exert on loan-granting organisations. It is these people who have had access to building land in both countries.

In Ghana, while there are no official rules making the grant of a public plot conditional on the applicant's occupation, an examination of the beneficiaries of grants of building lands in the public sector shows that senior public officers (staff of the state and parastatal corporations) and senior university staff stand the best chances of obtaining them.

The Nigerian situation is similar. Commenting on the activities of the Lagos Executive Development Board, Okpala (1979) observes that a very significant proportion of housing land under the control of the Board has gone to the elite who constitute a small percentage of the city's adult population.

Thus, public sector land management has often favoured those for whom such advantages can only marginally improve their situation; and has often ignored those for whom better accommodation is often a fundamental requirement. The reasons are not too hard to find. In the words of Okpala (1979):

This pattern of distribution is brought about in several ways. The first is the explicit government policy to provide land or housing to certain otherwise privileged groups of people. The middle and high income groups, particularly the senior civil servants, exert the greatest and most effective pressures on the Government to allocate land and housing to them. More often, too, these groups not only influence government policy but make the policies themselves, and so their disproportionate beneficiary share in publicly owned and managed lands is not surprising.

It is clear, however, that if the urban poor are to be meaningfully aided in the provision of shelter, this trend needs to be re-examined.


## THE POLICY OPTIONS

Within the constraints discussed above, it would appear that if the urban poor are to be helped to provide themselves with accommodation some conscious and direct effort must be made by African governments. Such effort must either enable the urban poor to participate freely in the land market or seek to make building land directly available to them. These options will now be discussed.


## PARTICIPATION IN THE LAND MARKET

In countries where the state has absolute control over ownership and use of land (e.g. Tanzania, Ethiopia, Uganda) this option does not necessarily arise since a land market in its pure definition does not exist. In those countries where a dual land market exists (e.g. Ghana, Kenya, Côte d'Ivoire) the discussion in this part will apply only to the private land market. The public land market will be discussed in the next section.

As already discussed, one of the reasons why the urban poor cannot participate in the land market is that they lack the ultimate weapon – money – with which to enter the market. If they are to be invested with the ability to participate in the market, therefore, they must either have access to funds or land prices must be reduced to a level which will enable them to feel able to enter the market.

*Provision of finance* It is of some significance to note that few schemes aimed at providing finance for house-building provide finance for the purchase of land. Almost invariably housing finance is provided after the house-builder has acquired the land (e.g. Ghana's Bank for Housing and Construction and the First Ghana Building Society only grant mortgage finance when the developer has completed the foundation stage of the building for which he needs the mortgage.) Purchases of building land by the urban poor could be financed through schemes that would provide them with 'soft loans'. There is little doubt that such a policy would result in subsidising landowners. It could mean creating rapid increases in land prices as demand for building land would increase relative to the supply and eventually lead to inflationary consequences in the economy generally. It could also lead to the unhealthy practice of land speculations as the urban poor, having had access to 'cheap' land, may themselves end up selling the land to the middle and high-income groups at comparatively high prices. For example, Kanyeihamba (1973:20) reports of cases in Kenya and

Uganda where the poor, having obtained 'cheap' lands, sub-let them at high premiums to the rich.

*Lowering of land prices* It would seem a more viable alternative to bring land prices down to a level the urban poor could afford. This could be most effectively done by legislation. As with the market in many other commodities, however, lowering land prices in this way would undoubtedly have the effect of encouraging a black market in land and lead to windfall profits for the landowners. Such profits would, under the circumstances, be illegal; the state would not have access to data on them to aid its economic analysis. India has a variant of this system under its Urban Land (Ceiling and Regulation) Act of 1976; excess vacant land in Indian cities can be acquired at a price equivalent to 100 months of the current productive income from the land.

*Vacant land tax* Another alternative open to African governments to manipulate the urban land market to the advantage of the poor is through the imposition of a tax on land value based on the unrealised development value of land. There is a potential in land taxation for the realisation of planning objectives which has not been tapped in many developing countries. In general, the reason for introducing a system of land taxation may be grouped under four main headings:

(a) To raise revenue for general expenditure or to finance specific projects.
(b) To promote social justice through the equalisation of land distribution, income and other benefits of land ownership and utilisation.
(c) To achieve an efficient allocation of land resources.
(d) To aid the orderly development of cities and other planned localities.

Unfortunately land taxation in the continent has often placed much emphasis on the raising of revenue and has altogether ignored the other objectives. In Ghana and Nigeria, for example, even though development on land is taxed for local development, the tax burden does not fall on land even when such land is vacant. The effect has been that landowners could hold on to land without any financial loss being incurred by them. On the contrary, such land increases in value and when the landowner eventually sells it, he creams off substantial profits. This has meant that owners can manipulate the land market to their advantage. A tax on vacant land in such a situation would have the effect of increasing the supply, at least in the short run, because landowners would rather sell their lands, thus releasing such lands for development, if holding on to such land would represent an economic loss. This would be the result if the tax is higher than land value increases. The increase in land supply would, holding demand constant, bring down the price of land in the short run and hence enable the poor to participate in the market.

In the long run, however, demand would outstrip supply, as more people who had hitherto been on the periphery of land demand would now enter the market and the supply could not be indefinitely increased. Unless other checks were introduced this could result in urban sprawl as the cities expanded to make peripheral land available for development. The state would therefore need to adopt, concurrently with land value taxation, a policy aimed at limiting the growth of the urban population.

## DIRECT PROVISION OF LAND

There are some options open to African governments to make a direct provision of land to the urban poor for housing purposes. These will now be discussed.

*Confiscation and re-distribution of land* Perhaps the most obvious of these options is the confiscation and redistribution of land. This could be at two levels – outright confiscation without compensation as in Ethiopia, or compulsory acquisition with compensation. Both options pose socio-political and economic problems, particularly in the circumstances under which land is held in Africa. Communal ownership of land, which is prevalent, ensures that there is no class conflict between a wealthy landowning class and a poor landless proletariat, or at least casts a veil over the existence of such a conflict. Confiscation of land or compulsory acquisition, even when coupled with the payment of compensation, thus serves to politically alienate some sections of the community. In Ghana it has been seen that even though the traditional political authorities have become a landowning class, they can often rely on the members of their communities to resist any efforts at dispossessing them of the land, because the community members still believe land belongs to them all, even though it is clear that such ownership functionally offers them no particular advantages.

Where the powers of compulsory acquisition with compensation are used, there is the added difficulty of the government having to find the money to pay the compensation. In the precarious situations in which the economies of most African governments find themselves, such payments could pose serious economic constraints.

*Vesting of land management in the state* Where confiscation or compulsory acquisition with compensation may not be a feasible option, African governments could take over the administration and management of all communally-owned urban land. This option is particularly useful in countries where communal landownership is prevalent. Because this option leaves ownership substantially in the landowner's hands it is likely to be less objectionable to landowners than the use of the powers of confiscation or compulsory acquisition with compensation. Ghana employs this system successfully. Under the Administration of Lands Act, 1962 (Act 123) the government of Ghana has vested the management of all communally-owned land in the state. Effectively, this means that even though the ownership of land is still in the hands of the communities and their leaders, all decisions relating to the releasing of land are taken by the government. This system is advantageous because it gives the state the same rights and privileges over land as does the use of compulsory acquisition; it does not involve payment of compensation and is thus less costly. Again it avoids the unsavoury political implications inherent in the use of the powers of confiscation or compulsory acquisition.

*Limiting amount of landholdings* The state could also limit the amount of land anybody could hold within the urban area. Those who held more than the legislated limit would have to release the surplus for development. The increase in supply could lead to a lowering of land prices. Alternatively the state could take over all such surplus land for redistribution to the urban poor. This option has many drawbacks. First, the effect could be minimal as the excess land may not significantly affect the supply situation in the market. Secondly, its effect could be very short-lived as once people relinquished their hold on the excess land there would be no more excess land to draw on for development. Thirdly, with the prevalence of communal ownership of land, defining 'excess land' could be extremely difficult. Fourthly, it may not work. This is because when landowners are faced with such drastic impositions they react by devising mechanisms which may be entirely legal within the general legal framework of the country but which work against the success of the imposition. Bolivia, India, and Nigeria have attempted to implement this option. In Bolivia, the Law on the Reform of Ownership of Urban Land placed a mandatory limit of 1 ha. on urban landownership (Hardoy and Satterthwaite, 1981:133). The Indian Urban land (Ceiling and Regulation) Act of 1976 also limited individual landownership in large urban centres to 500 sq. m.

According to Nigeria's Land Use Decree (No. 6 of 1978), in urban areas, where land had been developed before the Decree came into effect, the owner continued to hold it as if he had a statutory right of occupancy. Where the land was undeveloped the owner continued to hold a portion of land not exceeding ½ ha., the surplus being taken over by the state. According to Sada's assessment, owing to

some special provisions of the Decree and problems of implementation, the objectives of social justice in terms of equal access by the rich and poor became a farce . . . The implication of this situation is that the Decree had merely contributed to the artificial scarcity of land and further complicated the procedure for the acquisition of land to the greater disadvantage of the poor. (Sada, 1984:75)

Despite these limitations a policy aimed at limiting the quantum of landholdings could achieve the desired results if it were effectively monitored.

*Negotiations with landowners* The state could also enter into negotiations with landowners to obtain land for later distribution to the urban poor at prices they could afford (Asiama, 1984). This option is particularly attractive where traditional landowners possess, under the customary system, large urban land areas.

There are alternatives within this option. First, the state could bargain, on the basis of allocation of resources and facilities to the area, if the traditional political authorities would release land for redistribution to the urban poor. In the context of many countries in the continent where government is the prime mover in local development projects, this should be an effective means of securing land needed for housing the urban poor.

Secondly, the state could negotiate with large landholders on the basis of land readjustment schemes. Under this method, the state would take over the entire area of land, provide services and other infrastructural facilities such as roads, drains, water supply, electricity, sewage and parks. The state would retain part of the land to pay for the cost of services and infrastructural facilities provided and the remainder would be returned to the landowners. The state could reallocate the land retained to the urban poor for their housing.

Thirdly, the state could create, in its favour, pre-emption rights under which landowners wishing to sell their land would have to offer it first to the state. The state could then pass on such offers to the urban poor at low prices. Any revenue accruing could then be passed on to the landowners. Thus the state becomes an intermediary price-stabilisation factor between the landowners and the urban poor.

## CONCLUSION

In this chapter I have tried to focus attention on some of the issues which will need to be resolved in providing land for housing to the urban poor. It is important to remember that land for housing is not just the *terra firma*; it also means land prepared to receive shelter and to make the shelter both habitable and enjoyable. This means that some services must be provided on the land, such as clean water, storm-water drainage, electricity, etc. I have not gone into the details of how these should be provided because the prime importance of this chapter has been to consider how the land can become more accessible to the urban poor.

I have attempted to present various options which may be adopted by African governments in their efforts to aid the urban poor in providing shelter for themselves. No single option would fit all situations; some have been tried and failed, or succeeded, in some countries, others have not yet been tried. What is important is for the policy-makers in Africa to have the will to help the urban poor; each of these options could be evaluated in the circumstances of each country and each locality and the appropriate option, or combination of options, adopted.

It is equally important to remember that efforts at providing facilities for the urban poor to house themselves should be not seen as isolated activities, but as a continuing process. As we move from one stage of the process to the next we must evaluate the preceding stages so we can correct our errors. It is characteristic of urban problems that as they are resolved they create congenial environments which serve to attract more people into the urban areas to re-create the problems. It is therefore necessary that programmes aimed at alleviating the urban housing problem are conceived, and executed, as part of a general framework of urban and regional development.

## REFERENCES

Acquaye, E. and Asiama, S. O. 1986. 'Land policies for housing development for low-income groups in Africa', *Land Development Studies*, 3, pp. 127–43.

Asante, S. K. B. 1975. *Property Law and Social Goals in Ghana 1844–1966*. Accra: Ghana Universities Press.

Asiama, S. O. 1981. 'Chieftaincy – a transient institution in urban Ghana?' *Sociologus*, 31 (2), pp. 122–40.

—— 1984. 'The land factor in housing for low income urban settlers – the example of Madina, Ghana', *Third World Planning Review*, 6 (2), pp. 171–84.

—— 1985. 'The rich slum dweller: a problem of unequal access', *International Labour Review*, 124 (3), pp. 353–62.

Busia, K. A. 1951. *The Position of the Chief in the Modern Political System of Ashanti*. London: Oxford University Press for the International African Institute.

Chubb, L. T. 1961. *Ibo Land Tenure*. Ibadan: University Press.

Elias, T. O. 1956. *The Nature of African Customary Law*. Manchester: University Press.

Hardoy, J. and Satterthwaite, D. 1981. *Shelter: need and response*. Chichester: John Wiley.

Hoben, A. 1973. *Land Tenure among the Amhara of Ethiopia*. Chicago: University Press.

Kanyeihamba, G. W. 1973. *Urban Planning Laws in East Africa*. Oxford: Pergamon Press.

Marian, M. W. 1970. 'Problems of urbanisation'. *Report of Proceedings of the Third International Conference of Ethiopian Studies*, Addis Ababa: Institute of Ethiopian Studies, Haile Selassie I University.

Okpala, D. C. I. 1979. 'Accessibility distribution: aspects of public land management: a Nigerian case', *African Urban Studies*, 5, pp. 25–44.

Oram, N. 1979. 'Housing, planning and urban administration', in H. S. Murison and J. P. Lea (eds.), *Housing in Third World Countries*, pp. 43–8. London: Macmillan.

Sada, P. D. 1984. 'Land resources and requirements for national shelter strategy'. Paper presented at the *National Seminar on the Formulation of Shelter Strategies*, Lagos, Nigeria.

Siriboe II, Nana Otuo. 1975. 'Traditional values in the land ownership system'. Paper presented at the *Seminar on Land and Economic Development in Ghana*, Kumasi, University of Science and Technology.

Turner, J. F. C. 1983. 'From central provision to local enablement', *Habitat International*, 7 (5/6); pp. 210–14.

## RESUME

Ce chapitre examine les relations de bail foncier sur le continent et les rattache à la question de l'apport du logement. L'influence des politiques gouvernementales sur les relations de bail foncier et leurs effets sur l'accessibilité des terrains d'habitation à la population urbaine pauvre sont alors discutés. Finalement, certaines options politiques ouvertes aux gouvernements sur le continent pour rendre les terrains disponibles à la population urbaine pauvre sont suggérées. Ces options offrent à la population urbaine pauvre soit la possibilité de participer au marché foncier, grâce à l'apport de fonds, soit la baisse des prix du terrain et l'utilisation d'un impôt sur la valeur des terrains pour aider la population urbaine pauvre. Ce chapitre examine également les politiques qui pourraient rendre les terrains directement accessibles pour loger la population urbaine pauvre. A cet égard, la confiscation immédiate et la redistribution des terres; l'assignation de la gestion foncière dans l'Etat, la limitation du nombre de propriétés; et les politiques impliquant des négociations avec les propriétaires fonciers sont discutées.

# RENTAL HOUSING AND THE URBAN POOR: AFRICA AND LATIN AMERICA COMPARED

## INTRODUCTION

Housing tenure is intimately related to development. As we shall explore below, tenure affects a family's health, nutrition and income, as well as the satisfaction they derive from their housing. In addition, income distribution, community organisation, and levels of investment and employment are all related to the distribution of tenures in the economy. We cannot improve low-income housing unless we understand the significance of tenure at each of these levels.

Ten years ago, little was known about rental housing in either Africa or Latin America. Attention focused on low-cost home-ownership, since this seemed to be the form of tenure most families wanted. Over the last decade, however, more attention has been given to renting as it has become clear that many (and in some countries most) poor families do not, in fact, own their homes. The evidence presented in Table 14.1 shows that rental housing is extremely important throughout both continents. There are, of course, differences in definition which make comparison difficult. Some figures refer to all rented properties (including government and local authority), others to private renting, and still others to 'non-ownership'. In addition, the data often underestimate the true proportion of tenants among the urban poor because landlords and tenants are unwilling to admit their status for fear of official reaction such as rent control, taxation or eviction. Nevertheless it is clear that renters form a high proportion of the urban population in both Africa and Latin America, though intra-continental variations in each case are considerable. In Africa, renters are almost always in the majority: in Latin America this is less true, and there has been a significant decline in renting levels over the last twenty years (though this may no longer be the case).

This chapter summarises our knowledge of this neglected form of tenure in Africa (excluding the Republic of South Africa, Namibia and Arab North Africa) and Latin America (focusing on Colombia and Mexico). The first

Table 14.1

Renter households as a proportion of total households in selected African and Latin American countries, 1958–80

| Africa | 1958 | 1960 | 1961 | 1962 | 1963 | 1964 | 1966 | 1967 | 1969 | 1970 | 1971 | 1972 | 1973 | 1974 | 1975 | 1976 | 1980 |
|---|---|---|---|---|---|---|---|---|---|---|---|---|---|---|---|---|---|
| Cameroon | 42·2 | — | — | — | — | — | — | — | — | — | — | — | — | — | — | — | — |
| Congo | — | 57·0 | — | — | — | — | — | — | — | — | — | — | — | 33·2 | — | 53·0 | — |
| Egypt | — | — | 56·9 | — | — | — | — | — | — | — | — | — | — | — | — | — | — |
| Ethiopia | — | — | — | — | — | — | — | 56·9 | — | — | — | — | — | — | — | — | — |
| Ghana | — | — | — | — | — | — | — | — | — | — | — | — | — | — | 60·0 | — | — |
| Malawi | — | — | — | — | — | — | — | — | — | — | — | 60·4 | — | — | — | — | 75·0 |
| Mauritius | — | — | — | 55·0 | — | — | — | — | — | — | — | — | — | — | — | — | — |
| Morocco | — | — | — | — | — | — | — | — | — | — | 62·8 | — | — | — | — | — | — |
| Nigeria | — | — | 80·9 | — | — | — | — | — | — | — | — | — | — | — | — | — | — |
| Seychelles | — | — | — | — | — | — | — | — | — | — | 62·7 | — | — | — | — | — | — |
| Sudan | — | — | — | — | — | — | 28·3 | — | — | — | — | — | — | — | — | — | — |
| Tanzania | — | — | — | — | — | — | — | 62·3 | — | — | — | — | — | — | — | — | — |
| Tunisia | — | — | — | — | — | — | 32·7 | — | — | — | — | — | — | — | 25·3 | — | — |
| Zaire | — | — | — | — | — | — | — | 38·3 | — | — | — | — | — | — | — | — | — |
| Zambia | — | — | — | — | — | — | — | — | 21·0 | — | — | — | — | 30·0 | — | — | 64·6 |
| Zimbabwe | — | — | — | — | — | — | — | — | 48·2 | — | — | — | — | — | — | — | — |

Mean = 50·2%; range = 21·0% to 80·9%                Mean = 55·4%; range = 25·3% to 75·0%

| Latin America | 1958 | 1960 | 1961 | 1962 | 1963 | 1964 | 1966 | 1967 | 1969 | 1970 | 1971 | 1972 | 1973 | 1974 | 1975 | 1976 | 1980 |
|---|---|---|---|---|---|---|---|---|---|---|---|---|---|---|---|---|---|
| Argentina | — | 31·1 | — | — | — | — | — | — | — | 22·8 | — | — | — | — | — | — | — |
| Bolivia | — | — | — | — | 47·1 | — | — | — | — | — | — | — | — | — | — | 30·9 | — |
| Brazil | — | — | — | — | — | — | — | — | — | 30·8 | — | — | — | — | — | 31·5 | — |
| Chile | — | — | — | — | — | — | — | — | — | 31·9 | — | — | — | — | — | — | — |
| Colombia | — | — | — | — | — | 38·8 | — | — | — | — | — | — | 41·4 | — | — | — | — |
| Ecuador | — | — | — | 55·5 | — | — | — | — | — | — | — | — | — | 49·2 | — | — | — |
| Mexico | — | 62·2 | — | — | — | — | — | — | — | 45·8 | — | — | — | — | — | — | 33·2 |
| Paraguay | — | — | — | 19·9 | — | — | — | — | — | — | — | 18·2 | — | — | — | — | — |
| Peru | — | — | 44·7 | — | — | — | — | — | — | — | — | 27·9 | — | — | — | — | — |
| Uruguay | — | — | — | — | 51·2 | — | — | — | — | — | — | — | — | — | 32·1 | — | — |
| Venzuela | — | — | 31·1 | — | — | — | — | — | — | — | 22·5 | — | — | — | — | — | — |

Mean = 42·4%; range = 19·9% to 62·2%     Mean = 32·4%; range = 18·2% to 49·2%

Sources: All data from UN Compendia of Housing Statistics, 1972–74, 1975–77, and 1983, except Malawi, which come from O'Connor (1984) and Malawi Housing Corporation (1980).

section looks at the factors governing tenure 'choice', focusing on the differences which have been assumed to exist between the two continents. The second section examines the structure of the low-income rental market and the nature of landlordism among the poor. This is followed in the next section by a discussion of tenure and development, and in the last section by an analysis of rental housing policy. These issues are particularly important because academic interest in renting has yet to be transformed into practical action, and we need, quickly, to begin to articulate proper rental housing strategies. Throughout, the Latin American experience is used as a point of reference, made valuable because we know a great deal more about renting here than in Africa.

## RENTING AS A MAJOR FORM OF HOUSING: WHY?

If successful interventions are to be made in the housing market, we have to understand why people rent. Is the decision a matter of choice, or of necessity, or a mixture of both? This is a complex question to which there is no simple answer. As I have shown elsewhere, the factors governing decisions over tenure vary over space and through time, so that their interaction is very specific (Edwards, 1983). What can be done, however, is to identify what these factors are, and make some general observations about how they are likely to interact under certain conditions.

### MIGRATION MOTIVES AND HOUSING PREFERENCES

Traditionally, migration to African cities has been seen as temporary, while movements throughout Latin America are overwhelmingly permanent (Roberts, 1978; Gugler and Flanagan, 1978). Most urban Africans, it has been argued, will eventually return to their rural homes; most urban Latin Americans will stay on. Because urban residence in Africa is perceived as temporary, low-income families are reluctant to invest in permanent housing and are therefore prepared, as a matter of preference, to rent accommodation. This is the reverse of the Latin American situation, where a desire for home-ownership is almost universal. If this is true, then we have come a long way in explaining why so many Africans are renters.

However, *is* it true? Although reliable, recent data on migration motives are scarce, there is some evidence at least that permanent migration is now more common, particularly in East and Southern Africa.[1] This is certainly borne out by a number of individual city studies, which show that most low-income households in Lusaka, Blantyre and Lilongwe wish to own their homes (Norwood, 1972; Pennant, 1984; HUZA, 1986). A desire for ownership is not necessarily a reflection of permanent residence, but it can provide a useful surrogate.

In addition, the question of temporary versus permanent migration in Africa becomes less relevant as the proportion of urban growth taken up by natural increase continues to expand. In many African cities, natural increase is the most important component of urban growth, and second or third-generation city-dwellers are beginning to see their futures in urban, not rural, terms. Although there are considerable inter-country variations, the major spurt in rural–urban migration in Africa took place immediately after independence, when legal restrictions on movement were lifted and economic opportunities for Africans expanded rapidly (Dwyer, 1975; Lusaka Urban District Council, n.d.). This is less true of countries such as Malawi where levels of urbanisation are still very low, but the desire to 'return home', and the preference for rented accommodation which traditionally accompanies it are less common in contemporary Africa. This means that, as in Latin America, renting is becoming more a reaction to the difficulties of ownership than a matter of positive choice.

However, a desire for home-ownership is not universal among the urban poor. In Colombia, there is a small minority of families who prefer renting even though they could afford to purchase housing (Edwards, 1982a). Usually, they are higher-income households who see in renting positive advantages such as flexibility and the ability to invest in business rather than in housing. Interestingly, this group also exists in some African cities, notably Kampala (Muench, 1978), Lilongwe (Pennant, 1984) and Lusaka.[2] Hence even in situations where permanent migration is universal some poor families will choose to rent. This needs to be borne in mind throughout the discussion that follows.

## HOUSING COSTS AND HOUSEHOLD INCOMES

In any housing market where incomes are unequally distributed, housing 'choice' will be a positive function of income (Edwards, 1983). Those with the least income face the smallest range of housing alternatives, and there may only be one form of accommodation they can afford. Ownership is a more expensive alternative in the short term than renting (or sharing with kin), though this is less true where land invasion is permitted. It follows, therefore, that the poorest city-dwellers will be forced into rented housing. This process of 'sequential market bidding' is the most important factor in the allocation of housing in Latin American cities, where housing is heavily commercialised, migration is permanent, most poor families want to own their homes, and governments are unable or unwilling to bring ownership within reach for all who want it. The importance of market mechanisms in determining the proportions of owners and tenants among the urban poor decreases in situations where these other factors – migration motives, housing preferences and government policy – play a more important role. This may be the case in parts of Africa. However, the commercialisation of housing which is such a feature of Latin America is also well advanced in many African cities, particularly in the most overtly capitalist economies such as Kenya (Amis, 1984). Hence sequential market bidding operates in Africa too, restricting ownership to the better-off regardless of housing preferences. This process has probably been reinforced over the last five or ten years by the precipitate economic decline of many African countries suffering terms-of-trade problems. This decline has reduced real incomes while forcing up the cost of housing (particularly of credit and imported building materials) to such an extent that entry into owner–occupation is becoming progressively more difficult. This is certainly true of Zambia and Malawi.[3]

## GOVERNMENT POLICY

Government policy is an important determinant of the tenure situation in many African and Latin American cities. Housing is often used for political ends – as a form of patronage for political parties or individual leaders, and as a means at higher levels to reinforce or legitimise state power (Gilbert, 1981; Edwards, 1982b). The way in which housing is used varies considerably, so that, for example, squatting is tolerated in one city but not in others. This makes home-ownership more accessible in certain situations than in others, thereby also exerting an important influence over the proportion of renters among the poor. Detailed studies of Kenya (Stren, 1978), Tanzania (Stren, 1975) and Zambia demonstrate that wherever the state is tolerant of low-cost, 'illegal' home-ownership (particularly squatting), the proportion of renters is likely to fall, always assuming that people want to own in the first place. In cities where eradication of low-income settlements is the norm (for example, in Harare, and, during certain periods, Nairobi), renting will be more common (Cormack, 1983; Teedon, ch. 12 in this volume).

Furthermore, colonial housing policy (at least in Anglophone Africa) deliberately segregated Africans into rental housing in response to their perceived role as a source of temporary urban labour (Tipple, 1976; Rakodi, 1986). Prior to independence, the great majority of Africans had no choice of tenures anyway and rented whether they liked it or not. This was rarely the case in Latin America, where official encouragement of home-ownership became government policy at an earlier stage than in Africa.

## OTHER FACTORS

In addition to the factors described above, ethnicity, urban growth rates, city size, and physical site and situation, are all worth noting. Growth rates obviously alter the balance between supply and demand in the housing market, and this may restrict decisions over tenure still further. Unless squatting is freely tolerated, renting is likely to increase in cities which are growing rapidly. Similarly, the size, situation and layout of the city are bound to affect the structure of the local housing market. Where usable land is in short supply, ownership will be more expensive and less accessible.

## HOW DO THESE FACTORS INTERACT OVER SPACE AND THROUGH TIME?

The tenure profile of each city at any point in time will be determined by the interaction of the factors described above. The trouble is that interactions between so many variables are too complex to permit easy generalisation. Differences within the two continents are at least as great as those between them, even if we restrict the analysis to a single point in time. Nevertheless, there are some general points that can be made.

First, there are clearly some differences in tenure profiles between Africa and Latin America. Renting is still more common among the urban poor in Africa, and part of the reason for this lies in the different migration motives, housing preferences and government policies displayed in each continent. The factors underlying tenure profiles also seem to vary within Africa itself, Anglophone areas conforming more closely to the Latin-American model than the Francophone West, which has more of a tradition of renting in pre-colonial cities and perhaps a less pronounced move towards permanent migration (Peil, 1976).

Second, tenure patterns change in predictable ways over time. In most of Latin America, there has been a long-term trend away from renting in response to the rise of low-cost home-ownership in 'unauthorised settlements'. In Colombia (and perhaps in Mexico too) this trend has recently been reversed because the factors favouring ownership no longer apply (Edwards, 1982a). It is much more difficult to trace temporal variations in Africa, but the data available suggests a similar pattern. In many African countries such as Zambia and Senegal low-cost home-ownership has been deliberately encouraged since independence, partly in reaction to colonial housing policy (Keare and Parris, 1982). The rapid development of upgrading and site and service schemes during the 1970s should have led to a decline in 'enforced' renting, though it is difficult to prove this. As Table 14.2 shows, an overall increase in ownership among Zambia's three largest cities masks an underlying rise in private renting. There are no data available specifically for low-income groups, but one suspects that the declining economic climate of many African countries since 1975 has affected this trend by making ownership more expensive.

Table 14.2
Households by tenure in Lusaka, Kitwe and Ndola, 1969 and 1980 (%)

|  | 1969 | | | 1980 | | |
|---|---|---|---|---|---|---|
|  | Lusaka | Kitwe | Ndola | Lusaka | Kitwe | Ndola |
| Owners | 39·7 | 17·8 | 33·1 | 42·5 | 21·5 | 32·5 |
| Renters | 60·3 | 83·2 | 66·9 | 55·9 | 77·2 | 66·0 |
| of which: |  |  |  |  |  |  |
| Government | 16·3 | 7·5 | 11·4 | 10·4 | 5·5 | 7·9 |
| Local authority | 22·5 | 28·6 | 29·5 | 11·8 | 29·2 | 26·6 |
| Employer | 5·9 | 42·2 | 21·2 | 7·8 | 36·5 | 18·9 |
| Private | 15·5 | 4·8 | 4·7 | 25·9 | 6·0 | 12·6 |
| Total | 100·0 | 100·0 | 100·0 | 100·0 | 100·0 | 100·0 |

*Sources:* Census of Population and Housing, 1969 and 1980. Lusaka: Central Statistical Office.
*Note:* Figures for 1969 refer to rented dwellings; those for 1980 to renter households.


Third, there is one general trend which stands out in both Africa and Latin America: 'commercialisation', the process by which housing and related services come to be exchanged as commodities on an open market. Commercialisation has been well-documented in Latin America (Burgess, 1978), and is beginning to be analysed in Africa too (Amis, 1984; Stren, 1978). As many of the chapters in this volume show, while the process may be more advanced in Latin America, its major features are universal. Wherever housing is commodified, housing choice becomes a function of income. Since incomes are unequally distributed, these decisions become progressively more restricted the further one moves down the income scale, so that for the poorest families there is usually no choice at all. Now, under certain conditions, this process will result in renting becoming the only form of tenure accessible to the very poor. Chief among these conditions are restrictions on squatting, declining real incomes, spiralling building costs, and a desire for permanent residence in the city. This is what has already happened in many Latin American countries, and what seems to be happening also in some parts of Africa (for example, Lusaka and Nairobi). If present trends continue, it will happen in other African cities too.

Hence while the conditions which determine tenure profiles are specific, the underlying processes governing tenure choice in market economies are the same. Furthermore, tenure profiles can be predicted accurately given adequate information on the local factors governing the housing market: city size, situation and growth rates, housing preferences, migration motives, household incomes, housing costs, and government policy. It is therefore possible for Local Authorities to predict with reasonable certainty whether the proportion of the poor who rent their homes will increase or decrease, and to plan accordingly. This is a crucial point to which we return in the last section.

## LANDLORDS AND TENANTS: HOUSING MARKET STRUCTURES COMPARED

Who is it among the urban poor that rents accommodation, and who are the landlords? In Latin America, we know that there are two types of tenant: a majority who rent single rooms, usually young families at an early stage in their lifecycles, anxious to have a home of their own but unable to accumulate sufficient capital to do so; and a minority who rent apartments or houses, usually larger, older families with higher total incomes, who invest their savings in their own small businesses rather than in housing (Edwards, 1982a). For the first group, renting is a response to their inability to purchase the kind of housing they really want; for the second group, it is a positive alternative which allows greater freedom in making decisions over investment, employment, and residential location.

In Africa, the situation appears similar. Studies in Lusaka (Schlyter, 1984), Blantyre (Norwood, 1972), Lilongwe (Pennant, 1984), Dar Es Salaam (Stren, 1975), Kampala (Muench, 1978), and West Africa (Peil, 1976) all conclude that tenants are usually young families embarking on their independent lives in the city (usually after a period of sharing with kin). For example, in a survey of Lusaka carried out by the City Council in 1985, the average age among owner household heads was 43·6 years (in upgraded areas) and 36 (in site-and-service schemes), as compared to 32 and 33 respectively for tenants.[4] Similarly, household size among owners was 6·8 persons in upgraded areas and 5·6 persons in site and service schemes. The comparable figures for tenants were 4·8 and 4·3 persons respectively. These data are confirmed by the results of the 1980 Census.[5]

Equally interesting, however, is the fact that many authors recognise considerable heterogeneity within the tenant population. Pennant (1984), writing about Lilongwe, separates tenants renting rooms from those renting houses, something which also holds true for Lusaka.[6] A common observation for African cities is that tenants are often no poorer than owners, though this depends on one's definition of income. It is, in any case, what one would expect if many African urban-dwellers aim to return to their rural homes, and therefore do not want to invest their higher incomes in permanent housing. Indeed, if the temporary migration hypothesis still held true, one would expect a larger degree of heterogeneity within the tenant population than is actually the case.

Landlords tend to be a more homogeneous group than tenants.

Throughout urban Latin America, they are usually small-scale entre-preneurs, rarely owning more than one or two properties and living on the same plot as their tenants. Rates of return are not excessive, though income from rent is often crucial to the landlord. Renting is almost wholly informal, in the sense that it is not regulated by contracts and exists outside the law. In Africa, the pattern of landlordism is more variable; while it is usually a small-scale phenomenon, it does take on larger-scale and more avowedly capitalist characteristics in situations of high demand and a long tradition of renting in central tenements. The best documented example of this process is Nairobi, where ownership of rented property is highly concentrated and profits are very high (Hake, 1977; Amis, 1984). Amis (1984) estimates 'annual capital returns' at 131 per cent. This compares to 50 per cent in Blantyre (Norwood, 1972).

However, the case of Nairobi appears somewhat extreme. Elsewhere in Africa landlordism has not developed in this way. For example, in Lusaka, 73 per cent of landlords in upgraded areas (1986) lived on the same plot as their tenants, and only 16 per cent of rented dwellings contained five or more households.[7] Multiple property-ownership is rare, though it does occur among local political and business leaders. In West Africa, the hallmark of landlordism is flexibility, with rents varying according to the income of the tenant (especially if related by kin to the landlord: Brand, 1973; Marris, 1979; Aina, ch. 4 in this volume). This is very similar to the situation in central tenement areas of Colombian cities (Edwards, 1982a). Renting in Africa is also informal, unregulated by contracts and legal controls. Eviction is therefore common. But despite its small scale, land-lordism is an extremely important method of generating income for poor owners, particularly single-parent families headed by women (Urban Edge, 1984). In George compound (Lusaka), for example, the costs of building a room can be recouped from rental charges within ten months (Schlyter, 1984). It is probably true to say that no other investment offers the poor such attractive and easy returns. In situations of rapid economic decline, the additional income generated from letting may be crucial in preserving living standards among that section of the urban poor lucky enough to own their homes.

To conclude, throughout most of Africa and Latin America, landlordism is a small-scale phenomenon which does not reflect a highly-concentrated pattern of property ownership. However, this may not always be the case. In situations where the demand for rental housing outstrips supply, the profitability of landlordism increases, and with it the incentive to build up large stocks of rental housing. Nairobi has already reached this point, as have the central tenement areas of some other cities. It may only be a matter of time before cities elsewhere in Africa and Latin America follow the same pattern.

The structure of the rental housing market in which landlords and tenants play out their uneasy relationship is often complex. It is structured by type of accommodation (room, house) as well as by type of settlement (squatter, inner city). There are many different forms of rental accommodation, and the significance of each varies from city to city. Originally, rental housing in Latin America and in the pre-colonial cities of West and East Africa took the form of tenements, usually converted from housing abandoned by the elite in the centre of the city (Mabogunje, 1968; Stren, 1978; O'Connor, 1983). In some countries (such as Mexico, Nigeria and coastal Kenya and Tanzania) central tenements (often misleadingly called 'slums') still offer cheap rental accommodation to substantial numbers of the urban poor close to their sources of employment. These areas exhibit their own peculiar characteristics, and are usually more heterogeneous than more recent, 'unauthorised' settlements.

In the ex-British colonies, however, tenements are rare because most cities lack a historic urban core. Although renting was almost universal among Africans prior to independence, tenants lived in hostels (if single men) or township houses (if families) rather than in tenements (Seymour, 1976). This tradition of rental housing being provided by government, local authority or employer continued after independence, so that today between 30 and 60 per cent of all formal sector housing in Zambia falls into this category (see Table 14·2). In Latin America, public rental housing is comparatively insignificant.

Regardless of whether tenements or public housing dominated the rental market during the early stages of urban growth, the capacity of the existing urban infrastructure to absorb the demand for cheap rental housing from poor families was quickly exhausted. In Africa, the quickening of rural–urban migration and its replacement by natural increase as the motor of urban growth occurred rather later than in Latin America, but in both cases, demand for cheap rental housing quickly outpaced traditional sources of supply. There was only one sector of the housing market which could satisfy this rapid increase in demand – the 'unauthorised' settlements which began to spring up around Third World cities during the 1950s. The emergence of a rental market in squatter and other illegal settlements[8] and in site and service schemes has been well documented in both Africa and Latin America. For example, in George compound (Lusaka), the proportion of renters increased from 14 per cent in 1967 to 20 per cent in 1973 and 46 per cent in 1976 (Department of Town and Country Planning, n. d.; Schlyter, 1984). The proportion of renters in Lusaka's upgraded areas as a whole stood at 52·4 per cent in 1986, as compared with 29·1 per cent for site and service schemes.[9] These figures are replicated in many other compounds throughout Africa. While the proportion of tenants varies according to the age, location, and physical characteristics of the compound (especially levels of service provision, and security of tenure), one usually finds between 40 and 80 per cent of the population living in rented housing (usually rooms). Although tenements do exist in such settlements (especially in cities such as Nairobi where the demand for rental accommodation is very high), they are not common. The development of a small-scale rental sector in low-income settlements is a classic illustration of the process of commercialisation identified in this volume as the dominant theme in African housing today.

## TENURE AND DEVELOPMENT: THE MAJOR ISSUES

What is the significance of tenure in terms of development? To answer this question, we have to make a set of assumptions about the goals of development policy and the nature of development itself. So let us assume that economic growth, a reasonable degree of equity in income distribution, the satisfaction of basic needs in health, nutrition and shelter, and a maximum degree of popular participation in decision-making, are our objectives. Is tenure an important factor in retarding progress towards these goals?

First, consider the level and distribution of income within society. It is clear from empirical evidence that renting and ownership have different short-term and long-term costs (Shelton, 1968). Ownership (unless land and building materials are free) requires a substantial initial capital investment. Renting, on the other hand, involves lower short-term costs but a much higher expenditure in the long run. Since ownership is cheaper than renting after the first year or so, income is redistributed to landlords and overall distribution of income among the poor becomes more unequal. In Bucaramanga (Colombia), the payment of rent widens the disparity between the incomes of tenants and landlords by as much as 40 per cent (Edwards, 1982a). We have no data from Africa to compare with this evidence. Clearly, much depends on the city and type of settlement under scrutiny, because rents as a proportion of income vary among central tenement areas and 'unauthorised' settlements. However, some measure of negative redistribution of income is inevitable, assuming that most landlords have higher initial incomes than their tenants.

Similarly, renting reduces a family's 'investment surplus' (total income minus expenditure on housing) to a greater extent than ownership. This has serious consequences for health and nutrition among tenants, since it means less is available for expenditure on non-housing essentials. In Latin America, rents do not seem to have reached the point at which physical survival is threatened, but in African cities (such as Nairobi) where the rental market is much tighter, this is already a problem. Amis (1984) raises the spectre of an 'adequately-housed' but 'malnourished' population of tenants in Nairobi's squatter settlements. We lack the data on urban health necessary to confirm this prediction, but it seems certain that in countries such as Zambia and Tanzania which are experiencing rapid economic decline and restructuring along free-market lines, urban food prices will continue to rise in relation to wage levels.[10] It remains to be seen whether malnutrition will increase at a faster pace among tenants than among owners.

However, housing is not simply a vehicle for the satisfaction of physical needs. It also provides emotional security in situations which are difficult and threatening. Much of John Turner's work has been concerned with this 'existential' aspect of housing – the need for the poor themselves to control the environment in which they live so that they can produce and maintain their own housing more effectively (Turner, 1976). But of course this is precisely what tenants cannot do. They have no control over their housing, and renting does not provide a satisfactory environment within which the family can grow, physically or emotionally. Coupled with renting's higher long-term costs, this is why most tenants want to own their homes.

A second major area to consider is *participation*. This is something of a 'vogue' word among policy-makers, and it is obviously true that participation by all groups is essential if the benefits of development are to be accessible to all. As the experience of squatter upgrading in Lusaka has shown, participation can also render housing improvements more effective. In reality, however, many groups within the urban poor (notably women and, generally, tenants) are excluded from participating in development programmes, and genuine participation is opposed by governments and housing officials who fear the control of the development process by the poor themselves. In addition, the more heterogeneous a population, the more difficult it is to organise effectively to meet common goals. Tenure plays an important role here because owners and tenants tend to have different interests. Tenants are less interested in improvements to local infrastructure because they lack a permanent 'stake' in the community (Edwards, 1982b; UNCHS, 1984). That is why they tend to be less active in 'self-help' initiatives (Hoek-Smit, 1982). In city-centre tenement areas, community organisations are often even less effective (Boyden, 1985). But in all cases, tenure acts as a divisive factor in retarding popular organisation and preventing the poor from presenting a united front.

Finally, we should not ignore the possible influence of tenure on the wider economy. Renting and ownership imply different levels of saving and investment in housing, and must therefore have an effect on wage and employment levels. It has been shown in many countries that informal-sector construction contributes massively to the economy, albeit a contribution unrecognised by official statistics (Currie, 1975). A society of renters will do little to stimulate the economy in this way, though it is true that many higher-income tenants invest significantly in business rather than in housing. As yet, none of these possible influences on the economy have been quantified.

In conclusion, tenure does have an influence on the level of distribution of income among the poor, on health and nutrition, 'satisfaction' with housing, participation and community development, savings and investment. It would, however, be unfair to blame tenure for creating inequality or subverting popular organisation. In most cases, tenure is a secondary influence superimposed on already unequal or repressive social, economic, political and gender structures. Tenants are not poor because they rent; they rent because they are poor, and they are poor because of the structure of society in which they live. Manipulating housing tenure will not change this fact.

## LOW-INCOME HOUSING POLICY: WHAT SHOULD BE DONE ABOUT RENTING?

If more and more poor families are living in rental accommodation, is this a problem, and if so, what should we do about it? This is a difficult question to answer because the characteristics of renting vary so much over space and time – one need only compare Lusaka and Nairobi to appreciate this. In addition, the advantages and disadvantages of renting change from group to group, even within a single city. For low-income home-owners (landlords), renting is clearly beneficial since there is no other investment which brings in so much money so easily. For tenants who want to own their homes, renting has few advantages, because it is more expensive in the long term and brings no existential benefits. For the small number of higher-income tenants who prefer renting to ownership, the situation is different again. And for communities and societies as a whole, yet another range of costs and benefits apply.

One way out of this dilemma is to assume that every family should be offered the type of housing they want. In most cases, this will be ownership, though there will always be those who prefer the greater flexibility provided by renting. The task then becomes how to make ownership accessible to those at present excluded from this option – by reducing the costs of purchasing land and building materials, easing the provision of credit, and lowering building standards. In Latin America there is no sign that governments are prepared to do this. Most argue financial constraints, but political opposition to land nationalisation, price controls and other measures is at least as important. In Africa, the situation is similar. Admittedly, land constraints are less of a problem because in many countries, such as Zambia and Tanzania, land cannot be exchanged on the private market. But there are no signs that opportunities for home-ownership on the scale required are going to be provided. Indeed, the evidence presented in the first section points in the opposite direction. If this is true, it will not be possible for all families to be offered the tenure of accommodation they prefer. The question then becomes what to do in order to minimise the problems which inevitably arise when the poor are forced into housing they consider a secondary alternative – the problems we explored briefly in the above section.

First, in order to reduce the inequalities which may be accentuated by the payment of rent, full cost-recovery has to be imposed on low-income home-owners. Otherwise, the real costs of ownership are reduced and the gap between landlord and tenant widens still further (Keare and Parris, 1982). In reality, this has rarely happened in upgrading or site and service schemes in either Africa or Latin America, because governments have been unable or unwilling to enforce repayments. Not only does this foster inequality; it also makes such programmes unreplicable. Given adequate cost-recovery, there is no reason why small-scale letting in upgrading and site and service schemes should be discouraged.

Second, gross profiteering on the scale seen in Nairobi has to be prevented. Most criticisms of renting are really attacks on large-scale landlordism rather than the small-scale tenancies characteristic of most African and Latin American cities. There is a legitimate fear, particularly in countries with strong socialist ideologies, that landlordism exemplifies all that is worst in capitalism. However, limiting profits (which implies restricting rents and property ownership) is dangerous in market economies because it removes the incentive to let and thereby contributes to shortages of cheap housing. This is the traditional argument against rent control in all societies (United Nations, 1979). Certainly, the record of rent control in Africa and Latin America is not impressive. Either it has been ineffective, as in the case of Colombia or Kenya or, because it has limited rents below their market value, it has accelerated deterioration in the rental housing stock and led to landlords demanding a variety of extra-legal payments such as 'key money'. Does this mean that rent control is irrelevant? Some authors have begun to think more imaginatively about this question, recognising that success might be achieved given the right degree of flexibility (Malpezzi, 1984). Rents could be set by neighbourhood councils representing the interests of both landlords and tenants, reflecting a commonly-agreed rate of return and linked to wage rather than price movements. One has to recognise, however, that the best form of rent control is to facilitate access to home-ownership. This relieves the pressure on the rental market and automatically leads to lower rents. Research on how to reduce the costs of ownership therefore remains of paramount importance. Similarly, areas of rental housing should not be eradicated, since this merely increases the pressure on rents in the rest of the market (see the experiences of Nairobi or Dar es Salaam, for example, in Stren, 1975).

Third, steps have to be taken to strengthen the position of tenants in relation to their landlords, perhaps by encouraging the development of tenants' associations. Such associations do already exist in many countries (Colombia, Venezuela and Mexico, for example), but they are rarely effective and often ignore the interests of the poorest groups. Similar organisations have existed in Mombasa for many years, but have foundered through their members' fear of eviction (Stren, 1978). This is particularly important in central tenement areas, whose inhabitants are often less organised even than tenants elsewhere in the city (Boyden, 1985). Another way forward is to concentrate on tenants within general community development programmes. This is what Human Settlements of Zambia, a Lusaka-based NGO, is doing, by identifying tenants living in upgraded areas and helping them to find land, and credit with which to purchase building materials. In this way, tenants are encouraged to play an equal role in existing community organisations.

Nevertheless, it has to be accepted that measures such as these will never address the fundamental problem faced by poor tenants: the fact that they *are* tenants. Renting results from a range of economic and political factors which limit housing choice. Until these constraints are removed, poor families will continue to be forced into rental accommodation, with all the costs this entails. However, if governments are not prepared to take the steps necessary to facilitate home-ownership for all who want it, they must concentrate on curbing the harmful side-effects of the only other form of tenure – renting – which is available to the poor. Exactly how to do this requires a great deal more thought, but people should not be prevented from renting (and, therefore, from letting) unless they can be offered a better alternative. At present, this is rarely the case.

## CONCLUSION

Does renting among the urban poor in Africa differ significantly from Latin-American models? Certainly, plenty of differences exist between and within the two continents, particularly in the factors which interact to determine the proportion of the poor who rent. In other areas, however, there are striking similarities between Africa and Latin America. This does not obscure the fact that there are certain conditions in Africa (and migration motives may be one of them) which do differ from the Latin-American situation; nor that there are particular cities (such as Nairobi) which do not share the small-scale, informal character of renting throughout the rest of the two continents. All these differences can be explained by reference to the particular factors at work locally.

Underlying these differences is a deeper set of similarities which concern processes active in all housing markets. We saw in the first section how the process of commercialisation restricts housing choice among the poor, and how this, under certain conditions, leads to ever larger numbers of tenants among the low-income population. While predictions are dangerous, economic pressures, combined with an unwillingness on the part of governments to intervene more forcefully to facilitate access to home-ownership, may mean that more and more poor families will be forced into rented accommodation, and will remain there for longer periods of time. This is a natural consequence of the commercialisation of African housing. If this is true, we must start to give much more thought to the question of regulating rental markets so that tenants' interests are protected.

## NOTES

1  Many authors explore this issue; see particularly Odongo and Lea, 1977; Gilbert and Gugler, 1982; Gugler and Flanagan, 1978; Roberts, 1978; Peil, 1976; Peil and Sada, 1984.

2  Evidence from Lusaka comes from my conversations with staff of the Peri-Urban Section of Lusaka Urban District Council.

3  To my knowledge, no one has studied this phenomenon systematically. My evidence comes from newspapers in Zambia, and discussions with housing officials in Lusaka and Blantyre.

4  I am grateful to Mr I. Mwendapole, Chief of the Peri-Urban Section, Lusaka Urban District Council, for allowing me access to the raw data from this survey.

5  The 1980 Census of Population and Housing (CSO, Lusaka) shows household size among owners in Lusaka to be 5·7 persons, as opposed to 3·7 persons among private renters.

6  Personal communication, Research Department, National Housing Authority, Lusaka.

7  1985 survey, Peri-Urban Section, Lusaka Urban District Council.

8  The terms 'unauthorised' and 'illegal' settlement are used interchangeably to denote squatter settlements, illegal sub-divisions, and other areas where tenure is uncertain. The term does not include site and service schemes nor central city 'slums'.

9  1985 survey, Peri-Urban Section, Lusaka Urban District Council.

10  In Zambia, for example, the price of the basic staple (maize meal) rose by over 80 per cent in the six months following the devaluation of the Kwacha and abolition of part of the maize subsidy in October 1985, forced on the country as a condition of securing further IMF loans.

## REFERENCES

Amis, P. 1984. 'Squatters or tenants: the commercialization of unauthorised housing in Nairobi', *World Development*, 12 (1), pp. 87–96.

Bamberger, M., Sanyal, B. and Valverde, N. 1982. *Evaluation of Sites and Services Projects: the experience from Lusaka, Zambia*. World Bank Staff Working Paper No. 548, Washington DC.
Boyden, J. 1985. *Children in Development: policy and programming for especially-disadvantaged children in Lima, Peru*. Oxford: OXFAM/UNICEF.
Brand, R. 1973. 'Migration and residential site selection in five low-income communities in Kumasi, Ghana', *African Urban Notes*, 7, pp. 73–94.
Burgess, R. 1978. 'Petty-commodity housing or dweller control? A critique of John Turner's views on housing policy', *World Development*, 6 (9–10), pp. 1105–34.
Cormack, I. 1983. *Towards Self-reliance: urban social development in Zimbabwe*. Gweru: Mambo Press.
Currie, L. 1975. 'Interrelations of urban and national planning', *Urban Studies*, 12, pp. 37–46.
Department of Town and Country Planning. n.d. *Low-cost Residential Development in Lusaka: the development and characteristics of official and unauthorised low-cost housing in Lusaka*. Lusaka: Lusaka Urban District Council.
Dwyer, D. 1975. *People and Housing in Third World Cities*. London: Longman.
Edwards, M. 1982a. 'Cities of tenants: renting among the urban poor in Latin America', in A. Gilbert *et al.* (eds.), *Urbanisation in Contemporary Latin America*, pp. 129–58. Chichester: John Wiley.
—— 1982b. 'The political economy of low-income housing: new evidence from urban Colombia', *Bulletin of Latin American Research*, 1(2), pp. 45–62.
—— 1983. 'Residential mobility in a changing housing market: the case of Bucaramanga, Colombia', *Urban Studies*, 20, pp. 131–45.
Gilbert, A. 1981. 'Pirates and invaders: land acquisitions in urban Colombia and Venezuela', *World Development*, 9(7), pp. 657–78.
—— and Gugler, J. 1982. *Cities, Poverty and Development: urbanization in the Third World*. Oxford: University Press.
Gugler, J. and Flanagan, W. 1978. *Urbanisation and Social Change in West Africa*. Cambridge: University Press.
Hake, A. 1977. *African Metropolis: Nairobi's self-help city*. New York: St. Martin's Press.
Heisler, H. 1974. *Urbanisation and the Government of Migration: the inter-relation of urban and rural life in Zambia*. London: C. Hurst & Co.
Hoek-Smit, M. 1982. *Community Participation in Squatter Upgrading in Zambia*. Philadelphia: American Friends Service Committee.
HUZA. 1986. *Survey of Renters in George Compound, Lusaka*. Lusaka: Human Settlements of Zambia (HUZA).
Jere, H. 1984. 'Lusaka: local participation in planning and decision-making', in G. Payne (ed.), *Low-Income Housing in the Developing World: the role of sites and services and settlement upgrading*. Chichester: John Wiley.
Keare, D. H. and Parris, S. 1982. *Evaluation of Shelter Programs for the Urban Poor: principal findings*. World Bank Staff Working Paper No. 547, Washington DC.
Lloyd, P. 1979. *Slums of Hope? Shanty Towns of the Third World*. Harmondsworth: Penguin.
Lusaka Urban District Council. n.d. *Report on the Operations of the Housing Project Unit*. Lusaka: Social Secretary's Department.
Mabogunje, A. 1968. *Urbanisation in Nigeria*. London: University Press.
Malawi Housing Corporation. 1980. *Proposal for the Upgrading of Unplanned Housing Areas in Blantyre*. Blantyre: Malawi Housing Corporation.
Malpezzi, S. 1984. *Rent Controls: an international comparison*. Dallas: American Real

Estate and Urban Economics Association.

Marris, P. 1979. 'The meaning of slums and patterns of change', *International Journal of Urban and Regional Research*, 3(3), pp. 419–41.

Muench, L. 1978. 'The Private Burden of Urban Social Overhead: a study of the informal housing market of Kampala, Uganda', unpublished PhD thesis, University of Pennsylvania.

Norwood, H. 1972. 'Ndirande: a squatter colony in Malawi', *Town Planning Review*, 43(2), pp. 135–50.

O'Connor, A. 1983. *The African City*. London: Hutchinson.

Odongo, J. and Lea, J. 1977. 'Home ownership in Uganda', *Journal of Modern African Studies*, 15(1), pp. 59–73.

Peil, M. 1976. 'African squatter settlements: a comparative study', *Urban Studies*, 13, pp. 155–66.

—— and Sada, P. 1984. *African Urban Society*. Chichester: John Wiley.

Pennant, T. 1984. *Report on a Study of Traditional (Site and Service) Housing Areas in and around Lilongwe City*. Zomba: Centre for Social Research.

Rakodi, C. 1986. 'Colonial urban policy and planning in Northern Rhodesia'. *Third World Planning Review*, 8(3), pp. 193–217.

Roberts, B. R. 1978. *Cities of Peasants*. London: Edward Arnold.

Schlyter, A. 1984. *Upgrading Reconsidered – the George studies in retrospect*. Stockholm: National Swedish Institute for Building Research.

Seymour, T. 1976. 'The causes of squatter settlement: the case of Lusaka, Zambia, in an international context', in Institute for African Studies (IAS), *Slums or Self-Reliance?* Lusaka: Institute for African Studies.

Shelton, J. 1968. 'The cost of renting versus owning a home', *Land Economics*, 44, pp. 59–72.

Stren, R. E. 1975. *Urban Inequality and Housing Policy in Tanzania*. Berkeley: University of California Institute of International Studies.

—— 1978. *Housing the Urban Poor in Africa: policy, politics and bureaucracy in Mombasa*. Berkeley: University of California Press.

Tipple, G. 1976. 'The low-cost housing market in Kitwe, Zambia', *Ekistics*, 41(244), pp. 148–52.

Turner, J. 1976. *Housing by People*. London: Marion Boyars.

UNCHS. 1984. *Community Participation in the Execution of Low-Income Housing Projects*. Nairobi: UNCHS.

United Nations. 1979. *Review of Rent-Control in Developing Countries*. New York: Department of Economic and Social Affairs.

Urban Edge. 1984. 'Rental housing: a rediscovered priority', *Urban Edge*, 8(2). Washington DC: World Bank.

# RESUME

Utilisant l'expérience de l'Amérique latine comme point de référence, ce chapitre explore la nature de la location pour la population de faibles revenus dans un certain nombre de contextes africains. Les sujets couverts comprennent les caractéristiques des propriétaires et des locataires, la structure du marché de location immobilière, les facteurs qui déterminent les proportions de propriétaires et de locataires parmi les pauvres, l'influence du bail sur les objectifs de développement tels que la distribution des revenus et l'organisation de la communauté, ainsi que les principales questions à considérer pour définir des politiques efficaces de location d'habitations. A la fois en Afrique et en Amerique latine, la commercialisation du logement restreint le choix en matière de logement et oblige les pauvres à vivre en location. Bien que la location représente une alternative acceptable pour les familles pauvres, il existe des situations où le taux élevé de demandes et le manque d'offres contribuent à créer un grand nombre de propriétaires et des niveaux d'exploitation inacceptables.

# MAIS COMMENT FAUT-IL DONC LE DIRE? LES SOLUTIONS DE DEMAIN SONT INSCRITES SUR LE SOL DEPUIS LES LUSTRES

## D'HIER A AUJOURD'HUI

### LES VILLES CROISSAIENT SOUS LEURS YEUX ET ILS N'EN AVAIENT QUE FAIRE

Permettez-moi de commencer cet exposé par un souvenir personnel. A l'occasion du bien connu colloque de Talence, organisé en 1970 par le CNRS,[1] j'ai souhaité (mais cela me fut refusé au profit d'un titre plus 'scientifique') intituler ainsi ma communication (comparative): 'quatre villes ou comment s'en débarrasser' en transposant le titre d'une pièce d'Eugène Ionesco. J'y remarquais en effet que, quelle que soit la situation urbaine étudiée, l'attitude des pouvoirs publics revenait toujours à *refuser l'urbanisation populaire*. Les villes croissaient sous leurs yeux et ils n'en avaient que faire. Ou bien ils se couvraient d'un voile pudique (politique de non-intervention ou de *laisser-faire*), ou bien ils se livraient à une politique active d'*éradication*.

Les quatre cas étudiés étaient trés contrastés:
  (a) Brazzaville, ville pauvre (avant le pétrole). Non-intervention.
  (b) Douala, ville riche. Non-intervention également, au point que j'aie pu alors parler d'une ville vivant *en-dessous* de ses moyens, ce qui pouvait paraître surprenant et paradoxal s'agissant d'une ville du Tiers Monde.
  (c) Abidjan, ville riche, mais avec un pouvoir fort qui avait clairement opté pour une politique d'éradication.
  (d) San-Pedro enfin, cas particulier d'une *ville nouvelle*, dans le même contexte d'un Etat fort et riche.

San-Pedro offrait le spectacle d'une apparente inconséquence: dans la création de ce nouveau pôle de croissance à l'ouest de la Côte d'Ivoire, on avait tout simplement 'oublié' de prévoir le logement, l'approvisionnement et la vie sociale des classes laborieuses. Une 'ville-bis' spontanée y pourvoya, mais,    longtemps,    elle    fut    obstinément    considérée    par    les pouvoirs publics comme totalement illégale, vouée à la destruction, et donc inapte à recevoir le moindre équipement alors même qu'elle abritait plus de 80 pour cent de la population totale de la ville.

La lecture du cas de cette ville-éprouvette était particulièrement éclairante et pouvait se résumer ainsi:

(a) San-Pedro ne pourrait pas être s'il n'y avait pas la ville-bis (constation objective).

(b) 'La ville-bis? Connaîs pas; nous la casserons à mesure qu'elle grandira' (position officielle).

Donc une incohérence totale, en apparence. Et pourtant, cela marchait très bien. *No problem.*

Depuis l'époque de cette analyse, une décennie puis les deux-tiers d'une autre se sont écoulés. Comment cela s'est-il traduit? Y a-t-il eu cristallisation des positions et des politiques? Ou bien y a-t-il eu des révisions, voire, des virages ont-ils été pris? Richard Stren nous a donné sa vision des choses, qui est celle d'une dégradation progressive (Stren, 1986). De fait, le 'cadavre' a grandi plus vite encore que dans la pièce de Ionesco, en tout cas beaucoup plus vite qu'il n'était prévu.

Pourtant la question urbaine a fait couler beaucoup d'encre et fait courir de nombreux experts. Des *opérations pilotes*, toujours initiées de l'extérieur, ont pu faire croire, ici ou là, que les choses allaient changer. Mais les montages de ces opérations ont toujours été beaucoup trop compliqués, leur conception trop sophistiquée, de sorte que ces expériences n'ont pas eu de lendemain, à moins que leurs objectifs aient été déviés, dénaturés.

## DE BONS PETITS BLANCS VINRENT FAIRE DES CHOSES BEAUCOUP TROP COMPLIQUEES

Nous avons tous en tête les expériences conduites par le Centre Habitat des Nations Unies, par la Caisse Centrale de Coopération Economique (CCCE, aide française), par la Banque Mondiale et l'USAID, et maintenant par les ONGs (organisations non-gouvernementales), qu'elles aient porté sur des transferts de technologie (voir l'inépuisable histoire du 'géobéton' ou terre compactée), sur des préceptes de gestion foncière (voir la Banque Mondiale), sur des produits bancaires (les expériences d'épargne-logement) ou sur des modèles plus ou moins mythiques de fonctionnement social (mouvement communautaire ou participatif aujourd'hui, investissement humain et opérations 'castor' hier).

Pour bien faire comprendre ce que je veux dire par 'trop de sophistication', il suffirait que je détaille l'opération de Cissin (Ouagadougou), mais vous la connaissez tous.[2] J'en évoquerai deux autres, moins connues.

La première nous ramène à San-Pedro et j'en fus l'acteur initial.

Malgré ce que je vous en ai dit, j'avais réussi, en 1973/74, à faire passer l'idée que l'on pourrait résoudre honorablement le problème de la ville-bis en lui apportant un minimum d'équipement (pour commencer) sans bouleverser le parcellaire spontané. Grâce au concours de la CCCE, puis à la perspective de la Conférence de Vancouver (où chaque pays était convié à présenter une action exemplaire), le gouvernement ivoirien avait – contre toute attente – adopté ce point de vue qui prenait le contre-pied de toutes ses déclarations antérieures sur ce sujet. C'était un miracle. Pourtant, parvenu au stade de sa mise en chantier, le projet dut être abandonné: le consensus se brisa sur la question foncière lorsque l'expert sollicité par les promoteurs proposa un montage apparemment séduisant, mais complètement irréaliste, qui fut rejeté par la population et ses représentants.[3]

Le deuxième exemple est actuel. Il se déroule à Port-Bouet, banlieue sud d'Abidjan. Grâce à l'érection récente de cette banlieue en commune, une nouvelle disposition d'esprit des pouvoirs – devenus locaux – s'est instaurée vis-à-vis des habitats irréguliers. Un projet naquit, avec le concours de spécialistes français du développement social. Objectif: améliorer l'assainissement de ces quartiers. Mais les animateurs voulurent, de proche en proche, investir tous les secteurs de la vie sociale, instituant pour cela une association dont la gestion se révèle être un casse-tête et dont le mode de fonctionnement, en outre, marque une rupture avec les réseaux traditionnels de la mobilisation sociale. Résultat: pour justifier son existence, l'association regroupe aujourd'hui l'essentiel de ses efforts sur un type d'opération que l'on connait bien: un programme d'habitat pour classe moyenne, qui n'a évidemment rien à voir avec les objectifs initiaux.[4]

Ce sont là des tentatives et des déboires ponctuels. Ces opérations avaient (ont) au moins le mérite de chercher à faire des percées hors de la logique dominante des politiques urbaines des Etats. A l'échelle de cette politique, les observateurs attendaient beaucoup, en Côte-d'Ivoire, de la crise économique des années 80.

## LES IMPASSES DE L'URBANISME ELITISTE NE CONDUISENT DECIDEMENT PAS A L'URBANISME POPULAIRE

La brutale récession du tournant 1980 avait en effet accéléré la remise en cause, par le gouvernement ivoirien, de sa politique du logement 'social' (que Djamat-Dubois nous a exposée), politique à la fois généreuse et, cependant, globalement élitiste.[5] Beaucoup d'entre nous – et la Banque Mondiale aussi – esperaient que l'Etat en profiterait pour revenir aux techniques d'urbanisation les plus simples, et qui avaient fait leurs preuves, c'est-à-dire, en gros, aux parcelles assainies, pour une autoproduction plus ouverte au grand nombre.

Six ans plus tard, force est de constater qu'il n'en fut rien. On cherche seulement d'autres filières pour réaliser de nouveaux programmes de logements 'clé-en-main'. Par exemple en faisant appel aux employeurs (quelques gros employeurs institutionnels ont fait un geste), mais plus généralement en encourageant l'apparition de promoteurs privés. Bien entendu, ces nouvelles voies (alliées à la poursuite d'une politique foncière ultra-sélective) ne font qu'accentuer le caractère inégalitaire de l'urbanisation officielle. Autrement dit, la Côte d'Ivoire, par delà les vicissitudes, reste fidèle à son image. Et l'urbanisation illégale y reprend de plus belle, en attendant que l'Etat sévisse à nouveau contre elle.

Que faut-il dire ou en dire? Comment faire passer cette idée très claire et mille fois rappelée: que l'Etat devrait se borner à penser 'équipement' selon les trames les plus simples, et se reposer pour le reste sur les modèles d'une autopromotion populaire toujours performante; que ce soit le modèle de la cour multi-locative et ses modernes dérivés en étages (à Abidjan ou dans les villes qui lui sont comparables); ou que ce soit celui de l'enclos familial, aux composantes encore champêtres, dans des villes plus petites et plus calmes, ou dans des contextes économiques et culturels différents (Afrique sahélienne, Afrique bantoue)?

Sauf intervention directe de la Banque Mondiale, et avec les déviations que l'on connaît, ces modèles continuent d'être tenus pour indignes de la cité moderne, et techniquement incompatibles avec une conception de plus en plus normative de l'équipement urbain. On continue de tourner le dos à une urbanisation extensive pourtant inévitable, et parfaitement jouable pourvu que la puissance publique concentre ses ressources et son imagination sur la mise au point, la réalisation et la gestion de réseaux primaires efficaces.

## VENEZ VOIR, MONSIEUR IONESCO!

A quoi faut-il attribuer cet aveuglement apparent, ce refus d'épouser les solutions les plus simples et les plus naturelles, celles qui collent au plus près des pratiques populaires et que réclament, de ce fait, la plupart des citadins d'Afrique et d'ailleurs?

Où est le niveau d'explication? Y aurait-il une impossibilité purement mécanique, due par exemple à la perversité du jeu foncier, ou bien à la nature des circuits de financement, ou encore à une inadéquation du savoir-faire technologique? S'agirait-il de la persistance d'un réflexe malthusianiste lié au souci de ne pas faire le lit de l'exode rural par une politique d'accueil trop ouverte? Serait-ce plutôt une question de modèles culturels (importés) ou bien, sous le couvert de ceux-ci, un problème de classe dominante et de confiscation des resources? Faut-il, plus simplement, attribuer cette situation à une paralysie bureaucratique, à une impuissance administrative si souvent dénoncèe?

On est tenté, ici, de se retourner vers Ionesco et de lui emprunter à nouveau son allégorie de la désespérance absurde: le cadavre est là; qui grandit et menace, et l'on ne sait pas pourquoi.

## POUR UNE NOUVELLE DONNE

En dépit du constat qui vient d'être fait sur des exemples partiellement ivoiriens, la désespérance n'est pas un mot qui colle vraiment à la situation abidjanaise. On s'accorde généralement à dire qu'à l'échelle de l'ouest africain, Abidjan, joue un rôle de laboratoire pour la recherche et l'expérimentation urbanistiques. Or, parallèlement à la situation décrite ci-dessus, il se pourrait qu'à nouveau se dessine, dans cette ville, un dispositif innovant.

Si l'accentuation de la crise économique, au tournant de 1980, semble s'être essentiellement traduite, sur le terrain, par la cessation de tout programme significatif d'habitat 'social' (le fleuron d'une politique de vingt ans), si le vide semble avoir succédé à une évidente fièvre créatrice (qui s'exerçait en faveur sinon de la grande masse, du moins d'une large tranche de citoyens 'moyens'), si aucune politique de rechange n'a véritablement été mise en place pour les catégories pauvres ou moyennes, on ferait bien de s'aviser de deux réformes qui pourraient totalement changer, à terme, les règles du jeu. Elles ne concernent pourtant pas directement la politique de l'habitat.

## DEUX REFORMES

La première réforme est la *réforme municipale* (1980). Divisée en dix communes, l'agglomération abidjanaise connaît pour la première fois l'exercice d'un pouvoir local réel, électif (avec pluralité de candidature) et renouvelable tous les cinq ans. On ne peut certes pas dire, bien qu'on en soit maintenant au deuxième mandat, que la machine municipale ait donné toutes ses preuves: la définition des compétences, les attributions budgétaires, les règles du jeu local souffrent encore de nombreux flous. L'engagement des acteurs n'est pas toujours évident. Sa traduction en termes de réalisations est encore peu spectaculaire (Attahi, 1986).

Pourtant, de nombreux signes montrent bien que le regard porté par ces nouveaux pouvoirs sur la nature des habitats et sur leur caractère plus ou moins légitime n'est pas et ne peut pas être le même que celui de l'Administration centrale. Une catégorie jugée marginale à l'échelle de l'agglomération peut devenir l'élément dominant dans le cadre d'une commune d'arrondissement.

Il en est ainsi, par exemple, de l'habitat 'irrégulier' dans la commune déjà citée de Port-Bouet, ou bien des lotissements 'coutumiers' dans la commune d'Abobo. Les élus de ces communes ne peuvent pas contourner ces réalités et sont amenés à composer, voire à rechercher les conditions d'une stabilisation ou d'une viabilisation des habitats problématiques.[6] Il en va de même dans d'autres domaines que celui de l'habitat: par exemple dans celui des activités économiques, et singulièrement de celles qui relèvent d'un artisanat plus ou moins 'informel'.

La deuxième réforme n'a pas bénéficié de la même publicité que la loi municipale. Elle relève d'un tout autre genre, celui de la politique feutrée qui s'exerce à l'ombre du pouvoir présidentiel. Elle consiste à dépouiller peu à peu les grands ministères techniques de leurs responsabilités en matière de grands travaux. Ceux-ci seront désormais du ressort d'un puissant service placé directement sous la tutelle de la Présidence. Ce 'domaine réservé' va très loin puisqu'il englobe l'agence publique d'urbanisme, donc le niveau où s'élabore la cohérence des interventions de l'Etat sur la ville.

Ce service des *Grands Travaux* est dirigé, pour l'instant, par des ingénieurs français. On lui reconnaît généralement une très grande efficacité technique et l'on assure qu'il fait faire de grosses économies au Trésor public. Mais on voit bien aussi ce que son existence et sa toute-puissance, sous la seule gouverne du Président, ont de choquant, même si elles traduisent à l'évidence la lassitude du Père de la Nation après les multiples scandales d'incurie, de gabégie et de corruption qui ont flétri les institutions publiques au cours d'une période récente. Choquant sans doute, mais pourquoi se voiler la face? Si un système s'avère bloqué (et c'est bien le sens de l'analyse faite plus haut), ne faut-il pas se réjouir de l'avènement d'une nouvelle donne? Surtout si, en s'alimentant à deux sources contraires, elle relie deux exigences complémentaires et susceptibles de s'équilibrer. En tout cas, les perspectives ainsi ouvertes méritent examen.

## L'ESQUISSE D'UN NOUVEAU DISPOSITIF?

Les deux réformes (loi municipale et réorganisation des grands travaux) esquissent en effet, l'une associée à l'autre, un dispositif global qui ne manque pas de séduction. Je dis bien 'esquissent' car il ne semble pas que l'on puisse déjà parler d'un système. Mais on peut l'imaginer. D'un côté, à l'échelle du local, une sorte de démocratie directe conduisant à une prise en charge des populations par elles-mêmes. De l'autre côté, à l'échelle de l'Etat, un instrument technocratique libéré des circuits politico-administratifs et de leurs pesanteurs.

Est-ce qu'une ville multi-millionnaire peut vivre et se construire sur ce schéma? C'est-à-dire comme une juxtaposition de cellules vivantes, auto-produites et auto-gérées, où se concentrerait l'exercice civique et politique des citoyens (au moins en ce qui concerne leurs droits à la ville), et qu'une sorte de technocratie présidentielle se contenterait de mettre en cohérence technique en assurant le fonctionnement général des réseaux de circulation ou d'assainissement, la production de l'eau et de l'électricité, la répartition des zones d'emploi et des grands équipements sociaux, etc.?

## POUR ALLER PLUS LOIN

Pour pouvoir répondre positivement à la question ci-dessus, il faudrait évidemment en dire plus. Pour approfondir et nuancer, pour éviter la caricature. Par exemple, on ne peut imaginer ni souhaiter que les grands équipements puissent être simplement octroyés au nom d'une pure logique techniciste. Cette pureté n'existe pas.

La concentration au plus haut niveau du pouvoir de décision ne devrait pourtant pas être, en soi, un facteur aggravant d'arbitraire. Rien de pire, pour le défenseur des intérêts locaux qu'un pouvoir introuvable, dilué. On saura mieux, désormais, à quelle porte frapper. Mais il faut encore que le porte-parole des communautés locales soit écouté, reconnu ès qualité, ses doléances et ses propositions reçues.

A cet égard, la réforme municipale ne constitue qu'un premier pas. Elle établit des cadres-relais: la commune d'arrondissement (250.000 habitants en moyenne) et, au-dessus, la commune 'fédérale', celle du grand Abidjan, dont le maire est l'élu des dix maires d'arrondissement. Mais ce n'est pas à l'échelle de 250.000 habitants que peut se situer un sentiment d'appartenance à une entité solidaire.

Que l'on se place dans le cadre d'une urbanisation officielle ou dans celui d'une urbanisation 'spontanée', les unités de voisinage (qui coincident généralement avec les limites des opérations foncières ou immobilières créatrices de l'espace urbain) n'excèdent pas quelques centaines de mètres de côté. C'est à cette échelle que les besoins d'équipement sont ressentis et, éventuellement, exprimés ou pris en main par les habitants ou les mieux placés d'entre eux. C'est aussi et surtout à cette échelle que se pose, le cas échéant, le problème du statut des établissements 'spontanés' ou 'irréguliers'.

## OU L'ON RETROUVE UN SENTIMENT LEGITIMISTE INATTENDU

La logique d'un pari en faveur d'une responsabilisation des citadins exigerait donc que l'on fasse descendre la notion de pouvoir local jusqu'à ce niveau des quartiers de base, par exemple en redonnant consistance à la vieille notion de *chefferie* de quartier, que l'on pourrait moderniser.

A l'appui de cette idée on pourrait évoquer le système des kampungs indonésiens. Mais les réalités africaines offrent un autre modèle qui ne demande qu'à être mis à profit: celui du pouvoir *'coutumier'*. Le recours à celui-ci pourrait sembler anachronique, mais il ne l'est pas pour deux raisons. La première est que les villes africaines continuent, plus que jamais, à se construire partiellement à l'initiative (plus ou moins clandestine selon les droits nationaux) des lotisseurs coutumiers. La seconde est que les citadins eux-mêmes conservent un sens très vif des prérogatives du premier occupant: les récentes élections municipales à Abidjan ont montré que, pour être élu, il valait mieux appartenir à l'ethnie autochtone, pourtant numériquement insignifiante au sein d'une population urbaine extrêmement mélangée. Dans neuf communes sur dix, ce sont les candidats ébriés qui ont recueilli les suffrages, ce qui donne la mesure du 'légitimisme' des abidjanais.

## REHABILITER ET MODERNISER LE POUVOIR COUTUMIER

A la recherche d'une solution moderne au fonctionnement de la grande ville, nous trouvons donc, paradoxalement, la 'coutume' à la fois comme siège d'un pouvoir représentatif reconnu par les citadins d'aujourd'hui et comme source génératrice d'espace urbain, plus abondante et plus accessible, plus personnalisée et cependant plus égalitaire que celle de l'Etat.

Une reconnaissance officielle de ce niveau de pouvoir permettrait de rompre enfin avec l'épuisant scénario du chat et de la souris (Haeringer, 1982) qui oppose la puissance publique (et ses bulls) aux lotisseurs coutumiers (ou plus exactement à leurs clients une fois établis) dans une très dommageable alternance de répression et de laisser-faire. Au lieu de cet affrontement stérile, un statut positif et modernisé du pouvoir coutumier permettrait d'établir des relations *contractuelles* entre les organismes centraux de l'urbanisme métropolitain et les initiatives locales de l'urbanisation populaire.

Cet équilibre entre initiative locale et pouvoir central a sans doute tout à gagner, répétons-le, de la concentration de ce pouvoir en un organe unique et conçu pour l'efficacité. Mais, puisque cette concentration semble être en passe de devenir une réalité dans le cas d'Abidjan, il est bon de remarquer que cette évolution autoritaire – dans un pays qui fait peu à peu l'apprentissage de la démocratie – n'a des chances de paraître tolérable qu'à la condition, précisément, que la bride soit lâchée à l'autre bout du dispositif. Inversement, un tel retournement de l'attitude officielle vis-à-vis de l'initative locale, suspectée non sans raison d'être porteuse d'un risque de désordre urbain, n'est guère envisageable – à moins d'un renoncement des pouvoirs publics à la maîtrise urbaine – sans une autorité centrale univoque et 'performante'.

Nous n'entrerons pas davantage, ici, dans une logique qui n'est peut-être pas du tout, malgré les apparences, dans l'esprit des dirigeants actuels de la Côte d'Ivoire, et qui n'est effectivement pas nécessaire à la compréhension des deux réformes analysées. N'allant pas plus loin, nous nous éviterons, reconnaissons-le, d'aborder les écueils, les faiblesses et les contradictions, voire l'inacceptable d'un tel système, à supposer que l'on puisse tous et toutes les prédire ou les cerner.

Remarquons tout de même que l'innovation esquissée dans ces pages (et suggérée par l'expérience ivoirienne) perdrait une bonne part de son côté radical si nous prenions le temps de l'examiner plus en détail et d'une façon plus pragmatique. On notera, par exemple, que:

(a) Les attributions d'un organe de décision placé hors du champ gouvernemental n'engloberont jamais (ce ne serait pas conforme à la nature d'un tel organe) tous les domaines de l'administration publique concernés de près ou de loin par la vie des quartiers.

(b) En considération de ce qui précède, mais aussi dans la mesure où les ressources et les attributions de compétence des mairies ont été fortement augmentées par la réforme communale, le domaine de confrontation entre pouvoir central et pouvoirs locaux pourrait se réduire, en définitive, à quelques grands dossiers dont celui, justement, des 'grands' travaux.

Il n'empêche que les deux réformes ivoiriennes indiquent une direction et que cette direction rejoint une conviction: que la cité africaine d'aujourd'hui et de demain a besoin à la fois d'une plus grande efficience technologique (et gestionnaire) et d'une meilleure écoute de son génie propre; que la conjonction de ces deux exigences (et de leur satisfaction) est une condition nécessaire pour que l'absurde désolation n'étreigne pas trop les mégavilles du siècle prochain.


## POST-SCRIPTUM: REFLEXION SUR L'EMPLOI DE LA NOTION 'HOUSING THE URBAN POOR'

Cette expression semble, a priori, correspondre à une évidente priorité. Les grandes villes du monde enferment en effet de nombreux pauvres. Dans les villes du Tiers Monde, ce phénomène prend des proportions telles qu'il apparaît majoritaire. La grande misère de l'habitat urbain n'en est-elle pas la preuve?

A partir de là je ne suis plus d'accord. Nous savons tous très bien que la grande détresse de l'habitat urbain est loin d'être un simple corollaire de la pauvreté. Nous savons bien (Galila El Kadi nous l'a rappelé à propos du Caire) que le mal-habiter atteint des catégories sociales dont le niveau économique ne peut pas être mis en cause. Inversement, nous connaissons tous des situations urbaines où l'indigence populaire engendre des habitats tout à fait estimables, à la fois modestes et séduisants et, surtout, conformes aux modes de vie en vigueur.

Ces simples faits d'observation, confirmés par de nombreuses analyses, montrent bien que l'abomination des habitats urbains est d'abord le produit d'un *dysfonctionnement*, lequel peut être dû indifféremment ou tout à la fois à une politique urbaine déséquilibrée ou mal orientée, à une main mise des classes possédantes sur le foncier et l'immobilier, aux effets mécaniques d'une croissance démographique galopante, à d'autres causes encore.

Il est certes incontestable que les effets de ces dysfonctionnements frappent d'abord et surtout les 'pauvres'. Mais si la pauvreté accroît la vulnérabilité des citadins, elle n'est pas la cause véritable de l'éventuelle misère de leurs maisons et de leurs quartiers. Aborder la question de l'habitat des pauvres sous l'angle de cette pauvreté (et c'est bien ce que suggère l'expression 'housing the urban poor') serait donc une erreur, si toutefois on se propose de traiter cette question au fond. Une telle orientation ne peut à mon sens que conduire à des propositions de l'ordre de la charité (un niveau d'action il est vrai tout à fait nécessaire devant certaines situations)[7] ou relevant du bricolage (et qui peuvent être néanmoins utiles).

Il me semble que l'on doive au contraire partir de la conviction qu'à tout niveau économique correspond, pour un groupe ou une population donnés (le problème peut être différent à l'échelon du cas individuel), un habitat potentiel non seulement honorable mais conforme aux habitudes de ce groupe ou de cette population. En d'autres termes, il semble qu'il faille tenir pour une sorte de loi qu'une population quelle qu'elle soit est toujours en mesure de produire l'habitat qui lui convient, pourvu que les structures, les circonstances et l'environnement socio-politique en laissent l'occasion, ne lui interdisent pas de le faire.

S'agissant de l'Afrique noire, il suffit de se reporter à l'excellence des habitats produits par les populations rurales les plus indigentes, mais aussi à la simplicité des modèles les plus courants de l'habitation urbaine: modèles traditionnels comme la maison soudanienne en pisé banché, la case en briques adobes ou en torchis armé (sur clayonnage), la maison de carabottes (planches 'éclatées') ou la case en bambous et palmes tressées des banlieues côtières; mais aussi modèles plus actuels à base de parpaings au ciment, moulés sur place et parfaitement banalisés.

Nous savons très bien que le citadin le plus démuni, pour peu que lui soit accordé un accès paisible au sol urbain, saura construire la demeure qui lui conviendra le mieux – et qu'il fera belle – à moins qu'il ne préfère, dans un premier temps, louer dans la cour de son voisin, ce qui peut être une solution tout à fait satisfaisante si ce voisin a pu lui-même bâtir 'paisiblement' et s'il ne jouit pas d'une position de force trop marquée qui serait la conséquence d'un marché déséquilibré, dominé par une pénurie foncière et immobilière trop accablante. Bref, s'il n'y a pas un dysfonctionnement majeur.

On peut, certes, tenir cet idyllique tableau pour parfaitement irréaliste eu égard à la complexité d'un milieu urbain multimillionnaire et compte tenu du fait que le problème de l'habitat ne s'arrête pas à la réalisation du logement proprement dit. Le 'mal-habiter', c'est aussi l'absence de l'eau potable, les rues boueuses, l'éloignement des écoles et des emplois. Mais là, justement, ce n'est plus le domaine de l'économie domestique, ce n'est plus l'affaire des pauvres ou des moins pauvres. C'est pourquoi, pour conclure, je dirai que l'analyse théorique ou le montage opérationnel qui parviendraient à traiter de cet immense problème de l''infra-habitat' urbain sans utiliser le concept de 'pauvre' auraient les plus grandes chances d'être dans le vrai. Et inversement.

Il y a vingt ans, pour traiter du même problème, nous parlions beaucoup de l'habitat 'du grand nombre', expression quelque peu délaissée aujourd'hui. Il me semble qu'elle correspondait à un angle d'attaque plus juste.

## NOTES

1   Haeringer, 1972:625–51. Voir aussi, dans le même ouvrage, mon rapport général sur 'La dynamique de l'espace urbain en Afrique noire et à Madagascar: problèmes de politique urbaine' (pp. 177–88), où je poursuis mon argumentation.

2   Opération internationale conduite par le Centre Habitat des Nations Unies au milieu des années 70. L'originalité première de cette expérience de lotissement résidait dans l'adoption des techniques de la terre compactée ou 'géo-béton' (mais cette proposition était assortie de nombreuses autres suggestions touchant à l'architecture, aux conditions d'attribution des parcelles, aux activités féminines, etc.). Quelques années plus tard, un petit film produit par le Centre Habitat lui-même (dont il faut saluer le courage) démontrait l'échec à peu près total de l'opération, y compris sous l'angle de son principal apport: les constructions témoins s'étaient écroulées ou prématurément dégradées. On envisage à présent la mise au point de presses (à géo-béton) plus efficaces, mais quelle dérision dans un pays où les techniques traditionnelles de la brique séchée sont, elles, parfaitement maîtrisées!

3   Pour contourner la difficulté du bornage a posteriori d'un parcellaire 'spontané' quelque peu chaotique (mais peut-être aussi pour introduire en Côte-d'Ivoire un début de remise en cause de la privatisation du sol urbain), le juriste proposa en effet le principe de la parcelle collective s'étendant sur tout un îlot. Seules les emprises des constructions existantes devaient être attribuées en toute propriété aux individus. Outre les complications infinies qu'aurait causées la

révision de ces emprises à chaque modification du bâti (un bâti alors provisoire et impatient de se transformer), ce statut spécial ne pouvait plaire aux habitants de San-Pedro, que seul intéressait le régime 'normal' de la parcelle individuelle. La contestation qui s'exprima alors ouvrit une brèche et permit à ceux des responsables politiques qui étaient restés peu favorables à la réhabilitation de San-Pedrobis de reprendre peu à peu l'avantage.

4  Il faudrait beaucoup de lignes pour une restitution fidèle de la dynamique développée à Port-Bouet. Le raccourci ci-dessus est sans doute injuste à cause de la distance qu'il prend, tandis que foisonnent, sur le terrain, les bonnes idées. Il faudrait, par exemple, indiquer que l'opération d'habitat innove (par rapport aux pratiques antérieures de l'Etat-promoteur) en groupant les postulants en mutuelles d'épargne et en sociétés civiles de construction:   un grand pas vers le 'développement communautaire' à l'américaine, à condition que la greffe prenne. En attendant de savoir si ces ballons d'essai réussiront ou non, nous pouvons nous montrer bons joueurs en constatant que cette expérimentation multiforme, voulue par le Maire de Port-Bouet, contribue à donner une réalité à ce niveau de proposition et d'initiative que doit être la commune.

5  Djamat-Dubois, 1986. Près de 50.000 logements construits par les sociétés immobilières de l'Etat. Subventionnés à plus de 50 per cent, ces logements sont loués à des niveaux très avantageux, mais échoient surtout aux catégories sociales moyennes. Cet engagement massif de l'Etat en faveur d'un habitat 'clé-en-main' lui a fait abandonner ou négliger les autres filières d'urbanisation populaire. Voir aussi Haeringer, 1985.

6  Il est réconfortant de constater que cette attitude conciliante apparaît aussi lorsque l'habitat irrégulier n'est pas la dominante. Voir ce que dit A. Yapi Diahou des relations entretenues entre le maire de Yopougon (commune d'Abidjan dominée par les réalisations des sociétés immobilières d'Etat) et le chef d'un quartier illégal (Diahou, 1986). Comparer cette analyse avec celle d'une situation observée avant la réforme municipale dans la commune d'Abobo (Abidjan), où une incommunicabilité totale entre le pouvoir et les habitants aboutit à de grands gâchis (Haeringer, 1982).

7  Significative, à ce propos, l'ambiguité entretenue sur le champ d'étude et d'action couvert par l'*Année Internationale des Sans-Abris* (1987). Les termes anglais *Shelter for the homeless*, comme les termes français, évoquent *a priori* le cas de populations sinistrées, brutalement privées de leur habitat par un tremblement de terre, une guerre, une migration forcée, un statut de réfugié. L'emploi du mot 'abri' ou *shelter* suggère une intervention d'urgence, l'organisation de secours, une aide humanitaire. Il n'y aurait donc pas lieu de s'étonner qu'au Royaume-Uni, par exemple, le *trust* organisé pour regrouper les initiatives se réclamant de l'Année internationale soit légalement défini comme *a registered charity*. En réalité, dans les textes d'appel, il n'est pas question de réfugiés ou de sinistrés: c'est de l'habitat des pauvres que l'on parle, dans toutes ses dimensions (et de l'action communautaire comme panacée). Mais alors, la terminologie est-elle bien la bonne? On peut certes considérer les pauvres comme des sinistrés de l'économie, de l'urbanisation, etc. Mais la connotation apitoyée des mots 'sans abri' ou 'homeless', qui enferme les populations concernées dans un ghetto, dans une marginalité, incite en effet à une approche caritative du problème posé. Pourtant, celui-ci n'est certainement pas du ressort d'une telle approche.

## REFERENCES

Attahi, K. 1986. *Evaluation de la réforme de la gestion municipale en Côte d'Ivoire*. Abidjan: Centre de Recherches Architecturales et Urbaines, Université d'Abidjan.

Diahou, A. Y. 1986. 'Dépôt III–IV: conflits et alliances urbaines dans un quartier d'Abidjan', *Politique Africaine*, 24, pp. 53–67.

Djamat-Dubois, M., 1983. 'Les logements économiques à Abidjan: une politique d'habitat du grand nombre en Côte d'Ivoire' dans Colloques Internationaux du CNRS (voir Haeringer, 1972).

Haeringer, P. 1972. 'L' urbanisation de masse en question: quatre villes d'Afrique noire', dans Colloques Internationaux du CNRS, *La croissance urbaine en Afrique noire et à Madagascar* (Talence, septembre 1970).Paris: Editions du CNRS.

—— 1982. 'Stratégies populaires pour l'accès au sol dans la ville africaine: une grande partie de dés dans la banlieue d'Abidjan, ou l'impossible débat avec l'Etat', dans *Enjeux Fonciers en Afrique Noire*, pp. 341–59. Paris: Karthala.

—— 1985. *Vingt-cinq ans de politique urbaine à Abidjan, ou la tentation de l'urbanisme intégral*. Paris: ORSTOM. (Première partie parue dans *Politique Africaine*, 17, mars 1985, pp. 20–40.)

Stren, R. E. 1986. 'Urban housing in Africa since independence: itinerary of a problem', dans Colloques Internationaux du CNRS (voir Haeringer, 1972).

## SUMMARY

Despite years of facing the same housing problems that only worsen, African governments seem still not to accept the obvious fact that the best solutions to the housing problem are the simplest ones – ones that are rooted in popular habits and customs. A look at Abidjan suggests the possibility that something new is emerging as a result two administrative changes: the 1980 municipal reform which provided for decentralised elected local authorities and the gradual break-up of the big centralised technical ministries. Both these reforms potentially enhance the power of local neighbourhoods and may make official housing policy more responsive to popular demands and also lead to a revitalisation of a more legitimate traditional authority.

Peter Lloyd

# EPILOGUE

What kinds of society are being fostered by the housing policies of the several African states as outlined in the chapters of this book? What effect do these policies have upon emergent patterns of stratification among the urban poor? Is a more egalitarian society being created – or a less egalitarian one?

The term 'urban poor', as conventionally used, embraces two-thirds or more of the population of these African cities; it excludes only the 'middle class' of usually well-educated professionals and executives and of prosperous commercial entrepreneurs and an 'upper class'. We must expect a very wide range within the urban poor from the relatively affluent traders, artisans and skilled workers at one end of the spectrum to those who live by scavenging on the city rubbish dump at the other. We have moreover grown accustomed to the idea that capitalist development, at least in its early stages, often increases the differences between rich and poor – and this is manifest too in growing disparities within the urban poor. The depressed economic conditions of the 1970s to which so many of our authors have alluded serve only to exacerbate the poverty of those at the lower end of the spectrum.

But is housing a cause or a symptom of this poverty? Edwards has written 'Tenants are not poor because they rent; they rent because they are poor, and they are poor because of the structure of the society in which they live' (p. 266). One certainly cannot attribute all the ills of society to its housing system; but we have seen in the examples given that there are many who rent (paying a landlord) when they would prefer to own (repaying a mortgage loan); and whilst some tenants have benign landlords others are obliged to pay very high rents. The poverty of the very poor is exacerbated as the costs of consumer goods (of which housing is but one) rise faster than incomes; the affluence of the better-off is buttressed by home-ownership and the possibility of a rental income to set against loan repayments. The theme of many of the case studies in this volume is the increasing commercialisation of the housing market and the division of the urban poor into landlords, owner-occupiers and tenants. Housing and poverty are certainly closely linked – but the precise relationship between them is often obscured by the differences in the discourses within which the debate takes place.

One discourse is that of the bureaucrats, the planners, the housing experts. They start from the laudable premise that everyone has a right to decent housing – to an impermeable roof, to adequate space, to basic services. Housing is seen as the symptom rather than the cause of poverty.

Such housing may be provided for the poor – or by the poor; as Aina graphically states, there are elite-based responses and popular responses to the expressed needs. In the Industrial West we have, for many decades, assumed that housing should be provided for the poor, largely by the state or by large-scale private enterprise. But in African countries the state is usually too poor to embark upon more than a few token schemes of housing development, and these are, as often as not, financed by international aid; private enterprise can find far more lucrative enterprises than the provision of housing for those who can afford only minimal standards and whose capacity to pay is so insecure. We are apt to forget that the urban poor have migrated to the city from villages and small provincial towns where they would expect to build their own homes, albeit perhaps mud and thatch and with the help of relatives and friends. Most would presumably be prepared to build their own homes in the city – but they are constrained by the lack of access to land or by government-imposed controls on the type of building allowed (legitimated by fears of disease and fire that are generated by high-density slums of primitive shacks). But as Mangin (1967) trenchantly noted in the early 1960s, describing the situation in Lima, Peru, the invasion of land and the building of a shanty town is not the problem, but the solution to a problem.

Intermediate between these two polar opposites of 'state-build' and 'self-build' are the site and service schemes and the growth of small-scale landlordism. The former represent a response by the state: an infrastructure of accessed plot with minimal services is established which the owner may then develop. As we have seen, these schemes range from those where a substantial house is built, the new owner adding additional rooms as needed, to those with a minimal core of toilet and kitchen sink; they range too from schemes where the owner is expected to build with his own labour and with minimal constraints of design to others where improvements are limited to those set out in approved plans and implemented by approved local contractors.

Petty landlordism is a popular response. Urban migrants have, unless prohibited as in southern Africa, long accommodated kin and friends from their home villages who in turn seek to establish themselves in the city. As some of the earlier migrants, as in West African cities, have built substantial homes for themselves, they have rented rooms, on a more permanent and

less personalised basis, to later immigrants. From here it is but a short step
to the building of a second and a third home, each of better quality than the
previous one which is then exclusively used for renting. This is a process
which has developed both in those areas, in Lagos for instance, where there
has been easy access to a customary land market, and in state-sponsored site
and service schemes.

Elaborate each of these few responses and one can appreciate the wide
variety of African housing systems. Yet as Amis and Stren have both
indicated, and other authors exemplified, it is possible to see an overall
trend in the kinds of policy espoused. The fashions of the big international
aid agencies, such as their promotion of and their disillusion with site and
service schemes, affect all countries equally. The economic depression
affects most, though in different ways. Sudden or violent changes in
regime, such as in Rhodesia/Zimbabwe, produce specific ideological shifts
in policy orientation.

In the housing discourse the evaluation of policy – and in particular of
state-directed housing programmes – is in terms of numbers of units
constructed. Though the target is rarely achieved, an impressive suburb is
often created which can be displayed with pride to visiting dignitaries. Less
often is attention drawn to the fact that the new houses are not occupied by
the originally proclaimed target population but by wealthier people – either
the former could not afford the housing in the first place or they have
quickly sold out to others. Nor is it immediately seen that housing intended
for owner–occupiers quickly becomes occupied by tenants. Whilst the
planners may be satisfied with the physical existence of the houses, the
politicians may be embarrassed by their unfulfilled promises to the poor,
with the addition of further discontents to stimulate the unstructured
rioting that has occurred in so many cities in recent years.

In the second discourse the focus is not upon houses but upon the people
– the urban poor and their poverty. Attention is drawn to the continuing
growth of the cities as conditions in rural areas deteriorate and as the youth
of the migrants raises urban birth rates. This city growth, continuing
despite worsening levels of poverty, produces the deterioration in standards
of services which, as Stren notes, now constitutes the prime problem for city
planners. It is manifest too in the widening gap between rich and poor –
among the urban poor themselves as well as in wider society. There is, of
course, a dearth of reliable statistics by which one could quantify the
disparity. And we lack terms by which we could usefully make qualitative
distinctions. The 'labour aristocracy' defined by Western scholars in the
1960s and 1970s seem to have few artistocratic qualities; those described as
the 'lumpen proletariat' are not always downwardly mobile 'drop-outs' but
are often achievement-oriented migrants aspiring for upward mobility.
Differences in wealth create a heterogeneity of life styles; but one cannot

equate these with economic position; men and women move between informal and formal-sector employment, their households containing a wide diversity of economic status. Ties of kinship or ethnicity link those widely separated in income.

We can nevertheless see an ongoing process. Some people are able to save, invest and accumulate; others are consuming less as prices rise faster than incomes. The rich are getting richer, the poor poorer. For each, housing is usually an element in the process. There are many ways in which one might invest – in education, in purchase of tools, etc. – but the ownership of a house is certainly one of them. Again, housing is but one of many items of consumption. For both rich and poor housing is an important element in their daily budget. For both there is a degree of choice – one may live in squalor and invest in education; one may prefer to spend money on food and entertainment rather than on decorating or furnishing the house. The choices are, however, severely constrained by access to land, by controls on the standard of building permitted. For most the outcomes are determined more by the external constraints than by personal choices.

Again we must envisage a spectrum of situations. At one extreme land is freely available and building minimally controlled. Such was the situation in many West African cities in the past, when one could, for a customary gift such as a bottle of gin, acquire a plot on the periphery of the urban area from the indigenous landholding descent group and build a mud-walled house with a corrugated iron roof, the building inspectors concerned minimally with size of rooms, window provision and the like. Or in Lima, where invasion of unoccupied land was for several decades tolerated and then recognised, the invader first erecting a matting shelter and then gradually a more durable structure without any controls, for these areas were outside the formal local government structures. When anyone can acquire land in this way there is no necessity to become a tenant – though some may choose to do so, perhaps lacking an intention to reside permanently in the city, or preferring a residence in the city close to informal job opportunities, to one twenty miles out, poorly served by transport.

At the other extreme, access to land is limited or non-existent; land is held by the state, by expatriate companies and the like which have no interest in making small plots available to the poor. Squatting is vigorously prevented by eradicative measures. Projects are developed, access to which is severely limited – by ability to make a down-payment; by income security to permit a mortgage loan, by success in completing the stipulated building, to those with patrons in appropriate offices or carrying the right party membership card. Those who fail to get access to land have little or no alternative save to rent from those who do; the latter, in turn, may be positively encouraged to build houses with rooms designed specifically for renting, with the assumption that the rents received will facilitate regular mortgage repayments.

Thus at one end of the spectrum we find societies in which widespread owner–occupation is possible; the urban poor will still be divided into the more and less poverty-stricken but it will be not the housing market but other factors which create and reinforce these distinctions. At the other end we find societies which are stratified into owners and tenants, with a substantial proportion of the former exploiting the latter.

In reality the countries of Africa fall between these extreme examples, each having not one but many forms of housing provision. Yet as the chapters in this volume have indicated, the commercialisation of the housing market is increasing and landlordism, in one form or another, is becoming more widespread.

The distinction between landlord and tenant is a self-perpetuating one – the longer one is within one of the categories the less chance one has of leaving it for the other. In Britain, as in most industrial capitalist countries, the picture is familiar: a young couple cohabit to economise on living expenses; after marriage they postpone childbearing, so that both can continue in full-time employment; relatively soon they can afford to buy a flat or small house; over the years as mortgage repayments (reduced by tax relief) constitute a smaller proportion of income, their family expenses can rise and they may trade upwards to a larger house. Another couple with only slightly smaller resources or ambitions opt for tenancy, and are impelled towards the subsidised state sector because of the high costs of private rental housing; to qualify for the former they need children – so the wife ceases employment and family income falls; their chances of house purchase rapidly diminish unless they become eligible as tenants of long standing to buy their home at a nominal price. This pattern is not replicated exactly in Africa for there is little or no state subsidised rental housing. But nevertheless one can see similar processes at work whereby some are able to jump on the bandwagon – and stay on it – whilst others run fast and seemingly faster without ever being able to catch it.

As an alternative approach to that of the planners, focusing primarily on the construction of housing units, let us look at the choices available to the individual as he seeks shelter for himself and his family in the city. What, in the different countries, are the opportunities open to him; how far can he satisfy his expressed needs? Each choice and decision made will tend to establish the individual irrevocably on a given path – for all choices are constrained by previous decisions. And each decision also changes, albeit slightly, the opportunities available to others; each acquisition of a plot of land reduces availability to others. Wikan shows graphically how the opportunities available to the younger generation of the Cairo poor are so different from those of their parents.

Edwards rightly reminds us that not all who migrate to the city wish to build there. Much of the African literature still emphasises 'circular migration' – the migrant expects to spend but a few years, or even months, there before returning to the rural area. Such migrants are hardly likely to wish to build their own house in the city. But with the cities providing an ever-increasing proportion of skilled employment, migrants are more and more expecting to spend most of their working lives there. And with the primacy of few cities the likelihood of transfer to other urban centres is declining. Nevertheless some will still prefer to build their permanent home in their rural community of origin, for it is there that they expect to retire. Such was common in the relatively wealthy rural areas of West Africa, for instance – but less so where the countryside provided neither opportunities for income-earning in one's retirement nor the services necessary for comfort. Furthermore, as Wikan notes, there are many who prefer to invest in other ways – for instance in education; for whilst some will measure their prestige by the quality of their home, for others the levels of scholastic attainment are rated more highly. Again, as she describes, in some cultures privacy within the home is seen as important, in others overcrowding is quite acceptable.

We cannot, therefore, assume that all the urban poor in a city share the same goals. Much more obviously they do not have the same levels of resources. Few have, on migrating, much capital or savings for they tend to come soon after completing schooling and with little skill or past work experience. Whilst many do establish themselves quite satisfactorily in the city, financial insecurity is perhaps their most serious handicap; very many are employed in the informal sector and a high proportion of those in the formal sector are in relatively unskilled jobs with little permanence – the building trade, for instance. The availability of mortgages for such people is severely constrained.

With such goals and level of resources in mind let us look at the problems of access to land. Asiama, in his chapter, has set out many of the possible patterns. In many West African cities the peripheral land is still held in customary tenure by indigenous descent groups, from the elders of which land may be acquired. In the past a customary gift gave one the right to build – a right which lapsed if construction was delayed; cash payments are now the rule, the sums varying with the proximity to main roads and accessibility. But today one has to go far into the bush to find a cheap plot! Elsewhere peripheral land is held by the state or perhaps by multinational companies; it is extremely rare or, as Asiama notes, unlikely that such bodies will allocate plots cheaply to the urban poor; in as much as they accede that the land is for housing it is the large schemes that are promoted. Projects in which two or three-bedroomed serviced houses are built according to conventional Western standards of construction are clearly beyond the means of the urban poor. For them site and service schemes were to be the answer. But as the many examples cited in the earlier chapters show, they usually tend to attract participants who are wealthier than the claimed target population. For these schemes too are not cheap; many are facilitated by foreign aid loans which must be repaid; full cost recovery is expected. Grant of a plot requires variously a substantial down-payment, security for a mortgage (a secure job or other property) and evidence of ability to complete the building. Default in either repayments or house completion may result in eviction. On the other hand the interest on the loan may be below commercial rates; as in Western countries there are financial benefits accruing to home-ownership.

Our discussion has focused on access to land for building one's own house – not on the possibility of purchasing a house from a previous owner. In this respect the housing market in Africa is very weakly developed. Most of those who have already built a home intend that it shall pass through inheritance to their children – or if they cannot occupy it, to be rented so their children enjoy the income. The inadequacy and complications of legal titles are a further deterrent to transfer. In site and service schemes, as Teedon discusses in Harare, the ability of an occupier to transfer his rights is often obscure; the developing agency seeks to retain some form of control over the new estate, to preserve its character; the occupiers demand rights tantamount to ownership before they will invest further in construction; but once they have such rights it is difficult to prevent their transfer. However, most of such projects are still relatively new and wide-scale transfer is only beginning to be reported.

Across Africa a broadly similar picture emerges. Several decades ago it was possible, in non-settler colonies, to acquire a plot of land relatively cheaply. Today, in almost all countries it is both difficult and costly. So what alternatives exist for the city migrant and resident? Basically he can rent, or he can invade land and squat. His choices are constrained by the availability of rental housing and by the government's attitudes to squatting. For those who aspire to build their own home, squatting is obviously the preferred alternative but such a choice is feasible only when it seems likely that one's construction will be, at least, tolerated. Many writers have argued that squatters will build only when they have been assured of legal title to their plot; more plausible, I think, is a view that a substantial house itself gives *de facto* security – the political furore over the eradication of an established suburb is much greater than over a few flimsy shacks. But if a government is resolute in its eviction practices the poorest among the poor will have little choice but to sleep on the streets.

A rental market is composed of those who wish to rent (or see no other choice open to them) and those with houses to let. The size of the former category is determined by the numbers of those who do not wish to build or own a home in the city and of those who do so wish but cannot gain access to land through customary grant or purchase state allocation or squatting.

That of the latter category is constrained by a variety of factors.

Rented accommodation is not new in Africa. In the colonial period governments provided houses not only for their largely expatriate senior employees but also for junior African employees usually stationed far from home and subject to frequent transfer, just as mining companies in inaccessible locations housed their migrant labour. When the University College, Ibadan, was built upon its permanent site from 1950 onwards not only was housing provided for all senior staff but a 'village' of barrack-like quarters accommodated several hundred junior employees. Today this is no longer common practice. African governments cannot build to the scale required by the migrant flow to the cities; investors in industrial enterprises are unwilling to sink capital both in plant and in housing. But whereas in the non-settler colonies African ownership of urban property was never in question, elsewhere – as Teedon's discussion of Harare shows – it is only recently that the African has successfully claimed a right to own property in the city, an erstwhile settler enclave.

The rental market has been dominated by the small landlord; rarely, except perhaps in North Africa, have private investors built large blocks of tenements for the relatively poor – they have preferred to build for the middle classes. Nor have governments made more than token gestures towards providing such cheap accommodation. In contrast we see as typical the migrant who, as described above, first builds a one-storey house for his family, then adds a second storey to which he moves, renting the ground floor to tenants; later he builds a slightly better house for himself and the whole of the first house is let; again he might build a new house specifically designed for a few tenants. Landlordism of this type yields a return on investment which is usually modest but very secure. Education may be more highly valued but a rental income usefully guarantees the costs of future scholars. The spread of such landlordism depends on continuing access to land – through purchase from indigenous groups holding under customary tenure, through squatting, perhaps successively, and the like; over all such processes governments tend to have little or no control. It is indeed, in Aina's terms, a popular response.

The development of landlordism in the larger housing projects, in site and service schemes for instance, has been taken up here by several contributors, and Teedon in particular. As long ago as the early 1960s the Lagos Executive Development Board built complete houses on its Surulere estate which contained an end room with outside access – clearly designed for the tenant whose rent would defray much of the mortgage. But recent internationally-financed projects have stressed owner–occupation, and the restriction of allocation to those who did not already own a house. It is with a sense of outrage (at most) or disappointment (at least) that successive writers have described how, after only a couple of years or so, so few of the

houses are occupied by owners alone, so many have either owners and
tenants or tenants alone. In some cases tenants are taken only after the
owning family is well accommodated; in others the tenants are the initial
residents, paying in effect for the construction of houses around themselves, the owner having contributed little or nothing more than the initial
payments. Crass exploitation of the latter variety is clearly contrary to the
stated aims of governments and international agencies and to their promises
to the urban poor. But, it seems, governments have as little will or ability to
control this situation as they have had in the previously described mode of
landlordism, legislation on rent control or tenants' rights being absent or
completely ineffectual.

Thus the demand for housing by those who would wish to own their own
property is being met by a rapidly growing number of small landlords.
Landlords and tenants from clearly distinct categories, the former probably
accumulating wealth whilst the latter find it difficult or impossible to save
enough to set themselves on a path to ownership. Yet in social terms the
distinctions are blurred.

We have very little statistical data on the scale of petty landlordism but
several small surveys suggest that most landlords are the owners of one or
two houses other than their own residences. Pennant's study in Malawi
shows that landlords do differ in social character but only slightly from their
tenants – they owe their position to their earlier arrival in the city: they got
in first and took the land available – now it is scarce and vastly more
expensive. Thus the landlords tend to be older than their tenants, less well
educated and in consequence to have lower earned incomes. In Wikan's
Cairo, too, we see relatively affluent educated young people in rented
housing, whilst their own poorer parents were able to become property-
owners (a situation becoming common in contemporary Britain).

Where, too, does one draw the boundary between lodger and tenant?
Migrants have always, on arrival in the city, lodged with kin who have
helped them to establish themselves in the new environment; to do so is a
social obligation. We do not know how many tenants (enjoying presumably
exclusive occupancy of their rooms) are from the same home area as their
landlords. For the social rewards of landlordism may be perceived to be of
similar value to the economic gains; one enjoys the 'deference' of one's
'clients', one gains prestige from being a benefactor, from settling domestic
disputes among one's tenants. But Amis found in Kibera in Nairobi that the
landlords preferred to take their tenants from ethnic groups other than their
own in order that an economic relationship should not be constrained by
social ties. As we have seen many landlords co-reside with their tenants and
enjoy presumably close personal relationships; in contrast many absentee
landlords use agents to collect their rents. One would expect close personal
relationships to result in a benign landlordism in which rents might be

waived, deferred or reduced in times of hardship; yet the small landlord, relying perhaps on the rent from his co-resident tenant to meet his mortgage repayments, may not be able to be so generous; in contrast, an elderly landlord with several houses but satisfied with a simple life-style might prove much more flexible. Landlord and tenants are bound in a relationship that is both social and economic, and it is the combination of the two aspects that determined how benign, how exploitative each relationship proves to be.

Poor quality of housing, high rents, insecurity of tenure must certainly rank among the causes of urban social discontent. Commercialisation is likely to exacerbate the tensions experienced; for whilst owner-occupiers may merely be frustrated by their inability to complete the building of a decent house, tenants may be faced with rent increases which exceed wage increases and with greater threats of eviction when demand for rental accommodation rises. But how far, we must ask, does housing become a specific major political issue and to what extent are demands directed against either government or landlords?

Amis has referred to food riots which have occurred in several cities; in Nigeria in the 1970s there were massive waves of strikes following apparent government intransigence in implementing wage and cost of living awards. But we do not hear of rent strikes directed against the private landlords.

We have very little comparative data on levels of rent; examples cited show that they may range from the nominal to the exorbitant but it is difficult to judge how far they vary with the scarcity of housing or with wage levels. Aina notes, for instance, that in his sample in Lagos a slight majority of his tenants felt that their rents were fair and they did not consider looking for other accommodation.

There is probably a widespread feeling among tenants that governments should control rents and the security of tenancies – and an equally widespread recognition that governments will either fail to introduce the necessary legislation or will be quite inefficient in implementing it. The petty landlords, as we have seen, are not members of a governing class but are themselves among the urban poor. Many are even more poor than their tenants and most share with them all the other deprivations of urban life – high food prices, inadequacies in service and the like. Protests are probably more likely to be directed against the government in its failure to create sufficient access to land – as when it vigorously evicts squatters from land which is apparently vacant, or when, in a project advertised as being designed to meet the needs of the relatively poor, the plots or houses are seen to be taken by those much wealthier than the target group. To the urban poor issues may look simple, though as Asiama shows, each of the solutions available to governments may produce unintended or unwelcome consequences in the long-term operation of the housing market.

Whilst landlords and tenants may join together in opposition to the government on many national issues, in local issues their divergent interests may nevertheless divide them. In many African countries local self-help and community action is seen as a means of providing within a neighbourhood the basic services – electricity, piped water, a surfaced road. Governments and public agencies may provide materials and technical expertise but the members of the local community are expected to contribute financially or provide labour for the projects. There tends to be an emphasis on equality of participation for it is clearly very difficult to evaluate different abilities to pay or differences in benefits ultimately received. Whilst tenants undoubtedly benefit from many of these projects, it is the landlord who gains most from the increased value of his property, resulting perhaps in raised rents. The potential for community action – and the development which it promises – are likely to be greatly reduced where a neighbourhood is divided into landlords, owner–occupiers and tenants. The responsibility for providing basic services, which governments had hoped to delegate to the urban poor is restored to them; governments can no longer claim that, if the poor lack the services which they seek, the fault lies substantially with them.

The participants in this international African Institute Seminar, in the few days available for their discussions, focused on housing policies rather than on the more sociological issues of social stratification within the urban poor. Impressions of growing inequality were created, which, with more time, many participants would have ably elaborated. The ultimate consequences of urban poverty are all too easily seen – in malnutrition, in apathy, in political unrest; the role played by various economic factors and policies is less easy to unravel.

But it is clear that housing policies do have a marked effect and that planners in this area must consider the social implications of their activities.

## REFERENCES

Mangin, W. 1967. 'Latin American squatter settlements: a problem and a solution', *Latin American Research Review*, 2(3), pp. 68–95.

## RESUME

Quelles sortes de sociétés sont produites par les politiques et les stratégies de logement décrites dans les pages précédentes de ce volume? Le logement est souvent considéré comme un symptôme de pauvreté – mais c'est également un des facteurs qui renforcent les divisions parmi la population urbaine pauvre. Posséder une maison est un moyen d'économiser et d'investir, un apport de plus grande sécurité; le coût de location dans la ville représente une forte proportion des dépenses de la population urbaine pauvre, les empêchant d'économiser et d'accumuler et entraînant ainsi un accroissement de la pauvreté et du manque de sécurité.

Certains migrants s'installant dans les villes ne cherchent pas à y posséder une maison – ils se considèrent en transit. Mais la majorité recherche la propriété – ce qui signifie posséder un terrain pour y construire une maison. Dans certaines villes, il existe des parcelles de terrain détenues selon des formes coutûmières de bail, dans d'autres villes, les squatters sont tolérés. Au fur et à mesure de la croissance des villes, les possibilités offertes aux migrants il y a trois ou quatre décennies leur sont désormais fermées. Les anciens migrants sont devenus de petits propriétaires, les migrants plus récents sont obligés d'être locataires.

Le conflit potentiel parmi la population urbaine pauvre entre propriétaires et locataires est atténué car leurs relations sont souvent affables. Le petit propriétaire partage souvent les mêmes origines sociales que ses locataires; dans sa pauvreté relative, il se joint à ses locataires pour s'opposer aux gouvernements qui semblent favoriser les riches aux dépens de la population urbaine pauvre. Cependant, la pauvreté de nombreux locataires risque de déstabiliser les gouvernements.

# INDEX